Sociology

Neil J. Smelser

Copyright © UNESCO 1994

First published 1994

Blackwell Publishers
238 Main Street
Cambridge, Massachusetts 02142
USA

108 Cowley Road
Oxford OX4 1JF
UK

Library of Congress Cataloging-in-Publication Data

Smelser, Neil J.
  Sociology/Neil J. Smelser; with the contributions of Bertrand
  Badie . . . [et al.].
    p. cm. – (UNESCO/Blackwell series in contemporary social
  sciences; v. 1)
   Includes bibliographical references and index.
   ISBNS: 0–631–18915–7; 0–631–18916–5 (pbk.)
   1. Sociology. I. Badie, Bertrand. II. Title. III. Series.
  HM51.S636 1994.
  301–dc20.   93–37354
                                             CIP

British Library Cataloguing in Publication Data

A CIP catalogue record for this book is available from the British Library.

Typeset in 11 on 12$\frac{1}{2}$ pt Palatino by TecSet Ltd, Wallington, Surrey.
Printed in the United States of America.

This book is printed on acid-free paper

Contents

Foreword

UNESCO and Blackwell Publishers launch their Series "Contemporary Social Sciences" with the present volume, *Sociology*. The Series offers international surveys of the social science disciplines, each accurately representing the current state of the field and written for university and college professors, researchers, and graduate students. Subsequent volumes will cover political science, economics, anthropology, psychology, geography, demography, linguistics, history, international studies, statistics, and management sciences.

Volumes within "Contemporary Social Sciences" will be *authoritative*, involving world-class scholars as principal authors, and *comprehensive*, representing the widest range of perspectives in each discipline. Moreover, the emphasis is *international* in two senses: first, information and analyses are provided by contributing specialists throughout the world; and second, each volume reflects the ongoing transformations of the social sciences' basic units of analysis – including the concepts of the nation-state and society – that are brought about by accelerating forces of internationalization and globalization.

These international accounts of the disciplines are also intended as a contribution to the international circulation of social-scientific information. The internationalization of the social sciences has made notable advances, particularly since the end of the Second World War. At the same time, communication between social science communities across countries and regions – an essential ingredient of scientific progress – is still hampered by parochialism. The wide diversity of epistemological, theoretical and methodological perspectives of the social sciences themselves, differing cultural and institutional traditions among nations and cultures, and the realities of contemporary cultural and political competition among nations and regions, may impede free, unbiased scientific communication.

UNESCO has a long-standing commitment to and sustained experience in international scientific communication. It is the designated UN agency for promoting social science teaching and research, as well as fostering international cooperation within and among its disciplines. More particularly, the Organization has a comparative advantage in developing international state-of-the-art surveys, because of its global and regional perspectives and its involvement with the professional associations and networks it has helped to create and continues to support.

Some of UNESCO's past activities have been dedicated to purposes similar to those of this series. For example, between 1951 and 1968, the Organization produced a series of volumes surveying some 15 disciplinary and subject fields, under the title of "The University Teaching of the Social Sciences." UNESCO's professional periodical, the *International Social Science Journal*, now in its 45th year, is another such activity. Each issue of the *ISSJ*, published in six language editions (English, French, Spanish, Arabic, Chinese, and Russian) and distributed worldwide, is an international state-of-the-art assessment of a social science discipline or subject.

The most ambitious UNESCO survey, however, was the *Main Trends of Research in the Social and Human Sciences*, carried out between 1965 and 1978. The project produced three ambitious volumes, written by outstanding scholars, for example Jean Piaget, Claude Lévi-Strauss, Roman Jakobson, Paul Lazarsfeld, and Stein Rokkan. Several hundred specialists, national and international bodies, councils, foundations, universities, research centres, and professional associations from all parts of the world participated in the projects. The volumes themselves proved a landmark and the subsequent paperback editions of the individual chapters became large sellers in several languages.

Drawing on the collaborative approach of the *Main Trends* project, we designed a new method, combining speed and cost-efficiency in production with breadth of coverage, reliability, and quality of coverage for the current series. The major challenge was to combine two ingredients: the coherence of logic and style provided by a single author, and the wealth of information and breadth of coverage offered by an international team of specialists. We addressed that challenge by selecting a reputed scholar to act as designer and author of each volume, supported by contributing specialists selected from different countries and parts of the discipline. The author of each volume will use contributors' texts as resources from which to fashion and write the book. The contributions of the specialist scholars will be appropriately acknowledged in the volume, and their papers published in the *International Social Science Journal*.

The present volume conforms to this model. All those who have been involved in the enterprise consider it a success. With few exceptions, the contributors invited to participate understood and accepted their assignments, lived by the rules of the games entailed by those assignments, and delivered manuscripts of high quality. We thank them for their share in the enterprise.

The key person in the success of this volume is Professor Neil J. Smelser, as its intellectual leader and author. We selected him for the project because he corresponded to the ideal profile we had in mind: one of the foremost sociologists of our time; an impeccable record and reputation for scholarship; author of numerous important books; an extensive international experience; punctuality; and, last but not least, an openness to all significant trends, theories, and schools of thought in the discipline. On each of these counts he met our highest expectations. In addition, he revealed a high threshold of tolerance for the inevitable difficulties of an international collaborative scientific enterprise. It was a privilege and a pleasure to work with Neil J. Smelser.

Ali Kazancigil

Preface

Writing this international account of contemporary sociology has proved to be one of the most stimulating intellectual enterprises of my career. Much of the excitement, moreover, derives from the fact that preparing the book has been an experimental endeavor in several senses:

- It is the first volume in the new UNESCO/Blackwell Series in Contemporary Social Sciences, so we had few, if any, precedents.
- It involves a collaboration between myself and nineteen scholars from five continents, many of whom I have never met, and some of whose previous work I did not even know about beforehand.
- It rests on a particular pattern of collaboration. Contributors were to submit advanced and documented essays to me, on the understanding that I would have complete freedom and responsibility in rewriting, adapting, and supplementing their work in the interests of producing as representative, comprehensive, and stylistically integrated a book as possible.

No special sensitivity is required to appreciate that such an enterprise not only is exciting but also has elements of uncertainty and risk. In this preface I provide a brief account of how the project worked out.

At the outset, three strategies for organizing the volume occurred to me. The first, not unprecedented, was to prepare a series of essays that represented the distinctive intellectual and institutional characteristics of different national and regional sociologies: Indian sociology, the French sociological tradition, sociology in Africa, for example. This would have had the advantages of coverage and representativeness but would probably have taken the form of descriptive presentations – sociology around the world, as it were – missed the analytic foci of the discipline in general and failed to focus on distinctive sociological problems.

The second strategy was to prepare something resembling a handbook or textbook, organizing chapters according to subfields of sociology such as family, stratification, political sociology, and so on. This would also have had the advantage of comprehensiveness but would have tended to produce inclusive review articles which would have drifted toward the inconsequentially synthetic and which, to be frank, would have been bland and boring.

The third was to focus on specific sociological topics or a range of problems which would represent both the greatest challenges to human civilization at the end of the twentieth century and the foci of current sociological interest and work. This strategy too would have involved some potential costs – the danger of arbitrariness in selecting topics, for example, and the danger of leaving out large areas of contemporary thinking and research. At the same time, this strategy promised to represent the sociological enterprise at its most vital and to demonstrate the distinctive strengths of the discipline.

In June 1992 in Paris I met Ali Kazancigil, the Director of UNESCO's Division for the International Development of Social and Human Sciences and the Editor of this Series, along with his colleague Nadia Auriat and Simon Prosser of Blackwell Publishers. We weighed the costs and benefits of all three strategies and, in the end, enthusiastically endorsed the third. By good fortune, I had attended a meeting of the Executive Committee of the International Sociological Association immediately before the meeting in Paris, so I had been able to consult several colleagues about both topics and potential contributors. This proved very helpful, and we were able to devise the entire table of contents and decide on most contributors there and then.

The table of contents reveals the topics selected. Because we concentrated on problems, the chapter titles do not reveal the neatness of organization of a traditional text. The chapters do fall into a series of clusters, however, and can be grouped more or less comfortably in four parts. These clusters are:

- Chapters 1–3 (Part I) deal with the discipline of sociology itself – its perspective, its theories, and its methods.
- Chapters 4–7 (Part II) deal with the political realities and ambiguities found in most parts of the contemporary world – including crises of nations and nationalism, crises of democracy, and crises of the welfare state.
- Chapters 8–13 (Part III) are concerned with the organization of economies – both national and world – and their consequences for human life and for the relations between humanity and nature.
- Chapters 14–19 (Part IV) focus on institutions and culture, including the urban complex, community, religion, race, and family.

There is some imprecision involved in identifying such clusters. Chapter 18, for example, on women in societies, deals as much with economic and political dimensions as it does with community and family. Still, the clustering may provide readers with a guide to the larger conceptual organization of the book.

My relations with the contributors posed some potentially delicate issues. At the outset we agreed that each of the contributors would provide a topical essay of specified length, sufficiently developed that it could be published separately in the *International Social Science Journal*. We agreed explicitly in advance that I would have complete freedom and judgment in adapting the materials, as well as final responsibility for the contents of the volume. Despite these agreements, there remained several unwelcome potential prospects: intellectual disagreements between contributors and myself, conflicts concerning pride of authorship, and the possibility of bruised egos.

I am pleased to report that hardly any of these negative prospects materialized. The contributors were models of scholarly quality, cooperation, and civility. For my part, I made a point of showing my drafts to contributors immediately after I finished them, so that points of ambiguity and disagreement could be worked out before, rather than after, publication. There were no confrontations or standoffs. We experienced the usual quota of missed deadlines and threats of default, but these all proved to be soluble by one means or another, and despite the snags, the entire volume as originally conceived survived intact.

My appreciation goes first to the contributors, who, as I have already indicated, surpassed my expectations; then to Ali Kazancigil, who was skillful, gracious and sensitive in dealing with both me and the contributors, and Nadia Auriat, who facilitated progress on the manuscript. Simon Prosser's enthusiasm for, and consistent encouragement of, the project were helpful at every stage. Finally, I would like to thank my assistant of many years, Christine Egan, for orchestrating the enormous amount of computer work, mailing, faxing, and reproducing that an international project such as this necessarily entails.

Neil J. Smelser
Berkeley, California

Part I

Fundamentals

1

The Sociological Perspective

In the Preface to the newly published *Concise Oxford Dictionary of Sociology*, the editor, Gordon Marshall, ventured the following statement about the field of sociology: "Sociology itself has a clear theoretical core but irretrievably opaque perimeter" (Marshall 1994). This statement has a nice ring. It fails, however, to state what the core and perimeters *are.* To do this is a daunting task at the end of the twentieth century, but I shall try in this opening chapter to define and indicate the scope of the sociological enterprise, note some of its peculiar characteristics, elucidate the nature of its subdivisions, present some thoughts about its boundaries, and sketch some patterns of change in its development.

Definition and Scope

A Definition

Defined most simply, sociology is the scientific study of social relations, institutions, and societies. Sociologists describe and explain phenomena at the following levels of analysis (with reference to chapters of this volume in which each level has a significant place):

- The demographic, which refers to the size and composition of human populations, as affected by marriage, natality, mortality, and migration. In this emphasis sociology overlaps significantly with and complements demography, differing from it by emphasizing formal processes less and the cultural

---

This chapter was written solely by Neil J. Smelser. Parts of it are either taken from or based on four of his recent publications: Smelser, 1989, 1991a, 1991b, and Neidhardt and Smelser, 1992.

and social-structural sources of demographic behavior more (chapters 8, 11, 14).

- The social-psychological, which refers to the attitudes and behaviors of individuals in relation to their social environment and the interaction among persons. Here sociology overlaps with and sometimes becomes indistinguishable from that subdivision of psychology that is social (chapters 10, 17, 19).
- The group, which refers to the structure and behavior of more or less purposive collectivities, with individuals as members (e.g., cliques, parties, social classes, ethnic groups). The neighboring fields in this case are economics and political science, which deal respectively, with the generation and allocation of wealth and power among groups (chapters 8, 16, 18).
- The social-structural, which refers to the more or less enduring patterns of relations among individuals and groups (chapters 4, 5, 6, 9).
- The cultural, which refers to systems of values and beliefs that regulate, legitimize, and give meaning to social institutions and social behavior. Anthropology and sociology find common ground in this emphasis on culture and collective meaning (chapters 7, 15, 17).

As this characterization shows, the boundaries between sociology and other disciplines are less distinct than their more or less exclusive organization into academic faculties and professional associations would suggest. (The issue of sociology's relations with the other social sciences will be taken up later in the chapter.)

Some Enduring Sociological Preoccupations

There are some questions–many of them posed by the field's past giants such as Max Weber, Emile Durkheim, and Karl Marx – that stand as enduring preoccupations for sociologists. The following is a sample: What are the major patterns of change and modernization that occur in societies– for example, differentiation of social structures and rationalization of cultural patterns (Spencer 1897; see also chapters 4, 9, 13 in this volume). Are there special mechanisms, such as diffusion, social conflicts, and social movements, by which these changes are facilitated, inhibited, or deflected (Weber 1956; see also chapters 15, 16, 17)? What kinds of structural strains and "contradictions" lie behind those mechanisms of change (Marx and Engels 1848; see also chapters 5, 8, 16, 18)? What are the origins and causes of inequalities in society, and what are their consequences for human behavior and human welfare (Pareto 1935; see also chapters 5, 6, 10, 16, 18)? If differentiation belongs to the central processes of modernization, what kinds of integrating mechanisms ensure against anomie and instability (Durkheim 1984 [1893]; see also chapters 7, 9, 15, 17)? What are the functions and dysfunctions of bureaucracy in this respect? Which intermediating role is played by the main structures and processes of associational life, including religion, family, community, and voluntary associations (chapters 15, 17, 19)? How do these affect the workings of democracy and other processes in the larger society (de Tocqueville 1835; see also chapters 4, 5, 7)?

Methods and Data

The word "scientific" appeared in the definition of the field given at the beginning. Sociology had its origins in the development of the social science disciplines in the nineteenth century. All these modeled themselves, in one way or another, on the physical and life sciences. This modeling included a stress on empirical investigation and systematic explanation according to the scientific method. Most contemporary sociologists in the world describe themselves as social scientists, though, as we will see later in the chapter (and in chapter 2), the scientific status of sociology is a subject of deep controversy in the discipline.

In any event, insofar as the discipline aspires to scientific status, this means that its practitioners seek generalized explanations. The principal explanatory efforts involve the attempt to isolate, control, and establish the significance of causes of variations in phenomena at the several levels of analysis specified. In striving to do this, sociologists rely on several methods of analysis, involving different kinds of data. The first method, only occasionally employed, is the systematic analysis of experimental data produced by the deliberate creation of groups in order to study the effects when some of these groups are experimentally stimulated (experimental groups) and others are not (control groups). The second utilizes survey data, including census data, gathered by interviewing samples of people and subjecting the responses to statistical analysis. The third involves archival data, consisting of recorded evidence of events and situations as they have evolved in the historical process. The fourth entails ethnographic data, gathered as the investigator participates and observes behavior in actual empirical field settings in communities, factories, churches, and the like. Also under the heading of methods, attention should be called to the central importance of comparative studies in sociology, which involve the systematic gathering of social and cultural data from more than one nation, society, culture, or region and the systematic attempt to sort out the causes of, and thereby establish explanations for, the variations these data show (see chapter 3).

Subdivisions of Sociology

If we take the levels of analysis, the fundamental questions asked, and the data and methods listed, we have a reasonable working statement of the core of sociology. Most sociologists in most countries would agree that this characterization is a reasonable account of what sociology is and what sociologists do.

Table 1.1 Divisions of sociology, American Sociological Association and International Sociological Association

American Sociological Association*	International Sociological Association**
Applied Sociology/Evaluation Research	
Biosociology	
Sociology of Children	Sociology of Childhood
Collective Behavior/Social Movements	Collective Behavior and Social Movements
	Social Classes and Social Movements
Community	Community Research
Comparative Sociology/Macrosociology	Comparative Sociology
Criminal Justice	
Criminology/Delinquency	
Cultural Sociology	
Demography	Sociology of Population
	Sociology of Migration
Development	
Deviant Behavior/Social Disorganization	Deviance and Social Control
Economy and Society	Economy and Society
Education	Sociology of Education
Environmental Sociology	Environment and Society
Ethnomethodology	
History of Sociology/Social Thought	
Human Ecology	
Industrial Sociology	Participation, Workers' Control and Self-Management
Latina/o Sociology	
Law and Society	Sociology of Law
Leisure/Sports/Recreation	Sociology of Leisure
	Sociology of Sport
Marriage and the Family	Family Sociology
Marxist Sociology	
Mass Communication/Public Opinion	
Mathematical Sociology	
Medical Sociology	Sociology of Health
Methodology: Qualitative	Logic and Methodology in Sociology
Methodology: Quantitative	
Microcomputing	
Military Sociology	
Occupations/Professions	Sociology of Occupational Groups
Penology/Corrections	
Political Sociology	Political Sociology
Race/Ethnic/Minority Relations	Ethnic, Race, and Minority Relations
Rational Choice	Rational Choice
Religion	Sociology of Religion
Rural Sociology	Sociology of Agriculture
Sexuality and Homosexuality	
Small Groups	
Social Change	
Social Control	

Table 1.1 (Cont'd)

American Sociological Association*	International Sociological Association**
Social Organization/Formal/Complex	Sociology of Organization
Social Psychology	Social Psychology
Socialization	
Sociological Practice	Social Practice and Social Transformation
	Sociotechnics – Sociological Practice
Sociology of Aging/Social Gerontology	Sociology of Aging
Sociology of Art/Leisure	Sociology of Arts
Sociology of Emotions	
Sociology of Knowledge	Sociology of Communication, Knowledge and Culture
Sociology of Language/Social Linguistics	Sociolinguistics
Sociology of Mental Health	Sociology of Mental Health
Sociology of Science	Sociology of Science and Technology
Sociology of Sex and Gender	Women in Society
Sociology of Work	Sociology of Work
Sociology of World Conflict Resolution	Armed Forces/Conflict
Stratification/Mobility	Social Stratification
Theory	Sociological Theory
Undergraduate Education/Teaching	
Urban Sociology	Regional and Urban Development
Visual Sociology	
	Futures Research
	History of Sociology
	Sociology of Poverty, Social Welfare and Social Policy
	Sociology of Youth
	Alienation Theory and Research
	Conceptual and Terminological Analysis
	Biography and Society
	Housing and Built Society
	Labor Movements
	Clinical Sociology
	International Tourism
	Social Indicators
	National Movement and Imperialism
	Time Use Research
	Sociocybernetics and Social Systems Theory
	Famine and Society

*Listed under "areas of sociological interest" on 1993 membership application form.
**Listed under research committees, working groups, thematic groups, 1993.

At the same time, it is an incomplete account of the field, and much of the remainder of this chapter will be given over to qualifying it.

The first qualification results from examining the field according to its *internal* boundaries–that is, its division into subfields. Almost no sociologist would claim that he or she covers the whole of sociology as described, and almost every sociologist would be prepared to list a number of his or her specialized areas of interest and competence within the field. What are these subdivisions? There is no single answer to the question, but a good starting point is provided by the list of subfields recognized "officially" by the American Sociological Association and those represented by the Research Committees and Working Groups of the International Socio-logical Association. These are represented in Table 1.1. Inspection of the two columns of the table indicates that the overlap between the two associations' lists is considerable, especially if one allows for differences in terminology. There are certain "subfields" which would probably be listed by few outside the group that organized them–for example, "International Tourism" and "Housing and Built Society." Nevertheless, the list is enormous, and there is every reason to believe that it will continue to grow, as existing subfields subdivide further and as new social phenomena appear in the world and come to the attention of sociologists.

If one tries to detect a consistent rationale underlying the naming of subfields, one searches in vain. Some are named after the institution they study (law, medicine); some after a group (children, youth, the aged); some after an analytic dimension or social process (stratification, socialization, deviance); some after a social problem (famine, poverty, disasters); some after a theoretical approach or a method (Marxist sociology, rational choice); some after a specific method (microcomputing, social indicators); some after a use of sociology (applied sociology, sociological practice). Perhaps more classificatory threads could be identified. The reason for this somewhat hotchpotch character of sociological subdivisions is that their accumulation has been historical – as new ways of looking at the field have emerged, as new knowledge has been uncovered and has accumulated, and as new social phenomena and social problems have appeared – and hence not very systematic.

In all events, the lists of subfields yield two conclusions about the field of sociology as a whole:

- Its scope is enormous; in principle there is a sociology of virtually everything under the sun. It has been said in jest that there is, on a shelf in a certain American university, a Master's thesis with the title "Sociology of Spelling Errors in Southern American Cookbooks in the Nineteenth Century." One doubts that such a thesis exists, but it could exist.
- Sociology is specialized to the point of fragmentation. It is therefore not surprising that one finds in the literature comments to the effect that sociology has no common ground or core, that sociologists cannot converse with one another, that the field is in disintegration or disarray, that it has no identity,

and that it is in crisis (the review symposium edited by Calhoun and Land 1989). My own view is that such statements are exaggerated. It is not difficult, however, to appreciate why they are uttered.

Boundaries of the Field: Several Views

National Boundaries and the Internationalization of Sociology

At the outset it was asserted that sociology has a core set of analytic levels, substantive preoccupations, and research methods. By implication, there would be a general consensus – always *some* dissent, of course, or else it would not be sociology – among those people who call themselves or are called sociologists throughout the world. At the same time, there are certain differences in content and style among nations and among clusters of nations. These highlight certain themes and downplay others within the general corpus of sociology. Sociology – or any other field of inquiry, for that matter – never exists in isolation from the larger society but is embedded in it in complex ways. The differences between national sociologies can therefore be interpreted in part as an outcome of their different national environments. Consider the following illustrations:

- Sometimes a national sociology may reflect themes found in the larger culture of its own country–for example, themes of individual achievement, mastery, and equality in American culture; themes of authority and the state in German culture; themes of colonial suppression and collective alienation in Third World countries.
- Sometimes national sociological preoccupations reflect a special agenda or social struggle that is salient at that particular moment in its history. To take an example from economics, the late eighteenth- and early nineteenth-century preoccupation of British political economists reflected the societal fact that important groups of merchants, industrialists, and bankers were fighting against what they experienced as the shackles of mercantilism. Later, sociology in Britain came to be preoccupied with the struggles of the poor and organized labor against those very classes.
- National sociologies are shaped by the degree of friendliness or antagonism of national political regimes toward the field in general or to some of its expressions in particular. An example of this is the fate of sociology within the former Soviet Union and the former socialist countries of Eastern Europe. Many of these regimes expressed hostility to theories seen as inconsistent with Marxist–Leninist doctrines, and this restricted the development of sociological theorizing and research within these countries. Correspondingly, as thought control receded or disappeared and as the requirements for institutional rebuilding were seen as requiring social knowledge, reinvigorated sociological thinking and research appeared.
- Sociological research and its interpretations are influenced by the views and interests of those who sponsor and support it and the views and the interests of the audiences to which it is addressed. The "human relations" school of

industrial relations in the United States, for example, arose from research directly sponsored by industrial corporations and was primarily addressed to managers of those corporations and to others interested in controlling industrial struggles.

- The "nationalism" or "regionalism" of sociologies is influenced by the international conflict among nations and their stratification. Throughout its history, the International Sociological Association has been influenced by the international situation. For much of its existence the politics of the cold war accounted for much of the positioning and posturing of sociological groups within it. While that dimension has receded in recent years, the association experiences internal divisions based on those that exist in the larger world – between developed and undeveloped nations, North and South, and more specific regions (Western European, North American, Latin American, Middle Eastern, and so on).

Those factors work toward the diversification of, and conflicts within, sociology along national and regional lines. At the same time the field manifests a number of internationalizing tendencies as well. In fact, the internationalization of sociology can be regarded as, in part, the result of material and political changes in the world and international relationships among national societies. After the Second World War, the strong and somehow homogenizing influence of American sociology was only in part a result of the advanced development and professionalization of research in the United States. The transmission of American perspectives and standards would not have been so striking without the leading political and economic role of the United States, which manifested itself in sponsorship and participation in social research abroad, as well as by managing exchange programs so that foreign nationals could study and teach in the United States. When students and faculty go to another country on exchange programs, they are inevitably influenced by distinctive theoretical traditions, substantive preoccupations, types of research conducted, and methods employed by sociologists in their host countries. This influence is subsequently diffused or taken back into the home countries as students and faculties return, and this in turn may shape sociological traditions in the direction of the sociology absorbed in the country visited.

The internationalization of sociology is further facilitated by the increasing breakdown of boundaries among nations. The two most dramatic examples of this are the increasing unification of the European Community and the disintegration of the barriers between East and West occasioned by the collapse of the Communist and Socialist governments in the former Soviet Union and Eastern Europe. In connection with the latter, the possibilities for both receiving and developing sociology have been greatly increased by the downfall of regimes which maintained long-standing political hostility to academic sociology. The internationalization of sociology between North and South, however, is limited, largely because of the tilted economic and political relations between the regions and also because of the woefully inadequate infrastructure for the development of sociology in most southern countries.

Other barriers to internationalization are also observable (Rokkan 1979). Governments of many countries, especially in the Third World, believe that foreign scholars' research in their countries smacks of neocolonialist domination, and they have actively discouraged anthropologists and others from entering their countries to carry out work. Many national governments also have policies that permit research agencies to give financial support only to their own nationals, not to foreigners, and restrict the spending of their own currencies in other countries. More important, virtually all avenues for allocating research resources and career recognition and rewards are organized through universities, academies, and governments that are *national* in location and orientation; this, more than any other single factor, orients academics–including sociologists– toward the nation-state in terms of their career motivations and activities. Finally, international research is impeded by the fact that many agencies committed to support it cannot do so for lack of resources. This is certainly true of the International Sociological Association. Although it is a valuable medium for the international dissemination of theory and empirical research through its world congresses, the ISA produces very little international collaborative research, except for the occasional project organized through its specialized research committees.

Societal Boundaries

The contours and boundaries of sociology can be appreciated by considering its empirical subject matter. Recall the nature of that subject matter as set forth in the initial definition: social relations, institutions, and societies. That definition is adequate, but it does not convey the truth that this dimension of human life transpires in several different kinds of environment, which can be represented as one set of boundaries of the discipline. Consider the following representation of these societal boundaries:

The physical and biological It has been long acknowledged in intellectual endeavors such as social ecology, human geography, and rural and urban sociology that human society exists in physical space and that the constraints of space constitute a special set of parameters or limitations to the possibilities for the organizing social life. Those parameters are, of course, variable, as the revolutions in transportation and communication during the past two centuries amply demonstrate. It is equally evident that it is biological organisms that populate the systems of human interaction, institutions, and society and that the biological exigencies – including genetic potentialities and limitations on learning and adaptation – constitute both resources for, and limits on, the possibilities of organizing social life as well. More recently, the emergence of the specter of environmental spoliation, exhaustion, and destruction have further underscored the fragility of the natural environment, as well as the relations between economic and social life and that environment (see chapter 11).

A number of subfields found in table 1.1 reveal a preoccupation with the boundaries between society and nature – biosociology, human ecology, the sociology of aging, environment and society, and many parts of the sociology of health, sexuality and homosexuality, community, urban sociology, demography, and housing and built society. Despite the tangibility of these concerns with the physical and biological boundaries of society, it should be stressed that the concept of "boundaries"–which connotes some kind of dividing line–is itself misleading. The relationship is, rather, one of meshing through a highly permeable film. As modern developments in the sociology of medicine have demonstrated, the incidence of industrial accidents, occupational stress, and behavior–related disorders such as lung cancer and even AIDS reflect clearly the relations between social structure and biological functioning, malfunctioning, and trauma. Furthermore, the pollution and exhaustion of the natural environment are directly and indirectly conditioned by the patterns of production, consumption, and stratification associated with the social structures of industrial and urban life.

The cultural   At the outset the "cultural" dimension was identified as one of the central organizing perspectives of sociology. So it is, because it manifests the inescapable and universal fact that social interaction and organization are mediated and regulated by symbolic representations. At the same time, if the core preoccupation of sociology is with interaction, institutions, and society as such, then culture can legitimately be conceived as a kind of boundary which, like nature, sets constraints and actively determines the form and function of those social relationships.

Many of the subfields of sociology found in table 1.1 deal with this cultural boundary. Among them are cultural sociology, mass communication, sociology of the arts, sociology of religion, sociology of education, sociology of knowledge, sociology of science and technology, and sociology of language and sociolinguistics. Again, the relationship is one of meshing rather than separation by boundaries. Institutionalization, by virtue of which values and norms are tangibly embedded in the regulation of social interaction, illustrates that interpenetration of culture and society.

The person   In an early, forceful, and influential statement, Durkheim (1958 [1895]) set forth the argument that the proper study of sociology was the study of social facts, which exist and which can and ought to be conceived as independent of psychological facts, or the person. This line of thinking has often been contrasted with the perspective of Weber, that action, the proper unit of sociological study, is "social," insofar as "its *subjective meaning* takes account of others and is thereby oriented in its course" (1968: I, 4; my emphasis). The term "subjective meaning" suggests, *contra* Durkheim, that the person is the analytic starting unit of sociology, the ultimate conditioning element of all social interaction and social structure. Whatever the final resolution of this long-standing sociological debate – it might be called "structural sociology" versus "action sociology" – it reveals the analytic boundary between society and the person.

This boundary, like the two others mentioned, has also become the subject of sub-specialization in sociology. Referring again to table 1.1, the subfields of sociology of mental health, social psychology, socialization, and alienation theory and research lie on that boundary. But, once again, the phenomena of socialization, which include the learning and internalization of both social roles and culture, and the "social construction of society" – which is an account of how individuals in interaction create and sustain the "reality" of society – reveal the constant interplay and interpenetration of society and the person.

Conceptual Boundaries of Sociology

Yet another way of characterizing the scope and boundaries of the field is to attempt to set sociology off *analytically* from its sister disciplines in the social sciences. This is a difficult enterprise, largely because the arraying of the social science disciplines–and the conceptual territory they occupy–is the result of a somewhat unsystematic historical process. In both Europe and the United States, sociology was something of a disciplinary latecomer and found itself, as it were, attempting to occupy those empty parts of the conceptual map that had not yet been colonized by law, history, economics, political science, and psychology. Those who established the discipline found themselves continuously struggling to define the field and set it off from others. Durkheim's early efforts can be regarded in part as a struggle to differentiate sociology from psychology. Weber was deeply preoccupied with the differentiating characteristics of economics and sociology (1949 [1904]). The early American sociologists, especially Ward and Small, following Comte, attempted to characterize sociology as the great synthesizing science, incorporating the results of the more specialized sciences of economics and politics into a unified theory of society. In practice, however, sociology found itself concentrating on a range of institutions–family, community, class, and "society" as a whole–not explicitly formulated or covered by other disciplines and a range of social problems – inequality and poverty, social injustice, crime, divorce, and so on – that gradually came to constitute much of its subject matter.

It is possible, as an exercise in rational retrospection and reconstruction, to lay out some analytic bases of distinction between sociology and the other social sciences. Economics, for example, can be said to deal with the production, distribution, exchange, and consumption of scarce goods and services, whereas (economic) sociology can be said to deal with the institutional and cultural contexts in which such processes transpire (Smelser 1975). Political science deals with power in much the same way as economists deal with wealth, while political sociology treats the institutional and cultural contexts of political life. Anthropology concentrates on simple societies and, within those, on special phenomena such as kinship and culture; whereas sociology deals more with the organization of modern, complex societies. Psychology takes the elements of the person (motives, emotions, skills, traits) as the basic units of analysis, sociology the *relations* among persons. (For an attempt at a conceptual map of the social and behavioral sciences according to these kinds of divisions, see Smelser 1967.)

Or alternatively, the academic disciplines can be distinguished from one another by certain "first principles." The analytic foundation stone of economics, for example, is the conceptualization of the person as an individuated, self-interested, choosing, rational, calculating creature in a context of scarcity; whereas in sociology the perspective is of the human being as adaptive but constrained by the limits imposed by his or her institutional and cultural involvements.

In the end, however, all such efforts at a systematic and symmetrical ordering of the behavioral and social sciences fall short, largely because of the conceptual incompleteness and "messiness" of the distinctions, as well as the overlapping–in practice–of the conceptualizations and intellectual efforts of the practitioners in the various disciplines. Consider, for example, only a few examples of these complications:

- Sociology itself contains so many different perspectives and theoretical paradigms that it defies a single, consistent analytic characterization (see chapter 2).
- Economics and sociology differ in analytic starting points, but economics contains "institutional economics," and sociology contains "exchange theory," which incorporates many features of the rational-choice models of economics.
- Anthropologists now study modern, complex societies (e.g., urban neighborhoods), and comparative sociologists now catch less developed societies in their net.
- The investigations of historical sociologists fuse indistinguishably with the work of historians, and social historians borrow sociological concepts and frameworks freely.
- The fact that all social science frameworks entail some informing assumptions about the motivational primacies of the human actor (*homo economicus*, political man, the "oversocialized conception of man" [Wrong 1961]) constitutes an overlap, whether intended or not, with psychology.

The subfields of sociology, as represented in table 1.1, underscore this overlap. We find, for example, "economy and society," as well as industrial sociology, occupations/ professions, sociology of work, the sociology of leisure, and "rational choice," on the sociological edge of economics. We also find the sociology of law, political sociology, the sociology of world conflict, and "national movement and imperialism" on the sociological edge of political science. And, as indicated, the "person" appears as the central focus of interest in subfields such as social psychology, social structure and personality, socialization, and others.

Crossover and Nonboundaries: Interdisciplinary Work

The history of sociology reveals a continuous process of exportation and importation in relation to other disciplines. Examples of the former are the rise of behavioral political science in the 1950s and 1960s, which relied heavily on methodological tools (e.g., survey research), specific theoretical formulations (modernization), and general theoretical orientations (structural functionalism), all borrowed from sociology. Similarly, the rise and consolidation of a new social history in the past three decades, including, more recently, a new history of the family, have drawn on sociological frameworks and theories as well as demographic methods. Such developments tend to blur the disciplinary boundaries of both sociology and other fields, so that political sociology and historical sociology cannot properly be located within a disciplinary province.

Examples of importation by sociology also abound. The sociological study of the family and socialization in the 1940s and 1950s was influenced by psychoanalytic perspectives and the "culture-and-personality" emphasis from anthropology. Homans's (1974) behavioral sociology involved an implicit importation from psychological learning theory and economic theory. Other, more concrete illustrations include the possible takeover of some areas of the field of marriage and the family by practical agencies such as the National Council on Family Relations, the takeover of industrial sociology by psychologists (Borgatta and Cook 1988), and the shift in the center of gravity in the study of formal organizations from sociology departments to schools of business administration in the United States. Finally, the recent flurry of activity in sociology in the area of "rational choice" and "exchange" is an example of simultaneous exportation from economics, particularly the work of the economist Gary Becker (1976), and importation by sociologists, particularly in the work of Coleman (1990).

Another type of interdisciplinary endeavor involves the drawing together of the perspectives associated with different disciplines when considering a certain empirical phenomenon or problem. Many recurrent foci and issues are such as to defy disciplinary identification–for example, the study of the unequal distribution of rewards and power in society or the origin and consequences of revolutionary movements. The "sociology of welfare" (see chapter 6) is a complex amalgam of sociology, economics, political science, and "applied" areas such as social policy, social welfare (social work), and public health. The sociology of the environment (see chapter 11) incorporates simultaneously general sociology, the sociology of science and technology, economics, and political science. All such work is interdisciplinary (or multidisciplinary), in that a researcher makes use of materials, concepts, and theoretical frameworks from a variety of disciplines, develops synthetic approaches, incorporates ideas from many disciplinary sources, or actually collaborates with scholars from other disciplines.

So powerful is the interdisciplinary impulse that, in a recent American survey of promising research developments, a national group commissioned by the National Academy of Sciences/National Research Council (Gerstein *et al.*, 1988) reported that the most innovative and dynamic lines of research were interdisciplinary in character. Examples touching sociology reported by this group included health and behavior, information and decision making, and the internationalization of social, economic, and political life. The group recommended that funding and the development of research infrastructures be developed along interdisciplinary lines–in addition to disciplinary ones–in the coming decade. A parallel investigation in Western Europe–the European Social Science Commission (Dierkes and Biervert 1992)–also stressed the salience of interdisciplinary work and organized the chapters of its report partly along disciplinary lines and partly along the lines of "fields in transition" and global and synthetic problems.

From the standpoint of an academic discipline such as sociology, interdisciplinary work represents yet another example of forces of centrifugality and overlap in the social sciences. It involves simultaneously an enrichment of investigation and a diffusion of disciplinary rigor in the interest of the comprehensive solving of a scholarly or scientific problem. Furthermore, it renders more difficult any effort to place a given piece of research in a given discipline, as well as any attempt to characterize a discipline like sociology as a recognizable "thing."

Applications: The Boundary between Sociology and Society

One distinguishing characteristic of sociology is that it has never really made up its mind whether it is a "pure" science – with the trappings of analytical rigor, objectivity, and ethical neutrality–or an endeavor dedicated to the amelioration, betterment, or radical transformation of society. The European origins of sociology–found in history, the classics, and law mainly–generated a critical attitude toward state and society, which continues in that tradition and in sociology in general. Much of Weber's methodology involved a struggle between the dictates of scientific neutrality and the dictates of ethical commitment. The long-standing and uncertain overlap between the role of analytical sociologist and the role of critical "intellectual" reveals the same tension at the boundary of sociology and society. The early American founders of the field generated a persistent effort to set sociology off from both philosophy and ideology (primarily socialist ideology) by arguing that it was simultaneously *scientific* (as contrasted with speculative) and incrementally *ameliorative* (as contrasted with visionary and revolutionary). At present the field contains many sub-strands of "applied sociology," which is primarily problem-oriented in character, and "radical sociology," which is more transformative in vision and manifests itself in the Marxist and critical traditions.

To view the relations between sociology and society in a more dynamic way, the history of sociology is a story of its changing focus as the world changes and as sociology continues to "chase" new social problems that appear on the horizon. We can observe this dynamism working in the contemporary world with respect to the following situations:

- In the area of family sociology, there is likely to be an increased research focus on step-parenting, households with multiple members employed, "commuter marriages," and family implications of new "cottage industries," such as new forms of "putting out" by manufacturing firms and working at home with computers.
- In the area of sociology of religion, more research will focus on fundamentalism and other developments that have challenged the "secularization hypothesis" of modernization theory, new forms of religious conflict, and various manifestations of "privatized" religion.
- In the area of medical sociology, there is likely to be an increased emphasis on the problems of large organizational medicine and the economic and ethical implications of complex medical technology for professional practice.
- With respect to specific social problems, current and growing emphasis is being given to international sex tourism, the social epidemiology of AIDS, new forms of occupational and technological risk, and the social dimensions of environmental threats.

With respect to every one of these situations, sociologists will be called upon–and will take it upon themselves–to both understand and diagnose the problems and thereby contribute to dealing with them.

Given the history of the discipline, there is every reason to believe that both the applied and the radical sociological traditions will persist, albeit with vicissitudes. With respect to applied sociology, a number of national and world trends suggest that sociologists in search of problems to address will not be disappointed and do not face the prospect of unemployment through lack of subject matter. Among these trends are the increasing internationalization of world society (with the consequent lack of control of nation-states over their fortunes), the increasing complexity of all societies (with the consequent problems of coordination and integration), and the continuation, if not increase, of social problems associated with industrial and post-industrial societies. Governments and other large organizations will continue to experience the need to finance applied sociological and other social science research, and perhaps a greater proportion of sociologists will find employment in applied settings and a lesser proportion in universities and academies. Such trends may heighten certain divisions within the field, especially those between "theory" and "methods" and between "basic" and "applied" research.

Sociology as Intellectual Endeavor and as Organizational Endeavor

In this chapter we have looked at sociology from a number of angles, including its definition, its analytical foci, its subdivisions, the tensions between nationalizing and internationalizing forces within it, its substantive boundaries, its conceptual boundaries, its interdisciplinarity, and its boundaries with society. It is necessary to take this multiple view to appreciate the complexity of the field as an intellectual enterprise.

While the view from each angle yields a different description of the field, the consequences emerging from each view provide a single type of conclusion about sociology as an intellectual or cultural endeavor. Definite statements can be made about the foci, the internal divisions, and the boundaries of sociology. But in every case those statements require qualification, because of the complexity of the field. Furthermore, with respect to both internal subdivisions and external boundaries, the field defies systematic and consistent description. It is somewhat indistinct as to core, fragmented as to subject matter, fuzzy around the edges, and overlapping and interpenetrating with related academic disciplines and intellectual and practical endeavors.

Sociology displays a clearer unity and continuity from an organizational and social-structural point of view, however, than from an intellectual or cultural point of view. We use the word "sociology" as if it applies to a definite thing, and we use the word "sociologist" to apply to a distinct and identifiable class of persons. These usages are real in their consequences, since people so designated make their livelihoods in carrying that label and are employed under its umbrella. Sociology is certainly an institutional reality in terms of its organization in academic subdivisions–departments, divisions, and programs–of colleges, universities, and academies. Funding agencies such as national governments and private foundations include "sociology" and "sociological research" in their repertoire of programs to be funded. Sociologists join national and international associations bearing the name of their discipline, and, as a professional group, they constitute one of many "status groups" and "vested interests" in the prestige and political hierarchies of countries and regions in which they live.

When we look at the cultural and organizational facets of sociology simultaneously, then, we are greeted with a certain contrast: between the apparent complexity, diversity, and divisions of the first and the apparent unity, fixity, and continuity of the second. Or, speaking as sociologists, we might note this as an increasing tension or contradiction between the cultural and the social-structural levels. Furthermore, insofar as sociologists find themselves preoccupied with problems of imprecise self-definition, unclear academic professional identification, difficulties of communication inside and outside the field, and even a sense of "crisis" about their own discipline, it may be a reflection of that contradiction. That is to say, institutional realities suggest that sociology and sociologists are single, identifiable, and definite, whereas intellectual realities suggest that they are many, difficult to define, and elusive. My own sense is that in the long run the institutional realities of the academic social science disciplines will become more complex and flexible, thus bringing them into line with the intellectual realities of the field, but that the journey will be long and the path strewn with many organizational and political obstacles.

References

Becker, G. S. 1976: *The Economic Approach to Human Behavior*. Chicago: University of Chicago Press.

Borgatta, E. F. and Cook, K. S. 1988: "Sociology and its Future," in Borgatta and Cook (eds), *The Future of Sociology*, Newbury Park, Calif.: Sage Publications, 9–17.

Calhoun, C., and Land, K. (eds) 1989: "Review Symposium on the *Handbook of Sociology.*" *Contemporary Sociology*, 18: 475–7.

Coleman, J. 1990: *Foundations of Social Theory*. Cambridge, Mass.: Belknap Press of Harvard University Press.

De Tocqueville, A. 1835: *Democracy in America*. Paris: Éditions Minuit.

Dierkes, M. and Biervert, B. (eds) 1992: *European Social Science in Transition: Assessment and Outlook*. Frankfurt: Campus Verlag.

Durkheim, E. 1984 [1893]: *The Division of Labor in Society*. New York: Free Press.

Durkheim, E. 1958 [1895]: *The Rules of Sociological Method*. Glencoe, Ill.: Free Press.

Gerstein, D. R., Luce, R. D., Smelser, N. J. and Sperlich, S. (eds) 1988: *The Behavioral and Social Sciences: Achievements and Opportunities*. Washington, D.C.: National Academy Press.

Homans, G. C. 1974: *Social Behavior: Its Elementary Forms*. New York: Harcourt, Brace, Jovanovich.

Marshall, G. 1994: Preface to *Concise Oxford Dictionary of Sociology*, Oxford: Oxford University Press.

Marx, K., and Engels, F. 1848: *Manifest der Kommunistischen Partei*. London: Hirschfeld.

Neidhardt, F. and Smelser, N. J. 1992: "Sociology," in M. Dierkes and B. Biervert, (eds), *European Social Science in Transition: Assessment and Outlook*, Frankfurt: Campus Verlag, 244–67.

Pareto, V. 1935: *The Mind and Society*. New York: Harcourt, Brace.

Rokkan, S. (ed.) 1979: *1952–1977. A Quarter Century of International Social Science: Papers and Reports on Development*. New Delhi: Concept Publishers.

Smelser, N. J. 1967: "Sociology and the Other Social Sciences," in P. Lazarsfeld, W. H. Sewell and H. L. Wilensky, (eds), *The Uses of Sociology*, New York: Basic Books, 3–44.

Smelser, N. J. 1975: *The Sociology of Economic Life*, 2nd edn. Englewood Cliffs, N.J.: Prentice-Hall.

Smelser, N. J. 1989: "Sociology's Next Decades: Centrifugality, Conflict, Accommodation." *Cahiers de recherche sociologique*, 14: 35–50.

Smelser, N. J. 1991a: "The Social Sciences in a Changing World Society." *American Behavioral Scientist*, 34: 518–29.

Smelser, N. J. 1991b: "Internationalization of Social Science Knowledge." *American Behavioral Scientist* 35: 65–91.

Spencer, H. 1897: *The Principles of Sociology*. New York: D. Appleton.

Weber, M. 1949 [1904]: "'Objectivity' in Social Science Policy," in E. A. Shils and H. A. Finch, (eds), *The Methodology of the Social Sciences*, Glencoe, Ill.: Free Press, 49–112.

Weber, M. 1956: *Wirtschaft und Gesellschaft*. Tübingen: Mohr/Siebeck.

Weber, M. 1968: *Economy and Society: An Outline of Interpretive Sociology*, (eds) G. Roth and C. Wittich. 3 vols. New York: Bedminster Press.

Wrong, D. 1961: "The Oversocialized Conception of Man in Modern Sociology." *American Sociological Review*, 26: 183–93.

2

Sociological Theories

In discourse we typically refer to sociological theory as an entity and to sociological theorizing as a recognizable activity. We write articles and books and teach courses on sociological theory, and some of us say that we specialize in theory. In one sense such statements are misleading. Every item of empirical research in the field, however narrowly defined and circumscribed, is rooted in general propositions about human beings and society and contains the seeds of abstract reasoning and normative evaluation. These elements are often implicit but never absent. For this reason, theory should be regarded as an integral *aspect* of sociological inquiry rather than something separate from it. In another sense, however, theory is distinguishable. It is legitimate to consider the relations among the general elements in their own right; in doing so, we enter the realm of sociological theory.

The objectives of this chapter are two: first, to make some general remarks about sociological theory (at the beginning and the end); second, to lay out a rough, but comprehensive, map of theoretical thinking in contemporary sociology (in the middle). Each objective demands more than the total space allowed, and it is perhaps foolhardy to attempt so much. However, one cannot appreciate contemporary theory without addressing both objectives.

The Nature and Varieties of Sociological Theorizing

History and Theory

We frequently distinguish between the history of theory (or thought) and systematic theory. The former traces self-conscious thought about society

---

This chapter was written solely by Neil J. Smelser.

stemming from a person (Hobbes, Comte), a school (utilitarian), or a period (perhaps classical Greece). The latter deals with more contemporary thinking that is disciplined by reference to elements of scientific inquiry such as first assumptions, formal derivation of hypotheses, and empirical falsifiability. In reality, the distinction is a matter of shading. Many thinkers considered "historical" in their significance (e.g., Adam Smith, Jeremy Bentham, Karl Marx) were systematic and scientific both in aspiration and in mode of thinking. Furthermore, much contemporary thinking that we call "theory" is not especially systematic; it often involves advocacy of general perspectives, approaches, and ideological preferences, as well as formal theoretical statements and empirical propositions. Finally, many perspectives from the history of thought (such as classical evolutionary theory) continue to survive as ingredients of contemporary theories. For these reasons, "history" and "theory" fuse with one another in sociology.

Formal Varieties of Theory

One important continuum in theory involves the degree of formality it manifests; formality, in turn, implies the degree of attention paid to the scientific norms of theory formation. Some types of discourse that we call "theory" consist mainly of general perspectives or ways of thinking about human beings and society, with a somewhat imprecise, loose logical structure and few, if any, identifiable empirical propositions, to say nothing of efforts to confirm or disconfirm them. Sometimes these perspectives inform, or are incorporated into, more or less formal models, but much theoretical discourse involves argumentation about the analytical or normative importance of the perspective itself.

Other bodies of theory are formal verbal constructions of general assumptions and postulates, hypotheses, independent variables (or causes), dependent variables (or effects or outcomes), and evidence relating to empirical verification. For example, even though Robert Michels, in espousing his iron law of oligarchy, denied that he was creating a "new system" (1959 [1911]: viii), his insights can be represented as a systematic account organized according to the canons of scientific explanation (Smelser and Warner 1976: 237–476). Similarly, Durkheim's classic, *Suicide* (1951 [1897]), contains all the ingredients of a formally constructed theoretical explanation (Merton 1968a; Smelser and Warner 1976: 161–72). A definition of formal theory of this sort, still satisfactory in many respects, was put forward by Parsons half a century ago: theory is "a body of logically interdependent generalized concepts of empirical reference" (1954 [1945]: 212). As such, a theory contains a series of interrelated assumptions or postulates that approach logical closure, a derivation of general propositions statable as empirical hypotheses that are, in principle, testable. As indicated, not everything we call "theory" contains all these elements, so the definition must be regarded as a desideratum rather than a description.

The most formal expression of theory is a statement of relations, derivations, and hypotheses in mathematical language. Such theories are most commonly found in economics, but in sociology they have been used to generate explanations and predictions relating to demographic processes, social mobility, diffusion of inventions, and organizational behavior.

Another continuum concerns theoretical scope or generality. A model usually refers to a formally stated set of expectations about empirical outcomes–thus a model is a type of theory–but it is restricted to a narrowly identifiable range of situations. Middle-range theory is more encompassing, seeking to push explanatory principles over a wider range, while still dealing with "delimited aspects of social phenomena" (Merton 1968c: 39–40). General theory constitutes an effort to develop the most abstract principles to explain a vast range of regularities in social behavior, institutions, and change. This entire continuum is represented in the enterprise of sociological theorizing.

Uses and Value of Sociological Theory.

While theory is widely accepted as a legitimate ingredient of the sociological enterprise, the reasons for this acceptance are not always made explicit. It will be helpful, therefore, to give a reminder of the uses and value of theory for sociology itself and for the societies in which it is embedded:

- Theory is the mechanism by which discrete results of empirical research activities, often conceived independently of one another and reported in different conceptual contexts, are *codified* and related to one another within a single framework.
- Codification implies a second use, *generalization*. Theory presses sociological findings and insights beyond the boundaries within which they are formulated and extends the limits of their application.
- Theoretical formulations also have a *sensitizing* function–to alert investigators of, and commentators on, social phenomena to issues and questions that may not be readily apparent if the phenomena are approached naively (Blumer 1954).
- Theory has the potential for *application*–to be made useful in policy, organizational and institutional design and reform, even revolutionary transformation. This does not imply that such application is a literal and wholesale implantation of theoretical systems in social reality. Rather, application implies the provision of insights, perspectives, and ways of looking at social phenomena that may make practical activities more relevant and effective.

● Sociological theory is useful insofar as it enters into *general public discourse*, as one of the voices supplying intelligence, debate, and controversy to that discourse. In this sense sociological theory has a definite ideological aspect. Critics of the field may regard this aspect negatively–whether as reinforcing the *status quo* or as undermining it–but the general point is that sociological theorizing never occupies a neutral place in its sociocultural contexts.

The Issue of Accumulation

Sociology, including its theoretical aspects, is normally represented as a social *science*. Historically, the social sciences grew up as an effort to adapt the models and methods of the natural sciences to society, and most practitioners comfortably describe themselves as social scientists. In this connection, it is often asked whether social-scientific knowledge grows in a cumulative sense.

The scientific model of accumulation usually held out for comparison is that scientific knowledge, including theory, has validity only in a temporary sense. It is continually being displaced, absorbed, or replaced by the additive accumulation of new empirical discoveries and their theoretical interpretations. Accordingly, the history of science is of interest mainly as a matter of curiosity, not validity, because science is forever being rendered invalid by its own progress.

It has been argued (Kuhn 1962) that this idealized model does not apply even to the natural sciences; certainly it does not apply to the development of theoretical knowledge in sociology. The dynamics of sociological theory seem to be something like the following. From time to time, scholars formulate a timely, original, or creatively synthetic statement about social relations or society–for example, the idea of linear, or progressive, evolution. This statement excites immediate interest if it emerges in an appropriate intellectual or societal context; or it may lie dormant for a while, to be activated only when its time comes. In any event, the interest that is excited invariably gives rise to a number of theoretical and empirical challenges to the statement and the assertion or reassertion of alternative interpretations. Such criticisms, in their turn, invite statements of defense, adaptation, and elaboration of the original statement on the part of its advocates. As an outcome of this process, a perspective, an approach, or even a "school" takes its place in the history of theorizing. Over time that school may endure, be discredited, be revitalized, or be transformed as it is combined and recombined with other ideas and perspectives.

The history of sociological theory, as well as the current state of sociological theory, is the precipitate of dozens, if not hundreds, of such intellectual episodes. It is a history of invention, elaboration, synthetic combination and recombination, vitalization and revitalization, and occasional death of theoretical perspectives. This history is thus *not* one of additive accumulation–replacing the old by the new in light of more adequate or valid knowledge. It is, rather, a history of increase in numbers, complexity, and enrichment of more or less systematically expressed perspectives, frameworks, and theories about human society. It is also a history of continuous flux, as theoretical knowledge undergoes internal shifts through invention, controversy, and debate within the field and as it responds to the changing conditions in the societies in which it is generated. Finally, at any given moment, the map of sociological theory is a complicated mosaic, an aggregated product of that flux, rather than a rationally accumulated pattern. What coherence it possesses arises mainly from the interpretations of those scholars who subsequently discern patterns in its development.

A Contemporary Map of Sociological Theories

Sociology, a discipline of enormous scope, is divisible in several ways: first, in terms of subfields classified by content–stratification, sociology of the family, sociology of poverty, environmental sociology (see chapter 1); second, according to methods–mathematical, statistical, comparative, experimental, ethnographic (see chapter 3); and third, by alternative (sometimes competing) theoretical perspectives or paradigms. In this chapter I concentrate on the third.

Three qualifications are in order at the beginning:

- The map I am about to draw suffers from a certain ahistoricity; it is cross-sectional, with few references to the origins and development of the map's different parts.
- My own geography–like that produced by anyone else–involves some arbitrariness, because there are many legitimate ways to slice the theoretical pie. The work of Max Weber, for example, can legitimately be classified as "phenomenological," "structural," "middle-range," and "conflict" theory; Weber could therefore be located on one or many parts of the theoretical map, depending on the salience given to each of these facets of his work.
- The presentation of a map with distinct territories should not conjure up the imagery of a field occupied by multiple armies of scholars, each mobilized tightly around a theoretical perspective. Some scholars define themselves in that way, but most tend in practice to be somewhat eclectic in their theoretical choices, perhaps stressing one perspective over another, but also borrowing from and combining approaches when the intellectual problem at hand seems to demand it.

Now to the map itself. The fundamental division is between macroscopic perspectives that focus on organizations, institutions, societies, and culture and microscopic perspectives that focus on individuals' social psychology and interactive processes among them. In practice, the two levels overlap; all macroscopic theories contain at least implicit psychological assumptions, and most microscopic theories assume broader societal parameters within which micro-processes transpire.

Macrosociological Theories

The most frequent contrast is between theories that stress social integration and those that stress social conflict.

Integration theories The main tradition falling under this heading is structural-functional theory, traceable through the works of Herbert Spencer (1897), Emile Durkheim (1947 [1913]), Bronislaw Malinowski (1955), and Radcliffe-Brown (1952) and culminating in the formulations of Talcott Parsons (1951) and Robert Merton (1968b). All these regard society as a structure of mutually interrelated parts which are sustained, in varying degree, by equilibrating mechanisms. The structural-functional perspective is also associated with the consolidation of modernization theory in the decades following the Second World War. This theory treats the developmental process as breaking through tradition-based obstacles (located mainly in religion, tribe and caste, community, and kinship) and replacing them by the more "modern," differentiated institutions (including democratic governments) found in the developed countries. One other theoretical formulation–"the end of ideology" (Bell 1960)–also falls roughly under heading of functional analysis. Exponents of this point of view, which appeared in the post-Second World War decades, argued that a new consensus had been achieved in Western societies, in that workers had achieved political citizenship, the bourgeoisie had accepted the welfare state, both had accepted the democratic process, and the ideological issues dividing the Left and the Right had been reduced to marginal differences in emphasis over governmental ownership and economic planning.

The structural-functional perspective came under assault in the turbulent years of the 1960s and is still the target of criticism from radical and critical sociologists and from many sociologists in developing countries. The full apparatus of structural-functional analysis (including a systematic classification of functional prerequisites, the idea of societal survival, and stable equilibrium) does not survive intact, but much research still relies on a number of central ideas associated with it, namely:

- Institutions serve a positive purpose in the ongoing societal effort to guarantee that its main goals are realized.
- Institutions manifest a "strain toward consistency"; for example, the contours of higher education are shaped by the functional needs of a high-technology, service-based economy.
- Strains and contradictions in institutional life set up equilibrating processes that change these institutions in adaptive directions; for example, when both

parents in families enter wage labor in large numbers, alternative systems of socialization (extended kin, child-care institutions) tend to materialize.
- A principal form of change in developing societies is structural differentiation, the development of more complex and specialized social structures (Alexander and Colomy 1990).

The weakest aspect of structural-functional analysis in contemporary thinking is the idea that integration is achieved through consensus on common values, a view associated mainly with Parsons.

Elements of structural-functional analysis also survive in some recent theoretical perspectives. One is "population ecology," a perspective that invokes classical Darwinian principles. Its main application is in the area of formal organizations, in which the birth, growth, transformation, and death of economic and other organizations are seen as resulting from an interaction between the adaptive strategies of organizations and the constraints (mainly resource opportunities) in the environment (Hannan and Freeman 1977). A second is "systems theory," long associated with the idea that all natural, human, and social systems manifest the same principles of functioning. Its most important contemporary expression is found in the work of Luhmann (1982), who has carried forward some aspects of Parsons's theory and has generated theories regarding functional differentiation and the self-production of systems (*autopoesis*), as well as their evolution. A third perspective is "neo-functionalism," associated with Alexander (1985) and others. This approach stresses the interrelation of societal activities, analysis at the social-structural level (macrosociology), deviance and social control mechanisms, and structural differentiation as a central principle of social change. What is "neo" is the acknowledgment that cultural consensus is not the core integrating mode in society, but rather that coalitions, interest groups, and other agencies of conflict play a key role in social dynamics; that personal interaction must be taken into account as the basis of social-structural processes; and that sociology should deal not only with "systems" but also with "action." In a word, neo-functionalism builds a kind of bridge to theories that give a central role to conflict, theories which we will now consider.

Conflict theories   It is appropriate to begin with another statement bridging the integration and conflict perspectives. This is found in the thinking of Georg Simmel as consolidated by Coser (1956). Coser's starting point is a criticism of the functional view (mainly Parsons's) that conflict destabilizes the social order. Coser argues that conflict often constitutes the basis for community and unity among combatants and that conflict with an outside group (as in war or civil strife) is a solidifying force. In one sense this argument is an extension of the functional approach itself, because of its continued preoccupation with integration. In any event, Coser's aim is to incorporate various types of conflict within the functionalist perspective.

Most conflict theories in contemporary sociology derive from the formulations of Karl Marx: that all historical societies–and notably bourgeois capitalism–are based on an economic mode of production that produces a bipolar system of social classes, one exploiting, the other exploited. By virtue of that relationship, the classes stand in a relation of irreconcilable conflict with one another. This conflict, moreover, is the engine of historical change in Marx's theory, insofar as the ultimate victory of the exploited class ushers in a new type of society and a new phase of evolutionary history (Marx 1913 [1859]; Marx and Engels 1954 [1848]).

It is evident that the Marxist perspective has been an enormous intellectual and political force. It spawned a vast array of Marxist-inspired theories in the late nineteenth and twentieth centuries; it became the informing ideology of Communist, Socialist, and other left parties in most advanced and developing countries; and it was (or is) the legitimizing ideology for the former Soviet Union, the People's Republic of China, almost all Eastern European countries, and other countries such as Cuba and North Korea.

In recent decades the influence of Marxism has experienced a decline among Western European and (to a lesser degree) North American scholars and a virtual demise in Eastern Europe and the former Soviet Union, where the Socialist and Communist regimes erected on Marxism-Leninism have collapsed dramatically. Nevertheless, the materialist class perspective still finds expression in theoretical writings and political outlooks of scholars from the Third World and among some Western scholars. Among the latter, however, its vitality is seen not so much in its presentation as a total theory of society (with the exception of the theory of monopoly capitalism) but rather in its application to specific areas. Among these are Wright's (1985) statements on the continuing determinative influence of economic classes; Braverman's (1974) and Burawoy's (1979) analyses of change and domination in the workplace; certain interpretations of contemporary race relations in the United States–for example, the internal colonialism model of Blauner (1972), which borrows heavily from the neo-Marxist theory of colonialism; the interpretation of gender domination as a special manifestation of the capitalist domination of labor (Hartmann 1976); and the "new criminology" (Taylor *et al.* 1973), a perspective based on the premise that the definition and punishment of crime are mainly in the interest of the continued capitalist domination of the oppressed classes.

Most other contemporary conflict perspectives maintain one or more elements of Marxism, such as the idea of oppressing and oppressed classes or the idea of group conflict. These theories either abandon so many other elements of Marxism or combine them with so many non-Marxian ideas, however, that they can scarcely be said to be "Marxian" without overstretching that perspective. One example of this kind of theoretical formulation is that of Ralf Dahrendorf (1959), who rejects the fundamental Marxian proposition that economic relations are the basis of inequality in modern society and criticizes the Marxian theory of classes derived therefrom. At the same time, Dahrendorf retains the idea of domination as an organizing principle, tracing that domination, however, to a differential position in a relationship of authority (thus giving his work a Weberian cast). He also retains ideas similar to those of Marx to the effect that class groups based on authority relations gradually crystallize from latent interest groups into action groups as the interests become manifest through ideology, consciousness, leadership, and organization and that these groups are the main vehicles for conflict and change.

Another major conflict perspective which derives in part from the Marxian tradition is the "critical school" of sociology. Mainly German in origin–and within Germany, stemming mainly from Frankfurt–the critical school arose in the interwar period as a confluence of Marxian, psychoanalytic, and various cultural perspectives. Its more recent expressions are found in the works of Herbert Marcuse and Jürgen Habermas. Marcuse (1964) retained the Marxian notion that contemporary European and North American societies are divided into the two great classes of the oppressors and the oppressed and that oppression is related to the capitalist organization of the economy. However, because of the rise in affluence through technological advance, the distribution of wealth through welfare, and the continued transfer of wealth from the Third World to the advanced countries, the proletariat has become passive and is no longer a revolutionary force. Rather, domination works through technological manipulation by big government and is sustained through the mass media, which perpetuate a kind of false consciousness of material well-being in the population. As a result, the masses are subdued, and conflict is rare (except for occasional defiance and violence by outcast racial minorities and the unemployed underclass). The apparent consensus that exists is only a superficial cover for domination and suppressed conflict.

In a related statement, Habermas (1975) regards the main agency of domination in post-industrial capitalism not as class in the Marxian sense, but rather as the technical-administrative apparatus of the state, based on instrumental rationality. This apparatus intrudes on the life-world of individuals and groups and distorts it in an overly rational direction. The state involves itself in the organization and manipulation of the economy in its "steering performances." In addition, the state enters the economy directly, providing education and training, supervising and maintaining the infrastructure of transportation and housing, and sustaining huge military forces. The state secures the loyalty–often passive–of the populace by assuring a flow of consumer goods, providing welfare, and controlling the media. At the same time, Habermas viewed the technical-administrative state as constantly facing crises such as inflation, financial instability, failures of planning, administrative paralysis, failure to deliver on its promises, and the erosion of cultural values such as the work ethic.

Two additional lines of theorizing are consistent with the renewed emphasis on the state. The first is the work of Skocpol (1979) and others, who–under the rubric "bringing the state back in"–have reasserted that the state assumes an autonomy (not recognized in Marxist theory) and becomes a prime mover in the processes of bureaucratic growth, social domination, and the development of revolutions. The second is the European literature on the new social movements (Eyerman 1992). Noting that "new" movements such as the women's, environmental and anti-nuclear, anti-war, counter cultural, and racial-ethnic movements are not class-based in the Marxian sense, writers have attributed their rise largely to the bureaucratic state's intervention in the fabric of society and to cultural domination by the knowledge industry and the mass media.

Another feature of the classical Marxian world view is that culture (philosophy, religion, ideology) is derivative from the economic substructure in society and functions mainly in the interests of the dominant economic classes. Several recent theoretical developments have attributed greater independence to culture, however. One line of development concerns the analysis of cultural codes themselves, building on the seminal work of Lévi-Strauss (1963) and others; this view pervades cultural sociology in both the United States and Europe. Another line of development stresses the fusion of culture with power and domination.

Much of the impetus for this last view stems from Gramsci (1971). Himself a Marxist, he nevertheless assigned independent significance to the notion of "cultural hegemony," a process by which the ruling classes in society achieve domination by persuading the subordinate classes of the correctness of their cultural, moral, and political views through avenues such as the educational system and the mass media. Two French theorists, Michel Foucault and Pierre Bourdieu, have elaborated the power–culture link in various directions. Foucault (1980) was concerned especially with the significance of knowledge as a pervasive mode of domination–he maintained that power and knowledge are one and the same–in society's structural relations. His particular analyses treat the exercise of knowledge/power in medical, psychiatric, and correctional settings. The macrosociological theory of Bourdieu (1984) also stresses the struggle among classes in society. This struggle involves an economic element, but Bourdieu himself gave more weight to a cultural or symbolic dimension. Different classes possess different levels and kinds of "cultural capital"–generated through socialization, formal education, and "cultivation"–which serves as a major resource in the assertion and defense of class position.

Two final conflict-based perspectives have arisen from a critique of theories of modernization. Both have an international flavor. The first is dependency theory, associated with Fernando Cardoso and other Latin American writers (Cardoso and Faletto 1969). Arguing that development is not rooted primarily in intra-societal forces such as entrepreneurship and the overcoming of traditional obstacles, these theorists stress that international capital, multinational corporations, and debt give direction to economic change and shape patterns of class domination and conflict in the developing countries. Whereas early formulations stressed that international capital prevented or warped development, newer variants have analyzed cases (e.g., South Korea and Taiwan) where robust and successful economic development has occurred within the context of dependency. The second perspective is world-systems theory, associated with Fernand Braudel (1979) and Immanuel Wallerstein (1974). It is based on the premise that both the modern and the contemporary organization of societies are based not on indigenous conditions but reflect the shifting system of economic relations *among* societies. In particular, any historical period is characterized by the presence of a core (e.g., Great Britain in the nineteenth century, the United States in the post-Second World War decades), a periphery (colonial countries, Third World countries), and a semi-periphery of involved but weaker countries (e.g., Mexico and Argentina at the present time). At its most extreme, world-systems theory would write the internal histories of societies as ramifications of the international economic forces impinging on them.

Microsociological Theories

While social psychology and social interaction have long been parts of sociology, the 1970s witnessed a "microscopic revolution" in which theories based on interpersonal interaction were either revitalized or invented. These were brought forward as competitors to macrosociological theory, which, it was claimed, "reifies" social life as abstract organizations, structures, and cultures.

Exchange and rational choice   As the names imply, theories of this kind borrow from the fields of economics and psychology. Homans's social behaviorism (1974), for example, incorporated the principles of the maximization of utility and diminishing marginal utility from economics and the principle that regularities are based on connections between influences from the external environment (stimuli) and items of individual behavior (responses) from psychology. In particular, Homans argued that the more a person is rewarded (reinforced) for performing a certain act, the more solidly will that act be established in his or her pattern of behavior. The "exchange" component of Homans's theory arises from the assertion that two or more persons will behave toward one another in accordance with the principles of reward as reinforcement and that all types of interactive relationships (e.g., cooperation, authority) can be understood and explained as manifestations of such exchange. Another variation on exchange theory, that of Blau (1964), also relies on economic ideas of exchange, but his version is more nearly "social–structural" in character in that it envisages exchanges among persons located in organizational and structural positions and includes explicit analyses of the development of social differentiation, power structures, and collective values.

Rational-choice theory also arises from the application of psychological and market models current in economics to types of behavior and institutions not considered primarily economic. Becker, the economist, argued (1976) that the principle of rational calculation pervades all human life and applied that perspective to such diverse topics as racial discrimination, marriage choice, crime, and drug addiction. The most ambitious sociological statement of the rational-choice perspective is that of Coleman (1990). Starting from the utilitarian view of the actor as maximizing, rationally calculating, and unrestrained by norms, Coleman moved to wider settings and generated derivative analyses of interpersonal exchange, market and authority systems, collective behavior and social movements, and corporate and institutional structures.

Micro-conflict theories   The first illustration of this approach is found in the work of Collins (1975). His theory involves two or more actors in a situation of scarcity, oriented not to exchange but to gaining dominance over other actors. However, he envisions interaction as more than a simple power struggle, because he acknowledges and develops possibilities for negotiation and compromise. The existing distribution of power in the larger society is a kind of aggregated result of thousands of settled micro-conflict situations. The second illustration was developed in one subfield of sociology, deviance and social control, and generally goes under the headings of labeling theory (Becker 1963) or stigma theory (Goffman 1963). Whereas functional theory treats deviance as originating in individual motivation and as in violation of some societal norm, labeling theorists regard deviants (and deviance in general) as produced by the exercise of power of agents in positions of social control (doctors, judges, law-enforcement officials), who enforce their definitions upon "deviants." The problem of deviance thus emerges as a kind of struggle over meanings–indeed, a power struggle–with the more powerful usually able to impose their definitions, though those labeled "deviant" develop strategies to subvert or manipulate those meanings. New social structures are created as authorities assign deviants to a kind of disadvantaged underclass.

Phenomenological theories   Several microscopic approaches are based on the premise that the study of social reality must be based on the meaning systems of individual actors. An illustration of this approach is symbolic interactionism, rooted in the pragmatic philosophies of John Dewey, Charles Cooley, and George Herbert Mead and given later expression in the work of Blumer (1969). In one respect Blumer's starting point was a negative polemic: that human behavior cannot be characterized as the product of internal or external forces such as instincts, drives, social roles, social structures, or culture. Instead, the notions of subjective meaning and the self are central. Meaning is found, moreover–as the name of the perspective implies–in the interactive process. Individuals communicate with one another, create and derive meanings, and act on them accordingly. In addition, an individual engages in meaningful communication with himself or herself, making the same kinds of indications as are found in interaction. These processes are complicated, involving the reading of others' meanings, revising meanings on the basis of such reading, guessing others' readings, and modifying one's anticipations and behavior in line with these processes. Enduring social arrangements are treated in large part as joint actions and the "fitting together" of meaningful activity in more or less stable ways.

A related perspective is ethnomethodology, associated mainly with Garfinkel (1967). Ethnomethodologists likewise rejected social-structural accounts, in that they involve reification and lose sight of the realities of close interaction. The ethnomethodological perspective envisions a free, practical, improvising, negotiating actor who, in interacting with others has at his or her disposal a variety of action plans and "rationalities." The task of the ethnomethodologist is to investigate the lines of action taken, the accounts given for this action, and the ways that taken-for-granted understandings guide action. The structure of social reality is not given but is continuously constituted, reconstituted, reproduced, and accounted for in interaction. One line of research of ethnomethodologists has been to discover–or create–situations in which interaction is broken by ignoring or violating understandings of interaction and to track how existing meanings are restored or new ones negotiated. For this reason ethnomethodologists have been described as "microfunctionalists" who study the equilibrating processes of social interaction, just as macrofunctionalists focus on these processes in the larger society.

Habermas (1987 [1981]) has also generated a synthetic statement known as "the theory of communicative action," based partly on phenomenological sources. It is a theory of communication associated with individuals' and groups' life-world, which is a level of society set off from the world of cognitive instrumentality and rationality that is embodied in formal organizations–especially the state apparatus–in post-industrial society. Habermas regards communicative action as an "ideal speech situation" in which free (unconstrained) individuals engage in argumentative speech and thereby create objective definitions and intersubjective constructions. The criteria for validity of communicative action are not rational in the scientific-instrumental sense but, rather, are found in the truths that arise from the moral, aesthetic, therapeutic, and expressive dimensions of interaction. Furthermore, Habermas views communicative discourse as liberating individuals from the distortions of an overly rationalized world and containing the potential for criticism and reconstruction of that world.

A final theoretical statement by Berger and Luckmann (1967) is both phenomenological and microsociological in its origins but also journeys to the macrosociological level and back to the microsociological. According to this view, in the interactive process people stabilize what is an inherently complex and unstable–if not chaotic–world through a process of typification and objectification of social situations. The medium for this process is language. By a further process, objectifications are reified and given the stamp of legitimacy as they are forged into institutional and cultural expectations. Specialists in the definition and maintenance of "social reality" also arise. The circle is completed when this constructed reality of society becomes the basis for socialization and social control–processes carried out "as if" the constructed social reality were objective and real.

Some Qualifying Comments on the Map

Upon completing this tour of theoretical perspectives, which could have been more extensive and elaborate if space had permitted, the reader is likely to experience a certain weariness and frustration. The coverage of sociological theory is immense; its diversity is such that one searches in vain for unity; and most of the theoretical positions enunciated include a critical stance toward many of the rest. In many respects such perceptions are justified; sociological theory *is* sprawling, fragmented, and divided by polemic. To counteract this negative view to a degree, I now introduce a thread of continuity by venturing a few observations on the state of "theory in practice"–that is, on how sociologists regard theory in their ongoing empirical research.

Most sociologists would describe themselves as, in principle, favoring one or more of the perspectives found on the map and not favoring others. Statements of preference of this kind tend to highlight differences among sociologists. However, it is also clear that when theoretically informed investigators turn to the analysis of specific intellectual problems rooted in social reality, they are almost inevitably forced to "compromise" the purity of their first principles and incorporate others. For example, Durkheim's empirical studies of suicide (1951 [1897]) and Weber's empirical studies of religion and economic action (1958 [1904–5]) have much more in common than their methodological manifestos (Durkheim 1958 [1895], Weber 1949 [1904]), which are polemically opposed on almost all theoretical and methodological scores. The same can be said of most empirical research. Despite metatheoretical and substantive differences in starting points, the complexity of social reality and the methodological constraints of empirical investigation invariably force the investigator to break from the rigidities of first principles. In a word, empirical research imposes a tendency toward eclecticism and partial theoretical synthesis.

Furthermore, most of the theoretical perspectives reviewed here do not exist in some kind of pure state but are adapted continuously according to particular circumstances. For example, as theoretical perspectives, most of which have originated in Western Europe and North America, move to countries and regions of the world different from those of their origin, they are modified. They are combined and recombined with one another and shaped to apply to perspectives, outlooks, and conditions distinctive to those particular countries and regions. It is also to be expected that as these countries develop universities, academies, and other institutions that facilitate social inquiry, more independent theorizing will develop. It is a matter of contemporary debate as to the degree to which sociology is unified versus the degree to which there are distinctive national and regional sociologies (see chapter 1); surely the correct view is that contemporary theoretical sociology is a complicated mosaic, incorporating both universal and particular intellectual and social forces.

We should also acknowledge several activities and outlooks that counter the tendencies toward polemic opposition among theoretical positions. First, insofar as sociological research becomes increasingly interdisciplinary–and many signs point in this direction–interpretative perspectives that might be considered opposed in the abstract tend to blend together. Second, the contemporary scene reveals a number of serious efforts at theoretical synthesis. Among these are the following:

- the attempt to generate analytical and empirical links between the microsociological and macrosociological levels (e.g., Alexander *et al*. 1987);
- the effort to weld theoretical linkages between the purposive efforts of individuals and groups (agents) and the social-structural context in which they reside (Giddens 1984);
- the attempt to create focused theories, which nevertheless draw from a variety of perspectives; feminist theory, for example, while in large part formulated in conflict–domination terms, also incorporates other viewpoints, including the psychoanalytic and the phenomenological (Lengermann and Niebrugge-Brantley 1992).

Third, the past two decades have witnessed a decline in the polemic warfare that characterized sociology and many of the other social sciences during the 1960s and 1970s. The mood more characteristic of the 1990s appears to be one of "peaceful pluralism"–an acknowledgment that sociological inquiry legitimately harbors a diversity of perspectives and methods, even though clear preferences are apparent among identifiable groups of theorists and empirical investigators.

On Reading Sociological Theories

My career as an academic sociologist began with teaching a course in systematic theory at the University of California, Berkeley, in the fall of 1958, and I have continued to teach such courses over the decades until the present time. In this period of study and teaching, I have developed a series of questions that, in my estimation, are essential to understanding and criticizing sociological theories and comparing them with one another. I conclude by offering them to readers for reflection:

- What model or imagery of scientific knowledge informs or guides the efforts of a theorist or theoretical tradition? The reasons for asking this question are two: first, the social sciences developed historically in the shadow of the natural sciences and in most cases modeled themselves on them; second, sociology and the other social sciences continue to justify their legitimacy in academies and universities by the claim that they are social *sciences*. It is thus difficult for any theory not to take the canons and methods of science into account. This is not to say that all theories model themselves on a positivistic image of science. Some clearly do–rational-choice theory, for example–but the informing assumptions of many social theories are explicitly critical of positive science. Even when the orientation toward it is negative, however, some model of science remains as a point of reference.

- What specific formal and substantive elements of scientific imagery are incorporated or rejected? This query is a specification of the first.

- What is the theorist's conception of the individuals and groups that constitute the subjects of theorizing? Are they seen to be active, neutral, or passive as agents of change and history? Do their outlooks matter in the formulation of scientific knowledge (behaviorists say no, phenomenologists say yes)? In short, what is the theorist's image of human nature?

- What is the theorist's conception of his or her own role in the generation of sociological knowledge? Active or passive? Conservative, neutral, critical? This question arises because social scientists are, inescapably, intellectuals situated in society and invariably reflect on the implications of that fact.

- What is the theorist's commitment concerning the primary level of analysis–cultural, social system, social-structural, group, or individual? Closely related, what is it *about* that level–integration, conflict, freedom, oppression–that is most salient?

- How adequately does the theory fare with respect to *logical* canons of clarity, internal consistency, logical closure, and coherence between first principles and derived propositions? How adequately does it fare with respect to *empirical* canons of assembling evidence, assuring the reliability of that evidence, and demonstrating the validity of claims contained in propositions? Even theorists who deny the relevance or even the possibility of logical and empirical discourse invariably find themselves engaging in this kind of discourse, and their work can be assessed according to its canons.

If the student of theory asks such questions in a thorough, probing, and dispassionate way, that person will be well on the way toward charting his or her own map of sociological theory and toward stating, with reasons, a set of theoretical preferences.

References

Alexander, J. C. (ed.) 1985: *Neofunctionalism*. Beverly Hills, Calif.: Sage Publications.

Alexander, J. and Colomy, P. 1990: *Differentiation Theory and Social Change: Comparative and Historical Perspectives*. New York: Columbia University Press.

Alexander, J. C., Giesen, B., Münch, R. and Smelser, N. J. (eds) 1987: *The Micro–Macro Link*. Berkeley, Calif.: University of California Press.

Becker, G. S. 1976: *The Economic Approach to Human Behavior*. Chicago: University of Chicago Press.

Becker, H. 1963: *Outsiders*. New York: Free Press.

Bell, D. 1960: *The End of Ideology*. New York: Free Press.

Berger, P. and Luckmann, T. 1967: *The Social Construction of Reality*. Garden City, N.Y.: Doubleday.

Blau, P. 1964: *Exchange and Power in Social Life*. New York: Wiley.

Blauner, R. 1972: *Racial Oppression in America*. New York: Harper and Row.

Blumer, H. 1954: "What is Wrong with Social Theory?" *American Sociological Review*, 19: 3–10.

Blumer, H. 1969: *Symbolic Interactionism: Perspective and Method*. Englewood Cliffs, N.J.: Prentice-Hall.

Bourdieu, P. 1984: *Distinction: A Social Critique of the Judgment of Taste*. Cambridge, Mass.: Harvard University Press.

Braudel, F. 1979: *The Perspective of the World*. New York: Harper and Row.

Braverman, H. 1974: *Labor and Monopoly Capital. The Degradation of Work in the Twentieth Century*. New York: Monthly Review Press.

Burawoy, M. 1979: *Manufacturing Consent. Changes in the Labor Process under Monopoly Capitalism*. Chicago: University of Chicago Press.

Cardoso, F H. and Faletto, E. 1969: *Dependency and Development in Latin America*. Berkeley, Calif.: University of California Press.

Coleman, J. 1990: *Foundations of Social Theory*. Cambridge, Mass.: Belknap Press of Harvard University Press.

Collins, R. 1975: *Conflict Sociology*. New York: Academic Press.

Coser, L. A. 1956: *The Functions of Social Conflict*. Glencoe, Ill.: Free Press.

Dahrendorf, R. 1959: *Class and Class Conflict in Industrial Society*. Stanford, Calif.: Stanford University Press.

Durkheim, E. 1951 [1897]: *Suicide*. Glencoe, Ill.: Free Press.

Durkheim, E. 1958 [1895]: *The Rules of Sociological Method*. Glencoe, Ill: Free Press.

Durkheim, E. 1947 [1913]: *The Elementary Forms of Religious Life*. Glencoe, Ill.: Free Press.

Eyerman, R. 1992: "Modernity and Social Movements," in H. Haferkamp, and N. J. Smelser, (eds), *Social Change and Modernity*, Berkeley, Calif.: University of California Press, 37–54.

Foucault, M. 1980: *Power-Knowledge*. New York: Pantheon.

Garfinkel, H. 1967: *Studies in Ethnomethodology*. Englewood Cliffs, N.J.: Prentice-Hall.

Giddens, A. 1984: *The Constitution of Society: Outline of a Theory of Structuration*. Berkeley, Calif.: University of California Press.

Goffman, E. 1963: *Stigma: Notes on the Management of Spoiled Identity*. Englewood Cliffs, N.J.: Prentice-Hall.

Gramsci, A. 1971: *Selections from the Prison Notebooks*. London: Lawrence and Wishart.

Habermas, J. 1975: *Legitimation Crisis*. Boston: Beacon Press.

Habermas, J. 1987 [1981]: *Theory of Communicative Action*. 2 vols. Boston: Beacon Press.

Hannan, M. and Freeman, J. 1977: "The Population Ecology of Organizations." *American Journal of Sociology*, 82: 929–64.

Hartmann, H. 1976: "Capitalism, Patriarchy, and Job Segregation." *Signs*, 1: 137–69.

Homans, G. 1974: *Social Behavior: Its Elementary Forms*. New York: Harcourt, Brace, Jovanovich.

Kuhn, T. 1962: *The Structure of Scientific Revolutions*. Chicago: University of Chicago Press.

Lengermann, P. M. and Niebrugge-Brantley, J. 1992: "Contemporary Feminist Theory," in G. Ritzer (ed.) *Contemporary Sociological Theory*, 3rd edn, New York: McGraw-Hill, 308–57.

Lévi-Strauss, C. 1963: *Structural Anthropology*. New York: Basic Books.

Luhmann, N. 1982: *The Differentiation of Society*. New York: Columbia University Press.

Malinowski, B. 1955: *Magic, Science and Religion and Other Essays*. Garden City, N.Y.: Doubleday.

Marcuse, H. 1964: *One–Dimensional Man*. Boston: Beacon Press.

Marx, K. 1913 [1859]: *A Contribution to the Critique of Political Economy*. Chicago: Kerr.

Marx, K, and Engels, F. 1954 [1848]: *The Communist Manifesto*. Chicago: Henry Regnery.

Merton, R. K. 1968a: "The Bearing of Sociological Theory on Empirical Research," in *Social Theory and Social Structure*, rev. enlarged edn, New York: The Free Press, 139–55.

Merton, R. K. 1968b: "Manifest and Latent Functions," in *Social Theory and Social Structure*. enlarged edn, 73–138.

Merton, R. K. 1968c: "On Sociological Theories of the Middle Range," in *Social Theory and Social Structure*, rev. enlarged edn, 39–72.

Michels, R. 1959 [1911]: *Political Parties: A Sociological Study of the Oligarchical Tendencies of Modern Democracy*. New York: Dover Publications.

Parsons, T. 1951: *The Social System*. Glencoe, Ill.: Free Press.

Parsons, T. 1954 [1945]: "The Present Position and Prospects of Systematic Theory in Sociology," in *Essays in Sociological Theory*, rev. edn, Glencoe, Ill.: Free Press. 212–37.

Radcliffe-Brown, A. R. 1952: *Structure and Function in Primitive Society*. Glencoe, Ill.: Free Press.

Skocpol, T. 1979: *States and Social Revolutions*. New York: Cambridge University Press.

Smelser, N. J., and Warner, R. S. 1976: *Sociological Theory: Historical and Formal*. Morristown, N.J.: General Learning Press.

Spencer, H. 1897: *The Principles of Sociology*. New York: D. Appleton.

Taylor, L., Walton, P., and Young, J. 1973: *The New Criminology: For a Theory of Social Deviance*. New York: Harper and Row.

Wallerstein, I. 1974: *The Modern World-System, Vol. 1: Capitalist Agriculture and the Origins of the European World-Economy in the Sixteenth Century*. New York: Academic Press.

Weber, M. 1958 [1904–5]: *The Protestant Ethic and the Spirit of Capitalism*. New York: Scribner's.

Weber, M. 1949 [1904]: "'Objectivity' in Social Science and Social Policy," in E. A. Shils and H. A. Finch (eds), *The Methodology of the Social Sciences*. Glencoe, Ill.: Free Press, 49–112.

Wright, E. O. 1985. *Classes*: London: Verso.

3

Sociological Methods

In the last chapter, two requirements for an adequate sociological theory were specified: identifiable empirical propositions about social relations and society and efforts to confirm or disconfirm those propositions. In its simplest definition, sociological methodology consists of the rules and procedures to be applied in the confirmation or disconfirmation of such propositions. Although that definition is correct as far as it goes, we will see in this chapter that methodology is vast and complex and contains many ingredients not explicit in the simple definition.

Theory and/or/versus Method?

It is easy to think of theory and method as two distinct enterprises. One deals with concepts and frameworks in the world of ideas, the other with operations in the empirical world. In college and university curricula, the two are taught in separate courses with different names. Furthermore, the terms often connote some kind of tension–if not open warfare–between the two. This quality is caught in the following pair of unfriendly jests:

> *Methodologist*: Theory is what you talk about; methodology is what you do.
> *Theorist*: Methodology may be what you do, but theory is what you mean.

While the separateness and tension exist, they conceal the more important fact that sociology as a science cannot progress unless both theory and methods advance. A theoretical account of societal transformations, for example, rests on our ability to measure formally defined

---

This chapter is based on a contribution by Karl M. van Meter.

quantitative changes in rates of behavior and other institutional facts over time, and the quality of our measurement rests in turn on a sound knowledge, based on theory, of what it is we want to measure. Furthermore, a weakness in theory sooner or later appears as a weakness in method, and vice versa; and advances in either contribute to the development of the other and to the scientific status of the discipline.

One difficulty in relating theory intelligibly to methodology lies in the fact that there are many varieties of each. We scanned the great panorama of sociological theories in chapter 2. There are also a large number of commonly cited sociological methods–experimental, statistical, computer simulation and mathematical modeling, survey, depth interview, participant observation, historical/archival, comparative/illustrative, and ethnographic/case study, to say nothing of dozens of sub-varieties under these general headings. Sometimes there is an affinity between a certain type of theory and a certain type of method; for example, ethnomethodologists, who study subtle personal interactions based on taken-for-granted meanings, typically rely on interview and participant observation. Such affinities are loose, however, and what we observe in sociology is a vast array of theories and a vast array of methods, the relations among which are not always evident.

Things are not helped, moreover, by the fact that both theorists and methodologists speak many different languages, which constitute barriers to communication *among* both theorists and methodologists and *between* the two. One way to overcome such difficulties is to point out that, despite the different languages used, investigators using presumably different research methods are really pursuing identical explanatory strategies. For example, it could be argued that the major objective of social science explanation is to *control* as many possible causes (independent variables) of an effect (dependent variable), as possible, so that the actual influence of a single suspected factor can be assessed without contamination by the other factors. The experimental method achieves this control by directly manipulating these factors situationally; the statistical method achieves the same control by conceptual devices such as multiple or partial regression; and the comparative/historical method does the same by systematically comparing limited numbers of cases according to their similarities and differences with respect to causes and outcomes. In a word, the methods of inquiry are different, but the scientific objective is identical (Smelser 1976).

In the end, however, there are few interpreters and few schemes of translation available, and efforts to relate theoretical and methodological languages intelligibly to one another often result in offending the theoretical or methodological sensibilities of a subdisciplinary community and breeding accusations of distortion. One of the objectives of this chapter is to work toward a language that will help the translation process, while recognizing that such an objective is difficult and involves taking some risks.

The Program of the Chapter

The International Sociological Association has a committee called the Research Committee on Logic and Methodology (RC 33). As a preliminary to drafting this chapter, we surveyed all the members of this committee and asked them to specify the major issues confronting sociological methodology at the present time. We found a surprisingly wide agreement among the respondents, who identified the following three points:

- the diminishing significance of the "quantitative" versus "qualitative" issue in sociological methodology;
- the "nonuniversal" character of all methodologies, even though each has a distinctive domain;
- the value of multi-method analysis in obtaining reliable results and in opening up communication among subdisciplines.

The chapter is organized under these headings. Toward the end we will develop some practical suggestions for "doing methodology" for interested readers.

Two orienting definitions are in order at this point. Throughout, the terms "method" and "methodology" will be used. The first refers to a method of data analysis unless otherwise specified. Sometimes it will be used in connection with other terms to specify a specific phase of investigation, such as "methods of data collection" or "methods of data coding." The second term, "methodology", covers all the different aspects and steps involved in conducting sociological research. As such, it is very broad in its reference. Some methodology involves such nonformalized, practical research lore as assuring correct weightings on voting polls and having the right "street savvy" for locating drug-users to interview. "Methodology" also covers practical rules for making inferences from empirical data to propositions, as well as logical rules for relating propositions to theoretical frameworks and for criticizing the internal logic of theoretical frameworks. The label "logic and methodology," used to characterize the scope of RC 33, connotes this breadth of reference.

The Quantitative–Qualitative Distinction

Like the relations between theory and methodology, the relations between quantitative and qualitative methods have been obscured by the mistaken conception that the two are separate, identifiable entities. The major debates between exponents of each position before the Second World War produced a wide divide in sociology and a hardening of partisan, quasi-ideological positions. The massive use of survey research during and after the war led to a dominant institutional status for quantitative methodology. But with the development of critical, anti-positivistic thinking since the 1960s, qualitative methodologies have asserted themselves. More recently, the evident need for subtle and inventive methods for investigating difficult and evasive problems such as drug usage and AIDS has also confirmed the value of qualitative methods.

When examined closely, however, the distinction between quantitative and qualitative methods weakens. For one thing, the apparently single distinction contains a multiplicity of dimensions. A recent attempt (Hammersley 1982) to disaggregate the distinction produced a number of components: words versus numbers, natural versus artificial settings, meaning versus behavior, inductive versus deductive approaches, cultural patterns versus scientific laws, idealism versus realism. We might even add the ideological connotations of scientism versus humanism and dispassion versus moral commitment as sometimes contained in the distinction. In any event, we agree with Hammersley's conclusion that "[the] prevalence of the distinction between qualitative and quantitative methods tends to obscure the complexity of the problems that face us and threatens to render our decisions less effective than they might otherwise be" (1982: 172). Furthermore, any effort to find a consistent, binding distinction between quantitative and qualitative methods tends to founder. Consider the following:

- Even the most hard-line "qualitative" analyst will find him or herself sometimes using words such as "more" or "less" as descriptive terms. Whether it is acknowledged or not, such words imply a quantitatively representable universe populated by phenomena with different values.
- Some (Combessie 1986, Wilson 1986) have argued that no investigator does either qualitative or quantitative research but that the two approaches are always intertwined. This observation is reinforced by the fact that computers can easily formalize and analyze all kinds of data, whether they are categorical, scaled or numerical representations (i.e., "quantitative" data) or texts, conversations, and documents (i.e., "qualitative" data).
- As if to acknowledge the confusion, the American National Science Foundation does not now indicate any preference for "quantitative" methodology–despite its institutional commitment to "science"–but requires only that the methodology be adapted to the problem under study.

Consider also two examples that reveal the intermingling of the two kinds of methodology. First, ethnomethodology is generally regarded as having launched one of the most telling critiques of quantitative methodology. Moreover, the approach has produced rich qualitative findings about conversations between persons, which emphasize the subtleties of "turn-taking" and conversational "repair" activities. Recently, however, these two processes have been formalized and incorporated in an experimental computer program at the University of Surrey, in conjunction with British Airways. The computer is able to reply with a synthetic voice to telephone requests for information about arrival and departure times. The researchers have quantified the concept of "turn-taking" to a length of time between −0.8 and +1.2 seconds with a precision of 0.2 seconds. After that time, repair may be necessary in the conversation. So much for a methodology that is "intrinsically" qualitative!

Second, in an investigation a few years ago, French survey analysts encountered difficulties in distinguishing right-wing from left-wing political attitudes in relation to the reform of spelling in the French language. The usual quantified questionnaire variables, analyzed with classical multivariate statistical methods, were not providing an intelligible distinction. At one point in the research, the investigators introduced an open-ended question at the end of the standardized questionnaire. Respondents were simply asked to write what they thought of the proposed spelling reform. The resulting "qualitative" data–that is, the written texts–were analyzed by content-analysis methods, and the results were incorporated directly into the graphic results produced by correspondence analysis. The "qualitative" distinction became clear: right-wing responses included terms such as "our past," "our identity," and "cultural values," while left-wing responses included terms such as "government interference," "lack of debate," and "not consulting the public." In this case qualitative language furnished quantitative results.

Ascending and Descending Methodologies

One constructive way of breaking through the unsatisfactory distinction between quantitative and qualitative methods is to reframe the issue, without necessarily scrapping the whole enterprise of distinguishing among types of methods. A helpful way to reframe, moreover, is to introduce the concepts of "ascending methodology" and "descending methodology," keeping in mind that this distinction is between types of investigative tools and not types of scientific results. The distinction can be illustrated by looking at research on the current social problems of drugs and AIDS, whose study involves above all methodologically sophisticated efforts to study "hidden" or "covert" populations (van Meter 1990).

The difficulty in studying hidden populations reveals a kind of opposition between extensive survey methods and intensive data-collection methods. Put in other terms, this opposition is between descending methodology and ascending methodology. The former involves strategies designed and executed on large or general populations. It necessitates highly standardized measures, such as closed-response questionnaires and rigorously defined population samples. It also usually involves traditional statistical analysis. Descending methodology has been used by national governments to make statistical inferences and develop social policy. It has proved useful, though its strict scientific approach, even when applied in an exemplary manner, can be readily criticized (Guttman 1984). When data on hidden populations are needed, however, this methodology–which assumes ready accessibility to cooperative respondents–runs into difficulties.

Ascending methodologies involve research strategies designed for studying special groups or special behavior–for example, a population of prostitutes in a large city. To be effective, the means of data collection must be selective and intensive. The modes of data collection are life histories, ethnographic descriptions, and use of snowball samples. Methods of analyzing the collected data must also be adapted to the qualities of the data themselves and to the specific objectives of the research. Typical modes of ascending data analysis are content analysis, ascending classification analysis (often called "cluster analysis"), and analysis of ego-centered social networks.

Each method has its distinctive strengths and weaknesses. Ascending methodology is very sensitive to the peculiarities of the population being investigated, but it is difficult to generalize findings beyond that population. Furthermore, the issue of the bias of the investigator is especially acute in ascending methodologies, largely because the methods of collecting data are not standardized. In addition, however sensitive, these methodologies resist formalization of their sample biases, at least within the reach of current statistics. Sometimes, however, ascending methodologies, such as network analysis, can be applied to large populations, though only if standardized and then at great monetary cost; an example is Levine's (1984) effort to analyze network interactions ("overlapping directorates") among the entire world population of corporations.

For its part, descending methodology cannot reach hidden populations with specific adaptations. In a recent review article on drug use, Kozel and Adams (1986) noted the inadequacy of traditional medical epidemiological models (which are, in effect, descending methodologies) in this regard. They also criticized the practice of classifying drug-using behavior in terms of a few apparently distinct categories determined by simplified descriptive terms and proposed instead to deal with "patterns of abuse." Although the authors granted the usefulness of surveys for measuring rates and monitoring trends in drug use, they concluded that because drug epidemics are often localized and involved specific subpopulations, surveillance of these by methods using national data systems is clearly inadequate.

Kozel and Adams mentioned the household survey of the American National Institute of Drug Abuse as the single best measure of drug abuse in the American population. But this measure, too, is limited because of sample bias. It misses an important and very active hidden population: transient and nonresidential individuals and groups. The President's Commission on Organized Crime (1986) made the same point: the Household Survey and the High School Senior Survey "have been criticized because they do not include information from these populations that are frequently involved with drugs, high school dropouts and people without residence" (PCOC 1986: 340). The PCOC has proposed a solution of "over-sampling" to seek out specific types of persons in hidden populations; this is, in effect, an ascending methodology. The commission recognized that "surveys of cocaine users demonstrated that there is no 'typical' cocaine user" (1986: 25) and that the concept of different patterns of use must be employed. Correspondingly, it insisted that the community be the focus of the study, prevention, and treatment of drug abuse.

The PCOC's specific criticism of descending methodology included the lack of data on the price and quantity of drugs purchased, the sources of the funds, and the sources of the data. It also complained of the unreliability of "analysis by negotiation," with final estimates of drug use "resulting from a bargaining process among the member agencies" (1986: 343). These are the very lacunae that "community epidemiology" (Hall 1988), an ascending methodology, attempts to fill by focusing on the consequences of abuse rather than the prevalence of use. "For local purposes it is often more useful to determine answers to the questions of 'who' and 'where' rather than 'how many' so that limited resources may be most effectively applied to provide the greatest benefit" (Hall 1988: 2). Similar ascending methodologies are appropriate for monitoring the heterosexual spread of AIDS in the general population, since it is now recognized that AIDS as an epidemic "will be long and drawn out as it spreads through the different at-risk groups and in different localities over the coming decades" (Anderson 1987: 6140).

An example of recent research (Le Guen and Jaffeux 1989) illustrates the complementary character of ascending and descending methodologies. The authors used an ascending method of analysis–automatic classification analysis–to establish distinct classes in their data but confirmed this analysis by the use of factorial correspondence analysis, a typical "French" method of descending analysis. Using these classes, the authors then plotted the means for each class, permitting a decomposition of the means and variance according to specific classes that had been constructed originally in an ascending manner based on similarity. This method differs from the traditional "Anglo-Saxon" descending method of decomposing variance over an entire population. Moreover, this dual method (ascending *and* descending) offers a reliable way of locating specific parts of the variance in distinct classes or hidden populations while at the same time permitting the calculation of general population estimates.

"Nonuniversal" Methodologies

While stressing the diminishing significance of the quantitative–qualitative distinction in the preceding section, we were simultaneously stressing the limited applicability or generalizability of certain research procedures, such as the sample survey and the ethnographic community study. The same point has been made in other contexts. For example, in his detailed assessment of the famous "Hawthorne experiments" on group morale and industrial relations in the 1940s, Lecuyer (1988) observed that the methods and results of the experiments were not "false" when considered in the clearly defined and limited context of the experiments themselves. However, when generalized to cover industrial processes generally and to become a general school of thought (the human relations approach), these methods lost both validity and pertinence. Such an observation applies equally well to most methods developed and executed in specific research. It is the central point of the nonuniversality argument. We now develop that argument in more detail.

General Research Procedure

We may characterize research in sociology–and in all the social sciences for that matter–in terms of an abstract process of distinct phases. The starting point of this characterization is that sociological research is a process whereby the investigator treats (analyzes) sociological data in a certain way so as to produce results (findings) that he or she can then proceed to interpret. Accordingly, the quality of the research depends on four operations: (1) choosing individuals for study in the population under investigation; (2) choosing variables to describe those individuals; (3) choosing a system of coding data and, when relevant, a mode of collecting data; and (4) employing a method of analysis. The quality of any given piece of research depends on how well all–not just one or two–of these operations are carried out. Furthermore, different kinds of questions are asked for each of the several operations. We may use this scheme, finally, to look at many kinds of research in sociology, thus moving toward a kind of common language of research methodology that may work to break down barriers of communication among those who work with different theories, in different subfields, with different methodologies in the field of sociology.

Refining the points just mentioned, we may represent the typical sociological research procedure as a series of four steps that move from the initial data toward final results:

1 the choice of *descriptive variables* to characterize each of the individuals in the population examined;
2 the choice of *individuals* who constitute that population;
3 the *coding* (or recoding) of the initial data gathered and appropriately described and, when applicable, the *mode* of data collection;
4 the *methods* of analysis employed to treat the data so that formal, often statistical, results can be furnished.

(The use of the term "steps" implies only analytical, not temporal, priority; all the steps are intermingled in actual time.)

Actually, it is possible to specify two additional steps, one, (0), which occurs *before* the four mentioned and another, (5) which occurs *after*. By (0) we refer to the *initial transformation* of an individual's internal mental states or their external representation through discourse into stylized, formalized, or even numerical information. Simplifying matters somewhat, this step constitutes an "objectification" of the subjective experiences of the individuals being studied. By (5) we refer to the *final transformation* by the researcher of the formal results of the study into some kind of public discourse or scientific text.

It is widely appreciated that step 1, the choice of variables, is far from being a standardized, formalized, or "objective" process. It was Weber (1949 [1904]) who pointed out forcefully the impossibility of a "presuppositionless," completely objective science of sociology. He also pointed out that the choice of sociological problem to be studied–and, we might add, the choice of variables–always reflects certain "cultural preferences" on the part of the investigator. That is to say, they reflect his or her own cultural predilections, institutional position, and personal biography. In fact, if we are seeking the origins of different "paradigms" or "schools of thought" in sociology, we would do well to ferret out those important first assumptions that define what different investigators deem it important to describe about social relations and society. To undertake this operation, moreover, is to undertake an important enterprise in the sociology of knowledge (Desrosières *et al*. 1983).

As indicated, the initial choice of descriptive variables seems to have an almost inevitable "arbitrary" component, and, for that reason, we may regard this step as simultaneously *both* the most original and creative task of the research *and* the most remote from objectively based systematization. We know of only one empirically based attempt to solve this problem of arbitrariness. This is found in the survey methodology developed since the 1970s by the French Agorametrie group for its annual survey of the structure of French public opinion concerning social conflicts (Durand *et al*. 1990). In this instance, a formalized method is used to select the variables (questions) which enter into each year's questionnaire. One month before the survey is administered, an analysis is made of all French daily and weekly newspaper articles, as well as all radio and television programs. Each time a topic of social conflict is encountered in these sources, it is entered on a list which is then submitted to a panel of survey experts, with the relative importance of the topic indicated. Questions (variables) are then formulated to reflect the entire range of social conflict as experienced by the French public through its mass media. By this procedure, the researchers attain a certain independence (from themselves) in the definition of the variables to be studied and also guarantee that those variables are in some way representative in relation to the social universe under study.

In contrast to the "arbitrary component" of step 1, step 2 (the choice of individuals) has become virtually an exact science in itself, with an entire literature and research tradition. We refer to sampling theory and practice, which rely on sophisticated mathematical and statistical techniques, and which have developed a whole range of subtypes (random, stratified, block, sequential sampling), each of which is appropriate to different kinds of questions. In fact, we may place step 1 (choice of variables) and step 2 (choice of individuals) at the extremes of the "arbitrary–objective" continuum and treat the other two steps of our idealized research process as intermediate between those two.

Stability of Results

Within the framework of the four-step procedure we have put forward, we may add for consideration two further aspects of the organization and structure of the research process:

A   the properties and structure of the information contained in the *initial data*;

B   the relationship between the initial data and the *results* based on a formalized or statistical analysis of those data and announced or presented by the research in a report.

These aspects of the research process are related differently to each of the four steps of the scheme.

The relationship between steps 1 and 2 (choice of descriptive variables and choice of individuals) and aspect A (properties and structure of the initial data) is direct: the choice of variables and the choice of individuals *strongly determine* the properties and structure of the initial data. To put the matter in plain language, what you get is what you have chosen to get. Steps 1 and 2 also influence aspect B (the final results and their reporting). However, this influence works mainly via aspect A, the character of the initial data.

It is also true that the operations undertaken in step 3 influence the properties and structure of the initial data (aspect A). That is to say, how you code and gather the data also influences its character. These influences are often discussed under the headings of experimenter influence, interviewer influence, errors in recording data, and so on. Sometimes these influences can be assessed and taken into account in the research–for example, by noting the differential responses that male respondents give to male and female investigators, respectively. In other cases such sources of "error" in the initial data are unknown and for that reason beyond control.

This relationship between coding and mode of collection (step 3) and the nature of the initial information (aspect A) is often characterized as a problem of *isomorphism*, or changing between two equivalent codes, or *surjection*, or recoding initial information by using a new, more compact coding system. In these cases there may be some loss of information but supposedly no transformation of the data structure. In relation to survey research, we may mention yet another source of bias. This arises in step 0, the transformation of mental states and their representation as discourse into formal measures. The specific bias involved here is the compressing of complex and idiosyncratic dimensions of the meaning of personal experience into simple standardized coded responses, which omit and possibly distort those dimensions.

In assessing the impact of step 3 (coding) on aspect B (final results), it is necessary for the researcher to vary the codings–that is, to make them into recodings. In a research project on white-collar crime in France, van Meter (1981, 1983) showed that a typical recoding often used in social research (recoding numerical variables as categorical variables) greatly transforms the general structure of the data while leaving the detailed structure of the data nearly intact. This type of recoding–often described as part of "cleaning up a raw data file"–is a widely practiced process. In the area of survey research, some guidelines have been provided to assess the impact of coding systems, as well as the modes of collecting data.

Step 4 (methods of analysis) can be seen as supervening on aspect B (the relationship between initial information and final results). We note that formalized methods apply algorithms (often metrics or similarity indices), which tend to be specific for each research method, to generate results. Many computer systems of data analysis programs–such as SPSS, BMDP, OSIRIS, and SAS–provide the possibility of changing algorithms for any method chosen. This feature of selection of algorithms is becoming more common, even in smaller programs. In actual practice, however, the choice of the method of analysis usually determines the choice of a single algorithm and therefore influences the ultimate results. In any event, the only way to study the influence of the methods of analysis on the final results is to use several different methods (or algorithms when possible). This is one of the meanings of the term "multi-method analysis."

Finally, we mention the relation of aspect A (properties and structure of initial information) to step 4 (choice of methods of analysis). Cibois (1980) argued that researchers in sociology have a tendency to *anticipate a structure in their own data* in order to provide a descriptive or explanatory framework for the social phenomenon being studied. In a similar vein, Schiltz (1983) argued that a researcher often follows a nonformalized procedure that is guided by an intuitive conviction about what his or her data will reveal. And if, relying on this intuitive conviction, the researcher chooses but a single method of analysis, he or she has little chance of encountering unanticipated properties in the initial data. This is yet another example of the possibility of "loading the dice" in such a way that one or more of the four research steps is not guided by criteria independent of decisions taken with respect to the other steps.

Multi-Method Analysis

The upshot of the account given in the preceding section is the following: if a sociologist chooses only *one* strategy for each step, then the research results are influenced by–and thus cannot be considered stable or independent of–those choices. If a researcher uses only one type of coding, only one method of "cleaning up" the data file, and only one method of formal analysis, then the results–a correlation, a typology, an explanation–become the only ones possible, given the logic of the methodological choices made. Furthermore, such results can easily be contradicted by some other, thoroughly acceptable analysis of the same initial data (Florens 1984, Combessie 1984). The striking implication of this statement is that contradictory results in sociological research can have their origin not only in the complexity of the empirical world but also in the methods selected to study the empirical world. Further, one of the reasons why so much sociological knowledge may not be scientifically cumulative is that different researchers (both in the same and in succeeding generations) simply make different choices of strategies with respect to steps 1–4, each operating on their own as well as institutionally generated, choices of research strategies.

The moral to be drawn is that the quality of sociological knowledge will be improved if researchers undertake to treat the methods of dealing with the issues stipulated in the various phases of research (steps 1–4) *as themselves variables to be investigated.* That is to say, they should rely as much as possible on multiple methods of analysis. Such a program grows more feasible with time, since increasingly sophisticated means of employing different methods are available in computer systems. Despite the evident desirability of multi-method analysis and despite the capacity to carry out that kind of analysis, however, we find discouragingly few attempts actually to execute it. Those that exist, moreover, tend to be isolated from one another and restricted to a single discipline, so that they remain highly particularized and isolated from general social science thinking (Gower 1971, Conner 1982, Harter 1980).

Furthermore, these multiple-method exercises tend to present their results as an effort to develop a better *single* method of analysis, a strategy that fails to avoid the pitfalls that arise from the very use of single methods in steps 1–4. In fact, they have most often been efforts to correct what were perceived as "weaknesses" in other, particular methods by developing yet another, particular method. As we have seen, however, "weaknesses" in research are often a product of the overall *methodology* employed, not the shortcomings of a single *method* in and of itself. A full multi-method approach would address steps 1 and 3 and would not restrict itself to a single method of analysis, step 4. In the present state of the art, then, multi-method analysis is a helpful but limited way of generating stable results.

Two examples of helpful multi-method analyses may be noted. In the first, in research on child development, researchers carried out multiple analyses–factorial correspondence analysis, proximity analysis, hierarchically ascending classification analysis, and smallest space analysis–and arrived at the following conclusion: "The existence of a complex data structure has shown us the limits of the methods (employed) and the dangers of a too rapid interpretation of the results obtained separately by each method" (Pottier 1976).

In other instances only one method was used, but it was employed several times and often with a variation in relation to either step 1 (variables chosen), 2 (individuals chosen), or 3 (coding and mode of collection chosen). It is possible to find multiple factorial analyses in archeological work on Etrusco-Italic amphoras, statistical research on the stability of principal component analyses in which the research has varied the weighting of modalities or the subpopulation analyzed, and research on the factorial analysis of several different data files which share a strong mutual structure. In the context of these multiple analyses, one can find work on simulation with bootstrap and jackknife methods, including work on validation in which the subpopulation of individuals analyzed is systematically varied and work on "mean clouds" or "mean clusters" which result from several classification analyses of different groups of variables for the same individuals.

Beyond these technical arguments, there is a final, somewhat more down-to-earth case to be made for the use of multiple methods in sociological research. It goes as follows. If an empirical researcher is making an effort to give a coherent explanatory account of a given social phenomenon (e.g., changes in job segregation by gender over time in a given country), then he or she would be well advised to apply a *number* of different research methods, both ascending and descending. To continue the illustration, different facets of the topic of gender segregation in jobs will be illuminated and deepened if the analysis rests on trends revealed by census and survey data, community ethnographies, interviews with both employers and employees, and detailed case studies of individual plants and offices. Each method is limited, but each can deepen the analysis, and the several strategies taken together will tend to complement one another, particularly if the results obtained by each point in the same direction.

Conclusions

The foregoing analysis suggests that stability of research results is extremely difficult to attain at the present time, largely because research is carried out with little systematic attention to the implications of using different strategies with respect to steps 1–4 of the research process. One evident strategy for the future is to make efforts to ensure that stable research results are secured *under systematic variation of research strategies* for each of those steps.

A further implication of our analysis is that methodological choices, like substantive choices of sociological problems, are themselves socially determined. They depend on the cultural "temper of the times," the institutional locations and vested interests of researchers, on processes of influence and exercise of power within academic disciplines, and on idiosyncratic personal predilections. This truth holds for methodological choices in both the social and the natural sciences. The lesson we draw from this is not that research is destined to be arbitrary but that the social determination of choices of research strategies should *itself* be made the subject of study. Sociology, with its sociology-of-knowledge tradition, is perhaps best equipped among all disciplines to undertake this kind of research. Certainly, this line of inquiry seems more likely to generate payoff than a kind of constant endeavor, imitative of the physical sciences, to strive for increasingly "precise" methods and for "quantitative" rigor of definitions and measures, which now seems to be the strongest impulse.

We underscore this final point by quoting the powerful epistemological statement by Combessie (1984: 25), which leads to the same conclusion:

> Procedures and methods, which limit the number of points of view on an object by eliminating relationships and producing a feeling of closure and termination, are *also rhetorics of conviction*. They tend *to enchain* within limits they have assigned. Methods which on the contrary multiply the number of points of view, diversify the images of an object and juxtapose the partitions produced by methods and scales that sometimes differ, those methods tease conviction and hold it at a distance. One is tempted to label them "brilliant" and "attractive." Their virtue is to generate questions and inquiries; their major weakness is to give in to allusions or impressions. But this danger should not mask the fact that the objectifying intention is also an intention to find new approaches, tools, and objects.

"Doing" Sociological Methodology: Some Practical Leads

The reader interested in methodology might benefit from five kinds of knowledge: what groups to join, where to learn, where to find documentation, where to find books, and where to find periodicals. With respect to the last two, we list a few sources in the Selected Annotated International Bibliography at the end of the book; with respect to the first three, we conclude the chapter by giving a few pointers.

What to Join

Two major organizations are dedicated to sociological methodology. On the international scene there is the Research Committee on Logic and Methodology of the International Sociological Association (54 Boulevard

Raspail, 75006 Paris, France), which has an international membership of approximately 200. The Methodology Section of the American Sociological Association (1722 N Street N.W., Washington, D.C. 20036, USA) has about 400 members and produces an annual entitled *Sociological Methodology*. Some other major national associations also have methodology sections.

Where to Learn

Most universities with a sociology department have courses and programs in research methodology. Aside from this vast resource, there are three specialized institutes and organized activities that merit mention.

In the United States, the Survey Research Center (Institute for Social Research, University of Michigan, Ann Arbor, MI 48106–1248, USA) organizes a Summer Institute in Survey Research Techniques each year. A typical program includes courses in statistical research design, survey research, survey sampling, survey data analysis, questionnaire design, data collection, longitudinal survey data and analysis, evaluation research, cognitive psychology and survey methods, event history design and analysis, reliability and validity of survey measurement, plus special workshops.

In Europe, the Summer School in Social Science Data Analysis and Collection (Department of Government, University of Essex, Colchester, CO4 3SQ, UK) also organizes annual courses. A recent term included mathematics for social scientists, statistical methods for data analysis, causal modeling, basic scaling, multidimensional scaling, regression and principal components analysis, regression theory, social networks, probability and distribution theory, game theory, and bargaining set theory.

The European Science Foundation of the European Community (1 Quai Lezay-Marnesia, 67080 Strasbourg Cedex, France) organizes specialized international training programs and workshops in social science research methodology.

Where to Find Documentation

The Social Research Methodology Documentation Centre (SRM-Documentation Centre, Erasmus University Rotterdam, Department of Sociology, P.O. Box 1738, 3000, Rotterdam, Netherlands) provides specialized information on literature in the field of methods and techniques of empirical social research. It maintains an up-to-date data base which is available on-line or on CD-ROM disk, along with several other services. It also publishes the quarterly *SRM Bibliography* and the annual *SRM Abstracts*. The SRM classification scheme has twelve main categories: A. methodology of the social sciences (introductory category); B. research methodology, research design; C. types of research; D. selection of research units; E. data collection; F. measurement and scale analysis; G. statistical theory, univariate statistical analysis; H. bivariate and multivariate statistical analysis; K. types of analysis and interpretation; L. reliability of data and instruments; M. organization and application of research; and N. teaching research methodology, information sources.

We conducted a search of the first subcategory of each of the twelve main categories (containing general introductions, textbooks, handbooks, etc.). Entries since 1988 included 28 in A, 109 in B, 5 in D, 10 in E, 17 in F, 156 in G, 39 in H, 35 in K (types and uses of models), 5 in L, and 8 in M. Before 1986, there were 175 entries under "qualitative research," which represents 1.08 percent of all entries. Since 1986 there have been 241 entries in this category, representing 2.14 percent of all entries. Before 1986, the four most cited topics (key words) under qualitative methods were, in order of importance (with percentages of total entries before 1986), field research (0.80 percent), participant observation (0.63 percent), ethnomethodology (0.60 percent) and life history (0.53 percent). For entries since 1986 (with percentages of total entries after that date), the four most cited topics are, in order, field research (1.12 percent), life history (0.92 percent), ethnomethodology (0.58 percent), and case study (0.33 percent).

Another international source of documentation is *Sociological Abstracts* (P.O. Box 22206, San Diego, CA 92192–0206, USA). It has a specific Methodology section in each issue. *Sociological Abstracts* also has an on-line data base and is on CD-ROM. National sociological data bases include the German Informationszentrum Sozialwissenschaften (Lennestrasse 30, D 5300 Bonn 1, Germany) and the Dutch SWIDOC (Herengracht 410, NL, 1017 BX Amsterdam, Netherlands). Both have "methodology" as one of their categories and often publish separate entries for it. And, of course, any university library will also be of help.

References

Anderson, A. 1987: "President's Commission in Turmoil." *Nature*, 329: 6140.

Cibois, P. 1980: "L'Usage social de l'analyse factorielle des correspondences." *Informatique et sciences humaines*, 46–7: 56–135.

Combessie, J.-C. 1984: "L'Évolution comparée des inégalités: problèmes statistiques." *Revue française de sociologie*, 25: 233–54.

Combessie, J.-C. 1986: "À propos de méthodes: effets d'optique heuristique et objectivation." *Bulletin de méthodologie sociologique*, 10: 4–24.

Conner, R. F. (ed.) 1982: *Methodological Advances in Evaluation Research*. London: Sage Publications.

Desrosières, A., Goy, A. and Thevenot, L. 1983: "L'Identité sociale dans le travail statistique: la nouvelle nomenclature des professions et categories socioprofess-ionelles," *Économie et statistique*, 152: 55–81.

Durand, J., Pages, J.-P., Brenot, J. and Barny, M.-H. 1990: "Public Opinion and Conflicts: A Theory and System of Opinion Polls." *International Journal of Public Opinion Research*, 6: 390–427.

Florens, J.-P. 1984: "Inégalité et dependance statistique." *Revue française de sociologie*, 25: 255–63.

Gower, J. D. 1971: "Statistical Methods of Comparing Different Multivariate Analyses of the Same Data," in F. R. Hodson, D. G. Kendall, and P. Tautu, (eds), *Mathematics of the Archaeological and Historical Sciences*, Edinburgh: Edinburgh University Press, 138–49.

Guttman, L. 1984: "What is Not What in Statistics. Statistical Inference Revisited – 1984. The Illogic of Statistical Inference for Cumulative Science." *Bulletin de méthodologie sociologique*, 4: 3–35.

Hall, J. 1988: *The Community-Based Drug Epidemiology Network*. Brussels: Health Directorate of the Commission of the European Communities.

Hammersley, M. 1982: *What's Wrong with Ethnography? Methodological Explorations*. London: Routledge.

Harter, H. L. 1980: "Early History of Multiple Comparison Tests," in P. R. Krishnaiah, (ed.), *Handbook of Statistics*, Vol. 1: *Analysis of Variance*. London: North Holland.

Kozel, N. and Adams, E. 1986: "Epidemiology of Drug Use: An Overview." *Science*, 234: 970–4.

Le Guen, M. and Jaffeux, C. 1989: "La Conjonction Analysis de données et statistique inferentielle pour conduire à un meilleure perception visuelle." *Revue statistique appliquée*, 37: 75–97.

Lecuyer, B.-P. 1988: "Rationalité et idéologie dans les sciences de l'homme: le cas des experiences Hawthorne (1924–1933) et de leur reexamen historique." *Revue de synthèses*, 3–4: 401–27.

Levine, J. H. 1984: *Atlas of Corporate Interlocks*. Hanover, N.H.: Worldnet.

Pottier, F. 1976: *Analysis comparative de méthodes statistiques appliquées à des données de psychologie de l'enfant*. Paris: Université de Paris, Docteur de Troisième Cycle thesis.

President's Commission on Organized Crime (PCOC) 1986: *Report to the President and Attorney-General. America's Drug Habit: Drug Abuse, Drug Trafficking, and Organized Crime*. Washington, D.C.: Superintendent of Documents, US Printing Office.

Schiltz, M.-A. 1983: "L'Élimination des modalités non pertinents dans un depouillement d'enquête par analyses factorielle." *Bulletin de méthodologie sociologique*, 1: 19–40.

Smelser, N. J. 1976: *Comparative Methods in the Social Sciences*. Englewood Cliffs, N.J.: Prentice-Hall.

Van Meter, K. M. 1981: *Une analysis de la criminalité d'affaires par la classification automatique*. Paris: CNRS, rapport de recherche.

Van Meter, K. M. 1983: "Sociologie de la criminalité d'affaires – deux méthodes differentes, deux représentations sociales distinctes." *Bulletin de méthodologie sociologique*, 1: 3–18.

Van Meter, K. M. 1990: "Methodological and Design Issues: Techniques for Assessing the Representatives of Snowball Samples," in Elizabeth Y. Lambert, and W. Wayne Wiebel (eds), *The Collection and Interpretation of Data from Hidden Populations*, Washington, D.C.: National Institute on Drug Abuse, Research Monograph 98, 31–43.

Weber, M. 1949 [1904]: *The Methodology of the Social Sciences*, tr. and ed. by E. A. Shils and H. A. Finch. Glencoe, Ill.: Free Press.

Wilson, T. P. 1986: "Qualitative 'Versus' Quantitative in Social Research." *Bulletin de méthodologie sociologique*, 10: 25–51.

Part II

Polity and Society

4

The Sociology of the State Revisited

Through its use in ordinary language and especially in the context of controversy, the word "state" has been progressively drained of conceptual rigor. This drift is observable even in the social sciences: the political analyst and the historian, in particular, have a regrettable habit of regarding all political structures as states, as if the differences between the Han Empire and the modern Western nation-state are only secondary or marginal and do not appear to merit consideration in the formation of the concept. Everything seems to indicate that the social sciences are devoted to some kind of substantialist preoccupation: namely, that there is some "essential" political force that structures all power relations, no matter what the social and cultural contexts.

Origins of the State

The return to a historical sociology of the state–with contributions from scholars such as Bendix (1964), Eisenstadt and Rokkan (1973), Tilly (1975), Badie and Birnbaum (1983), J. Anderson (1986), Gledhill (1988), Genet (1990), Poggi (1990), and Greengrass (1991)–is a healthy corrective to this way of thinking, even though it has raised a number of questions in its turn. This change took place in a definite context; the 1970s witnessed the first rupture in an international order which proclaimed the universality of a state that decolonization had consolidated everywhere. That decade also witnessed the crisis of the welfare state in industrial societies, casting doubt on the state's capability of adapting itself to all new situations. Putting the

This chapter is based on a contribution by Bertrand Badie and Pierre Birnbaum.

state into historical perspective accomplished the proper contextualization of the state. Historical sociology thus revived Max Weber's methodology, which, however, he never applied fully to the analysis of the state, committed as he was to its essential rationality. In any event, this method takes the state to be a historically specific structure, nestled in a definite social and cultural context.

The works that sustain this tradition depend on historians such as Strayer (1970) and Guénée (1971) or sociologists like Elias (1975). All take the crisis in feudal society as the historical starting point for the rise of the state. It is difficult to dissociate this thesis–which is equally in evidence in P. Anderson (1974) and Tilly (1975)–from the idea that the state emerged as an *invention*, which involved a definite break with the past and a creative act. The break is seen as a decline in the political power of the traditional feudal order, whose lords could no longer wield authority, contain rural migration, or safeguard the security of social actors. The break also refers to the disintegration of social relations, the emergence of class conflict, and the separation of the economic and political realms.

At the same time, these disruptions were accompanied by a continuity of meaning which made the invention of the state possible. The structures of the invented state, by and large, were copies of the structures of the Church; Roman law was revived, but with a mixture of subjectivism borrowed from Christian beliefs; dynastic centers imposed their authority by asserting their sovereign powers; the state rested on a political community, the identity of which derived directly from the concept of *universitas* which had been formulated in medieval Christian thought. In sum, the invention of the state was seen as a product of selective political strategies. Several authors, notably P. Anderson (1974), put forward the questionable idea that the state was invented on the initiative of collective entities: *the* bourgeoisie, in order to protect its interests, or *the* aristocracy, in order to reassert its authority. Such formulations help account for the state in its later phases but fail to account for its origins.

It was Hobbes who ventured the most convincing strategic analysis of the origins of the state. The state is established on the basis of a contractual exchange of utilities, with individuals giving up part of their freedom to the sovereign, who, in return, assures their safety. Individuals, acting rationally, agree to entrust their security to a third party, but only in a specific sociopolitical context. By contrast, some sociologists, following Toennies and Durkheim, argue that individuals find their primary communities more satisfactory and less restrictive than the remote structures of the state. Putting the two observations together, consent to a Hobbesian contract may be seen as a rational device for binding together governors and governed in polities in which communities have failed (see chapters 5, 7, and 15). Such a hypothesis is helpful in explaining why the crisis in feudal society was conducive to the emergence of strategies of state-building.

The double idea of a break with the past and a creative venture thus provides a kind of operational definition of the invention and accounts for the characteristics of the new political order. Regarded as such, the state is a distinct and specific type of political system, but it cannot be seen–as some would see it–as a priori more effective than other possible forms. It developed in specific circumstances, in response to specific issues, and in a specific cultural context. The state's distinguishing feature is that it marked the *separation* of politics from social relations and thus set up the requirement for a bond of citizenship and a claim to special loyalty on the part of individual citizens (see chapter 7).

There are thus some functionalist assumptions associated with the historical sociology of the state; as an invented type of political system, it can be evaluated only according to its ability to resolve the crises which gave birth to it. Following this logic, we can suggest further that the *degree* of state development was a function of the scale of the initiating crisis. For example, the polity became more differentiated in France than in England, where feudalism was less deeply entrenched in the social fabric and the tensions relating to its breakup were less in evidence (see Petit-Dutaillis 1971 [1933] and Corrigan and Sayer 1985). To proceed further, the state is seen as a kind of ideal-type category, and post-medieval political entities can be ranked according to how far their political systems were differentiated from the social to create a public realm. Differentiation, of course, is never complete; that being said, it remains true that strategies of differentiation should be more effective in those cases where the associational mechanisms of communities are unable to cope with emerging challenges.

By using such a socio-historical paradigm, it may also be possible to gauge the chances of survival and universalization of the state in functionalist terms. The key question is this: how can the state, as a type of political system invented in a specific time and place, function everywhere and for all time? This question implies that the concept of the *invented* state needs to be supplemented by the concept of the *imported* state and a state invented in the West that *adapts* to new, different conditions (see Badie 1992). These additions are absolutely essential if we are to avoid a deterministic view of the state, a view that locks social actors into a "dead-end" trajectory within which they can merely elaborate the essential structures of a universal state form.

There are limits to this kind of functional explanation. First, its methodological rigor is limited; a sociological approach to the state has great difficulty in explaining the perfect match between the state-builders' strategies and the collective needs of a deteriorating medieval order. Some historians have probably overestimated the conflicts and tensions–and hence the violence–which accompanied the birth and development of the Western nation-state. Political sociologists, however, have certainly underestimated these elements, taking refuge in the general hypothesis that the differentiation of the functional sphere was functional for all social actors. Taken in totality, moreover, these kinds of functional explanations seem to cover the whole waterfront and so to lose determinacy. Thus:

- According to Wallerstein (1974), the state satisfied the needs that arose from the emergence of a market economy; in fact, the origins of the state may be traced back to the rural economy that antedated capitalism.
- P. Anderson (1974) maintains that the state emerged in response to the needs of an aristocratic society liberated from the constraints of feudalism; he probably underestimates the role of needs specific to the emerging state itself.
- According to Hechter and Brustein (1980) the state is the regulatory mechanism of a civil society characterized by the growing social division of labor and class conflict.
- Still others have regarded the state as the defender of the rural social order, as the harbinger of a form of neo-mercantilism that hindered trade and as the generator of a bureaucracy as a new source of obstacles.

At this point functionalism emerges as an enemy of functional analysis. Functional analysis can identify some elements of the state and how they first took shape. If, however, these insights are ossified into a general, universal theory of the state, those who espouse such a theory lose sight of the possibility of combinations and innovations that cannot be ascertained or predicted from the conditions of origin of the state

The Differing Logics of States

Consideration of the social origins of states does shed some light on their diversity. At the same time, states, regarded as a universe, display very dissimilar features, insofar as each is called upon to perform the greatest variety of functions. In appreciating this dissimilarity and attempting to avoid the pitfalls of evolutionist or developmental approaches, some sociologists have put forward the distinction between "strong" and "weak" states (see Badie and Birnbaum 1983, Evans *et al.* 1985, Migdal, 1988).

Strong States

The notion of a "strong" state conjures up several possible models: de Tocqueville's image of the state with absolutist pretensions, Hegel's powerful state as it aims to impose its order and rational values on society as a whole, and Weber's model of the rational-legal state.

One way of gauging the strength of the state is to discern the ability of that state to expand its scope until it coincides with the entire public realm (see Arendt 1958, Habermas 1989). At this point citizens regard the state as the focus of *all* their expectations and demands and make themselves a function solely of the extended state; they are then unwilling to commit themselves to intermediate structures such as political parties, voluntary associations, and social movements, which, under other circumstances, interpose themselves between citizens and the state.

Thus viewed, the strong state is not conducive to the establishment of a pluralist democracy, in which independent and partisan interest groups occupy a conspicuous place. Contrary to the hopes of advocates of participatory democracy, the strong state strives to minimize the distinction between the state realm and the public realm–or, better, to expand the state to fill the public realm. The strong state attempts to minimize its citizens' "voice" (Hirschman 1983), because the expression of voice–the organized statement of citizens' values and interests–constitutes an encroachment on the supremacy of the state. In this sense the strong state approaches the incarnation of "public well-being" and does not wish to hear citizens' language of public well-being.

Even more, the paradigm of the strong state tends to reduce private well-being to public well-being, the latter goal being established by the state. The strong state does not appear to allow scope for independent action on the part of subjects, even within the confines of the state itself, to say nothing of society apart from the state. The logic of the strong state is one of an institutionalized and differentiated structure that governs according to its own account of things and ignores the values and strategies of its subjects (see the discussion of totalitarianism in chapter 5). The main risk associated with this paradigm is that it tends to reify actors as ultra-passive, thereby flying in the face of other contemporary theoretical developments that stress intentionality and rest on paradigmatic assumptions of methodological individualism.

In more concrete terms, the strong state appears as a powerful bureaucratic structure populated by civil servants in carefully circumscribed roles, who hold themselves aloof from the citizenry's individual values, group loyalties, and interests. The strong state is impelled to assume direct responsibility for the management of society. It imposes its values through a government system of socialization (formal education) served by teachers who are also government employees; it excludes the expression of religious values from the state realm, separating Church from State and making civil religion impossible; it controls public memory by managing museums, libraries, and historical archives; it resolves conflicts that pit social groups against one another; it takes over social welfare, economic intervention, economic planning, and sometimes the direct management of enterprises.

It is possible to regard the contemporary state in France as a close approximation to the model of the strong state. From the time of the absolute monarchy to Gaullism–and even to recent socialist policy–appeal to the state has seemed to be a natural course for all those in positions of political power. The state is the seat of legitimacy upon which aspiring future elites set their sights; its educational socialization operates more or less satisfactorily, and its control over society is extensive. Such a state renders the introduction of mechanisms of participatory democracy almost impossible.

Such a model of the strong state has been exported to other societies–from the Turkey of Kemal Ataturk to Tunisia–and, despite the backlash stemming from those societies' independent cultural traditions, it gradually brings about its own secularization of the public realm (see chapter 15). Indeed, many of its features are incorporated by societies that officially favor a weak state. The United Kingdom, for example, has, to a degree, adopted the French model for training its senior civil servants (see Kazancigil 1986, Heper 1987, Birnbaum 1988).

Weak States

Weak states, by contrast, tend to solidify their existence by conferring on the public realm a structure that makes it easier for people to find a voice. Private interests find more fertile ground for expression. In such polities, the distinction between the private realm and public well-being is less meaningful. Social actors can gain a hearing for their interests through agents in authority who are not mere functionaries of a state. The paradigm of methodological individualism seems appropriate for the weak state, because, in fact, the weak state gives greater leeway to the posited intentionality of actors. In such a setting, publicly acknowledged private interests can be taken into consideration, since citizenship does not entail being absorbed in the larger civic society. Weak states foster a different understanding of citizenship, one that is less militant and universalistic and permits the simultaneous expression of political, ethnic, racial, regional, and religious allegiances without these involving any kind of anti-state intent or stigma (see chapter 7).

Weak states, with their federal or confederational structures, also limit the privileges and growth of the bureaucratic apparatus. They are favorably disposed to localism and the spread of associations, partisan structures, interest groups, and pressure groups, even though they may also harbor elements of vested interests and inequalities that inihibit the effectiveness of these. Weak states, epitomized by the British or American model, show little inclination to confront churches head-on, do not wish to control the mechanisms of political socialization themselves, and tolerate peripheral allegiances and their symbolic affirmation. Needless to say, weak states are permissive of, if not coterminous with, the spread of pluralist democracy.

Limitations of the Strong–Weak Dichotomy

Like so many ideal-typical dichotomies, however, the opposed visions of strong and weak states run into difficulty when the empirical world is confronted. Local society frequently continues to defend its autonomy to the point where even the strong state cannot impose its control completely (on France, see Dupuy and Thoenig 1985, Suleiman 1987); also, the strong state cannot resist the influence of specific clienteles. It continues to be invaded by particularist interests, and its definition of public well-being cannot escape the intrusion of private interests. The strong state is often incapable of imposing its authority on various social groups mobilized against it, particularly when they emerge from behind their functions and introduce particularist, individualist strategies in universalistic language. Similarly, weak states are forever developing "strong state pockets," that are able to overcome the resistance put up by private interests and impose policies on them (Nordlinger 1981, Krasner 1978). The weak state is often strong when it comes to economic affairs, even when its direct control over the economy is limited (Vogel 1986). In these ways, then, the ideal logic of weak and strong states cannot remain unadulterated when confronted with historical reality.

Beyond such limitations, it is clear that the world offers examples of states that display contradictory logics. In confronting these anomalies, historical sociology becomes weaker in its explanatory power. Armed with only its few favored variables, it cannot account for the multiplicity of variables and unpredictable strategies and structural variations manifested in these anomalous or contradictory cases. So, we find the formation and functioning of states in contexts that are not, according to functionalist logic, conducive to the formation of states at all (e.g., in some African societies). In other cases we find a single group or party monopolizing the state for its own advantage, though sometimes only temporarily. It is difficult to assimilate such cases to the logic of historical sociology or to idealized dichotomies such as weak–strong.

The Crisis of the State

Whatever their structure, and whether strong or weak, contemporary states have to contend with a number of challenges. As managers of increasingly complex, post-industrial societies that have generated whole new ranges of values and demands, states are exposed to the obvious risk of "overload." This metaphor, taken from systems analysis, seems an apt one to apply to states experiencing crises in governance. Inheriting both their histories and their present situations, states are struggling to cope with a veritable explosion of demands with respect to wages, health, education, the environment, economic assistance to businesses, associations, territorial communities, and a wide variety of other groups ranging from shopkeepers to manual workers to people employed in the health professions–all of them making entitlement-like demands that their interests be responded to and nurtured. The presence of a democratic polity seems to foster such an overload, since it is built on the premise that groups can *legitimately* make such claims and that the state is obliged to respond to them. Furthermore, within a democratic context, if a government fails to respond, it risks the reactions of alienation, privatism, and clientelism, all of which can be regarded as indictments of the legitimacy of a democratic state that has refused to serve its publics.

The Economic Sphere

The reasons for this kind of political crisis are numerous, especially in post-industrial societies, but attention must first be called to the economic sphere. O'Connor (1978), for example, has pointed to the contradictions that arise when a state is *both* required to foster the activities of large private enterprises by providing them with facilities or bailing them out of troubled situations *and* responsible for managing the social consequences of their activities for society as a whole. The state is thus seen as in crisis, struggling to secure resources to meet multiple and contradictory economic demands that are structural in character.

The development of corporatism in its various forms can be interpreted as a reaction to the economic crises of the state. By calling into question the conventional theory of political representation–and by restricting plural-ism–corporatism fosters the role of private socioeconomic groups (businesses, trade unions, professional groupings) capable of controlling their own representatives and in return enjoying privileges of their own. Corporatism thus creates a kind of quasi-private form of management of public interests *within* the state. It involves a conflation of the public and private realms and compromises the autonomy of the state in that it allows "intruders" to penetrate more deeply into its fabric. Put another way, corporatism–whether at the level of individual firms, specific sectors of the economy, or highly structured organizational complexes–implies a kind of *dedifferentiation* of the idealized model of the state.

The kinds of demands faced by different post-industrial societies are very similar. However, every state copes with these challenges in a unique way, the uniqueness being determined by the special features of each society's history and current circumstances. In this respect the present is no different from the past. States have always coped in different ways with the difficulties entailed in establishing welfare states and in superintending their evolution (see chapter 6); they have also varied in how they have managed strikes and other kinds of conflicts; and, at present, they may be disposed in unique ways toward the introduction of corporatist practices. France, Germany, the United Kingdom, and the United States continue to display distinctive features of their own, despite common challenges. Even though a strong state on the French model may give way in certain specific sectors, it is still less favorably disposed toward a corporatist-type approach that would encroach on its long-standing position of pre-eminence. By contrast, no difficulty is experienced in accommodating corporatist demands in Germany, where they are consistent with a long-standing political tradition and with the politics of German social democracy. Depending on a combination of inherited historical patterns and contemporary adaptations, each post-industrial society responds to crisis in its own way.

The Management of Conflicts

States also vary in the ways they contend with internal conflicts and threats. In weak states voluntarism governs industrial relations and gives rise to socioeconomic conflicts in which the state is something of a by-stander, at least until these conflicts reach critical dimensions. Strikes may be long and bitter but have little political content; above all, the antagonists are pitted against one another, not the state. If the state is strong and interventionist, the interplay of social forces is different. Social actors in conflict may then wait for their confrontation to be resolved through the authoritarian (but legitimate) intervention of the state. In strong states the state is the absolute tutelary power on which all hopes are pinned but against which people also feel inclined to rebel, since it is the key player in society. Many collective actions, ranging from peasant revolts to the virtually insurrectionary strike, are launched *against* the state. Each camp attempts to enlist the state on its side in order to avail itself of the state's power.

To illustrate this theme from French history, during the internecine French wars that have marked the past two centuries, the state has always been in the center of the fray. From the abortive coup of General Boulanger to the seditious movements of the 1930s, hostility toward the Republic took the form of populist currents representing different political values, all having in common the principal aim of taking over the state. Extremist political movements of every hue mobilized their forces against the state and readily resorted to violence, since they regarded the state as *the* formidable obstacle to taking over society. On its side, the machinery of the state–with both its civil and its military faces–was instrumental in breaking up every one of these attempts at political dedifferentiation fomented in the name of radical ideologies of various political leagues and movements. The strength of the French state yielded only in the face of some exceptional events, such as military defeat and enemy occupation. In this connection, comparison with Germany yields the observation that the significantly less institutionalized and less differentiated German state proved incapable of facing up to Hitler's political movement and military mobilization.

Needless to say, massive mobilization directed against the state rarely occurs in weak states, since conflict is shunted into civil society with a minimum of state involvement. In the United States, for example, the few populist movements of any significance have not set themselves the goal of overthrowing the state but have ended up working through the mechanisms of social movements or political parties to influence the state to respond to their demands.

Even at the present time, new social movements adapt themselves to the logic of state organization. When they collide with a strong state, they often take it as their target and threaten to destabilize it. In weak states, however, the action of social movements remains more locally circumscribed and decentralized. The "political opportunity structure," as it might be called, proves to be of enormous significance. For example, the anti-nuclear movements in Germany, France, and the United States are all quite different from one another (see Jasper 1990, Joppke 1993), and the same is true of consumer and feminist movements.

It is sometimes claimed that the more politically "closed" a system is (e.g., the former Soviet Union), the less likely are social movements to attract a large membership. On the other hand, a strong state may witness particularly bitter collective actions directed against it. Complete exclusion engenders violence, because it rules out other political options. To illustrate by a negative example, in Switzerland, a sort of "co-opting" process helps new social movements to gain a hearing in a fragmented political system. In France, the student movement has formed along highly centralized lines–after the manner of the state university system itself–whereas in the United States it is highly decentralized. In a centralized state like France, which often turns a deaf ear to the demands of social movements (having utter confidence in its own rationality), the mobilization of movements such as the anti-nuclear one often takes a violent, almost insurrectional form. In "open" systems like the United States, where the parties are fragmented, the demands of such movements are more readily accommodated. Negotiation has won over violence and, in the end, has been more successful in imposing a program that is hostile to the development of nuclear power.

Similar differences in political structure and style can be seen in the even more fundamental challenges found in the growing presence of immigrant groups who simultaneously defend their own cultural values and demand citizenship and its associated rights in the host country. Consider the following contrasts among three European countries in the interaction between state, nationality, and citizenship.

In Germany, ties between citizens are grounded in the concept of a cultural community; hence it has been virtually impossible for immigrants to gain access to German nationality and to the various advantages of citizenship. Even after several generations, the same resistance remains. In addition, Germany is the site of some xenophobic reactions, although these do not go so far as to constitute an actual nationwide mobilization on the basis of identity. This crisis of the state in Germany is more like a crisis of morality, given the specific German cultural context.

In a weak state like the United Kingdom, the considerable presence of immigrants derives from the country's colonial past. Immigrants from Commonwealth countries enjoy British nationality and citizenship. They are both electors and eligible for election, and some have become members of the House of Commons. The fact that they may reside legally in the country accounts both for the significant numbers of them that concentrate territorially and express their cultural preferences openly in the United Kingdom. Xenophobic reactions do occur, but it is even rarer than in Germany for these to take a collective form that might conceivably threaten the state.

France, with a strong state, persists in trying to impose its universalist values on all citizens; at the same time, as a secular state, it manifests very unfavorable attitudes to the public affirmation of cultures that have a salient religious dimension (Brubaker 1989). French-style secularism has always supported the cause of the state, and this implies the rejection of allegiance to other cultural communities. In contrast to Germany, it is relatively easy to acquire nationality in France. At the same time, nationality implies integration into the imagined political community built from the time of the French Revolution on the model of a militant citizenry with rationalist ideals (see chapter 7). The main modes of integration are education and military service. The French polity is still built on a model of citizenship that leaves traditional values exclusively to the private realm. Unlike Germany, the United Kingdom, or the United States, it rejects any collective form of ethnic-based organization. Even so, this principle of the strong state has not been carried to completion; there have always been undercurrents of intolerance toward outsiders within the state, whereas in theory the French strong state implies universal toleration of all those who have become French citizens.

However, the principle of universalistic integration supported by a strong state such as France gives rise to two unanticipated kinds of difficulties. Despite the designs of the state, a significant proportion of immigrants and their offspring will always wish to preserve collective values associated with their ethnic or national backgrounds. In reaction, xenophobic forces against immigrant minorities become organized on a nationwide scale. Groups manifesting these forces are often violent, and they strive *both* to expel immigrants *and* to blame the state for its universalist values and its tolerance of foreigners. As a result, the French polity faces a fresh crisis, more acute than those of Germany or the United Kingdom. The extreme right wing is managing to consolidate its position throughout the country, creating a kind of counter-society which, like many earlier collective movements in French history, is determined to challenge the differentiation of a state that is perceived as too remote from the true values that make up French identity.

The State and International Disorder

It may be claimed that the state has not only endeavored to shape society in its own image but that it has also imposed its own distinctive pattern on international relations. It has commonly been observed that since the treaties of Westphalia in 1648, the world has been structured as a community of sovereign nation-states and has functioned as such. All the characteristics of the state system have been reproduced in the world order: the territorial basis of politics, the principles of sovereignty and power, and the adoption of a system of international public law based on the counterreformational effort to revive the state when it faced the first serious threat to its existence (Caporaso 1989, Haimson and Tilly 1989). In keeping with the principle of projection of the national mode onto the international sphere, the pattern of international or inter-state relations has come to be seen as possessing the same kind of naturalness and inevitability as the "way to do things" as has the state itself.

In the 1980s, however, this seemingly permanent international order was subject to a set of disturbances more serious than any experienced heretofore. This resulted from the convergence of three disruptive factors: the questioning of the universal validity of the state model, the rise of other forms of transnational relations, and a crisis in the machinery for regulating inter-state relations. At the analytical level, the realist theory of international relations came to be supplanted first by independentist theories, then by transnational theories, both of which rested on different fundamental assumptions.

The universal spread of the state in the last half of the twentieth century may have generated a temporary illusion. The wars of colonial independence and the process of decolonization, far from challenging the nationalist model, imposed it almost everywhere in Africa and Asia. It was as though the architects of the post-colonial political systems were eager to import the Western state model because it was well known (as the vehicle for their own past domination) and because of their urgent need to establish political order in the wake of independence. In the absence of such urgency, one might have envisioned the invention of political systems better suited to the problems and cultures of the newly independent societies. In any event, the adoption of the Western state model created a kind of international society of elites (both North and South), with shared interest in governing and a kind of derived solidarity among themselves.

At the same time, the imposition of a "foreign" system of meaning via the establishment of the Western-type nation-state separated the political elites from the peoples they governed in the new nations. These elites were increasingly challenged by local political forces based mainly on communitarian (regional, religious, and tribal) groupings which drew their meaning and support from symbols of the indigenous cultures. In this way a certain vicious circle was initiated: the more the opposition groups succeeded in mobilizing support against the new regimes, the more the official governments were constrained to rely on foreign models, policies, and aid, all of which put them in a posture of dependency on the developed countries. This in its turn further eroded the legitimacy of the rulers and their claim to represent a legitimate governing entity, the state.

The net effect of this vicious circle was to discredit the ideal of the state as an organ which could be transplanted and thereby claim universal legitimacy. It also had the dysfunctional side effect of casting alternative political movements into the mold of permanent oppositions, thereby postponing or preventing their establishment as alternative forms of government. Consequently–and *pace* its claim to be a universal institution–the state became a source of tension and exclusion, which led to political disintegration and loss of political capability. Political interaction between governed and governors showed signs of a breakdown in political communication; it witnessed the rise of populism, the manipulation of neo-traditional symbols, and an upsurge in authoritarian practices. These were not indicators of ongoing institutional and political development; rather, they expressed a state of tension between an imported product, the state, and social structures that were speaking a different political language (Migdal 1988, Lee 1988, Médard 1992).

This failure of the state manifested itself in many different forms:

- the disintegration of political and administrative institutions (Liberia and Somalia);
- the development of populism as the obligatory medium for all political movements (Latin America);
- the progressive takeover of the claim to legitimacy by revivalist movements (Muslim and Hindu worlds);
- the almost universal challenge to efforts to promote a secular, "public" sector that would transcend narrow group loyalties;
- the attack on the territorial basis of the political order, which is one of the pillars of the state system, and the increasing incompatibility between established state frontiers and the demands of communal (ethnic, religious, national) movements (the former Yugoslavia, Czechoslovakia, and the Soviet Union).

All these add up to a steadily weakening allegiance to the state, the proliferation of alternative modes of political identification, and an increase in political volatility and the potential for violence. The state model now seems to be only one of many possible paradigms of public order.

This international crisis of the state has affected the ways in which a state gains legitimacy, even in Western societies, where authority has been based on claims to a legitimate universality and its effectiveness in the politico-diplomatic handling of domestic problems, conflicts, and crises. The weakening of these bases has been aggravated by the effects of transnationalization–that is, the worldwide development of relations which arise, intentionally or indirectly, outside the framework of the nation-state and the traditional network of relations between nation-states and thus escape state control or intervention (Badie and Smouts 1992).

The intrusion of transnationalization has been most pronounced in societies where the resources of the state are weak. These include especially the Third World countries, in which informal economic circuits bypass the formal economy and thus complement the corrosive effects which cultural, and especially religious, movements are having on state sovereignty. The effects of transnationalization are not limited to the Third World, however. The Western state has been circumvented in various ways by the strategies of transnational corporations, some of which are even difficult to locate in any given nation (see chapter 8). Individuals, too, with varying degrees of awareness, undermine their own national citizenship by replacing it with ties of solidarity that cut across national lines. These take the form of economic and financial circuits, the proliferation of trans-frontier associational lines, the increased flow of information, and the boom in transnational communication.

In the West, too, states are experiencing increasing difficulties in controlling their own frontiers and territories, as evidenced by their failure to control population movements–movements of individuals and groups which defy boundaries and which operate independently of the international arena. Some of these problems are of states' own making–the weakening of frontiers as part of the development of the European Community and the "open border" movement by the United States and Mexico are examples–but, be that as it may, the consequences are equally profound. The "individualization" of decision making has tended to destabilize the state by taking from it its main prerogative: namely, its sovereign right to conduct and control foreign policy, which, along with the principle of territoriality, has been one of its mainstays.

It seems realistic, therefore, to recognize that the inter-state world is giving way to a kind of dualistic world, in which the logic of the state continues to be a principal fixture of the political world but coexists with a growing number of individual and collective actors who occupy nooks and crannies not encompassed by the logic of the state. One cannot agree with neo-realist thinkers such as Waltz (1979), who play down this fundamental transformation and foresee a return of the strength of the state and the practice of conventional power politics. There are signs of this to be sure: the battleship diplomacy of the Falklands War and the policing action of the United States and its allies in the Gulf War, as well as the general thinking about a new kind of "policeman" role for the United States, now that there is only one superpower. More generally, it should be anticipated that the state, which itself has become a bastion of solidly entrenched social interests, will not take its own erosion lying down. Correspondingly, we should expect to see continuing efforts on the part of the state to reassert its traditional roles, both domestically and internationally. That fact conjures up a curious but accurate image: a weakening state simultaneously attempting to reestablish its strength.

The major fact remains, however: the logic of the state is weakening precisely because of the growing diversification of the international arena. This logic is based on the status and monopoly of control and force, which the state can no longer assert effectively. There is a proliferation of international actors which the state can no longer control or contain; and this perforce narrows the scope of the security role which the state has traditionally played in the international arena. This proliferation also tends to sap the state's legitimacy. When it is constrained to negotiate or compromise with those actors whom it cannot effectively control, the state becomes just one of those actors, rather than the officially designated and legitimate referee, judge, and controller of their actions.

The "de-statification" of international relations takes a variety of forms. There is a spawning of formal and informal (sometimes Mafia-like) networks that escape the control of the state, jeopardize economic policies, and render policies of economic regulation and embargo ineffective. The proliferation of transnational bonds of allegiance that bring together individuals in socio-occupational as well as religious, linguistic, and ethnic networks builds up a set of loyalties that compete with those to the nation-state and tend to erode the supposed unity between the notions of citizenship and state.

The occurrence of violence in the world is also becoming more complex. The international order is split along the lines of state violence and group violence (Wilkinson 1986, MacFarlane 1974). Terrorism, guerrilla actions, and uncontrolled ethnic conflicts affect the credibility of the state and undermine it potency; they also weaken the distinction between public violence and private violence, bringing to mind a similar ambiguity in medieval times. International illegality such as that involved in drug trafficking grows increasingly difficult for the state to control, if for no other reason than that millions of people pass across frontiers daily, posing insurmountable monitoring problems. These developments are also effectively part of the conspiracy to diminish the international powers of the state and reduce its ability to function effectively.

The de-territorialization of the international arena stems from a paradoxical cultural fragmentation of the world at precisely that time in its history when international communication and interchange have reached their highest level ever (see chapter 8). The collapse of the former Soviet empire greatly compromised the nation-state model when it proved impossible to build political communities on a territorial basis without running the risk, one among others, of attempts at ethnic cleansing. Most networks of religious and ethnic transnational solidarity defy all efforts at territorial delimitation–witness the development of the pan-Islamic, pan-Hindu, and pan-Slav movements. Finally, we learn from the works of Susan Strange (1988) that the most effective hegemonic strategies no longer depend on a territorial power base; indeed, as the cases of the former Soviet Union and Yugoslavia demonstrate, political direction can prove counterproductive in the long run. Economic strength is coming to be built, rather, on a highly effective system of economic, financial, and cultural networks.

The demonstration that the state is an unstable, precarious, fragile entity that is not universal but rather a product of a distinctive history poses a special challenge for social scientists. They, too, have shared in the illusion of universality, taking the country–nation-state–culture fusion as a natural one, and have made that imagined entity their primary unit of analysis for setting the parameters for all economic, political, and social processes. The day of that illusion now seems to be over, and the state must be relativized in the minds of its investigators. It may be regarded as a valid, continuing subject for sociological study; yet it must take its place as but one of many fundamental bases for the structuring of power and integration in society.

References

Anderson, J. (ed.) 1986: *The Rise of the Modern State*. Brighton: Wheatsheaf Books.

Anderson, P. 1974: *Lineages of the Absolutist State*. London: NLB.

Arendt, H. 1958: *The Human Condition*. Chicago: University of Chicago Press.

Badie, B. 1987: *Les Deux États*. Paris: Fayard.

Badie, B. 1992: *L'État importé*. Paris: Fayard.

Badie, B. and Birnbaum, P. 1983: *The Sociology of the State*. Chicago: University of Chicago Press.

Badie, B. and Smouts, M. 1992: *Le Retournement du monde*. Paris: FNSP.

Bayart, J.-F. 1989: *L'État en Afrique*. Paris: Fayard.

Bendix, R. 1964: *Nation-Building and Citizenship*. New York: Wiley.

Birnbaum, P. 1988: *States and Collective Action: The European Experience*. Cambridge: Cambridge University Press.

Birnbaum, P. 1992: *Les Fous de la République, histoire politique des Juifs d'État*. Paris: Fayard.

Brubaker, W. (ed.) 1989: *Immigration and the Politics of Citizenship in Europe and North America*. Lanham, Md.: University Press of America.

Caporaso, J. (ed.) 1989: *The Elusive State–International and Comparative Perspectives*. Newbury Park, Calif.: Sage Publications.

Cawson, A. 1986: *Corporatism and Political Theory*. Oxford: Blackwell.

Corrigan, P. and Sayer, D. 1985: *The Great Arch-English State Formation as Cultural Revolution*. Oxford: Blackwell.

Dupuy, F. and Thoenig, J.-C. 1985: *L'Administration en miettes*. Paris: Fayard.

Eisenstadt, S. N. and Rokkan, S. (eds) 1973: *Building States and Nations*. Beverly Hills, Calif.: Sage Publications.

Elias, N. 1975: *La Dynamique de l'Occident*. Paris: Calmann Levy.

Evans, P., Rueschemeyer, D., and Skocpol, T. 1985: *Bringing the State Back In*. Cambridge: Cambridge University Press.

Genet, P. (ed.) 1990: *L'État moderne, genèse*. Paris: CNRS.

Gledhill, J. 1988: *State and Society: The Emergence and Development of Social Hierarchy and Political Centralization*. London: Hyman.

Greengrass, M. (ed.) 1991: *Conquest and Coalescence*. London: Edward Arnold.

Guénée, B. 1971: *L'Occident au XIVème et XVème siècles. Les Etats*. Paris: Presses universitaires de France.

Habermas, J. 1989: *The Structural Transformation of the Public Sphere: An Inquiry into a Category of Bourgeois Society*. Cambridge, Mass.: MIT Press.

Haimson, L. and Tilly, C. (eds) 1989: *Strikes, Wars and Revolutions in an International Perspective*. Cambridge: Cambridge University Press.

Hall, P. 1986: *Governing the Economy: The Politics of State Intervention in Britain and France*. New York: Oxford University Press.

Hechter, M. and Brustein: W. 1980: "Regional Modes of Production and Patterns of State Formation in Western Europe." *American Journal of Sociology*, 85: 1061–94.

Heper, M. (ed.) 1987: *The State in Public Bureaucracies*. New York: Greenwood Press.

Hirschman, A. 1983: *Bonheur privé, action publique*. Paris: Fayard.

Jasper, J. 1990: *Nuclear Politics: Energy and the State in the United States, Sweden, and France*. Princeton, N.J.: Princeton University Press.

Joppke, C. 1993: *Mobilizing against Nuclear Energy: A Comparison of Germany and the United States*. Berkeley, Calif.: University of California Press.

Kazancigil, A. 1986: *The State in Global Perspective*. Aldershot: Gower/UNESCO.

Kitschelt, H. 1986: "Political Opportunity Structures and Political Protest: Antinuclear Movements in Four Democracies." *British Journal of Political Science*, 16: 58–85.

Krasner, S. 1978: *Defending the National Interest*. Princeton, N.J.: Princeton University Press.

Lee, S. H. 1988: *State-Building in the Contemporary Third World*. Boulder, Colo.: Westview Press.

MacFarlane, J. 1974: *Violence and the State*. London: Nelson.

Médard, J. F. (ed.) 1992: *États d'Afrique noire*. Paris: Karthala.

Migdal, J. 1988: *Strong Societies and Weak States*. Princeton, N.J.: Princeton University Press.

Nordlinger, E. 1981: *On the Autonomy of the State*. Cambridge: Cambridge University Press.

Nye, J. and Keohane, R. 1977: *Power and Interdependence*. Boston: Little, Brown.

O'Connor J. 1978: *The Fiscal Crisis of the State*. New York: St Martin's Press.

Peters, G. 1978: *Can Government Go Bankrupt?* New York: Basic Books.

Petit-Dutaillis, C. 1971 [1933]: *La Monarchie féodale en France et en Angleterre*. Paris: Albin Miche.

Poggi, G. 1990: *The State*. Stanford, Calif.: Stanford University Press.

Rosenau, J. 1990: *Turbulence in World Politics*. Princeton, N.J.: Princeton University Press.

Schmitter, P. and Lehmbruch, G. (eds) 1979: *Trends towards Corporatist Intermediation*. London: Sage Publications.

Strange, S. 1988: *States and Markets*. London: Pinter.

Strayer, J. 1970: *On the Medieval Origins of the Modern State*. Princeton, N.J.: Princeton University Press.

Suleiman, E. 1987: *Private Power and Centralization in France: The Notaires and the State*. Princeton, N.J.: Princeton University Press.

Tilly, C. (ed.) 1975: *The Formation of Nation States in Western Europe*. Princeton, N.J.: Princeton University Press.

Vogel, D. 1986: *National Styles of Regulation: Environmental Policy in Great Britain and the United States*. Ithaca, N.Y.: Cornell University Press.

Wallerstein, I. 1974: *The Modern World-System*, Vol. 1: *Capitalist Agriculture and the Origins of the European World-Economy in the Sixteenth Century*. New York: Academic Press.

Waltz, K. 1979: *Theory of International Politics*. Reading, Mass.: Addison-Wesley.

Wilkinson, P. 1986: *Terrorism and the Liberal State*. London: Macmillan.

5

Varieties of Authoritarianism and Democracy

Over the past three decades, political scientists have come to understand how democracies sometimes break down. They understand less about how nondemocracies become democracies, and to remedy this deficiency, they will have to seek help from sociologists and anthropologists. We raise some of the sociological issues involved in this process in this chapter. We proceed by three stages: first, by tackling the difficult distinction between democracy and nondemocracy; second, by referring to the literature on breakdown and on "redemocratization" in the contemporary world; and third, by looking at some nondemocratic settings in the world and assessing their relevance for the comparative study of democratic development.

A Metaphor: Launching Democratic "Satellites"

In attempting to become and remain a democracy, a society makes an effort to *detach* its political system from its more authoritarian roots and make it work under new, more democratic rules. The analogy of launching a satellite into orbit provides some helpful pointers in understanding this process. To put a satellite into orbit, it is first necessary to have established some technological (in this case, social) conditions and to have an appropriate fuel (here, social commitment) available. Once launched, a democratic "satellite" will have some self-correcting mechanisms, but the society must also be able to exert some control to correct its position as it moves into its trajectory. Most countries in today's world have launched neither successful space satellites nor working democracies. Except for small intellectual and political segments within these countries, most lack

---

This chapter is based on a contribution by Bolivar Lamounier.

the conditions even to aspire to full democracy. Some have tried and failed; a few appear to have succeeded, but in some of those, the democratic experiments may be malfunctioning.

Pursuing the satellite imagery a step further, we may regard a democracy as a subsystem "bounded" by society, not something completely autonomous. Within this kind of framework, we may define democracy as a macro social arrangement that has the following characteristics:

- Authorities (decision-makers) are chosen by means of a competitive, *formalized process* (elections).
- Power is exercised under competitive *pressure*; parties and interest groups continuously attempt to influence policies.
- Power is subject to a measure of popular *consent*, exercised through some institutional mechanism, such as a parliament.
- Power is exercised under *institutional restraints* (constitution, rule of law) designed to protect individual, minority, and private interests.

In the past few decades there has been a tendency to abandon language regarding the *source* ("will of the people") and *purpose* ("common good") of democracy and embrace instead Schumpeter's (1947) focus on *mechanisms* that ensure political competition.

The definition given above is in keeping with traditional thinking, but it is a tough one. To be in democratic "orbit," a country must measure up to all four requirements. Borderline cases do exist, but in order for a democratic system to be stable, all four elements must be present. A *breakdown* in democracy occurs when the boundaries specified by the criteria are overstepped: when legislatures are bypassed or dissolved, when individuals are imprisoned on trumped-up charges or without due process, when the press is censored, and so on (see Knudde and Neubauer 1969, Dahl 1971).

In normative or politico-ideological discourse, "democratic society" is represented as a kind of undifferentiated, holistic thing. For proper sociological analysis, however, it must be disaggregated into components that are only sometimes correlated with one another empirically. For example, a country may have a competitive (i.e., democratic) political system but at the same time have a highly regressive income distribution or a rigidly stratified status structure. A democratic polity may possess the apparatus of legislature, executive, courts, coercive machinery, and party system, but these may or may not be consonant with patterns of authority in other arenas, such as business, labor unions, and churches. Another peril of thinking about democracy in holistic terms is that it may have unfortunate political consequences. In some countries religious groups and altruistic reform organizations assume that a society may become truly democratic only after it has entirely shed its authoritarian culture. Such thinking may be counterproductive, in that it projects the perfect democracy far into the future–as some kind of utopian ideal–and thus indirectly tolerates current authoritarian ideologies and practices.

One must distinguish, then, between the general *concept* of democracy and its concrete implementation. There seems to be no question that the idea of democracy is, worldwide, much stronger than it has ever been in human history. But this does not mean that it is everywhere implemented or consolidated into stable, "irreversible" forms. What has transpired is that Western-style democracy, while not fully accepted as legitimate worldwide, can no longer be written off as "bourgeois" or "merely formal" in the way that it was by the Fascist right in the interwar period and the Marxist left until very recently. Surviving versions of such authoritarian ideologies must now somehow incorporate the idea of representative democracy into their world views. The key question, of course, is in what way these modifications of formerly nondemocratic ideologies are grafted onto polity and society. They may involve efforts to enlarge direct, "participatory" mechanisms (Barber 1984), or they may involve a partway move toward "oligarchic pluralism," a kind of waystation for more sweeping reforms to come (see Macpherson 1975, Weffort 1992, Lamounier 1990).

As indicated, democracy is a political subsystem, not a total society. A question must still be asked, however: how sharply can we draw the line between political institutions and the substantive organization of the surrounding society? This question assumes particular significance when we consider, first, the processes that transpire between the "launching" and the consolidation of a democratic polity and second, the conditions that ensure that a democracy, once consolidated, will stay in place and avoid breaking down.

Democratic Consolidation and Breakdown

We noted earlier a kind of tension between substantive and procedural definitions of democracy. This tension is a source of conflict in the scholarly literature on democracy, especially when the notions of democratic consolidation and breakdown are discussed. It is not a "left–right" conflict, but rather a tension between those who stress the importance of political leaders and authorities for democratic stability versus breakdown and those who stress structural processes. On the one side, both traditional liberals and modern rational-choice theorists rest their analysis on assertions that democratic survival is primarily a matter of how key elites choose to behave within the institutional rules of the political game. On the other side, both system-theorists like Parsons and modern Marxist theorists would (in a rare moment) agree to take a structural approach and emphasize the fragility of the boundaries of the polity in times of crisis. Such theorists would argue that societal factors such as extreme inequalities in income, rampant ethnic tensions, or nondemocratic cultural values can overwhelm the *procedures* of democracies with *substantive conflicts*. As is true of many dialogues in the social sciences, this one has major normative underpinnings, concerned mainly with the issue of political responsibility. Was the collapse of the Weimar Republic and the rise of Nazi fascism, for example, primarily the result of a disorder within the political system, something that political leaders and elites could have avoided? Or were the latter overwhelmed by a much larger, complex set of conditions (Lepsius 1978)? When we speak of a "crisis of ungovernability," in India, for example, are we referring to the incapacity of political leaders and the resulting inadequacy of the political institutions or to large, inexorable, irresistible conflicts (Kholi 1990)?

The World of Nondemocracy

Huntington (1991) dates the contemporary "wave of redemocratization" in the world from an apparently implausible moment: the military coup of April 24, 1974, against the authoritarian regime in Portugal. Since that time, Huntington calculates, about 30 countries have shifted from authoritarianism to democracy, and perhaps 20 more were directly affected. The term "*re*democratization" locates the process: a movement toward, or a return to, democratic forms in Southern Europe, in the former Soviet Union and Eastern Europe, and throughout Latin America. These are all countries with a high level of institutional complexity and at least minimal prior experience of representative democracy. Some have asked whether countries such as Haiti fit this characterization, but most of the cases qualify.

In looking at the recent experiences of these countries, we are aided by the distinction between *totalitarian* and *authoritarian* regimes built on the pioneering work of Friedrich and Brzezinski (1985) and others. Huntington summarizes this distinction as follows:

> Totalitarian systems are characterized by a single party, usually led by one man; a pervasive and powerful secret police; a highly developed ideology setting forth the ideal society, which the totalitarian movement is committed to realizing; and governmental penetration and control of mass communications and all or most social and economic organizations. A traditional authoritarian system, on the other hand, is characterized by a single leader or small group of leaders, no party or weak party, no mass mobilization, possibly a "mentality" but no ideology, limited government, "limited, but not responsible pluralism," and no effort to remake society and human nature (Huntington 1991: 12)

This distinction is helpful, though the range of countries covered by it is limited in number. To deepen our understanding of the relations between democracy and nondemocracy, the universe should be expanded to include other regions, levels of socioeconomic development, and cultures. We undertake this expansion in the remainder of the chapter, considering four types of situations:

- countries in which a sense of a common social "order" or political "community" scarcely exists;
- societies which seem to lack even the initial impulse for democratization ("primitive dictatorships");
- societies in which a combination of religious and political beliefs seem inimical to Western-style democracy (mainly Islamic countries);
- totalitarian and authoritarian regimes proper, in the semi-industrialized and industrialized countries of Latin America and Eastern Europe.

From "Order" to "Community"

It should come as no surprise, Whelan wrote, "that democracy, which is a method for group decision-making or self-governance, cannot be brought to bear on the logically prior matter of the constitution of the group itself, the existence of which it presupposes" (1983: 40). He counterpoised this insight against the view that democracy is "the sole foundation of democratic government": "that democratic methods cannot be brought to bear on the determination of political boundaries–even though this is usually an important political decision, about which people may have strong preferences–has the effect of rendering controversies over boundaries among the most intractable and bitter types of political conflict" (ibid.).

Whelan's observation extends beyond physical boundaries. Democracy is a political "order" in a territory; this is what Weber had in mind when he stressed the monopoly of the means of violence as the most important defining characteristic of a state (1968: 56). Violence is a last resort, imposed when other political means are insufficient or inapplicable. In the last decade or so, a number of "orderly" countries have seen their political "order" dissolve. Somalia is the obvious case, but others are Peru, Colombia, El Salvador, and, of course, the former Soviet Union and the former Yugoslavia. These episodes have given Hobbes's "war of all against all" a less abstract meaning. Hobbes, of course, saw the solution to this problem as the imposition of rule by a sovereign. Rousseau and others since him have countered with the idea that a sense of "community" is more relevant for political order.

The literature on democracy has ignored situations which lack a basic order, possibly because, following Whelan's observation, it shares the assumption that political democracy presupposes a societal community or order. However, the issue is more complex than the presence or absence of order. In the case of Peru, for example, it is important to ask which came first: the erosion of democracy on account of a rigid stratification system and ethnic and linguistic differences or the erosion of community because of ineffective democratic government. In any event, the question is informed by the plausible assumption that a strong sense of community enables a democracy to weather difficult times and, correspondingly, a fragile community makes democratic government very difficult. Jelavich's point about the situation in interwar Austria underscores that assumption:

> The issue of Austrian patriotism dominated the entire history of the First Republic. Under the empire . . . the inhabitants of the German-speaking areas had been in varying degrees, and depending on the individual, loyal to the empire, their provinces, or the wider concept of a German nation. No one had fought for, or believed in, a specifically Austrian idea–apart from the empire. Like the republic, the Austrian state was a second choice for all concerned. (Jelavich 1989: 171)

Dependence on Fascist Italy and the *Anschluss* of 1938 demonstrates that foreign events weighed heavily in the Austrian equation, but they do not tell the whole story. The Austrians lacked an "Austrian idea." This fact contributed to the fact that Left and Right were so strongly polarized, that each major party had its private army, and that political leaders could not sustain a constructive dialogue on national goals. For each Austria there are probably several Angolas, but the Austrian example indicates that "disorder" is not a preserve of underdevelopment or of countries emerging from a civil war.

Citing the Austrian example is not meant to suggest either that interwar Austria was in the same situation as India, Peru, Colombia, the former Yugoslavia, or the USSR today, or that all cases of disorder are of the same cloth. But all those cases share a problematic relationship between the group as a national community and its aspirations for and capability of democratic government.

Primitive Dictatorships

During the past half-century a number of small Third World countries have been governed by what might be called "primitive dictatorships." No pejorative evolutionary connotation is intended by this term. What it implies is a situation with little structural differentiation in which there is a "primitive" political structure based on a corrupt police apparatus built around one ruler–in vivid contrast to the elaborate bureaucratic mechanisms of authoritarian regimes proper. Examples of primitive dictators are the Duvaliers (Papa Doc and Baby Doc) in Haiti, Stroessner in Paraguay, and Somoza in Nicaragua. Haitians elected Père Aristide (later deposed) after the demise of Baby Doc; Paraguay went through an ambiguous transition of military government; and Nicaragua fell to the

Sandinistas; but the legacy of such dictatorships remains, and their appearance in other Third World countries is not impossible.

At the same time, this kind of open, personal dictatorship is an extreme case. In other countries, mainly African, the failure of initial democratic experiments sometimes gave way to unstable rule by rival military cliques and sometimes to strong-man regimes disguised thinly by some kind of electoral process. A journalistic description of M. Houphouet-Boigny during the Ivory Coast presidential contest of 1990 illustrates one such situation and raises some relevant sociological issues. Jacques de Barrin gave the following account under the title "La Revanche de M. Houphouet-Boigny":

Confronted for the first time by a political opponent, the old dictator of the Ivory Coast, whose power had been shaken, won hands down in the presidential election. The "old one" had, in all probability, won his bet: more than 80 percent of the voters gave him a seventh term as head of state. In referring to the preceding presidential vote, when he had obtained, purely and simply, 100 percent of the vote, he could savor it, to be sure. But today, things were not exactly as they were yesterday, since Felix Houphouet-Boigny found himself, for the first time in the history of the Ivory Coast, opposed by an adversary in the person of Laurent Gbagbo.
. . . Democracy requires a long apprenticeship. It seems impossible to conceive that this democratic exercise had finally evolved into a "masquerade," to the point of perverting the results of that presidential election.

In reality there were two opposing profiles: the old planter versus the young professor. And there were two conceptions of power as well. Under the pressure of mob action, on the day after the April disturbances, the chief of state had been forced to relax his grip to the point of renouncing the one-party system and even to imagining his fall from power. He had thus lost the first round. But, as an experienced politician who had never been conquered, he quickly recovered himself. . . .

M. Houphouet-Boigny, at eighty, can now coolly look forward to his own succession, forecasting its unfolding . . . but he will no longer be able to direct his country as the father of a family. (De Barrin 1990)

It is not at all remarkable that M. Houphouet-Boigny won a seventh term in office; President Kekkonen held power in Finland for 25 years. Nor is the massive majority unusual; this kind of noncompetitive pattern prevailed in Brazil in nine of 11 direct presidential elections held during the First Republic (1889–1930), and only in the last one (1993) did the proportion of voters in the total population reach 5 percent. What is remarkable is contained in de Barrin's last point: either there is hope for democracy, or increased conflict is on the horizon. Three distinct sociological issues arise from the Houphouet-Boigny election.

The effectiveness of international control of elections in adverse situations
Huntington stressed the increasing importance of international oversight of
elections:

> In any society, the sustained failure of the major opposition political party to
> win office necessarily raises questions concerning the degree of competition
> permitted by the system. In the 1980s, the free-and-fair elections criterion of
> democracy became more useful by the increasing observation of elections by
> international groups. By 1990 the point had been reached where the first
> election in a democratizing country would only be generally accepted as
> legitimate if it was observed by one or more reasonably competent and
> detached teams of international observers, and if the observers certified the
> election as meeting minimal standards of honesty and fairness. (Huntington
> 1991: 8)

On a more informal basis, the international press functions as a kind of
watchdog, sometimes actually inhibiting governmental repression of
democratic movements, as in the revolutions in Eastern Europe in 1989–90.

The relationship between a country's size and its democratic development   The
received wisdom, building on the ancient Greek city-state, the New
England town meeting, and other exemplars, is that smallness favors
democracy. But Dahl and Tufte have challenged that assumption:

> the effectiveness of the citizen who is in concord with the preponderant
> majority of other citizens in his unit may well be maximized, as Rousseau
> thought, when the unit is small and homogeneous. Yet in such a unit the
> effectiveness of the dissenting citizen is minimized by his difficulty in finding
> an ally, and by the weakness of political competition. (1975: 138)

At the same time, large size is no guarantee of democracy, as Fascist and
Communist dictatorships themselves testify.

Smallness is often combined with simple economies and repressive
political traditions in Third World countries, thus confounding any effort
to isolate the influence of size as a factor in explaining democratic
development. In much of European history, intellectuals and dissident
groups could cross borders and continue their efforts as expatriates. In the
contemporary Third World, distances are often forbidding and frontiers
closely guarded (consider Birmania). Poverty is such that middle-class
citizens, even intellectuals, cannot readily emigrate. Under these kinds of
circumstances, cooptation and intimidation may be effective, and this
contributes to the judgment sometimes ventured that democracy in such
contexts is a lost cause.

The precise nature of the obstacles to democracy in adverse contexts   Do we
settle for simple explanations such as that democracy is impossible in the
midst of mass poverty? or fall back on de Barrin's notion that "democracy

needs a long apprenticeship?" We seem by now to have abandoned two orders of explanation: that of quasi-evolutionary political "modernization" or "structural differentiation," whereby urban life, the autonomy of the middle classes, the spread of education, and the growing autonomy of the churches were rolled into one large explanation for the advent of democracy; and that of Marxist approaches, which argued that less developed countries were organized too simply for class consciousness and class politics to arise. Having left these behind, however, we seem to be without satisfactory explanations.

Islamic Theocracy: "Culture" as a Causal Factor?

The social science literature comes up with many supposed obstacles to the development of democracy in the Islamic countries of the Middle East. Not the least of these is the involvement of this region in possibly the world's most difficult geopolitical situation, the politics of oil and Israel. Other favored candidates for obstacles are the militarism of the area; its steep and regressive social stratification systems; the model of "state-led" development, which subordinates large sections of the economy to government control; and a residual "lack of democratic experience." The greatest theoretical challenge, however, is found in the cultural argument: Is the Islamic "political culture" compatible with political democracy? This question immediately triggers two methodological ones: What do we mean by "political culture?" How can we deal with the issue of cultural causality–that is, how, in this case, religious beliefs and symbols affect political behavior and shape political institutions? A word or two on these methodological issues is in order.

The attempt to explain political developments by referring to a people's "national character" is not new. It has been invoked frequently in considering Latin countries. Building in a kind of reverse way on Weber's insights about Protestantism and capitalism, many writers have asserted that Catholicism is inimical to both capitalism and democracy. The latter religious system, often in combination with plantation patterns of land ownership and poverty, is said to encourage excessive submission to authority, a sense of personal inefficacy, and cynicism about public institutions. The argument proceeds by asserting that, with this mentality, it is only a short step to nepotism, extreme inequality, the appropriation of public institutions for private gain, and the emptiness of formal rules and rights.

Cultural explanations of Brazil's uneven democratic development touch on the social formations associated with the plantation economy and its extended family clusters. Even today, many writers revive Holanda's (1936) reference to an "Antigona complex," the persistence of blood ties, which inhibits any clear, normative distinction between the private and the public, a distinction essential for the consolidation of democratic practices.

More generally, the argument brings to mind the tension residing in Aristotle's distinction between the limited *oikos* and the enlarged *polis*. Inherent in the colonial experience and the social organization of the plantation is a kind of eternally reenacted cultural or family drama that impedes the fulfillment of Brazil's democratic aspirations (see Lamounier and de Souza 1993).

The cultural case is plausible, but, as a viable explanation, it encounters evident difficulties. Brazil is no longer such a country. Its population is nearly 150 million, of which three-quarters live in urban areas, one-third in metropolitan centers, and less than one-quarter in agricultural regions. There are 90 million registered voters. The complexity accompanying these gross facts is such that refuge in simple "national character" explanations is analytically hopeless. When Almond and Verba (1965) put forward their original notion of "political culture," they stressed its statistical character, the empirical distribution of attitudes and preferences in different countries. This formulation takes into account the multidimensionality and changeable character of national attitudes and thus appeals for caution in appealing to political culture as a causal factor. Yet this qualified version often gives way to simpler causal arguments.

This issue points up the major intellectual challenge to "cultural" interpretations of "nondemocracy" in Islamic countries. At first glance the cultural account is an attractive one, since Islam presents an extremely coherent set of religious beliefs. Lewis, a historian, put the issue as follows:

> From a historical perspective it would seem that of all the non-Western civilizations . . . Islam offers the best prospects for Western-style democracy. Historically, culturally, religiously, it is the closest to the West, sharing much–though by no means all–of the Judeo-Christian and Greco-Roman heritage that helped to form our modern civilization. From a political perspective, however, Islam seems to offer the worst prospects for liberal democracy. Of the forty-six sovereign states that make up the international Islamic Conference, only one, the Turkish Republic, can be described as a democracy in Western terms, and even there the path to freedom has been beset by obstacles. (1993: 89)

The central question for Islam, according to Lewis, does not affect Islamic fundamentalists. For them, the concept of democracy is irrelevant, and they rarely utter the word. The question is, rather, whether liberal democracy as a political system is compatible with Islam itself. Variations notwithstanding, Western democratic institutions usually encompass some kind of council or assembly, in which representatives participate in the formation, policies, and sometimes the replacement of a government. This is the heart of the matter, according to Lewis. We can do no better than quote his words:

[The effective functioning of democratic councils] was made possible by the principle embodied in Roman law and in systems derived from it, of the legal person–that is to say, a corporate entity that for legal purposes is treated as an individual, able to own, buy, or sell property, enter into contracts and obligations, and appear as either plaintiff or defendant in both civil and criminal proceedings. [Though] there are signs that such bodies existed in pre-Islamic Arabia, they disappeared with the advent of Islam. . . . From the time of the Prophet until the first introduction of Western institutions in the Islamic world there was no equivalent among the Muslim peoples of the Athenian boule, of the Roman Senate, of the Jewish Sanhedrin, of the Icelandic Althing or the Anglo-Saxon witenagemot, or of any of the innumerable parliaments, councils, synods, diets, chambers, and assemblies of every kind that flourished all over Christendom. . . . One obstacle to the emergence of such bodies was the absence of any legal recognition of corporate persons. . . .

Almost all aspects of Muslim government have an intensely personal character. In principle, at least, there is no state, but only a ruler, no court, but only a judge. (Lewis 1993: 94).

Without legislative or any other kind of corporate bodies, there was no need for any principle of representation or any procedure for choosing representatives. . . . Such central issues of Western political development as the conduct of elections and the definition and extension of the franchise therefore had no place in Islamic political evolution. Not surprisingly . . . the history of the Islamic states is one of almost unrelieved autocracy. The Muslim subject owed his obedience to a legitimate Muslim ruler as a religious duty. That is to say, disobedience was a sin as well as a crime. (Ibid.: 96)

Lewis's formulation touches on the main methodological issue, mentioned above, concerning the causal role of culture. Some social scientists go further than Almond and Verba's notion of culture as a statistical distribution of opinions and beliefs. Parsons (1966), for example, considered culture as a superordinate system that exercises a kind of cybernetic control over systems "below" it, including the social and political system. Geertz (1973) differed from Parsons in many particulars but, if anything, went further in assigning an "active" role to society's organized symbolic activity. Lewis's analysis of the political implications of Islam is closer to Parsons and Geertz. If he is correct, the obstacles to liberal democracy which he cites are serious ones, characterized by a kind of intractability and repetition compulsion that cultural values often impose. Furthermore, Lewis's formulation derives strength from his effort to establish *specific* causal connections: between cultural elements (in this case the idea of the corporate) and organizational ingredients of the democratic enterprise (in this case deliberative assemblies).

Yet, in the last analysis, Lewis tends to hedge on the precise role of culture in the evolutionary prospects for democracy in Islamic nations. On the one hand, he treats modernization as reinforcing the authoritarian character of Islam: "Modernization in the nineteenth century, and still more in the twentieth century, far from reducing . . . autocracy, substantially increased it, insofar as it made powerful repressive technology available to the autocrats and enfeebled or abrogated the religious constraints and intermediate powers that had in various ways limited earlier autocracies" (1993: 96). How could the democratic impulse gain strength under these historical circumstances? An answer seems difficult to conceive, but Lewis himself, in an almost contradictory moment, anticipates democracy's advance: "Despite all these difficulties and obstacles, the democratic ideal is steadily gaining force in the region, and increasing numbers of Arabs have come to the conclusion that it is the best, perhaps the only, hope for the solution of their economic, social and political problems" (1993: 98).

It would be easy to dismiss Lewis's analysis as simply contradictory; but it is more helpful to point up the general problem involved in the use of political culture as an explanatory category. Too often it is used as a residual category, a wastebasket into which we throw a variety of explanatory factors whose status we do not understand. As such, cultural explanations will inevitably turn out to be inconsistent, circular, or even contradictory. What is called for is a greater specification of the precise connections and the causal role of symbolic beliefs in structuring political activity and the formulation of these connections in the form of hypotheses that can be evaluated systematically in relation to other, competing explanations.

Latin America and Eastern Europe

We began this chapter by sketching the course of the ongoing, worldwide "wave of redemocratization." It began with the collapse of authoritarian systems in Southern Europe (Portugal, Spain, and Greece) and Latin America (Brazil, Uruguay, Argentina, and Chile) and later the totalitarian regimes of the former Soviet Union and Eastern Europe. There are, of course, great cultural and social-structural differences among the many countries affected. At the same time, it is legitimate to set these cases apart from those considered in the earlier sections, because their political systems are far more developed institutionally than those of the countries with "primitive dictatorships" and even Islamic countries and because, as a rule, they have had more prior exposure to the democratic experience.

At the moment, the prospects for democracy in Southern Europe are intimately tied to the future of the European Community, so we will set them aside. As for Latin America, Eastern Europe, and the former Soviet Union, they occupy center stage with respect to the consolidation of democratic systems, just as they did in the breakdown of authoritarian and totalitarian ones. We should look at the differences among them and assess the sociological issues they pose. Discussion of that transition is informed by the following queries:

- What does prior democratic "learning" really mean, and how important is it?
- What are the key links between economy and polity, in particular, the connections between market-oriented reforms and inequality on the one side and democratic stability on the other?
- How relevant are the classical political-institutional issues in building democracy–monarchy versus republic, presidentialism versus parliamentarianism, majoritarian versus proportional electoral systems?
- How central is the reemergence of "neo-primordialism" based on ethnic, linguistic, religious, or regional factors? In certain areas (notably the former Yugoslavia) they seem overwhelming. Moreover, reference to them returns us to the earlier topic of the importance of "community" as a prerequisite for a democratic polity.

The concept of prior democratic learning has an intuitive appeal, but in using it, one flirts with the possibility of producing only a residual or circular explanation: one can say of democracies that there has been prior learning and of nondemocracies that there has not, but that does not carry us very far toward an explanation. In this case, too, specification is required. One initial line of specification is to sort out the role of the external imposition of democracy. How much prior democratic learning did Germany and Japan have in 1945, or Spain and Portugal in the mid-1970s? One can argue plausibly that democratic stability in West Germany and Japan owed as much to the imposition of a democratic design by the Allied occupying powers and that an important impulse in Spain and Portugal was the incentive to join the European Community.

Turning to internal historical learning, a central element would appear to be the level of prior experience with electoral and party competition. Within that, it is important to ask whether the society has developed a consensus on a legitimate "umpire" (for example, the courts) or some other mechanism to decide finally about what "rules of the political game" are actually institutionalized and apply to the polity. Dahl's (1971) notion of "peaceful contestation" is relevant here, as is Higley and Gunther's (1992) emphasis on "elite settlements" regarding the rules and procedures whereby power is shared and opposition is considered legitimate (for the American case, see Hofstadter 1969).

On this particular score, most Latin American countries would seem to be in a more favorable position than the former Soviet Union and Eastern Europe. The word "most," however, immediately suggests exceptions. Central America, with a long history of factionalism and violence, and Cuba, where the one-party system associated with the communist experiment now seems doomed, are the obvious ones. Even Mexico, now standing to benefit from integration with the United States, may face serious difficulties. Mexico has a quasi-authoritarian system: an ultra-dominant party, though not a one-party system and pervasive authoritarian practices, but a substantial *de facto* pluralism and public debate. Paradoxically, it may be more difficult for Mexico to speed up the democratization process than it has been for countries like Brazil and Argentina, where the transition was from a more clear-cut authoritarian regime. In the latter cases there is a critical moment at which the military must extricate itself from the political process, one way or the other. In Mexico, further democratic progress must contend with a large and ossified political machine, historically connected with the Revolutionary Institutional Party (PRI). It is not clear that the evolving integration with the United States will be decisive in moving Mexico from its state of "incompleteness" of democratic evolution.

The second query deals with stratification and democracy—more particularly, the degree to which democracy depends on the elimination of mass poverty, the reduction of differences in income, and the improvement of basic social services. Marxists and non-Marxists appear to agree that democracy is not really viable until some authoritarian enclaves are removed. Moore's (1966) discussion of labor-repressive agriculture is an illustration. His hypothesis is that countries with a highly concentrated land distribution and a large peasantry face a major handicap in the development of democracy. By this measure, the former socialist countries of Eastern Europe would appear to have an advantage over those of Latin America. But this simple equation requires some qualification as well.

First, the "agrarian question" in Latin America has changed significantly. Though large and sometimes unproductive holdings still occupy much of the usable land, much of it has been converted for use in highly productive capitalist enterprises. The main problem no longer appears to be the repressive stratification of the countryside so much as the inability of the urban economies of the region to absorb the enormous labor surplus that has poured into the urban centers in the past 30 or 40 years.

Second, another qualification emerges from the distinction between authoritarian and totalitarian tendencies. In Latin American countries, the powerful interests and ideologies (sometimes including the Catholic Church) associated with large landed property were clearly authoritarian, but the traditionalism associated with that political constellation may have proved an obstacle to full-fledged totalitarian rule—a combination also present, to some extent, in the interwar Iberian peninsula and in Austria.

Third, the potential for authoritarianism should not be reduced to long-term poverty or income differentials. Democratic breakdowns have a certain suddenness about them. Although mass poverty, as in India or Brazil, clearly poses long-term threats, it is the short-term economic dislocations that constitute graver dangers to democracy in the short term. As a rule, abrupt, extreme dislocations, whether they result from left-wing revolutionary or market-oriented reforms, subject large sections of the population to painful economic adjustments. Both Latin America and the former Soviet Union are vulnerable on this score at the moment. In both regions, the state-led development model is discredited and exhausted. Brazil, after 60 years of successful industrialization, now suffers from a large fiscal deficit, stagnation, and chronic, galloping inflation, all superimposed on a huge, poor, urban population that is politically mobilizable. Likewise, in the former Soviet Union and in some Eastern European countries, efforts to move in the direction of a market economy have resulted in severe dislocations and have split the countries politically between reformists and nostalgic socialists or Communists, with many unstable movements, parties, and coalitions forming in the crevices of this split (see chapter 9).

Finally, the institutional format is an issue on the agenda of democratic development. This refers to the structure of constitutions, the unitary or federal character of states, electoral systems, the separation of powers, and the like. Two issues of special salience are, first, the contrast between "consociational" and "majoritarian" models of democracy, and, second, presidential versus parliamentary systems. These issues are matters of concern in both Latin America and Eastern Europe. The contrast between consociational and majoritarian democracy has to do with the degree to which minorities, however defined, are granted specific guarantees, regardless of their numbers. The former is aimed at preventing a tyranny of the majority; the latter gives a greater role to majority rule (usually bounded by legal restraints, however). There is a presumption in favor of the consociational mode in countries with severe ethnic, linguistic, or religious cleavages; in such countries one finds consociational arrangements such as federal organization, multiparty systems, and proportional (or even minority quota) representation. The majoritarian mode is, as a rule, more appropriate in more homogeneous societies.

Yet in practice the correlations between homogeneity (or lack of it) and representational type do not always work out. Brazil is certainly more homogeneous than India, by almost any measure, yet government structures appear to be more consociational in Brazil. For example, Brazil has a highly permissive form of proportional representation, whereas India has adopted single-member districts, which tend to leave minorities unrepresented in any given district. In any event, the consociational–majoritarian dilemma reflects a complex set of possible trade-offs between the desire to "mirror" diversity in political representation, on the one hand, and movement toward a system in which workable support for the executive government is facilitated, on the other.

The respective effectiveness of presidential and parliamentary systems may also be represented as a series of trade-offs along an axis extending from rigidity to flexibility. Presidential systems are based on a rigid separation of powers. The Chief Executive does not depend on the legislature for his election, and he or she is less accountable to the legislature because of the fixed term of office. The Executive is both a player in the political game (chief of government) and an arbiter (chief of state). The parliamentary system contrasts with the presidential on all these counts. The key question is: Which system is more favorable to democracy, and under what conditions? The American presidential system has proved durable and effective; but is that because of its own characteristics or because of the "unique" American situation–affluence, a nonpolarized two-party system, almost universal allegiance to the Constitution, a strong judiciary, and a deep commitment to the rule of law? By contrast, in the parliamentary system the legislature may vote an executive out of office, and the executive may dissolve the legislature at any time. This may constitute an advantage (flexible government) or a disadvantage (instability), depending on the kind of society in which the government is embedded. So while the presidential versus parliamentary question is a matter of avid concern in both Latin America and Eastern Europe (see Linz and Valenzuela 1993), those who ponder the issues cannot ignore the institutional and cultural characteristics of the larger society.

Epilogue: Some Queries for the Future

The arguments presented in this chapter clearly underscore the fact that democracy is, if nothing else, a dynamic system and one subject to a complex and varying set of reinforcements and threats at all times. To conclude, we posit a series of challenges lying on the horizon for democracies. We list these queries as a kind of ongoing, unfinished agenda:

- Confusion on the Left–blessing or curse? The collapse of communism in the East and the uncertain state of socialist parties in the West must necessarily occasion a major realignment of parties, but the implications of this realignment are uncertain.
- Trouble on the Right? What are the political implications of continuing political apathy, disenchantment, and cynicism, as well as extremist (neo-Nazi, skinhead, racist) eruptions?
- Neo-primordialism and the loss of community? Will increasing racial and cultural diversity of the West, fostered mainly by continuing immigration, enrich or tax democracies" political fiber (see chapter 7)?
- The end of monarchical democracy? Will the British Crown survive, and if not, will this constitute a threat to other monarchical systems?
- Economy and polity–will the apparent functional dependence of a stable democracy on some kind of competitive market system continue to hold?

If, as Lipset (1960) argued three decades ago, democracy is dependent on economic growth, will the long-term threat to growth posed by the menace of environmental wreckage (see chapter 11) threaten the viability of democratic systems as well?

References

Almond, G. and Verba, S. 1965: *The Civic Culture: Political Attitudes and Democracy in Five Nations*. Boston: Little, Brown.

Barber, B. 1984: *Strong Democracy: Participatory Politics for a New Age*. Berkeley, Calif.: University of California Press.

Dahl, R. A. 1971: *Polyarchy: Participation and Opposition*. New Haven, Conn.: Yale University Press.

Dahl, R. A. and Tufte, E. R. 1975: *Size and Democracy: The Politics of the European Smaller Democracies*. Stanford, Calif.: Stanford University Press.

De Barrin, J. 1990: "La Revanche de M. Houphouet-Boigny." *Le Monde*. Oct. 30, 1990.

Friedrich, C. I. and Brzezinski, Z., 1956: *Dictatorship and Democracy*. Cambridge: Harvard University Press.

Geertz, C. 1973: *The Interpretation of Cultures*. New York: Basic Books.

Higley, J. and Gunther, R. 1992: *Elites and Democratic Consolidation in Latin America and Southern Europe*. Cambridge: Cambridge University Press.

Hofstadter, R. 1969: *The Idea of a Party System: The Rise of Legitimate Opposition in the United States, 1780–1840*. Berkeley, Calif.: University of California Press.

Holanda, S. B. 1936: *Raizes do Brazil* (Brazil's Historical Roots). Rio de Janeiro: Editora Jose Olympio.

Huntington, S. P. 1991: *The Third Wave: Democratization in the Late Twentieth Century*. Norman: University of Oklahoma Press.

Jelavich, B. 1989: *Modern Austria: Empire and Republic, 1815–1986*. Cambridge: Cambridge University Press.

Kholi, A. 1990: *Democracy and Discontent: India's Growing Crisis of Governability*. Cambridge: Cambridge University Press.

Knudde, C. F. and Neubauer, D. E. 1969: *Empirical Democratic Theory*. Chicago: Markham Publishing Company.

Lamounier, B. 1990: "Brazil: Inequality against Democracy," in L. Diamond *et al.* (eds), *Politics in Developing Countries*, Boulder, Colo.: Lynne Rienner Publishers, 87–134.

Lamounier, B. and De Souza, A. 1993: "Attitudes towards Democracy and Institutional Reform in Brazil," in L. Diamond (ed.), *Political Culture and Democracy in Developing Nations*, Boulder, Colo.: Lynne Rienner Publishers, 295–326.

Lepsius, M. R. 1978: "From Fragmented Party Democracy to Government by Emerging Decree and Nationalist Takeover: Germany," in J. Linz and A. Stepan (eds), *The Breakdown of Democractic Regimes. Europe*, Baltimore: Johns Hopkins University Press, 34–79.

Lewis, B. 1993: "Islam and Liberal Democracy." *Atlantic Monthly*, 271: 89–98.

Linz, J. and Valenzuela, A. (eds) 1993: *Democracy – Presidential or Parliamentary*. Baltimore: Johns Hopkins University Press.

Lipset, S. M. 1960: *Political Man: The Social Bases of Politics*, Garden City, N.Y.: Doubleday.

Macpherson, C. B. 1975: *Democratic Theory: Essays in Retrieval*. Oxford: Clarendon Press.

Moore, B., jr. 1966: *Social Origins of Dictatorship and Democracy*. Boston: Beacon Press.

Parsons, T. 1966: *Societies: Evolutionary and Comparative Perspectives*. Englewood Cliffs, N.J.: Prentice-Hall.

Schumpeter, J. 1947: *Capitalism, Socialism, and Democracy*. New York: Harper.

Weber, M. 1968: *Economy and Society: An Outline of Interpretive Sociology*, ed. G. Roth and C. Wittich, Vol. 1. New York: Bedminster Press.

Weffort, F. 1992: *Qual Democracia?* São Paulo: Companhia das Letras.

Whelan, F. F. 1983: "Prologue: Democratic Theory and the Boundary Problem," in J. R. Pennock and J. W. Chapman (eds), *Nomos XXV: Liberal Democracy*, New York: New York University Press, 13–47.

6

Social Welfare Systems and Their Limits

Reflecting on the history of industrial societies in the past century, one readily observes a general association between that history and the development of the welfare state. While the origins of state responsibility for the weak and needy go back centuries–the first Poor Law in England was enacted in 1572—the massive development of state welfare is associated with the rise of modern industrialism. Germany led the way with innovative legislation in the areas of health, work, and old age in the 1880s, and by the end of the first decade of the twentieth century, many European countries had begun to formulate comprehensive social welfare programs. The passage of the Social Security Act in the United States in 1935 constituted a major landmark. The quarter-century after the Second World War marked the high point of the romance of governments with social welfare, with the consolidation of comprehensive policies and programs in almost all the developed countries and the spread of programs to post-colonial and other less developed societies. In the past two decades, however, a whole range of concerns have arisen about the viability of the welfare state–concerns which, if they do not threaten its existence, at the very least portend future changes of direction for it.

Before considering some of the major sociological issues that systems of social welfare pose, a few distinctions are in order:

- "Welfare" itself is a generic term, referring to the condition of well-being of the individuals and groups of a population, defined in relation to some idea of *needs*. Needs are acknowledged to be historically variable, but they typically include subsistence levels of necessaries such as food and housing, health,

This chapter is based on a contribution by Olayiwola A. Erinosho.

protection from risk, education, and sometimes opportunities for work. The idea of needs sets the social conception of welfare off from that employed in welfare economics, where it refers more to the distribution of the gratification of utilities, or *wants*.

- The "welfare state" is a notion of relatively recent vintage, dating from the 1940s; it refers specifically to the increased responsibility assumed by the nation-state for guaranteeing the survival and well-being of populations. The benefits provided by the welfare state are variable, but they commonly include provisions for retirement and old age, sickness and accident compensation, unemployment compensation, health insurance and health delivery, and family benefits such as maternity leave and child care. Public education is sometimes, but not always, included in the definition of the welfare state. The "welfare state" as such is often considered to be the type of nation-state appropriate to advanced capitalist or even post-capitalist societies.
- "Social policy" is a broader term, encompassing social welfare policy but referring also to a broader range of activities that affect inequality and poverty, risk, and well-being generally. It often focuses on special institutions such as the family and the community. Social policy includes not only direct welfare policies, but also fiscal and monetary policies concerning employment, inflation, and economic growth (which themselves have implications for welfare) and the encouragement or discouragement of nongovernmental forms of welfare and redistribution, such as private charity and philanthropy.

Religious, Ideological, and Social Antecedents

The world religions invariably include doctrines relating to social justice and the poor. An early study of Christian views on community (Mathews 1896) stressed Jesus's acknowledgment of inequality in social life and his simultaneous advocacy on behalf of the poor and in favor of uniting rich and poor in a community of brotherhood. Yet the Bible itself also contains the seeds of Western ambivalence toward the poor. On the one hand, one finds encouragement of independence and self-sufficiency: "Seest a man diligent in his business, he shall stand before kings" (Proverbs 22: 29); on the other, an embryonic philosophy of welfare: "We who are strong ought to bear with the failings of the weak, and not please ourselves; let each of us please his neighbor for his good, to edify him" (Romans 15: 1). The Koran contains similar injunctions about helping the needy.

The history of Christianity reflects this biblical ambivalence. The Catholic tradition is a mixed one, containing both a certain fatalistic thread concerning the inevitability of suffering and a long history of almsgiving and help for the poor in the form of orphanages, burial provision, hospital care, and poorhouses (Girvetz 1968). Radical Protestantism, with its selective insistence on individual discipline and asceticism, tended toward the other extreme, stressing the conception that those who were socially and economically disadvantaged were, with some exceptions, to be regarded as those who had failed in their responsibility to God and society (Weber 1958 [1904–5]). Yet the dominant Protestant/capitalist tradition has produced traditions of individual philanthropy which are still vital in countries like the United States, where some 23 million citizens donated at least 5 percent of their annual salary to charity in 1989 (Magat 1989).

The nineteenth century produced a corresponding array of positions with respect to welfare-oriented social policies. The most consistent antagonism toward government involvement in social welfare was found in the Manchester school of political economy, which held that the sole distributional mechanism is (and should be) the free market and that any guarantee of income for able-bodied persons is a source of market inefficiency. Malthus came to the same conclusion, arguing that poor relief only generates more poverty. Even so, some classical economists favored state support of education, on the grounds that its cost is much less than that of pauperism and crime among uneducated people (West 1964). Later exponents of political economy, notably John Stuart Mill, relaxed the stridency of this doctrine and envisioned collective responsibility of the state in the areas of guaranteeing individual freedoms and mitigating social injustices. Even today, however, liberal theory has spokesmen who argue that social welfare policies undermine both distribution and market incentives and are thus economically inefficient (Lindbeck 1981, Gilder 1981).

The liberal hostility to welfare systems has engendered profound criticism and the formulation of alternative positions on welfare since the nineteenth century. From the "right"–mainly conservative and Catholic quarters–has come the view that the free cash nexus engenders social conflicts and social disorder. Wagner's (1872) argument was that a strong economy *requires* a strong social policy and that its payoff in reducing class conflict and related social strife is more than worth the cost. This view has appeared in a number of papal encyclicals and is echoed in the concept of "social capitalism" stressed by contemporary Christian Democratic authors (van Kersbergen 1991).

From the "left," which includes Marxian and critical theorists, has come a similar diagnosis but a different ideological conclusion. That is to say, welfare measures have been regarded in this tradition primarily as a strategy on the part of the capitalist classes and the state to minimize social disorder by "pacifying" the working classes (Milliband 1977, Peusner 1982). Both Marcuse (1964) and Habermas (1975) argued that massive welfare programs have been notable factors in diminishing class conflict in post-industrial societies. At the same time, positive legitimization for welfare has been found in the ideologies of the Left. Classical Marxism, with its themes of the abolition of private property and "from each according to his ability, to each according to his need," justified the most active state intervention in social institutions of redistribution. More specifically, socialist writers (Strachey 1956, Crosland 1967) have regarded welfare programs as a source of emancipation and empowerment of the working classes, and in Sweden socialist writers have argued that an active, egalitarian social policy is a precondition for both an efficient economy and a democratic socialist society (Tilton 1990).

On the more political-social side, it is apparent that individualist, meritocratic societies which stress social mobility (such as the United States) are less receptive to the growth of state welfare than those with more collectivist, paternalistic, or authoritarian traditions (some European societies). Wilensky (1982) discovered that welfare "laggards" typically spent heavily on education (designed to encourage and justify the ideology of meritocratic achievement), and he found a *negative* relationship in advanced countries between post-secondary school enrollments and other welfare expenditures.

Theories and Findings on the Welfare State

Socioeconomic Theories

The preceding section has dealt with the larger cultural and social context of welfare and social policies in general. Theories of the welfare state attempt to account for the rise, vicissitudes, and variations of that phenomenon as a historically unique institutional invention. We now survey, sketchily, some sociologists' and others' theories and research on this topic.

No doubt the most influential account of the rise of the welfare state is that of T. H. Marshall (1950), which tied it closely to the development of citizenship and what was later to be called nation building in the West. For Marshall, welfare rights follow historically on the development of two other classes of rights. The first are civil rights, such as freedom of religion, association,and expression; the second are political rights, such as the rights to vote and to seek political office. Social and economic rights, which come next, include welfare, which becomes a matter of legal entitlement rather than discretionary policy.

It might be argued that social and economic rights are a natural consequence of the first (which free a people) and the second (which empower them). Viewed in this way, welfare rights can be regarded historically as a special aspect of the history of the middle classes in industrial capitalist societies. The history of the late eighteenth and nineteenth centuries can be written in part as an attempt on the part of those classes to rid themselves and society of entitlements "from above" – that is, of the residual claims of privilege and advantage on the part of the landed, aristocratic classes. Much of this process involved a struggle for religious, civil, and political rights *for* the middle classes. The late nineteenth century witnessed the extension of political rights to the working classes, and the twentieth century marked the activation of new demands for entitlements "from below," as it were, in the form of universal social and economic rights, including welfare rights. Be that as it may, socialist advocates of the welfare state (Crosland 1967) saw it as an important bridge across the social-class divide and joined with Continental colleagues in regarding the establishment of welfare institutions as an integral step in the direction of social democracy or socialism.

Marshall's thesis can be regarded as a sort of appeal to the "logic of industrialism"–that is to say, to a natural course of historical events rooted in the class structure and polity of modern Western society which eventuated in the full-blown welfare state. Another "logic of industrialism" account, more explicitly functional in character, is associated with the names of Wilensky (Wilensky and Lebeaux 1958, Wilensky 1975) and Rimlinger (1971). The early version of this argument stressed the loss of functions of the family, church, guild, community, and neighborhood and the assumption of these functions by the state. Industrialization, urbanization, and the development of wage labor necessitate individual mobility, weaken the family, and increase risks for workers and their families. The state, responding to economic changes, takes over functions that were handled differently by preindustrial institutions.

Later work by Wilensky sought to explain *variations* in welfare systems. Basing his analysis on large samples of nations, Wilensky found a direct, strong relationship between the extent of welfare state development, on the one hand, and the society's level of economic development, on the other. In addition, the extent of welfare spending depended on the age structure of the population (the more aged, the more spending) and the age or duration of the welfare system itself (the older, the more welfare spending). Wilensky interpreted his results as follows:

> Over the long pull, economic level is the root cause of welfare-state development, but its effects are felt chiefly through demographic changes of the past century and the momentum of the programs themselves, once established. With modernization, birth rates declined, and the proportion of aged was thereby increased. This increased importance of the aged, coupled with the declining economic value of children, in turn exerted pressure for welfare spending. Once the programs were established they matured, everywhere moving toward wider coverage and higher benefits. Social security growth begins as a natural accompaniment of economic growth and its demographic outcomes; it is hastened by the interplay of political elite perceptions, mass pressures, and welfare bureaucracies. (Wilensky 1975: 47)

These relationships appear to hold independent of type of political regime and political ideology (capitalist, socialist, communist).

Two other socioeconomic theories, distinct from, but consistent with, the "logic of industrialism" explanation, are convergence theory and diffusion theory. The first states that, as they develop, or "modernize," countries, one after another, discover common economic and social-structural exigencies bearing on them and tend to deal with these in similar ways, welfare spending being one of them (Cutright 1965, Pryor 1968). This process of convergence also cuts across all types of political system. The diffusion argument is that welfare systems begin in a center of some kind–continental Europe–and then are noticed and spread to other countries. Some studies (Flora and Alber 1981, Heclo 1974) note the special historical importance of Germany in this regard, but they also stress the unevenness of the process and the supplementary role of internal national determinants as welfare programs are adopted in other countries.

Political Theories

The rise and consolidation of systems of welfare did not appear on the scene automatically and effortlessly. Their enactment has typically been accompanied by ideological and political–including class–conflict. Furthermore, because one of the intended effects of welfare measures is to redistribute economic and other resources, they inevitably raise the classical political question of who gets what, when, and how. Accordingly, many scholars have argued that the political, as well as the socioeconomic, context is an important determinant of the extent and form of welfare programs.

In a recent survey, Hicks and Swank (1992) identified three major political approaches to explaining variations in welfare systems: the social-democratic corporatist, the political democratic, and the statist.

The social-democratic corporatist approach This approach regards political ideology and political agency as determinative and in this way stands in sharp contrast to the "logic of industrialism" approach, which explains the rise and extent of welfare programs and spending independently of the type of political system and political ideology. The main argument is that countries that have strong left (i.e., Socialist, Labor, and Social Democratic) parties also manifest more highly developed welfare systems than those with strong right parties (Korpi 1983). Sometimes this works out in the form of direct political control by the Left; in other cases, it may take the form of political pressure that leads more conservative governments to adopt welfare reforms (Esping-Andersen 1990). Others have argued that centrist secular and Christian Democratic parties have also been active in advancing welfare policies (Castles 1982). In all cases, the prediction is that the kinds of political forces which are represented concretely in strong labor unions, strong left parties, and significant working-class presence in decision making will foster the development of welfare programs.

The political-democratic approach Scholars taking this approach have tended to move away from the partisan aspects of political life and to stress more formal features of political competition as affecting the development of welfare programs. One simple prediction is that large voter turnout is conducive to greater welfare effort, largely because it signals the entry into politics of lower-status voters–the greatest beneficiaries of welfare measures, as a rule–to whom politicians then respond. Another version of this perspective is that if electoral politics are highly competitive (i.e., result in very small majorities or the necessity of relying on coalitions to establish governments), then those governments are more likely to undertake redistributive–that is, welfare–policies in order to appeal to groups of voters who may make the difference between being in or out of power (Lijphart 1984, Masters and Robertson 1988).

The statist approach This approach to welfare systems takes its lead from an observation by Alexis de Tocqueville that it is the "instinctive desire of every government to gather all the reins of power into its own hands" (1955 [1856]: 58). The state itself is an interest group of sorts, and bureaucracies of states act to increase budgetary spending of all sorts. In particular, the degree to which the state is centralized, the degree to which it is bureaucratized (and, correspondingly, the numbers of bureaucrats employed), and the solidity and duration of the establishment of state programs, will all affect welfare expenditures (Skocpol 1985, Weir *et al.* 1989). The most recent work in this tradition is Skocpol's study of welfare benefits to civil war veterans and mothers in the United States in the late nineteenth century, on the basis of which she takes exception to the generally accepted view that the American welfare system lagged behind until the Great Depression of the 1930s. Instead, she argues, the state was very active in promoting welfare more than half a century earlier (Skocpol 1992).

Hicks and Swank (1992) carried out a time-series analysis of some 18 contemporary capitalist democracies between the years of 1960 and 1982, in an attempt to test the propositions derived from the various political approaches to welfare development. Interestingly, they found some support for all three lines of thinking. That is to say, that "electoral turnout, as well as left and center governments, increase welfare effort; that the welfare efforts of governments led by particular types of parties show differences and vary notably with the strength of oppositional (and junior coalitional) parties; and that relatively neocorporatist, centralized, and traditionalistic polities are high on welfare effort" (Hicks and Swank 1992: 658).

In a word, both partisan and nonpartisan features of modern democracy appear to play a role in accounting for differences in welfare spending.

The Effects of Welfare Systems

Economic Performance Effects

Different models of the welfare state envision contrasting relationships between it and the economy. In perhaps the most influential typology of welfare systems, Titmuss (1958, 1974) outlined the following variations:

- a residual model (typified by the United States), which is minimalist in its coverage and based on a traditional liberal view that only people unable to work in the market deserve to be protected;
- an institutional model, which extends the compass of welfare enormously and is aimed toward guaranteeing equitable living conditions, income distribution, and life chances for individuals;
- an industrial achievement model, closely approximating continental European systems, in which social benefits are geared to individuals' past economic status and performance.

The differences in economic impact of these three different types of systems are, in principle, very great.

The actual economic effects of welfare programs can be considered at both the microeconomic and the macroeconomic levels.

The microeconomic level   This level is frequently a subject of ideological concern. In the United States, where a high value is assigned to individual achievement, many people hold opinions antagonistic to welfare schemes–especially unemployment payments and the prospect of retirement on a generous pension–on the grounds that they constitute a disincentive for people to work and thus sap the work ethic. Regardless of the correctness or incorrectness of this representation of incentives, a considerable amount of research shows that, in the United States, the higher the income guaranteed in retirement, the greater the retirement rate and, correspondingly, the greater the decline in the labor supply (Hurd and Boskin 1981).

This relationship does not appear to hold on a comparative basis, however; countries with very generous and liberal pension systems, such as Norway and Sweden, have retirement rates that are among the lowest. High mass retirement rates also appear to be correlated with high unemployment rates (Kolberg and Esping-Andersen 1991), a finding which tends to place the "disincentive" onus on the market, not the retirement system. There is also some evidence that generous sickness and unemployment benefits discourage job searching–thus supporting the disincentive position (OECD 1985). This kind of argument is clouded by other considerations, however. Absenteeism rates in Scandinavia are extremely high, but these are accounted for not by sickness benefits but by women taking time off work to care for young children, thus suggesting a positive effect on family life and gender equalization of such programs rather than a simple work-disincentive effect. A separate line of research dealing with the relationship between personal self-esteem and welfare dependency has failed to turn up support for the proposition that people with low self-esteem seek welfare benefits. The literature does offer some support for the idea that chronic welfare dependency has a negative effect on self-esteem, however (Schneiderman *et al.* 1989).

On the macroeconomic side, there are a range of theories about how the welfare state affects the economy. The most straightforward, negative hypothesis is found in classical and neoclassical economic theory, which maintains that the market is the most rational allocative mechanism from the standpoint of efficiency and that any interference with it–including "artificial," nonmarket distributive mechanisms–is irrational. Most challenges to this viewpoint involve not so much attacks on the "efficiency" aspect of the market as the allegation that unrestrained capitalist markets generate poverty, risk, and social injustice and that these provide the principal legitimation for welfare interventions such as compensation for injury and sickness benefits, unemployment compensation, and provision for old age.

Other approaches stress the positive effects that welfare states have on economic performance. One of the central tenets of Keynesian economic views is that fiscal policies directed toward the progressive redistribution of income (most welfare policies are) have a positive effect on economic performance via their impact on demand. According to Keynesian assumptions, lower-income groups save a smaller proportion of their income than higher-income groups. A shift in the distribution downward thus constitutes a stimulus to demand, which in turn stimulates investment, production, and employment. A related argument is that welfare measures, by distributing benefits downward, improve the quality and quantity of the labor supply. This reasoning lies behind Myrdal's argument that "welfare reforms, rather than being costly for society, actually lay the basis for more steady and rapid economic growth" (Myrdal 1970: 51).

Empirical research makes it clear that states with strongly developed welfare systems also tend to maintain higher levels of employment over long periods of time. It is doubtful, however, that the welfare state as such plays a direct causal role here. Most full-employment policies rest on a kind of bargain between organized labor, on the one side, and capital and the state, on the other; the bargain is that if government will guarantee full employment (including many jobs in the welfare sector), then unions will forgo short-term wage gains (Crouch 1985). As for the general impact of welfare systems on long-term economic growth, the empirical results are very mixed, with studies informed by neoclassical assumptions arguing in the negative and studies by political scientists and sociologists pointing in the other direction. As Esping-Andersen (1994) has pointed out, however, research in this field is plagued by methodological problems and by the possibly erroneous strategy of trying to treat welfare as a distinct factor in economic growth, when in fact it is intermingled with so many other factors.

Redistribution or Equality Effects

The explicit ideological justification of welfare programs for most proponents is that they have a positive effect on redistribution of the good things of life, however these may be defined. This is certainly the thinking underlying almost all support for welfare positions coming from the Left–whether they have a Marxist, socialist, or social-democratic, corporatist, or liberal flavor. Certainly, also, egalitarian values were among the main legitimizing points for the Socialist/Communist regimes in the former Soviet Union and Eastern Europe, whose ideologies were clearly redistributive and egalitarian. In a way, neoclassical and conservative opponents of welfare programs concede the point–that is to say, they oppose those programs precisely because they involve an *illegitimate* redistribution of resources, one that is not "earned" by the recipients.

The study of redistributional effects is bedeviled by definitional problems contained in the phrase "the good things of life." Society is made up of a multiplicity of overlapping, but partly independent, systems of stratification, depending on the "good" specified–wealth, power, prestige, risk, legal privileges and immunities, even "religious grace" according to some religious belief systems. To assess the full distributional impact of *any* social policy, not one but many of these distributions have to be taken into account, and complicated trade-offs among them have to be considered. For these reasons, the difficulties of specifying any simple redistributional impacts of welfare policies become clearly apparent.

When the redistribution of economic resources and life chances is considered, the general impact of highly developed welfare systems is positive. Studies flowing from the Scandinavian Level of Living research show that, over the long haul, an index of social and economic resources has demonstrated a long-term, positive redistributional effect in the Scandinavian countries, which have the most developed systems of welfare (Eriksson and Aaberg 1985). On a more comparative basis, the extensive research carried out by the Luxembourg Income Studies group (Mitchell 1991) indicates generally that–following Titmuss's definitions–institutional welfare states such as those in Scandinavia have produced a considerably greater redistribution on several measures than have residual welfare states such as that of the United States.

A Case Illustration: Welfare in Africa

Much of the literature on the welfare state is frankly ethnocentric, focusing especially on Europe and North America and dealing with the problems of welfare in those societies. To a certain extent this bias is understandable. These areas were the first to develop industrially and thus the first to confront the institutional structures and anomalies of industrial capitalism that fostered the welfare state. Furthermore, the history of the welfare state in many of the less developed countries is one of diffusion outward from the advanced countries. In the post-Second World War period, as independent nations emerged from colonial status, many of them fashioned versions of the Western countries' civil service, legal systems, electoral and other political arrangements, and educational systems in their new societies. Welfare was among these. We close the chapter with a sketch of welfare arrangements in some African nations.

The history of state involvement in welfare in Africa dates from colonial times. The colonial powers began the process by extending their domestic welfare programs to cover only European workers in the colonized territories. This extension obviously reflected the colonial powers' differential interest in their own nationals; but it also reflected the fact that these colonials were not involved in the indigenous–mainly kinship and tribal–support systems already in existence among the local populations. Subsequently the colonial powers extended welfare measures to segments of the indigenous populations, notably urban African workers who were uprooted from their surroundings and unprotected from risk in industrial jobs. The impetus to cover these workers came from the need to stabilize the labor force and also from pressure by nascent trade unions, who sought the same kind of social security enjoyed by workers of the colonizing countries (ILO 1977).

Both the content and the coverage of social welfare broadened with the attainment of political independence in the majority of African countries by the 1960s. Social welfare was widely regarded as an essential aspect of the process of mobilization of the populations for nationhood. In addition, the sheer growth of numbers of wageworkers, especially in the ballooning state bureaucracies of the new nations, increased the need for coverage (Ayoade 1988). But progress was mixed, as indicated in the language of the report of the International Labour Organization in 1977: "Over the last 20 years, the progress of social security in many African countries has been remarkable and often impressive. But in some cases, this undeniably vigorous spirit has somewhat unbalanced results" (ILO 1977: 6). The United Nations Global Survey of welfare programs in 1986 confirmed this progressive trend in Africa (UN 1986). However, the supply of welfare services continued to lag far behind demand. It remained an inadequate complement to traditional modes of support for the poor. The facts underlying this diagnosis illustrate a general principle: the extent and effectiveness of a social welfare system depend directly on the capacity of the economic infrastructure of the society to sustain it, and this depends in turn on its level of economic development.

The limited scope and coverage of African welfare programs are typified by the case of Zimbabwe. Before 1976, the only kind of old-age pensions were the noncontributory pension benefits to non-Africans over the age of 60 by the (then) colonial government of Rhodesia. In 1980, when the country gained independence, this program was scrapped, with the understanding that expatriates and nationals of non-African origin would continue to receive benefits. A more general system, the Occupational Pension Scheme, began in 1980. This provides for funds contributed on an equal basis by employers and employees–involving between 5 and 7 percent of a worker's monthly income. The Government makes no supplementary contribution. Benefit levels are calculated on the basis of years of contribution plus interest. A nontransferability provision, however, works a hardship on workers who change employers; those who do so cannot carry benefits to the new employment situation but, instead, receive a lump sum of only their own contributions to date.

Zimbabwe has institutionalized further welfare provisions under an arrangement called Workmen and War Victims Compensation. The former covers workers (excluding casual and domestic workers) who are injured or permanently disabled as a result of occupational accidents or diseases. In cases of death, dependents receive compensation. The funds for the scheme are contributed exclusively by employers. The scheme covers workers with monthly incomes not exceeding $1,333. Benefits payable extend to a maximum of only $2,000 to meet medical costs, 75 percent of the most recent earning level in the case of permanent disability, with 12 percent and 5 percent of the worker's benefits going, respectively, to the oldest child and each of the five younger children of the worker. Funeral expenses up to $800 are provided, and a dependent widow receives two-thirds of what the worker would have been paid if permanently disabled (Kaseke 1988).

The War Victims Compensation Act of 1980 provides for those who sustained injuries or families who lost wage earners in the war preceding independence. The state finances the entire scheme. Benefit levels range between 50 and 90 percent of the earnings prior to injury for unemployable veterans and between 30 and 45 percent for those who can still work to some degree. The pension benefit for a widow or widower of the war is in the neighborhood of 60 percent of the deceased's earning level immediately prior to death.

For Zimbabwe and for the 40–odd other African countries which have benefit schemes, however, the general picture is that these schemes are confined to certain categories of wage earners and leave much of the population without protection. In recent years, moreover, African welfare systems have been affected by the same winds of change that have affected such systems elsewhere in the world. African leaders, after a long period of commitment to a pattern of a single-party state providing active guidance to economic development, are gradually accepting multiparty democracy and a market-driven approach to economic development. These developments are not without their impact on the fragile welfare programs of those countries, as governments tend to limit their involvement in many public expenditure programs and to cut the costs of those programs. As a result, the welfare systems of Africa share in the uncertainty facing those of virtually all other regions of the world.

Threats and Limits to the Welfare State

Without question, the decades following the Second World War marked the heyday of positive and expansive thinking about the growth of welfare programs and the welfare state. It was the "Keynes-plus-Beveridge" period, marked by the recovery of Europe and a period of decades of sustained growth, of the gradual subsiding of the threat from the Communist left in Western Europe, of social contracts between labor and capital, and of widespread governmental intervention in both employment policy and welfare. In this period, the liberal/conservative "end-of-ideology" theorists (Bell 1960) and radical/critical "crisis" theorists (Habermas 1975) concurred–though with different accounts and diagnoses–that the welfare state was a significant part of the package of growth, social stability, and social peace that characterized those decades.

The welfare state and its philosophies remain a solid fixture in most modern nation-states. Yet the past two decades or so have witnessed the development of an umbrella of uncertainty and a cooling of the romance with the welfare state in the developed Western democracies–their historical birthplace and haven. There is no single cause for this historical shift, but, by way of speculation, the following factors might be evoked to account for it:

- Among the critical left there remain residual claims that the welfare and related engineering efforts on the part of the post-industrial state "have not worked" as pacifying strategies and that the state continues in a kind of perpetual crisis. Those ideas have been expressed by O'Connor (1973), who views the chronic budgetary struggles and crises of the capitalist state as indications of its inability to stem the endless stream and variety of demands arising from continuing, capitalist-based contradictions. A similar message emerged from Habermas's (1975) diagnosis, which found the post-industrial state in a kind of continuing crisis of legitimation, despite its deployment of steering mechanisms to stabilize its economy and polity. While these diagnoses did not involve a direct attack on welfare programs as such, their impact, such as it was, was to generate a cynical attitude toward them.
- A decline of the social-democratic and socialist left. The past two decades have seen an undermining of moderate left, generally class-based parties in a number of countries–for example, the confusion and indirection of the Democratic party in the United States and the Labour party in England–and

a general waning of the class basis of politics in various European countries. This development may be the outcome in the longer run of factors such as the *embourgeoisement* of certain parts of the working class, its incorporation into the post-industrial state apparatus, or its undermining by capital through its new, "flexible" employment of immigrant and Third World labor. Whatever the mix of causes, it is apparent that the political forces that supported the welfare state–the traditional working classes–are less at center-stage at the end of the twentieth century than they were several decades ago.

- A corresponding resurgence of the conservative right. This was vividly concretized in the 1980s, which saw the triumph of Reaganism in the United States and Thatcherism in Britain. Both Reagan and Thatcher espoused a form of neoclassical economics which included themes of private incentives, market mechanisms, deregulation, and minimal government. They also made an assault on, and a rolling back of, the welfare state under the guise of privatization. Reagan was consistently hostile to the idea of welfare. As early as 1966, in his campaign for the governorship of the state of California, he made anti-welfare the centerpiece of his campaign. In that campaign he described social welfare as "prepaid vacations for a segment of our society which has made this a way of life" (quoted in Smelser 1987: 326). His policies were consistently anti-welfare, and while the worsening distribution of American income in the past two decades (Jencks and Petersen 1991) may have resulted primarily from other causes, it also coincided with Reagan social policies. Echoes of the conservative impulse were experienced in continental Europe as well, though in less extreme form. It remains to be seen to what degree the electoral victory of President Clinton, as well as the continuing troubles of the Conservatives in England, will signal a reversal of the Reagan–Bush political philosophy and social programs. But in any event, the prolonged episodes of Reaganism and Thatcherism, with their associated resurgence of the market principle, constituted a profound shock for the idea of the welfare state as an integrative device and an instrument for social justice in post-industrial society.
- The disintegration of the Socialist/Communist bloc. The years 1989–90 saw the collapse of the authoritarian left regimes of the Soviet Union and Eastern Europe. With that collapse came a global discrediting of what these regimes represented, together with an almost millenarian resurgence of the ideology of the free market as an integrative mechanism in those countries. That ideology, of course, is the one that is most incompatible with ideologies of welfare, and the reform of those countries along capitalist lines–insofar as it succeeds–will raise serious questions about the encompassing responsibility of the state for its citizens under the earlier regimes.

So much for some political-economic shadows that have been cast on the welfare state. Beyond these, there may be an even more important set of global economic forces at work that will call for profound modifications of the welfare state as we know it. After all, the welfare state itself is a uniquely constructed historical phenomenon, reflecting the societal realities of its historical moment. Among those societal realities were the following: the assumption of a *nationally based* labor force that was, in principle, under the jurisdiction of a government of a nation-state, and the assumption of a lifelong career of employment of adult males with "dependent" spouses and children, with identifiable and insurable risks and a foreseeable number of retirement years to which benefits could be applied.

It may well be that contemporary trends in the capitalist world economy will work to undermine these fundamental assumptions. Multinational world capitalism has already undermined the national base of labor in two ways: first, it has accelerated the rates of economically induced international immigration and the deployment of the migrant labor force, a trend especially visible in Europe and North America; second, it has decentralized production in its continuing search for cheap labor, which takes in newly developing countries like Mexico and many Third World countries. Furthermore, the employment policies of multinational economic enterprises have tended to parallel the "flexibilities" of their production policies with a corresponding flexibility with regard to labor. This includes hiring enormous numbers of low-wage female workers, often on a temporary basis (see chapter 18). It strikes one that this creation of armies of standby workers is the latest rendition of Marx's idea of an industrial reserve army. In any event, the implications for welfare are profound. It is now increasingly the case that the formation and deployment of labor forces observe the boundaries of national states less and less and that the assumption of a typical life cycle of a worker and his family is no longer operative, given the fluidity and fragility of much of the world's labor force. Insofar as they continue to be viable, welfare programs will have to adapt to these new socioeconomic realities.

It would probably be going too far to speak of a "crisis" or the impending "death" of the welfare state. There are too many economic and political forces and groups throughout the populations of nations that live in one, and have a vested interest in continuing it–the aging population (increasing in proportions and political significance), the unemployed, the unions, the ill and potentially ill, those at occupational risk, to say nothing of those professionals, government workers, and others who dispense welfare services. At the same time, like most institutions in post-industrial society, it is up for question, and this questioning may lead to changes in the responsibilities that societies are prepared to assume for the welfare of their citizens.

References

Ayoade, J. A. A. 1988: "State without Citizens: An Emerging African Phenomenon," in D. Rothchild and N. Chezan (eds)., *The Precarious Balance: State and Society in Africa*, Boulder, Colo.: Westview Press, 100–118.

Bell, D. 1960: *The End of Ideology*. New York: Free Press.

Castles, F. 1982: *The Impact of Parties*. Beverly Hills, Calif.: Sage Publications.

Crosland, C. A. R. 1967: *The Future of Socialism*. New York: Schocken.

Crouch, C. 1985: "Conditions for Trade Union Wage Restraint," in L. Lindberg and C. Maier (eds), *The Politics of Inflation and Stagnation: Theoretical Approaches and Case Studies*, Washington, D.C.: Brookings Institution, 105-39.

Cutright, P. 1965: "Political Structure, Economic Development, and National Security Programs." *American Journal of Sociology*, 70: 537–50.

Eriksson, R. and Aaberg, R. (eds) 1985: *Welfare in Transition*. Oxford: Clarendon Press.

Esping-Andersen, G. 1990: *The Three Worlds of Welfare Capitalism*. Cambridge: Polity Press.

Esping-Andersen, G. 1994: "Welfare States and the Economy," in N. J. Smelser and R. Swedberg (eds), *Handbook of Economic Sociology*, Princeton, N. J.: Princeton University Press and the Russell Sage Foundation, forthcoming.

Flora, P. and Alber, J. 1981: "Modernization, Democratization, and the Development of Welfare States in Western Europe," in P. Flora and A. J. Heidenheimer (eds), *The Development of Welfare States in Europe and America*, Rutgers, N.J.: Transaction Books, 37–80.

Gilder, G. 1981: *Wealth and Poverty*. New York: Basic Books.

Girvetz, H. K. 1968: "Welfare State," in D. L. Sills (ed.), *International Encyclopedia of the Social Sciences*, New York: Macmillan, XX, 512–20.

Habermas, J. 1975: *Legitimation Crisis*. Boston: Beacon Press.

Heclo, H. 1974: *Modern Social Politics in Britain and Sweden*. New Haven, Conn.: Yale University Press.

Hicks, A. M. and Swank, D. H. 1992: "Politics, Institutions, and Welfare Spending in Industrialized Democracies, 1960–82." *American Political Science Review*, 86: 658–74.

Hurd, M. and Boskin, M. 1981: *The Effect of Social Security on Retirement in the Early 1970s*. Washington, D.C.: National Bureau of Economic Research, Working Paper No. 659.

International Labour Organization 1977: *Improvement and Harmonization of Social Security Systems in Africa*. Geneva: ILO.

Jencks, C. and Petersen, P. J. (eds). 1991: *The Urban Underclass*. Washington, D.C.: Brookings Institution.

Kaseke, E. 1988: "Social Security in Zimbabwe." *Journal of Social Development in Africa*, 3: 5–19.

Kolberg, J. E. and Esping-Andersen, G. 1991: "Welfare States and Employment Regimes," in J. E. Kolberg (ed.), *The Welfare State as Employer*, Armonk, N.Y.: M. E. Sharpe, 3–35.

Korpi, W. 1983: *The Democratic Class Struggle*. London: Routledge and Kegan Paul.

Lijphart, A. 1984: *Democracies: Patterns of Majoritarian and Consensus Government in 21 Countries*. New Haven, Conn.: Yale University Press.

Lindbeck, A. 1981: *Work Incentives in the Welfare State*. Stockholm: Institute for International Economic Studies, University of Stockholm. Reprint Series No. 176.

Magat, R. (ed.) 1989: *Philanthropic Giving*. New York: Oxford University Press.

Marcuse, H. 1964: *One-Dimensional Man*. Boston: Beacon Press.

Marshall, T. H. 1950: *Citizenship and Social Class*. Cambridge: Cambridge University Press.

Masters, M. F. and Robertson, J. D.. 1988: "Class Compromise in Industrialized Democracies." *American Political Science Review*, 82: 1183–1201.

Mathews, S. 1896: "Christian Sociology. Social Life." *American Journal of Sociology*; 2: 108–17.

Milliband, R. 1977: *Marxism and Politics*. London: Oxford University Press.

Mitchell, D. 1991: *Income Transfers in Ten Welfare States*. Aldershot: Avebury.

Myrdal, G. 1970: *Beyond the Welfare State*. New Haven, Ct.: Yale University Press.

O'Connor, J. F. 1973: *The Fiscal Crisis of the State*. New York: St Martin's Press.

Organization for Economic Cooperation and Development 1985: *Employment Outlook.* Paris: OECD.

Peusner, Y. 1982: *State-Monopoly Capitalism and the Labour Theory of Value.* Moscow: Progress Publishers.

Pryor, F. 1968: *Public Expenditures in Capitalist and Communist Nations.* Homewood, Ill.: Irwin.

Rimlinger, G. 1971: *Welfare Policy and Industrialization in Europe, America and Russia.* New York: John Wiley and Sons.

Schneiderman, L., Furman, W. M. and Weber, J. 1989: "Self-Esteem and Chronic Welfare Dependency," in A. Mecca, N. J. Smelser and J. Vasconcellos (eds), *The Social Importance of Self-Esteem*, Berkeley, Calif.: University of California Press, 200–47.

Skocpol, T. 1985: "Bringing the State Back In: Current Research" in P. M. Evans, D. Rueschemeyer and T. Skocpol (eds), *Bringing the State Back In*, New York: Cambridge University Press, 3–43.

Skocpol, T. 1992: *Protecting Soldiers and Mothers: The Politics of Social Provision in the United States, 1870s-1920s.* Cambridge, Mass.: Harvard University Press.

Smelser, N. J. 1987: "Collective Myths and Fantasies," in J. Rabow, G. M. Platt and M. S. Goldman (eds), *Advances in Psychoanalytic Sociology*, Malabar, Fla.: Robert E. Krulger Publishing Company, 316–28.

Strachey, J. 1956: *Contemporary Capitalism.* Oxford: Oxford University Press.

Tilton, T. 1990: *The Political Theory of Swedish Social Democracy. Through the Welfare State to Socialism.* Oxford: Clarendon Press.

Titmuss, R. 1958: *Essays on the Welfare State.* London: Allen and Unwin.

Titmuss, R. 1974: *Social Policy.* London: Allen and Unwin.

Tocqueville, A. de. 1955 [1856]: *The Old Regime and the French Revolution.* Garden City, N. Y.: Doubleday.

United Nations. 1986: *Development of Social Welfare: A Global Survey of Issues and Priorities since 1968.* New York: United Nations.

Van Kersbergen, K. 1991: "Social Capitalism: A Study of Christian Democracy and the Postwar Settlement of the Welfare State." Ph.D. dissertation, European University Institute, Florence..

Wagner, A. 1872: *Rede über die Soziale Frage.* Berlin: Wiegandt und Grieben.

Weber, M. 1958 [1904–5]: *The Protestant Ethic and the Spirit of Capitalism.* New York: Scribner's.

Weir, M., Orloff, A. S. and Skocpol, T. 1989: *The Politics of Social Policy in the United States.* Princeton, N.J.: Princeton University Press.

West, E. G. 1964: "Private vs. Public Education: A Classical Economic Dispute.' *Journal of Political Economy*, 72: 465–75.

Wilensky, H. L. 1975: *The Welfare State and Equality.* Berkeley, Calif.: University of California Press.

Wilensky, H. L. 1982: "Ideology, Education, and Social Security," in I. Garfinkel (ed.), *Income-Tested Transfer Programs: The Case For and Against*, New York: Academic Press, 166–73.

Wilensky, H. L. and Lebeaux, C. 1958: *Industrial Society and Social Welfare.* New York: Russell Sage.

7

Nations, Nationalisms, and Citizens

Many contemporary political scientists–but only some sociologists–continue to struggle with the classic questions about nationhood: What is a nation? Do nations have a right to self-determination? If so, does this imply that the national identity of citizens is best guaranteed by a democratic system of government? What is nationalism? Does it differ from national identity? If not, can its growth be controlled so that democracy can survive and grow? If anything, these questions loom larger than ever before at the end of the twentieth century, when some might argue that the great era of nation building threatens to give way to a season of nation crumbling. This chapter will focus on the European experience, but the principles invoked will be at a level of generality to be relevant to other regions of the world.

Early Modern Origins

The classic questions have their roots in early modern Europe. With the decline of the Carolingian empire, a new sense of collective identity–national awareness–began to emerge. This nascent process of nation building was initially championed by some nobility and some clergy, who activated derivatives of the Latin word *natio* to highlight a people's linguistic and historical continuities (Beumann and Schroeder 1978, Guénée, 1981). At this early stage, "nation" did not refer to a region's entire population, but only to those classes in it who had developed and

---

This chapter is based on a contribution by John Keane.

begun to act on a sense of identity based on a common language and history.

From the fifteenth century onward, "nation" came to have an increasingly political cast. According to Diderot's classic definition, a nation is "une quantité considérable de peuple qui habite une certaine étundue de pays, renfermée dans de certaines limites, et qui obéit au même gouvernement" (Diderot 1751–65: 36)–that is, people in a given territory who shared common laws and political institutions. This conception included the idea of *societas civilis*–those citizens entitled to participate in politics and share in sovereignty. This component profoundly shaped the process of state-building, because it became linked with the struggles between privileged classes and monarchs for participation in state affairs. The former designated themselves advocates of "the nation." They insisted that *they*, not only the monarch, were the representatives and defenders of "national liberties" and "national rights" (Elton 1986, Bickart 1932). If the sovereign monarch was from a different nation–as in the Netherlands during the war against Habsburg Spain–then such struggles were fused with movements for national emancipation from a foreign tyrant (Huizinga 1948–53).

By the eighteenth century, claims for national identity and inclusion in "the nation" were broadened to include the nonprivileged classes–the self-educated middle classes, artisans, rural and urban laborers, and others. Henceforth "the nation" included everybody, not only the privileged classes; "the people" and "the nation" became the same. Paine's *Rights of Man* (1945 [1791–2]) symbolized the democratization of national identity. His statement generated bitter public controversies about the legitimacy of monarchies and republics, forced Paine into permanent exile from England, and led to a crackdown on "Painites" who argued for a system of representative government.

Paine's thesis manifested the democratic enthusiasm of both the American Revolutionary War and the French Revolution. Paine declared the natural and civil rights of a sovereign people of a nation, including the right to resist unlawful government and the establishment of a new kind of republican democracy. Paine warned George III and all other monarchs that the outbreak of revolution in Europe constitued a new dawn for democratic principles. "Monarchy is all a bubble," he wrote, "a mere court artifice to procure money." He painted the world as a struggle between the citizens of all nations, united in their commitment to republican democracy, and monarchic despots, accountable only to themselves, who were engaged in taxing hypocrisy, fraud, and aggressive warfare. Each nation had the right to determine its own destiny and its own representative government–a right which included periodic elections, fixed-term legislatures, a universal franchise, and civil liberties such as freedom of assembly and the press. "Sovereignty," he proclaimed, "is a matter of right, appertains to the nation only, and not to any individual; and a nation has at all times an inherent and indefeasible right to abolish any form of government it finds inconvenient, and establish such as accords with its interest, disposition, and happiness" (Paine 1945 [1791–2]: 341).

Paine's fusion of nation and democracy proved to have great staying power. The emergence of Germany and Italy as nations in the nineteenth century was based on the principle of national self-determination. So were the partition of Austria-Hungary after the compromise of 1867, the revolts of Poles in support of their reconstitution as a nation-state, and the formal recognition of a number of lesser states, including Luxembourg, Belgium, Bulgaria, Serbia, Greece, and Rumania. After the First World War the principle of "the right to national self-determination" became a virtual slogan among international lawyers and political philosophers, as well as among both national governments and their challengers. Under this principle, the claim that people should govern themselves became identified with the claim that nations should determine their own destiny. By this logic, furthermore, "state" and "nation" came to mean the same and to be used interchangeably, as in official expressions such as "League of Nations," the "law of nations," and "nation-state." "National" has come to mean anything run or regulated by the state–as in "national health insurance" or "national debt." So strong was this fusion that Deutsch could define "nation" simply as "a people who have hold of a state" (1969: 19).

The principle that nations should be represented within a territorially defined state carries over into the present. To mention only a few European examples that manifest it: the birth of Solidarity and the defeat of martial law in Poland, the velvet revolution in Czechoslovakia, the collapse of the Berlin wall to the sounds of "Wir sind ein Volk," and the struggle of the Demos government and its supporters to achieve Slovenian independence. The same principle was at work in the collapse of the Soviet Union. Prior to its dissolution, the Soviet Union was an empire of separate nationalities dominated by a Russian-centered Communist party that subordinated federal units' claims for autonomy and repressed demands for "national communism" by political crackdown and military force. At the same time, this system harbored a deep contradiction. While insisting on a Russian style of "socialism," the regime simultaneously governed through national cadres, promoted national cultures, encouraged education in local languages, and spoke of the eventual rapprochement (*sblizhenie*) and assimilation (*slyanie*) of nations. From the Khrushchev period on, these practices fostered the growth of national *nomenklatura* who ran the republics–especially in Transcaucasia and Central Asia–as fiefdoms controlled by Party "mafias" rooted in networks of kinship, friendship, and patronage. It also fostered a kind of "civil society" in these nations, which could protest, using the national idiom, against Russification, enforced industrialization, and ecological damage and could demand "democracy" and "independence" from the Russian-centered party (von Beyme 1991, Michnik 1991).

National Identity and Citizenship

The collapse of the Soviet empire under pressure for national self-determination is only the latest chapter in the overwhelming historical demonstration of the proposition that a shared sense of national identity is a precondition for creating and strengthening citizenship and democracy. Viewed as an ideal type, national identity implies that a people share a common language or dialect, inhabit or are familiar with a defined territory which they regard with loyalty and affection, share customs and memories linked to the history of their nation, and experience pride in the nation's achievements and shame in its failures (Schlesinger 1987, Gellner 1983, Anderson 1991).

National identity also provides an organizing basis for cognitive and affective experiences. As nationals, people experience purpose, confidence, and dignity. They experience the comforts of common membership. They understand and develop affection for items in the everyday world that are associated with the nation—food, clothes, products, songs, jokes, gestures, and adages. Correspondingly, that which falls outside that world tends to be regarded as strange and suspect. The borders between national identities and "neighboring" identities of class, gender, religion, and race are often vague, and the "border guards" between them are unreliable and tolerant (Barth 1981). Within a nation there is room for disagreement about the meaning and extent of nationhood. Common membership in a nation permits people to say "we" and "you" without sensing that their own "I," or sense of self, is thereby threatened.

The idea of national identity implies further that if citizens experience a denial of access to a felt sense of nationhood, they react with feelings of alienation from an unfriendly world. After all, democratic regimes, while free, are most encompassing and demanding. They are built on the expectation of the fullest and best participation of their interested peoples (Keane 1988, 1991). At the minimum, democracy implies equal and universal adult suffrage; majority rule and guarantee of minority rights, freedom from arbitrary arrest and respect for the rule of law among citizens and their representatives, constitutional guarantees of civil freedoms and political liberties, and, more recently, entitlement to the fruits of social policies in the areas of health, education, child care, and basic income provision (see chapter 6). Put differently, democracy involves an institutional division between a certain form of state and civil society. It is an openly structured system of institutions that facilitates the control of the exercise of power. It is a system in which political decision-makers at the local, regional, national, and supranational levels are expected to serve the *res publica*. Citizens, within their civil society, are obliged to be vigilant in preventing one another and their rulers from abusing their powers and violating the spirit of the commonwealth.

Although maintenance of democracy does not require the full-time participation of its citizens—indeed, a certain balance between over-participation and apathy seems optimal–it thrives best when certain virtues exist in the civil society. Among these are prudence, patience, common sense, self-reliance, courage, the capacity to make public decisions, the ability to criticize oneself and accept criticism from others, and the capacity to join voluntarily with others to resist threatening situations.

Finally, national identity constitutes a mechanism whereby citizens can confront and resist that which is feared politically–especially illegitimate domination and corruption. This strength is derived from a sense of belonging to a collectivity called "the nation" and sharing in a common language, a common place, a common sense of history, and a common culture. The experience of Poland is instructive in this regard. The century after the partitions of 1772, 1793, and 1794 witnessed a period in which Poland was carved up by the Russian empire, the Habsburg monarchy, and the kingdom of Prussia. A by-product of this was the nurturance of a distinctive national consciousness among the nobility (*szlachta*) of the country. During that century the Poles defined themselves–and were defined by others–as a nation martyred in the cause of democratic liberty. They refused, consistently and gracefully, to be bullied by power. The leader of the revolt of 1794, Tadeusz Kosciuszko, a friend of Paine, became a hero to democrats in Europe, America, and as far away as Australia. The Polish legions organized by Henryk Dabrowski took "For our liberty and yours" as their slogan, and Polish patriots played a role in the 1848 revolutions in Hungary, Germany, and Italy. And while strands of anarchism and messianic visions of a "Catholic State of the Polish State" still survive, the main thread of contemporary Polish national identity is its embrace of the language of democratic freedom. As Michnik (quoted in Lipski 1982) remarked, the Polish struggle for freedom against military dictatorship and Communist empire was simultaneously a struggle for the freedom of humanity.

The Rise of Nationalism

The preceding account suggests that Paine and others were correct in thinking that the defense of the nation and struggles against political despotism and for democracy are identical. When national feelings materialize, so do strivings for independence and democracy. Yet history has demonstrated that this simple equation is too simple. The French Revolution, the watershed for many movements of its sort the world over, itself demonstrates its oversimplicity. That revolution destroyed faith in the unchallengeable right of monarchs to govern, and it solidified the struggle against the privileged classes in the name of free and equal individualism. At the same time, it bred a species of national*ism*, which appeared in some respects to be a kind of substitute for the old absolutism. Those acting in the name of the nation now stressed faith in *la patrie*, which included citizens' obligations to their state, which in turn was the guarantor of the "one and indivisible" nation. The motto of the ancien régime, "Une roi, une foi, une loi" (One king, one faith, one law), was replaced by "La Nation, la loi, le roi" (The nation, the law, the king). The nation was to make the law which the king was responsible for implementing. And when the monarchy was abolished in 1792, the nation became the fountainhead of sovereignty. The battle cry of French soldiers at Valmy in the same year was "Vive la Nation." What had been royal now became national. The tricolor replaced the white flag of the house of Bourbon. This was nationalism proper, and in the end it overwhelmed the democratic potential of the revolution by establishing, in France under Louis Napoléon, the first nationalist dictatorship of the modern world.

This transformation of the impulses of national identity and democracy into despotism in the name of the nation has since proved attractive and manifested itself in many other parts of the world (Godechot 1983, Hobsbawm 1990, Seton-Watson 1977). This in turn has led to a much more complex understanding of the relations among national identity, nationalism, and democracy.

Perhaps in a cynical moment, Weber once defined democracy as a political system in which the people choose a leader who then says, "Now shut your mouths and obey me" (quoted in Weber 1975: 653). While perhaps understandable as an expression of impatience with the level of public clashes of opinion in a democracy, Weber's definition misses one of the latter's essential features. Democratic procedures, when they operate effectively, maximize the reversibility of public decision making. They invite dispute and encourage the expression of public dissatisfaction, even anger and direct action. Under classic conditions of despotism–Salazar's Portugal or Brezhnev's Russia–politics tend toward the boring, and time appears to stand still. Individuals continue to be born, to mature, to work and to love, to play and to fight, to have children and to die, but in a political context that is petrified and repetitious.

In a working democratic system, by contrast, the rule is motion, not stasis. Under conditions of liberty, citizens live in a state of perpetual unease about the distribution and exercise of power. The stress is on difference, openness, and constant competition among a plurality of power groups to produce and control the definition of reality. Outcries about public scandals erupt when publics learn about events kept secret. Democracy institutionalizes a condition of political uncertainty about who does and who should govern. Relations of power are understood as contingent and transient and as lacking transcendental guarantees of absolute certainty and hierarchical order.

Yet it could be argued that this very open–self-questioning, self-destabilizing–quality of democracy may increase the magnetism of ideologies such as extreme nationalism, which may be turned in an anti-democratic direction. Democratic conditions and processes may test citizens' shared sense of the unreality and instability of their political life, to the point where they may engage in some kind of "quest for certainty." Such a quest increases citizens' tolerance for suppression of the diversity, complexity, and openness of civil society. Democracies are never in a state of static equilibrium; they are process, not product. They are constantly in disagreement about public ends and means and constantly experience uncertainties, confusions, gaps in policy and programs, and overt and covert conflicts. As such, they tax citizens' tolerance for ambiguity and may generate that search for certainty that suppresses pluralism and imposes unity and order.

This, then, is a risk of democracy: it may be seduced by the language and power fantasies contained in nationalist ideologies. The French Revolution revealed this dynamic for the first time and revealed the fundamental difference–if not opposition–between national identity and nationalism. Nationalism is the child of democratic pluralism both in the special sense that the existence of open institutions and civil liberties enables nationalists to organize and propagate their nationalism and in the more general sense that democracy breeds uncertainty, insecurity, fear, and perhaps paranoia (Hofstadter 1965) about political life and the corresponding yearning for refuge in more sealed forms of life.

In contemporary Europe, nationalism is among the most virile and magnetic of these closed systems of life–or ideologies, to use Keane's (1992) preferred term. Like many ideologies, nationalism possesses a great appetite for power and justifies this appetite in the form of universal claims. It represents itself as part of the natural order of things and claims that the Nation (with a capital *N*) is an immutable–often biological or racial–fact, while at the same time attempting to stifle the plurality of nonnational and subnational forces within the established civil society and state in which it has arisen. Nationalism feeds upon national identity but parodies it by turning the nation into the Nation. Nationalism as an ideology includes a kind of fanatical core, which includes the ready identification–perhaps the necessity–of domestic and foreign enemies. By contrast with a sense of national identity, which tends to have fluid boundaries and a tolerance of ambiguity, nationalism demands that adherents believe in themselves and believe in the belief of nationalism, believe that they are unified in a community of believers known as the Nation, which is represented as a kind of timeless entity, a kind of secular guarantee of immortality. In its simplicity, it often contains a myth of participating in a continuous, renewed plebiscite. Its simplicity is manifested, above all, in the idea that some generalized, even mystical force is at work–or, as Bismarck instructed his people, "Germans! Think with your blood!"

If democracy involves a continuous struggle against the simplification of the world, nationalism and related ideologies can be regarded as struggles against complexity. Such struggles are perforce intolerant. They continuously invoke symbols of unity–a unity carrying a conviction of unconditional pride that permits no national shame. Nationalism invents ancestors, heroes, and martyrs. It also carries with it a conviction of invincibility associated with intolerance, and that conviction leads easily and almost necessarily to a portrayal of a world that is easily divisible into friends and enemies.

The enemy in nationalist ideology, as in other generalized beliefs (Smelser 1962), is portrayed as a creature that is simultaneously omnipotent and worthless. Nationalists warn of the menace to their own way of life of the growing presence of aliens. The logic of intolerance of "enemies in one's midst" has an odd, zero-sum quality about it, in that it regards every gain made by a foreign group as a corresponding loss on the part of the true members of the Nation. The world is thus portrayed as an arena of deadly struggle, a kind of jungle in which the outsider lives only at the expense of the Nation. Consider only some examples of this mentality in the contemporary European scene. The speeches of Jorg Haider in Austria are laced with insinuations that "East Europeans" are endangering the state, the constitution, and democracy. The literature and speech of neo-Nazis in the new half of Germany base their appeal on the slogan "Auslander 'raus!" and characterize Poles as hungry pigs, attribute shortages of bicycles to the Vietnamese and the lack of food to Jews, and accuse Turks of taking over German communities. French supporters of Jean-Marie Le Pen warn of the Arab "invasion of France." Lithuanian anti-Semites revive tales of Jews who once sacrificed Christian children and made Passover bread of their blood and stories of Jewish grain merchants and millers who put glass in their flour to make Gentile women's hands bleed when they kneaded the dough. Croatian extremists denounce Serbians as Cetniks or as Bolshevik butchers who murder their victims and mutilate their bodies; Serbian extremists reciprocate by denouncing Croats as Ustase Fascists bent on eliminating the Serbian nation; and both curse Muslims as foreign invaders of a land in which they have lived for five centuries.

The omnipotence of the ideologue manifests itself in an arrogant rejection of everything about the outsider as worthless and disgusting. Practically any supposed trait can be chosen to symbolize the enemy's unworthiness for respect and recognition: strange food, smelly breath, unhygienic habits, loud offbeat music, laziness, or an incomprehensible, ugly language. On account of this imputed sense of unworthiness, it follows that outsiders are unworthy of entitlements, even when they constitute a significant proportion of the population in or near the Nation.

Of course, nationalism varies in its manifestations. Lenin once observed that the nationalism of a conquering nation should be distinguished from the nationalism of those whom they conquer and that a conquering nationalism always seems uglier and more culpable. Nationalism can also be more or less extreme or militant. Its substantive themes are highly variable and may include material attachment to dietary patterns and a "truly national" form of currency, cultural attachment to language or myths of national origin, or geographical advocacy of political separateness. Despite all the variations, there is a common theme of omnipotent arrogance and scapegoating. Outsiders are taunted, labeled as wogs, Scheiss, and tapis, and discriminated against institutionally and informally. Use of their language may be discouraged or prohibited ("linguicide"). And in the most dire cases the rabidity of nationalism presses for the expulsion or even mass murder of outsiders for the purpose of creating a homogeneous territorial and cultural nation.

One of the ugliest and direst expressions of nationalism emerged on the southern fringes of Europe during and after the First World War. That period witnessed the mass expulsion of Armenians from Turkey in 1915 and, after the defeat of the Greek army by the Turks in Anatolia in 1922, the expulsion of some 400,000 Turks and a reciprocal expulsion of perhaps 1,500,000 destitute Greeks from Asia Minor, where they had lived since Homeric times (Eddy 1931, Macartney 1931). The herding and murdering of nations was repeated during the rules of Stalin and of Hitler, who insisted on the elimination of the Jews and others and organized the transfer of South Tyrolians and other Germans living outside the *Vaterland* to Germany itself.

The most recent manifestations of bloody nationalism have been the armed defense of "Serbian autonomous republics" and Serbia's military occupation of Kosovo in the former Yugoslavia. The Kosovo region has proved to be an arena for the classic expression of the excesses of nationalism. Serbian nationalist spokesmen, expressing that invariable mix of fear, rage, and arrogance, have attacked Albanian Kosovans as dirty, backward Muslims who are not a genuine Yugoslav nation (*nacija*) but an unimportant nationality (*nacionalnost*) of non-Slavs. At the same time they view this group as fanatical conquerors and call for "the severing of the right hand of all those who carry the green flag of Islam" (Vuk Draskovic) in the historic cradle of the Serbian nation, where King Lazar and his army were slaughtered while defending Christendom against the crescent and scimitar of Islam. These national and racial hatreds have torn Bosnia-Herzegovina to shreds. The European Muslims in the region have become something like late twentieth-century Jews in their persecution, incarceration, and mass murder.

Democracy

The above account should suffice to demonstrate that rampant nationalism is both serious and ignoble, a modern manifestation of the excesses that Erik Erikson has associated with the illegitimate elevation of a "pseudo-species" to the basis for defining all reality. Its manifestations have torn apart the Indian subcontinent, the Russian empire, and southeastern Europe and have resulted in millions of dislocations and deaths. The great question, however, is: How can movements of this kind be explained?

It is well understood that nationalism has a kind of primordialism about it–an atavistic and emotional projection of the community and the self according to an encompassing, undifferentiated principle such as *Blut und Boden*. To acknowledge this, however, should not lead us to make of this feature an explanation, because to point to the primordial characteristics of nationalism does not explain its variable character or when and where it emerges. Furthermore, the emergence of contemporary nationalism–whether in Serbia, France, England, or Georgia–cannot be well understood in neo-Marxian terms as the political response either of a beleaguered or expansionist bourgeoisie (Austro-Marxism) or of classes exploited by capitalist imperialism (Tom Nairn) or by the reckless destruction of the global capitalist economy (Slavoj Zizek). To structure economies by commodity production and exchange does generate class domination, deindustrialization, unemployment, and the formation of a new underclass, but such forces do not automatically generate a growth of nationalism. For that to happen, there has to be a distinctively psycho-political process: some preexisting, shared sense of nationhood that is, in its turn, capable of manipulation by power groups that take advantage of the openness and *deracinement* cultivated by the political mechanisms of democracy.

If the explanation for nationalism cannot be laid entirely at the door of capitalism, neither is it traceable to the operations of "real socialism." The ruling Communist bureaucracies of countries such as the former Soviet Union, Rumania, Hungary, Slovenia, and Poland undoubtedly stimulated nationalist tendencies in their efforts to legitimize their hold on power, but the conclusion that nationalism is a by-product of communism is not warranted. Nationalism (as the Magyar resistance to the Habsburg empire suggests) predated the era of twentieth-century communism in power; further, in central and eastern Europe nationalism has emerged more forcefully in the recent, post-Communist phase.

Since the "velvet revolutions" of 1989–92, the nationalist card has been played not only by Communist organizations struggling to retain their power–witness Milosevic in Serbia, Karavchuk in the Ukraine, and Iliescu in Rumania. It has also been used by anti-Communist opponents of the ancien régime–Gamsakhurdia in Georgia, Tudjman in Croatia, and Yeltsin in Russia. Both Communists and anti-Communists appear to have learned that in the early stages of democratization, when anti-Communists lack money and Communists' convictions are outworn, nationalism can change minds and win votes, give hope, and protect against the ongoing disequilibrium and disorientation produced by the uncertainty of the early transition from totalitarianism to democracy.

Finally, the close historical relationship among national identity, democracy, and nationalism should not invite us to throw out the baby with the bathwater–that is, to conclude that national identity, as the breeding ground or raw material of nationalism, is necessarily a force to be discouraged or to conclude that democracy is somehow the "real" cause of nationalism and so to fall into an anti-democratic posture. In a word, it seems futile to search for single-cause or one-sided explanations of nationalism. At the same time, none of the above-mentioned "schools" are irrelevant in accounting for it. To regard nationalism as the result of a complex interaction of historical forces serves to generate a more complicated view of the phenomenon in its contemporary manifestations, and thereby to avoid the kind of simplistic thinking that characterizes the accounts of causality in nationalist ideologies themselves.

With this new way of explaining nationalism, two ideas fall by the wayside: Paine's thesis that the defense of national identity is a basic condition of democratic government and the corresponding vision, championed by Paine, Mazzini, and Woodrow Wilson, of a holy alliance of self-governing nations working in harmonious partnership for the common good of humanity. These visions obscured the difference between national identity and nationalism, underestimated the anti-democratic potential of the struggle for national identity, and failed to foresee the degeneration of nationalism into extremism and violence. For those reasons nationalism has clouded the scene, as it were, leaving a trail of confusion about the proper relationship between national identity and democratic institutions.

National Self-Determination?

The confusions surrounding the complex relations among national identity, democracy, and nationalism are not dissolved in over-general and speculative arguments between those who assert that "nationalism is the ideology of the twenty-first century" (Conor Cruise O'Brien) and their opponents who suggest, hopefully, that "the Owl of Minerva is now hovering over nations and nationalism" (Hobsbawm 1990: 183). Such generalizations underestimate the variability and uneven distribution of European nationalism, oversimplify its causes, and provide little guidance on how to defuse nationalist forces. A more promising approach is to focus on democracy itself, which is simultaneously both a fruitful setting for the development of nationalism (in the circumscribed sense indicated) and the source of possibilities for containing its pathologies.

Such an approach would work from the principle that, since democratic mechanisms facilitate the transformation of national identity into nationalism, democracy can perhaps be best served by abandoning the indiscriminate principle of national self-determination—which is, in the end, fragmenting and so nonrational—and regarding a shared sense of national identity as a legitimate but *limited* basis for organized social life and community solidarity. This thesis contains a corollary that is paradoxical only on its face: namely, that national identity, which supports democratic institutions, is best preserved by restricting its scope in favor of *nonnational* identities that reduce the probability of its transformation in an anti-democratic, nationalistic direction. The paradox is diminished when we realize that two of the defining assumptions of democratic society are diversity of interests and mutual toleration. In the contemporary European context, four mechanisms come to mind that would tend to curb the forces of nationalism and at the same time guarantee citizens access to their respective national traditions and identities.

Decentralization of the nation-state   This occurs mainly through developing interlocking networks of democratically accountable sub-national and supranational institutions, thereby creating a system of crisscrossing lines of political power which would reduce the room for maneuvering by national state governments and diffuse nationalist fantasies of securing and aggrandizing national power by launching war on neighbors or crushing domestic opponents in the name of national preservation or salvation.

This kind of strategy would both renew and democratize the more complex patterns of political power typical of the late medieval and early modern periods. The process of European state-building eclipsed numerous alternative units of power–free cities, principalities, provinces, estates, manors, and deliberative assemblies–such that the some 500 political units that dotted the region around 1500 were reduced to about 25 in 1900. Some contemporary developments point to a reversal of the process of building centralized state institutions. One of these is the renewed interest in local government as a flexible forum for politics and policy implementation, partly in response to the declining effectiveness of economic macro-management and the apparent retreat of the national welfare state in western Europe (Batley and Stoker 1991, see also chapter 6).

The same decentralizing of the nation-state "downwards and sideways" is seen in the development of regional ideas and power in areas such as Catalonia, Wallonia, Emilia-Romagna, Andalucia, Scotland, and the Basque region. Economic cross-cutting of national entities is seen in the rapid growth and competitive success of industrial regions comprising interdependent networks of firms (Sabel 1989).

Finally, the trend towards a *Europe des régions* has been supplemented by the accelerating growth of supranational institutions like the European Parliament, the Council of Europe, and the European Court of Justice. An earlier phase of experiments with intergovernmental negotiations and economic cooperation has been complemented by a process of treatymaking and legal unification which, while still undemocratic, may shape the European political scene as radically as the Congress of Vienna in 1814-15, the Treaty of Versailles in 1919, or the Yalta summit of 1945. Community-wide decision making is moving from decision by consensus towards decision by majority vote; and member states are increasingly required to accept the treaties, laws, and directives enacted. These measures are growing in number, too–from 345 regulations, decisions, and directives in

1970 to 623 in 1987. The concerns of these measures reach to standards of central heating and housing, the purity of beer and wine, the cleanliness of beaches, and the conditions of women's employment. Some may see an international bureaucratization in this process; but from another standpoint it serves to hasten the decline of nation-state sovereignty and looks toward a post-national Europe. Derivatively, it adds to the pressure on nationalist movements, parties, governments, and leaders to recognize the fact and legitimacy of a countervailing supranational power that touches even "national economic policy" and the resolution of "national conflicts."

International legal guarantees of national identity   These also tend to break down the nation-state's sovereignty. Foreshadowed by the work of four Geneva conventions beginning in 1929, these guarantees received formal expression in the Universal Declaration of the Rights of Man of the United Nations in 1948: "Everyone is entitled to the rights and freedoms set forth in this declaration, without distinction of any kind such as race, color, sex, language, religion, political or other opinions, *national* or social *origin*, property, birth, or other status" (emphasis added).

The Badinter proposal for resolving the Yugoslav crisis extended and refined this principle of guaranteeing citizens' entitlement to national identity by means of international supervision, thus breaking with Paine's maxim that sovereignty and the territorially bounded nation are one. The proposal, contained in a European Community report in 1992, called for applications for EC recognition of the statehood of several Yugoslav republics and subsequently recommended the recognition of Slovenia, Croatia, and Macedonia, *subject to* their governments' guaranteeing civil and political freedoms to their national minorities, accepting international arms-control agreements, and renouncing force as a means of redrawing existing nation-state boundaries.

The report contains far-reaching implications for the links between nationhood, nationalism, and democracy. It posits that governments have an obligation to respect the wishes of their peoples, but it avoids J. S. Mill's premise that each nation requires a territorially based sovereign state: "Where the sentiment of nationality exists in any force, there is a *prima facie* case for uniting all the members of the nationality under the same government, and a government to themselves apart." The Badinter report uncovers a flaw in this doctrine of national self-determination: namely, that it generates endless boundary disputes, since the contours of nations, generically defined, do not coincide with territorial lines. Every border of each "nation" is tenuous, because states forever envision the possibility of reaching out territorially and annexing some space where members of one's "nation" live. This definition of "national autonomy" thus contains the seeds of "territorial cleansing," pushing and shoving, rescue missions and invasions, pogroms, and ultimately war. Civil wars touched off by nationalist pressures thus become the major threat to regional stability.

The Badinter report also reminds Europeans of the long-existing but increasingly multinational character of their respective states, accelerated by large-scale migrations. The past half-century has witnessed more than 15 million non-EC migrants, and as a result, even the most culturally "homogeneous" countries, such as Spain, England, Portugal, France, and Germany, have become mosaics of nationalities which increasingly challenge their institutional definition as sub-national satellites. The report thus challenges the axioms that national loyalties are exclusive and that democracy is possible only in a nationally homogeneous state. In this challenge the report seeks a new compromise *between* nations *within* states. It envisions a situation of supranational monitoring and enforcement of the principle that the various nations of a single state are entitled to their nationhood and to live as nationally different but free equals. The Badinter report thus "depoliticizes" and "de-territorializes" national identity, so bringing to mind the eighteenth-century view that nationality is a cultural entity belonging not to a state but to a civil society. Nationality is a *civil* entitlement of citizens, to be protected against the exercise of state repression in the name of nationalist fervor.

The development of a pluralist mosaic of identities within civil society This arrangement provides places for citizens to act upon *multiple* chosen or inherited identities, thus limiting the force of *specific* national identities in the civil society. The historical parallel is that of religious tolerance: the practice of a particular religion in a multi-religious society presupposes the principle of freedom of religious worship and recognizes the value of other religions and the right to have or practice no religion. The same principle can be extended to groups based on national identity, and in so doing, a force can be generated that fosters a pluralism that operates against differential privileging of one group over another and the pretense that one national identity can become the basis for a one-dimensional nationalism.

Slavenka Drakulic has described the straitjacketing effect of nation-centered politics in Croatia: "Nationalism has been forced on people like an ill-fitting shirt. You may feel that the sleeves are too short and the collar too tight. You might not like the color, and the cloth may itch. But you wear it because there is no other. No one is allowed *not* to be Croatian" (Drakulic 1991: 3). The point can be made conversely: in an open, self-governing civil society room is made for the cultivation of spaces where citizens can protect themselves against "uprootedness" by cultivating roots, memories of a national past, and identity-based orientations toward the present and future.

International civil society This is a final, important antidote to nationalism but is probably the most difficult to foster. That kind of society would involve an arena in which citizens of various nationalities could intermingle, display at least a minimal sense of mutual understanding and respect, and generate a sense of solidarity, especially in times of crisis.

In the second half of the eighteenth century this kind of friendship among citizens of various nations was called "cosmopolitanism". It manifested itself in a diversity of ways: young men were sent abroad to study; foreigners were invited and welcomed as teachers; wars took "nationals" elsewhere in Europe; "respectable" classes traveled; courts maintained diplomatic relations; commerce expanded; and the circulation of fashions in philosophy, letters, instruction, and dress accelerated. Thinkers as diverse as Kant, Paine, and Pietro Verri viewed the "loyal patriot" and the "true cosmopolite" as one and the same, involving no contradictions of membership (Venturi 1972, Schlereth 1977, Lemberg 1950, Texte 1899). But with the French Revolution the era of cosmopolitanism declined, and into its place moved nationalism, nation-state-building, and nation-state rivalry. "Internationalism" of various sorts continued to be stressed, for example, in Marx and Engels's conviction that "in proportion as the antagonism between classes within the nation vanishes, the hostility of one nation to another will come to an end." By and large, however, the word "patriot" became infused with all the emotions of modern nationalism, and the word "cosmopolite" became at best the fleeting symbol of an ideal political unity that was beyond reach.

A pressing theoretical and political question for contemporary Europe is whether a new form of cosmopolitanism is developing with the process of supranational integration in the West and the struggle to dismantle the totalitarian regimes in the East. Is the growth of an international civil society in Europe possible? Two decades ago Raymond Aron said not:

> Rights and duties, which in Europe, as elsewhere, are interdependent, can hardly be called multinational. In fact, they are quintessentially national . . . Though the European Community tends to grant all the citizens of its member states the same economic and social rights, there are no such animals as "European citizens." There are only French, German, or Italian citizens. (Aron 1974: 652–3)

Aron's conclusion has proved arguable on both theoretical and historical grounds. It was based on the premise that individuals are citizens by virtue of belonging to a sovereign state that is the sole guarantor of citizenship rights and duties. It did not take account of the future growth of multinational states and societies and the definition of the rights of *European* citizenship. Europe may be witnessing the slow, painful growth of a new species of political animal, the European citizen, whose institutional linkages are simultaneously local, regional, and state-national and whose meaningful political and cultural contacts reach through all of them.

The development of an international civil society in Europe faces many well-understood counterforces. Among them is the continued reinforcement of national markets through nation-based policies on the part of transnational corporations. It is certain, moreover, that the very forces described in this chapter, the forces of xenophobic nationalism, continue to reassert themselves in many corners of the continent. Yet, at the same time, there is a perceptible growth of European-wide exchanges among citizens whose political views lie within a universe of republican and democratic discourse. These exchanges move beyond specific ideologies and reach toward a pluralistic vision of Europe. Dramatic signs of the pressure for international democratic republicanism are the velvet revolutions of 1989 and the references to citizenship rights and duties across frontiers, detailed in the Maastricht treaty. But mainly the movement is a silent and undramatic one, unattended to by the very actors taking part in it. Nevertheless, the topic of the new European citizenry merits investigation from the sociological and other points of view, constituting as it does the ultimate antidote to the paradoxes of democracy and the perils of nationalism.

References

Anderson, B. 1991: *Imagined Communities. Reflections on the Origin and Spread of Nationalism*. London: Verso.

Aron, R. 1974: "Is Multinational Citizenship Possible?" *Social Research*, 41: 638–56.

Barth, F. 1981: "Ethnic Groups and Boundaries," in *Process and Form in Social Life: Selected Essays of Fredrik Barth*, London: Routledge and Kegan Paul, 198–227.

Batley, R. and Stoker, G. (eds) 1991: *Local Government in Europe: Trends and Developments*. New York: St Martin's Press.

Beumann, H. and Schroeder, W. (eds) 1978: *Aspekte der nationenbildung im Mittelalter*. Sigmaringen: Thorbecke.

Bickart, R. 1932: *Les Parlements et la notion de souveraineté national*. Paris: Felix Alcan.

Deutsch, K. 1969: *Nationalism and its Alternatives*. New York: Knopf.

Diderot, D. 1756–65: *Encyclopédie*. Paris: Vol. 11.

Drakulic, S. 1991: "The Smothering Pull of Nationhood." *Yugofax*, 31: 3.

Eddy, C. B. 1931: *Greece and the Greek Refugees*. London: G. Allen and Unwin.

Elton, G. R. 1986: "English National Self-Consciousness and the Parliament in the Sixteenth Century," in O. Dann (ed.), *Nationalismus in vorindustrieller Zeit*, Munich: Oldenbourg, 73–82.

Gellner, E. 1983: *Nations and Nationalism*. Ithaca, N.Y.: Cornell University Press.

Godechot, J. 1983: *La Grande Nation*, 2nd edn. Paris: Aubier.

Guénée, B. 1981: *L'Occident aux xive à xve siècles*. Paris: Presses universitaires de France.

Hobsbawm, E. 1990: *Nations and Nationalism since 1780*. Cambridge: Cambridge University Press.

Hofstadter, R. 1965: *The Paranoid Style in American Politics*. New York: Knopf.

Huizinga, J. 1948–53: "How Holland Became a Nation," in *Verzamelde Werken*, Haarlem: H. D. Tjeenk Willink, II, 266–83.

Keane, J. 1988: *Democracy and Civil Society. On the Predicaments of European Socialism, the Prospects for Democracy and the Problem of Controlling Social and Political Power*. London: Verso.

Keane, J. 1991: *The Media and Democracy*. Cambridge: Polity Press.

Keane, J. 1992: "The Modern Democratic Revolution: Reflections on Lyotard's *The Postmodern Condition*," in A. Benjamin (ed.), *Judging Lyotard*, London: Routledge, 81–98.

Lemberg, E. 1950: *Geschichte des Nationalismus in Europa*. Stuttgart: C. E. Schwab.

Lipski, J. J. 1982: "Two Fatherlands – Two Patriotisms." *Survey*, 26: 159–75.

Macartney, C. A. 1931: "Refugees," in *Encyclopedia of the Social Sciences*, New York: Macmillan, XIII, 200–5.

Michnik, A. 1991: "Nationalism." *Social Research*, 58: 757–63.

Paine, T. 1945 [1791–2]: *Rights of Man. Part First* and *Rights of Man. Part Second*, in P. S. Foner (ed.), *The Complete Writings of Thomas Paine*, New York: The Citadel Press.

Sabel, C. 1989: "Flexible Specialization and the Re-emergence of Regional Economies," in P. Hirst and J. Zeitlin (eds), *Reversing Industrial Decline? Industrial Structure and Policy in Britain and her Competitors*, Oxford: Berg, 17–70.

Seton-Watson, H. 1977: *Nations and States: An Enquiry into the Origins of Nations and the Politics of Nationalism*. London: Methuen.

Schlereth, T. J. 1977: *The Cosmopolitan Idea in Enlightenment Thought: Its Form and Function in the Ideas of Franklin, Hume and Voltaire, 1694–1790*. Notre Dame, Ind.: University of Notre Dame Press.

Schlesinger, P. 1987: "On National Identity: Some Conceptions and Misconceptions Criticized." *Social Science Information*, 26: 219–64.

Smelser, N. J. 1962: *Theory of Collective Behavior*. New York: Free Press.

Texte, J. 1899: *Jean-Jacques Rousseau and the Cosmopolitan Spirit in Literature: A Study of the Literary Relations between France and England during the Eighteenth Century*. London: Duckworth.

Venturi, F. 1972: *Italy and the Enlightenment. Studies in a Cosmopolitan Century*. New York: New York University Press.

Von Beyme, K. 1991: "Social and Economic Conditions for Ethnic Strife in the Soviet Union," in A. McAuley (ed.), *Soviet Federalism, Nationalism and Economic Decentralization*, New York: St Martin's Press, 89–109.

Weber, M. 1975: *Max Weber: A Biography*. New York: Wiley.

Part III

Economy and Society

8

Global, Regional, and Local Forces

International and global dimensions appear in many guises in this book–as threads in the organization of sociology itself (chapter 1), as parts of sociological theorizing (chapter 2), as sources of new challenges to welfare states (chapter 6), as features of economic development and the organization of work (chapters 9, 13, and 18), as major components of the distribution of population, urban complexes, and racial-ethnic distribution (chapters 12, 14, and 16), and as ingredients of contemporary environmental problems (chapter 11). So pervasive is the thinking about international systems and globalism that some question the centrality of the notions of nation, culture, and society as the fundamental units of analysis in the social sciences. In this chapter we focus directly and explicitly on the phenomenon of globalism itself.

Historical and Conceptual Notes

Theoretical Antecedents to Modern Thinking

As in most areas of social inquiry, historical scholarship often reveals that what is advertised as new is sometimes really new, sometimes not new at all, and sometimes a new variation on an old twist. The conception of the world as some kind of unified whole, or system, is no exception to this rule. We find three identifiable threads of thought that echo in contemporary formulations: diffusionism, domination, and syncretism of organization and culture.

This chapter is based on a contribution by Alan Warde.

Diffusion Toward the end of the nineteenth century a number of anthropologists focused on the international (or rather, culture-to-culture) diffusion of cultural traits (for a review, see Lowie 1937). One impulse underlying this interest was a critique of classical evolutionary theory, which argued that cultures were more or less self-contained and evolved from one cultural stage to another through a series of identifiable stages of technology, social organization, and culture. The diffusionists' counterclaims were that the history of civilization was in large part a history of cultural borrowing, and that this confounded any neat picture of societal evolution. Kroeber summarized the principle of diffusion as follows:

> The vast majority of culture elements have been learned by each nation from other peoples, past and present . . . even savages shift their habitations and acquire new neighbors. At times they capture women and children from one another. Again they intermarry; and they almost invariably maintain some sort of trade relations with at least some of the adjacent peoples. . . . There is thus every *a priori* reason why diffusion could be expected to have had a very large part in the formation of primitive and barbarous as well as advanced cultures. (Kroeber 1923: 197–8).

This emphasis on the borrowing of things seemed to restrict the diffusionists to a descriptive account of the travels of cultural items, such as calendars, tools, and ideas (e.g., the concept of zero). They seldom asked why certain items were diffused and others were not, how items were modified after being incorporated, or what new internal changes were stimulated by borrowed items, even though Lowie (1937) was aware of these issues. Diffusionism as an approach no longer has a clear identity, though its logic has survived in some thinking about international emulation in economic development (Bendix 1977 [1964]) and in the current preoccupation with the transfer of technology among nations.

International domination The Marxist tradition early on developed an international dimension. For Marx, internationalization was a logical extension of the general dynamic of capitalism, which, in the interests of competitive advantage, seeks to secure raw materials and labor at the lowest cost and to develop markets for its products. An ultimate consequence of this dynamic was to internationalize capitalism. Through this "a new international division of labor, a division suited up to the requirements of the chief centers of modern industry springs up, and converts one part of the globe into a chiefly agricultural field of production, for supplying the other part which remains a chiefly industrial field" (Marx 1949 [1867]: 451). In applying the principle to India, Marx interpreted the British efforts to unify that country politically and to build a network of railroads as a strategy to convert India into a supplier of cotton and other raw materials to British industries (Marx 1853).

Lenin carried the theme of internationalization further. His starting point was that competition as the driving engine of capitalism was disappearing. The main reason for this was the development of monopolies that controlled raw materials, prices, and production by virtue of the gigantic size of firms. Banks had also become monopolized and formed links with industry to create a system of finance capital. Through the export of capital–as contrasted with the earlier pattern of export of goods–this system had "divided up the world" economically. This development was accompanied by a political division of the world through colonial domination, which *"completed* the seizure of unoccupied territories on our planet" (1939 [1917]: 76, emphasis original).

The Marx–Lenin perspective moves in the direction of seeing the world as a single system dominated, at least temporarily, by a single economic system (capitalism). This viewpoint tended to regard internal economic and class developments–such as the destruction of the Indian caste system–as by-products of the international process. This stress is found in modern internationalist formulations, notably dependency theory (Cardoso and Faletto 1979), which traces the nondevelopment or warped development of dependent nations in large part to the strategies of international capital, and world-systems theory (Wallerstein 1974), which carries the idea of the world as an economic system to an extreme, in that the internal dynamics of nations are seen as overwhelmed by world forces.

Organizational and cultural syncretism   Under this head we do not locate a single "school" or even a consistent "literature," but rather a theme that has appeared in several strands of social-scientific research. The main thrust of this theme is that in the processes of international migration, diffusion, and cultural domination, institutional and cultural forms are influenced by new contexts and evolve into something new. Studies of assimilation of migrants and acculturation of natives by sociologists and anthropologists provide examples of the modification of culture through systematic exposure to other cultures. Studies of religious syncretism–for example, the cargo cults of Melanesia, which emerged as a rich mixture of indigenous and Western/Christian ingredients (Worsley 1957)–provide others.

Malinowski's (1945) classical conception of changes in culture under conditions of cultural domination stressed the theme of syncretistic change as well. He concentrated on African cultures under British colonial domination. He considered these cultures unstable. The main reason for this is that colonial societies are dominated politically; this implies the "impact of a higher, active culture upon a simpler, more passive one" (Malinowski 1945: 15). But this impact is not a matter of the simple transfer of Western prototypes versus the retention of African prototypes. Rather, it is a dynamic fusion of the two types into qualitatively new forms:

> The concept of the mechanical incorporation of elements from one culture into another does not lead us beyond the initial preparatory stages, and even then on subtler analysis breaks down. What really takes place is an interplay of specific contact forces: race prejudice, political and economic imperialism, the demand for segregation, the safeguarding of a European standard of living, and the African reaction to this. (Malinowski 1945: 23)

Accordingly, Malinowski viewed colonial societies in terms of what he called his "three-column approach," which delineated several kinds of social forces: "the impinging culture with its institutions, intentions, and interests"; "the reservoir of indigenous custom, belief, and living traditions"; and "the process of contact and change, where members of the two cultures cooperate, conflict, or compromise" (ibid., p. vii).

In the short run, the dynamics of culture change are confrontation, adaptation, accommodation, and syncretism. In the long run, however, Malinowski held out little hope for the survival of colonially dominated cultures. He predicted that the incessant pressures of European political and cultural domination would "sooner or later . . . gradually . . . engulf and supersede the whole of [the surviving African tradition]" (ibid.: 81). Malinowski's prediction was rendered moot by the ending of colonial domination in most of the world, but it was not rendered irrelevant. Much post-independence thinking about the developing areas has also focused on whether traditional cultures in those areas will be "modernized," retain an integrity of their own, or strike some evolving, synthetic mix (Eisenstadt 1992).

Analytical Levels of International or Global Relations

Diffusion, domination, and syncretism, considered analytically, are typical processes observable in the intersocietal arena. Implied in those relations is a fourth, that of interdependence, which implies that, once in some kind of relation, units such as nations or societies come to depend on one another for certain valued assets, whether that dependence works out in a context of equality or one of inequality. All these analytic threads work their way into more contemporary thinking about the world as some kind of system.

Also observable in the antecedent discussions are several analytical levels at which the several types of processes are played out.
To make these sometimes implicit levels explicit, we mention the following:

Economic   The focus of Marx and Lenin was the importance of capital and its domination, but the following economic dimensions have proved important in characterizing the world dimensions of the economy: trade, production (e.g., multinationals), finance and credit, international movement of labor through migration, and international economic organizations (e.g., the World Bank and the International Monetary Fund).

Political The contributions of Marx and Malinowski concern political domination, but additional political dimensions include military and political alliances and conflict, regional political unions, the role of international organizations (United Nations, ILO), and the state in relation to international economic trends.

Cultural The analyses of the diffusionists and Malinowski rested on anthropological conceptions of culture dominant at the time they wrote. Contemporary manifestations of cultural processes are the internationalization of technology, science, and related forms of knowledge through academies, universities, and international professional associations and their exchange and communication programs; the spread of "popular culture" through the mass media; the development of "global cultures" through academic disciplines, social movements, and the diffusion of ideologies such as democracy and modernization. Of special interest is the modification of cultural influences as they work their way into diverse regional, national, and local contexts.

Societal This dimension is least explicit in the antecedent theoretical discussion. By it we refer to the evolution of new rules of the game that guide and to some degree stabilize, international interaction and, if they are mutually acceptable, involve the relevant actors in some kind of transnational community or society. The best example of this is the growth of new understandings in the area of international security; even the cold war, confrontational and hostile as it was, developed a set of mutual understandings among superpowers and other nations about what limits were not to be exceeded, how communications were to be understood, and the like. After the end of the cold war and the decline of the former Soviet Union as a superpower, a new set of understandings is in the process of coalescing, with events such as the Gulf War of 1991 and the role of outside powers during the deterioration of former Yugoslavia constituting key situations for the groping efforts to formulate new norms for international conduct.

New Interpretations of the International and the Global

While the international dimension and efforts to understand it are thus very old, it is certain that the processes of internationalization of the world in the past several decades, along all the dimensions just outlined, have been so massive, spectacular, and unprecedented as to constitute something qualitatively new under the sun, a global order which has not before been witnessed and which calls for qualitatively new kinds of understanding. Many scholars and other observers believe this to be the case and have been struggling correspondingly to capture the essence of that order with new lines of thinking. We present a sample of these efforts now; then later, in the remainder of the chapter, we will focus on two representative areas–the globalization of economic activity and the globalization of culture.

New Preoccupations with Space

The history of sociology has incorporated the dimension of space, but only in selected fields of study. Among these were face-to-face interaction, usually in urban settings ("urban ethnography"); various facets of human ecology and urban sociology, such as residential zones, residential succession (usually ethnic), urban places and their hinterlands, and so on (see chapter 14); and the stress on territoriality as the central defining characteristic of a nation-state (see chapters 4, 7, and 16). It can be argued that the rise of special, "spaceless" research methods, such as statistical analysis and the survey method, abstracted behavior and attitudes from their space-specific embeddedness. Some theoretical developments may have contributed to this effect. Among these are economists' neoclassical and sociologists' neo-evolutionary and "modernization" theories of growth, both of which tend to treat abstracted analytical processes that are putatively universal–that is, applicable without reference to space and time. Such theories have been challenged by dependency and neo-Marxist theories of underdevelopment and uneven development, which suggest more space–time specificity; but even these theories have tended toward the analytic.

The 1980s witnessed a revival of interest in spatial forms. Among the signs were a heightening of attention to the boundaries between sociology and geography (Gregory and Urry 1985, Soja 1989). Part of this stemmed from dissatisfaction among some geographers with what they saw as the theoretical aridity of descriptive geography. A number of theoretical discussions about the ontological and epistemological status of space also appeared (Giddens 1989, Urry 1981). The most important work in this genre dealing with international and global processes is Harvey's recent book *The Condition of Postmodernity* (1989).

Harvey was concerned with the changing spatial scale of social organization, particularly the organization of capital, and argues that this has been so radical as to signal a new stage of development of Western societies. More particularly, the economic crisis of the 1970s called for a new approach to economic practice called "flexible accumulation," which generated new global economic and cultural forms. That shift has "entailed a new round of space–time compression in the capitalist world–the time horizons of both private and public decision-making have shrunk, while satellite communication and declining transport costs have made it increasingly possible to spread those decisions immediately over an ever wider and variegated space" (Harvey 1989: 14).

Only apparently paradoxically, this spatial extension of economic interdependencies on a wider scale entails, reciprocally, a heightened importance of the peculiarities of space:

> the more unified the space, the more important the qualities of the fragmentations became for social identity and action. The free flow of capital across the surface of the globe, for example, places strong emphasis upon the particular qualities of the spaces to which that capital might be attracted. The shrinkage of space that brings diverse communities across the globe into competition with each other implies localized competitive strategies and a heightened sense of awareness of what makes a place special and gives it a competitive advantage. This kind of reaction looks much more strongly to the identification of place, the building and signalling of its unique qualities in an increasingly homogeneous but fragmented world. (Harvey 1989: 271)

Following this line of reasoning, Harvey interprets the worldwide efflorescence of nationalism (e.g., in Eastern Europe and the former Soviet Union) and localism (e.g., regional language and cultural movements in Brittany, Spain, Italy, and the United Kingdom) as a kind of protest: the time–space compression constitutes a kind of human violation and thus stimulates a "quest for the security that place always offers" (ibid.). More generally, this great compression constitutes the backdrop for the transition to the cultural fragmentation of postmodernism, which Harvey considers another episode in the annihilation of space and time.

Harvey's formulations have proved to be provocative and have earned him criticisms for being reductionist, economistic, even sexist (Massey 1991) in his effort to link the phenomenon of flexible accumulation to its presumed cultural consequences. The precise merits of his central assertion, however–that the essence of very recent economic changes is best understood with respect to space and time dimensions–has been neither confirmed nor discredited. It is difficult to contest the fact that the recent historical modification of spatial relations, especially in the urban-regional arena (see chapter 14), has been profound.

Globalization As early as the 1960s, some sociologists (Nettle and Robertson 1966, Robertson 1968) began invoking the notion of "global" to challenge the *Gemeinschaft*-to-*Gesellschaft* kinds of modernization theories that were dominant at the time. That line of thinking was greatly accelerated by the appearance and debate of world-systems theory in the following decade (Wallerstein 1974). In the 1980s, the idea "took off," as it were, and became a common element in macroscopic sociology. Between 1981 and 1986, the word "global" in titles recorded in the *Social Sciences*

Citation Index averaged only one a year; by 1992 the figure was 14. The change is more than one in terminology alone; it is an indicator of the increasing salience of world trends and is one of the many ways of acknowledging the phenomenon that the world is becoming a single social system–"the increasing interdependence of world society" (Giddens 1989: 520).

In the discussions of globalization many of its manifestations have been noted: in the economic sphere, the growth of transnational corporations and a new international division of labor; in the sphere of communications, the intensified international transmission of media messages and cultural forms; and in the political realm, the entrenchment of powers of bodies like the United Nations, the European Community, and the Organization of Petroleum Exporting Countries (OPEC) and the ever-present risks of world nuclear war and environmental devastation. These and other changes have been debated under the umbrella of the unification and homogenization of the world and its culture, a debate initiated by McLuhan's prediction of cultural uniformity in the global village (1967).

These linear kinds of development associated with the process of globalization have been thrown into doubt with the recognition of the evidently opposing tendencies toward localism and national and sub-national fragmentation that have accompanied the process. To illustrate those tendencies, local audiences interpret and assimilate mass media fare to their own cultural experiences and interests. International inequalities highlight differences and make those residing in local pockets of poverty and wealth more aggressive and defensive, respectively. Established nation-states pursue their own interests and defy the authority and influence of supranational bodies, and sub-national and ethnic groupings give their parent states the same kind of treatment.

Some observers have noted these counter-tendencies and tried to account for them. As noted, Harvey explained localism by referring to the time–space processes of globalization. Others write of a global–local dialectic (Lash and Urry 1993), as though globalization and localization are both parts of some larger process. These kinds of formulations have an intuitive appeal, but they are found wanting when it comes to specification of the actual *mechanisms* by which the two processes are causally linked to one another.

The Eclipse of the Nation-State

If the process of globalization implies, as it necessarily does, the increasing salience of supranational forces, recognition of these would seem to lead naturally to a perception of a corresponding weakening, or "hollowing out," of the principal actors on the international scene. One version of the argument goes something like this. The state is, by its nature as a controlling institution, a kind of balance-wheel between the international and national economies. Not immediately responsible for fluctuations in import–export ratios and with very limited control over international fluctuations in currency rates, states, as guarantors of the integrity of the national economy, must meet accumulated obligations either directly or through borrowing. In addition, in the newly industrializing, Third World economies, the state is the agency to which falls the task of executing and implementing–or resisting–the strictures imposed by other national governments and by international banking agencies, such as the International Monetary Fund. In this role the state has less control over the fate of its economy–and therefore its own political fate–than before. It could be argued further that by virtue of the massive growth of the international press and television, nation-states have increasingly greater difficulty in keeping their peoples from learning about conditions and events outside their country (as the rulers of the former Soviet Union and Eastern Europe discovered) and in keeping outsiders from learning about events in their own countries (as Chinese leaders at the time of the 1989 Tiananmen Square uprising also learned). All these things point to a lessening of control of states over the conditions and fortunes of the peoples they presumably govern.

Besides these economic and cultural developments, we might suggest several other historical forces that have contributed to the general erosion of the states' control. First, many of the environmental problems of the world are regional, crossing state boundaries (spoilation of forests), or global (the hole in the ozone layer) and surely lie beyond the power of individual states to control (see chapter 11). Second, viability of the "state" as domestic guarantor of citizens' welfare has taken something of a lashing at the hands of Reaganism, Thatcherism, deregulation, and the "welfare crisis" (see chapter 6). Third, the end of the cold war also coincided with the death of some states (the former Soviet Union, the former Yugoslavia, the former Czechoslovakia) and the collapse of the definition of the world in terms of two large blocks of states standing in hostile confrontation with one another. If one adds to the picture the corrosive forces "from below"– in the form of forces of localization and sub-national movements–it becomes apparent that the state tends to become a victim squeezed both by overriding global forces and undermining local forces.

Sensitivity to this eclipse of national sovereignty seems especially great in a country like Great Britain, which now shares a position in the new world order with all other nations having gone from being a major industrial and imperial force to merely a deindustrialized, relatively poor, and increasingly less significant international power. Such a decline concentrates the national mind, as it were, and makes it more sensitive regarding the error of having ever imagined that it and those who governed it actually had sovereign control over its national affairs. The debate about the eclipse of the nation has been especially conspicuous in Britain, though certainly not absent in other countries.

We might suggest, however, that a picture of uniform national eclipse is overly simple. Other forces are at work to strengthen the state, or at least to make it strive to become a stronger agency. Because it is cognizant of its own vulnerability, the contemporary state tends to throw itself into economic and political processes with greater assertiveness in the interests of its own survival: assertiveness in encouraging the productivity and exporting capacities of its own industries, in maintaining monetary stability and low rates of inflation, and with respect to regulating and working out a symbiosis with foreign firms and banks that establish themselves in its territory.

To this must be added another paradox: while the economic, political, and cultural forces impinging on the state are more powerful than ever before, its political *process* remains national in character. National elections and political infighting are conducted *as if* the most important issues are domestic–or at least domestically controllable–because the national state (better, the national parties that are in power) remains the agency that is defined as being responsible for political problems. This paradox generates a special kind of squeeze on contemporary states: they must respond to forces that are not of their own making and not within their control within a framework of political democracy that is built on the myopic national-political premise that the national government is sovereign and that nationally based political procedures make accountability a national matter. This also presses states and politicians to insist that they have more power in a world situation in which they actually have less.

Two Examples Elaborated: World Industrialization and Global Culture

As indicated, other chapters in this book deal with migration, labor conditions, urban structure, the environment, and topics that are intricately associated with globalization, and the reader is referred to these. In this chapter we select two less well covered but central examples for documentation: world industrialization and global culture. Both are striking; but the documentation of the former is clearer, and the understanding of the latter is hobbled by some unclarity and speculation.

World Industrialization

In addition to its extraordinary growth during the past three decades, world industrialization has experienced dramatic locational shifts. By the 1970s the newly industrializing countries (NICs), mainly in Latin America and East Asia, were becoming as industrialized as the "developed" countries–sometimes more so (Arrighi and Drangel 1986). Manufacturing has surpassed agriculture as the major economic sector in many Third

World countries. By now the richest countries in the world (in terms of per capita income) are no longer the most industrial ones (World Bank 1991). With this change, world trade has expanded 30-fold in the past three decades. And within this explosive growth of trade, the place of manufacturing goods has become progressively more central, growing from 55 percent of the goods traded in 1980 to 75 percent in 1990. The leaders in manufacturing export are, as expected, Thailand, South Korea, Taiwan, and China, followed by Singapore, Hong Kong, Brazil, Mexico, and then Malaysia and Indonesia. By measures of dispersion and international trade, then, the world economy has experienced a sea change along the lines of both growth and interdependency.

When we turn to the specifics and the mechanisms involved in this development, the dimension of global interdependency becomes even clearer. As early as the late 1970s, Frobel pointed to a phenomenon he called the "new international division of labor" (1980). He documented the shifting of physical capital from West Germany to the NICs. Mass production processes, particularly of textiles and electronic components assembly, were being moved abroad. The dynamics were fairly clear; cheap labor costs and other factors in these regions clearly offset the increased transportation and other costs, and capital could be shifted quickly into the new regions. The immediate by-product of this development, which was also occurring at an accelerating rate in the United States and the United Kingdom, was to devastate certain regions of those countries–for example, the manufacturing north in England–with further consequences of unemployment, shifts in male and female employment, the undermining of trade union power, and the reconfiguration of whole towns and regions.

Further research showed that whole new industrial districts were developing (Storper and Harrison, 1991). In the manufacture of shoes, for example, South Korea was found to specialize in athletic footwear, Taiwan in vinyl and plastic shoes, Brazil in low-priced leather shoes, Spain in medium-priced women's leather shoes, and Italy in high-priced fashion shoes. The dominance of any given district depends on a variety of economic factors, including the cost and quality of the labor force; but some have suggested less tangible factors such as local trust and "civil society" networks that facilitate the productive process (Mingione 1991). The situation is extremely competitive for these industrial districts, with other districts and countries forever threatening to seize their shares of the market. These varieties of late twentieth-century international capitalism have a scope that is truly global in organization. Gereffi and Korzeniewicz (Gereffi and Korzeniewicz 1990, Gereffi forthcoming) have characterized this organization in terms of the concept of "global commodity chains." This concept focuses on manufacturing but stresses the trans-world dispersion not only of the process itself but also of the linkages between various economic agents–raw material suppliers, factories, traders, and retailers. Gereffi has distinguished between two kinds of global commodity chains, producer-driven and buyer-driven.

Producer-driven commodity chains refer to transnational and other industries that are both capital-intensive and technology-intensive. Examples are the automobile, aircraft, and electrical machinery industries. These industries are thoroughly internationalized. Both US and Japanese automobile companies carry out their production activities in a network that involves thousands of firms, including parent firms, subsidiaries, and subcontractors (Hill 1989). These industries are centralized in two senses: first, because of the nature of the products, there are centralized places which assemble the subproducts manufactured throughout the world into a single product; and second, corporate control headquarters are located in central places, usually a major world city. Despite these remnants of centralization, it is difficult to say of any automobile or other durable that it is "made in Japan," "made in the USA," or made anywhere in particular.

Buyer-driven commodity chains are even more fascinating from the point of view of their extreme specialization. These are industries in which large retailers, brand-name merchandisers, and trading companies set up production networks in a variety of countries, many of them Third World. The industries covered are consumer goods, labor-intensive ones such as garments, consumer electronics, toys, footwear, furniture, and ornaments. The familiar names are Nike, Reebok, Mattel Toys, and The Gap. While these firms sell manufactured products, they are not manufacturers at all. They typically do not own the factories that make their products–or more often, parts of their products–and sometimes they do not own their own retail outlets. These firms are huge and profitable, but they are basically corporate merchandisers that coordinate the activities of thousands of factories, traders, overseas buyers, and retailers throughout the world. They are all but "unlocated" in a central place except for their corporate headquarters, and this fact underscores Harvey's stress on the revolution in space that the global economy has achieved.

As indicated, and as demonstrated throughout this book, the social and political ramifications of these kinds of industrial globalization are virtually endless. We will look at just one more example of those ramifications here. When Bill Clinton was campaigning for the presidency throughout the United States in 1992, he repeatedly stressed two sore spots in the US economy: that real wages of American workers have been stagnant since the early 1970s and that there has been a regressive shift in the distribution of income in the United States during the same period, with its consequences of unacceptable unemployment rates and increased poverty and homelessness. Figures demonstrate that most of Clinton's assertions were correct. The political message he conveyed, however, was that these developments could be laid at the door of the retrograde domestic policies of the Reagan and Bush administrations over the previous twelve years and that he, Clinton, could do something about those trends if elected.

The key problem, unanalyzed in Clinton's political messages, was the following: what were the origins of the economic changes of which he complained? Were they the combined effect of tax changes, deregulation, and privatization and the employment, welfare, and housing policies of the Republican regimes? Or were they the consequences of the international migration of American manufacturing industry outward and the international migration of foreign labor inward, the further shift to services in the economy, and the increasing reliance of firms on "temp" rather than "perm" labor? The answer is that both sets of forces were involved, and involved in such ways that it is almost impossible to unscramble the relative effects of each. It is equally evident that if the global part of the equation is left out of the analysis, the answers are grossly incomplete.

The Globalization of Culture

Sociological interest in this topic has grown in recent years. Part of the reason is simply that the field is no doubt reflecting the reality of cultural processes in the world. The second is that the cultural dimension has enjoyed something of a resurgence in sociology in the past couple of decades (see chapter 2), and, as part of this, the interest in the internationalization of culture, or global culture, has also increased (Robertson 1992). Four questions command our attention: What are the main mechanisms of diffusion of culture throughout the world? Have there been, through that diffusion, any identifiable tendencies toward homogenization of world culture? If such tendencies are apparent, what kinds of local responses are observable? And what is the world cultural scene emerging from all these processes? (The last question raises the issue of cultural syncretism, identified above in the work of Malinowski.)

The first three questions have merged in recent discussions of the impact of the electronic mass media, whose spread throughout the entire world is clearly established. The "homogenization" side of the case has been stated by Tenbruck (1990). At the outset, he noted the enormous global potential of television: "Whereas the media formerly relied on language and were therefore geared primarily to national audiences, they now can by their reliance on sounds and pictures jump across linguistic and cultural frontiers and thereby become the direct bearers of cross-cultural images and messages" (Tenbruck 1990: 205). Like others in the past, Tenbruck saw the advent of television as an avenue for increased American influence, partly because American television and movie programming dominate the medium and because English has become the major international language (partly *because* of that medium).

Tenbruck regarded the current world television scene as a kind of struggle, between the more powerful cultures (mainly Western) seeking to impose their cultures and the weaker ones struggling to survive the impact of the stronger. Thus conceived, he saw the outcome as one of greater conquest and greater homogenization:

"Generally, individual cultures are losing their autonomy as they are being drawn into the network of electronic mass media that are instrumental in creating cross-cultural audiences, movements, issues, images, and lifestyles" (ibid.).

Other authors have envisioned the outcome as a complex interaction between global communication and local cultural form and thus as far less likely to produce a homogeneous outcome. Hannerz (1990), for example, has argued that cultural flows are complex, without any definite pattern of cultural imperialism–that is, no single direction from center to periphery. Various mediators and brokers intervene between source and audience and adapt the mass media communication to local circumstances. Furthermore, no matter how clear the message, it cannot determine the spirit in which it is received and interpreted: individual viewers "syncretize" common messages by adapting them to their own cultural wishes, attitudes, and outlooks. So, while television sends standardized messages over the world, they are diffused and differentiated as they penetrate their targets.

The debate between homogeneity and heterogeneity, thus phrased, appears to be too general and possibly too laced with ideological preferences to be decided either way; ample illustrative evidence can be amassed on either side. A more helpful approach is that taken by Appadurai (1990), who rejected the idea of the cultural homogenization of the world by arguing that cultural messages are "indigenized," repatriated, and adapted to highly variable local conditions. But he went further and disaggregated cultural flows into several distinct types, which have different kinds of consequences.

Appadurai explored five types of "global cultural flows"–people, technology, money, images, and ideas–that create the impression of globalization. He described these in terms of "types of landscape," to indicate that they are all perceived and interpreted differently throughout the world by different people. The world's peoples, then, live in what he called, respectively–and somewhat jarringly–"ethnoscapes," "techno-scapes," "finanscapes," "mediascapes," and "ideoscapes." So complex are the flows that it is oversimple to characterize the world's cultural scene as reflecting any of the center–peripheral models current in thinking about the world. What Appadurai regarded as happening is a kind of disjuncture of flows of materials in the various "scapes": "people, machinery, money, images, and ideas now follow increasingly non-isomorphic paths; of course at all periods in human history there have been some disjunctures between the flows of these things, but the sheer speed, scale and volume of each of these flows is so great that the disjunctures have become central to the politics of global culture" (Appadurai 1990: 301).

Migration through the world's labor markets is an example. Through the process of de-territorialization, migration sets up new social networks between migrants and their home culture, new cultural conflicts, and new opportunities for the media. These complex effects work their way into the fabric of different nations and turn out to be shaping influences for ethnic politics:

> The central paradox of ethnic politics in today's world (whether of language or skin color or of neighborhood or of kinship) is that they have become globalized. That is, sentiments whose greatest force is in their ability to ignite intimacy into a political sentiment and turn locality into a staging ground for identity, have become spread over vast and irregular spaces, as groups move, yet stay linked to one another through sophisticated media capabilities. (Appadurai 1990: 306; see also chapter 16).

The cultural effects of the globalization of communication are best understood according to the logic of syncretism. Abu-Lughod (1991) presents vignettes of markets in Tunis, which feature Egyptian rock singers who belt out Bedouin rhythms in Western style. The Japanese "country-and-western" rage is another example. The complexities of the Salman Rushdie controversies over his publications about Muslim religion–which led to actual threats against his life emanating from the Middle East–make the same point. Abu-Lughod suggests that because cultural flows are multidirectional and complex, the meanings given to them in different communities are so contrasting as to yield both misunderstandings and conflicts. She argues that in an unspecified past time, cultural boundaries were clearer, so that an author could expect that his or her messages would convey their intended meanings because they would be received in an environment whose cultural context and ambience were the same as his or her own. Now, increasingly, messages flow unhindered in and out of communities which do not share cultural understandings. In such a context "innocent" messages may offend, and insults may not be taken as such. Such seems to be the basis for the massive, conflictual misunderstandings arising from Rushdie's writings.

In the mélange of permeable meaning contexts that characterize the contemporary world, neither cultural absolutism nor cultural relativism seems a helpful way to approach matters. Surely it is not feasible to assert universal truths such as are envisioned in the great religious traditions or in the ages of Enlightenment and Reason. A bland relativism does not work either, however, because multiple perspectives abound, and people still carry strong, even passionate, convictions as to the rightness or wrongness of certain of these perspectives, even though they may be understood in very different contexts. We seem to be in need of some new logic of syncretism to gain the proper appreciation of the contemporary world's cultural kaleidoscope (see Abu-Lughod 1991).

Urry (1990) identified tourism as a key instance of the contemporary compression of space and time. An enormous industry, reflected in the expanding capacity to travel globally (Strange 1988), tourism enables people to link themselves with locality. The powers of tourists' myths are enormous and seemingly unshakable; tourists are drawn to exotic local color and local cultures even when they may be aware that what is presented is culturally inauthentic. If different cultures are indeed becoming homogenized, tourists' insistence on the different, the distant, and the exotic constitute a counter-tendency. The wish to gaze upon the faraway and the past has some economic impact as well, as governments and private entrepreneurs find profit in preserving historical sites, museums, and countrysides, all of which become part of the "heritage industry."

So great is the spread of "the foreign" that one need not travel to be a tourist. Shopping malls, advertising brochures, ethnic restaurant menus, movies, and television all play on the exotic and come to be anticipations or substitutes for the "real" thing. An English tourist, on viewing a splendid Sierra meadow near Yosemite National Park in California, was heard to exclaim, in a moment of aesthetic bliss, "What a perfect backdrop for a Western!" Further, localities manufacture cultural distortions for anticipated hordes of currency-bearing tourists in the form of kitsch products and performances, and sellers of artifacts profit from tourists' passion for discriminating between "genuine" and "mass-produced" cultural crafts and handiwork.

The mutual impact of locality on tourists and tourists on locality also serves to underscore the themes of permeability and syncretism that are so apparent in the globalization of culture.

Concluding Note: Understanding the Global

It is not especially fortuitous in our efforts to fathom the confusing novelty of a world that has changed so radically in the span of half a lifetime that the terms "global," "globality," and "globalization" have taken on something of an undifferentiated, almost mystical meaning. From a methodological standpoint, it would seem to be the better strategy, following Appadurai's lead, to disaggregate the phenomenon, though not precisely along his lines necessarily. The various analytical dimensions–spatial, temporal, economic, political, cultural, social, and perhaps even more–should be distinguished. For each level, the items that travel globally–for example, products, credit, people, ideas, images, commands–should be specified, as should the interactive contexts in which they are exchanged or move in other ways. The gains from viewing globalization as a complex grid of this sort, rather than as an undifferentiated process, might be that we would come to understand its full complexity and unravel the chains of causes and consequences that flow into and away from it.

References

Abu-Lughod, J. 1991: "Going beyond the Global Babble," in A. King (ed.), *Culture, Globalization and the World System: Contemporary Conditions for the Representation of Identity*, London: Macmillan, 131–8.

Appadurai, A. 1990: "Disjuncture and Difference in the Global Cultural Economy." *Theory, Culture, and Society*, 7: 295–310.

Arrighi, G. and Drangel, J. 1986: "The Stratification of the World Economy: An Exploration of the Semiperipheral Zone." *Review*, 10: 9–74.

Bendix, R. 1977 [1964]: *Nation-Building and Citizenship*. Berkeley, Calif.: University of California Press.

Cardoso, F. H. and Faletto, E. 1979: *Dependency and Development in Latin America*. Berkeley, Calif.: University of California Press.

Eisenstadt, S. N. 1992: "A Reappraisal of Theories of Social Change and Modernization," in H. Haferkamp and N. J. Smelser (eds), *Social Change and Modernity*, Berkeley, Calif.: University of California Press, 412–29.

Frobel, F. 1980: *The New International Division of Labor*. New York: Cambridge University Press.

Gereffi, G. 1994: "The International Economy and Economic Development," in N. J. Smelser and R. Swedberg (eds), *Handbook of Economic Sociology*, Princeton, N.J.: Princeton University Press and Russell Sage Foundation.

Gereffi, G. and Korzeniewicz, M. E. 1990: "Commodity Chains and Footwear Exports in the Semiperiphery," in W. Martin (ed.), *Semiperipheral States in the World Economy*, Westport, Conn.: Greenwood Press, 45–68.

Giddens, A. 1989: *Sociology*. Cambridge: Polity Press.

Gregory, D. and Urry, J. (eds) 1985: *Social Relations and Spatial Structures*. London: Macmillan.

Hannerz, U. 1990: "Cosmopolitans and Locals in World Culture." *Theory, Culture, and Society*, 7: 237–52.

Harvey, D. 1989: *The Condition of Postmodernity*. Oxford: Blackwell.

Hill, R. C. 1989: "Comparing Transnational Production Systems: The Automobile Industry in the USA and Japan." *International Journal of Urban and Regional Research*, 13: 462–80.

Kroeber, A. L. 1923: *Anthropology*. New York: Harcourt, Brace.

Lash, S. and Urry, J. 1993: *The Economy of Signs and Spaces*. Cambridge: Polity Press.

Lenin, V. I. 1939 [1917]: *Imperialism: The Highest Stage of Capitalism*. New York: International Publishers.

Lowie, R. H. 1937: *The History of Ethnological Theory*. New York: Rinehart and Co.

McLuhan, M. 1967: *Understanding Media*. London: Routledge and Kegan Paul.

Malinowski, B. 1945: *The Dynamics of Culture Change: An Inquiry into Race Relations in Africa*. New Haven, Conn.: Yale University Press.

Marx, K. 1853: "The Future Results of British Rule in India." *New York Daily Tribune*, Aug. 8, 1953.

Marx, K. 1949 [1867]: *Capital: A Critique of Political Economy*, vol. 1. London: Allen and Unwin.

Massey, D. 1991: "Flexible Sexism." *Environment and Planning D: Society and Space*, 9: 31–57.

Mingione, E. 1991: *Fragmenting Societies: A Sociology of Economic Life beyond the Market Paradigm*. Oxford: Blackwell.

Nettle, J. P. and Robertson, R. 1966: "Industrialization, Development or Modernization." *British Journal of Sociology*, 17: 274–91.

Pyke, F. and Sengenberger, W. (eds) 1992: *Industrial Districts and Local Economic Regeneration*. Geneva: International Institute for Labor Studies.

Robertson, R. 1968: "Strategic Relations between National Societies: A Sociological Analysis." *Journal of Conflict Resolution*, 12: 16–33.

Robertson, R. 1992: "Globality, Global Culture, and Images of World Order," in H. Haferkamp and N. J. Smelser (eds), *Social Change and Modernity*, Berkeley, Calif.: University of California Press, 395–411.

Scott, A. 1988: *New Industrial Spaces*. London: Pion.

Soja, E. 1989: *Postmodern Geographies: The Reassertion of Space in Critical Social Theory*. London: Verso.

Storper, M. and Harrison, B. 1991: "Flexibility, Hierarchy and Regional Development: The Changing Structure of Industrial Production Systems and Their Forms of Governance in The 1990s," *Research Policy*, 20: 407–22.

Strange, S. 1988: *States and Markets*. London: Pinter.

Tenbruck, F. H. 1990: "The Dream of a Secular Ecumene: The Meaning and Limits of Policies of Development." *Theory, Culture and Society*. 7: 193–206.

Urry, J. 1981: "Localities, Regions and Social Class." *International Journal of Urban and Regional Research*, 5: 455–74.

Urry, J. 1990: *The Tourist Gaze*. London: Sage Publications.

Wallerstein, I. 1974: *The Modern World-System*, vol. 1: *Capitalist Agriculture and the Origins of the European World Economy*. New York: Academic Press.

World Bank 1991: *World Development Report 1991*. New York: Oxford University Press.

Worsley, P. M. 1957: *The Trumpet Shall Sound: A Study of 'Cargo' Cults in Melanesia*. London: MacGibbon and Kee.

9

The Vicissitudes of the Market Principle

The organization of economies–and to a certain extent societies–on the market principle was the dominant theme in the theory and ideology of capitalism in the early nineteenth century. The principle came under attack with the governmental-regulatory and collectivist (including socialist) impulses later that century. It was definitely rejected by the Socialist and Communist regimes that assumed power in the Soviet Union, Eastern Europe, China, and other countries in the first half of the twentieth century, many of which imposed administered, "command" economies with an accompanying hostility to market-determined pricing and profits. Toward the end of the twentieth century–and in unexpected ways–the market principle has enjoyed a massive, widespread resurgence.

Three special turns of history have conspired to produce the current revitalization. The first is its dramatic reconquest of politics in the United States and the United Kingdom in the 1980s under Reagan and Thatcher, with its pro-market, anti-government, anti-welfare, anti-communist ideology and the irregular spread of that mentality to other Western countries. The second is the revolutionary collapse and more or less total de-legitimization of the Soviet-type economies as a result of the 1989 revolutions, so profound that some observers have spoken of its effects as a new world disorder (Jowitt 1993). The third is the somewhat manic resurgence of the market principle in former Socialist and Communist societies, a movement that has demonstrated not only the strengths of that principle but also its limitations. This chapter will focus on the political and social consequences of implementing a market economy in the post-Communist countries of Central and Eastern Europe.

This chapter is based on a contribution by Edmund Wnuk-Lipiński.

Basic Assumptions and Arguments

The market principle has at least a double functional significance: regulative and ideological. Its regulative function, well described in neoclassical economic theory, is as a mechanism that determines, through exchange, the allocation of resources, goods and services, and shares of income in the economy. Its ideological function is to legitimize fundamental institutional characteristics of the economy (production, banking, contracts, wage labor) of the society in which it is embedded and especially to legitimize market outcomes that result in social inequalities. In addition, the market ideology has proved a powerful ideological weapon in *de*-legitimizing systems–especially command economies–organized on presumably less efficient principles.

Historically, the consolidation of the industrial market economy (the British Industrial Revolution) and the rise of political democracy (the French Revolution) coincided, and commentators such as Karl Marx regarded them as two facets of the same larger world process. But, as the history of European fascism and Latin American authoritarianism demonstrates, the market principle is also compatible with authoritarian political systems. By contrast, a command economy seems to be incompatible with a democratic order. Hayek puts it as follows: "If [capitalism] means here a competitive system based on free disposal over private property, it is far more important to realize that only within this system is democracy possible. When it becomes dominated by a collectivist creed, democracy will inevitably destroy itself" (Hayek 1979: 52). Perhaps too extreme, this formulation nevertheless underscores the point that civil liberties are likely to be more stable if rooted in economic liberties, particularly private property. A post-Communist economic planner, Balcerowicz (1993), argues, in a similar spirit, that replacement of an administered economy by a market economy is facilitated by the dismantlement of an authoritarian political system and the establishment of a democratic order. Przeworski makes the same point:

> The strategy which is most likely to succeed is not the one that minimizes social costs: radical [economic] programs are more likely to advance further under democratic conditions even if voters would have preferred to start with a more gradual strategy. Hence, if politicians are concerned about the progress of reforms, they have an incentive to impose a radical strategy even against popular preferences and even when they know that this strategy will have to be moderated under popular pressure. (Przeworski 1991: 28–9)

This line of argument leads to an initial thesis. In the 1950s and 1960s the cold war, with its ideological and military rivalry bipolarization, left little room for experiments in the application of the market principle in the communist system. Such experiments threatened to undermine the otherwise coherent ideological system of totalitarian political and economic structures. After a brief period of détente, the bipolar world entered what amounted to a second cold war (Lewis 1992) in the 1980s. During this period the Communist bloc cautiously applied some market-like measures to revive declining economic output and to keep pace with enormous progress in the West. All attempts–applied mainly at the periphery of the Soviet empire–failed, because they challenged the Communist party hegemony and undermined the political system. After these episodes, democratic oppositions in Communist countries adopted the idea that political liberalization and democratization must *precede* radical market reforms.

A second thesis follows. The market ideology had great mobilizing power in overthrowing the command economy in Poland and elsewhere in Central Europe. The failure of the latter became the basis for a widespread conviction that the market is superior to administrative-political regulation as a mechanism to allocate and utilize resources. The evident difference in consumption standards between the West and the Soviet bloc lent substantial weight to this line of thought. All this contributed to the great initial popularity of neoclassical market solutions.

When it came to implementing the neo-liberal version of the market economy, however, both psychological and social-structural barriers soon surfaced. This led in turn to a political division–evident in Poland, at least–between those who supported neo-liberal reforms outright and those who believed that implementation of market reforms in a post-Communist setting had to be accompanied by state intervention in the interests of social justice and equalization of the burdens of transition. The second position, in its turn, broke into two options. The first was the social democratic, which stressed collective property rights; the second was the Christian democratic option, which, following the thinking of the Catholic Church, emphasized private property as well as solidarity, participation, the value of work and trade unions vis-à-vis the power of capital, and limitations on market principles in the name of the "common good" (Romanow 1992). Even with all these qualifications, however, the market remained the only alternative to the command economy.

In Poland, the radical economic reforms of Balcerowicz, designed along neo-liberal lines, became the pivotal political issue. All parties, including the surviving ("post") Communist party, rejected the command economy and embraced the market principle, but they differed on how far and how fast to carry the market reforms. As of 1993, the following positions had crystallized in relation to the neo-liberal reforms:

- the state as a protective umbrella over the industrial giants inherited from the command economy (appealing to the post-Communists and to a lesser degree the left wing of Solidarity);
- moderate state intervention on behalf of victims of unemployment and other deprivations in the new market environment–the doctrine of the "social market economy" derived from the Catholic Church (appealing to the

moderate center-right political parties, including the powerful Democratic Union);

- a kind of populist sentiment, arising from declining consumption standards (appealing to the radical right-wing parties, including the powerful Confederation of Independent Poland).

In the end, the divisions boil down to a tension between the principles of market efficiency and the principles of social justice. The neo-liberals stress efficiency; the moderate parties try to combine the two principles, while the populist groups put efficiency on the side and focus their attention on the equal distribution of wealth (Hausner 1992).

The emerging picture, then, is of a commitment to the market principle, but with deep political divisions about its implementation. In the larger world picture, the market also assumes a more central place in post-Communist societies, with the bipolar world replaced by a situation of competition for the economic interests of nations, accompanied by an increase in the activities of multinational corporations.

Elaboration of the Arguments

The Bipolar World and the Problem of Economic Efficiency

Until 1989 the world order was bipolar, consisting of Western democracies led by the United States and Communist regimes subordinated to the Soviet Union. The world was divided militarily, politically, and economically, with conflicts and confrontations occurring in all three spheres. The Third World was also an arena of rivalry between the two major superpowers.

As is characteristic of polarized situations, stereotypes abounded. The average Westerner conceived of the East in terms of masses of people enslaved under an offensive, dictatorial system. After the Stalinist period, some of the Communist countries emerged, in the eyes of the Western left, as more politically "civilized" and more attentive to issues of economic distribution. Among the stereotypes harbored by the masses under communism was a dream about a better Western world, which appeared in the imagination as a paradise of consumption.

In the context of these stereotypes, the shortcomings of market economies were perceived only as somewhat remote threats in Central and Eastern European countries. (Among these shortcomings are the priority of short-term interests over long-term ones, domination by monopolies, the existence of extreme regional and social inequalities, failures in the areas of law and order, education, and family stability, and above all subordination of the "common interest" to "particular interests" [Jänicke 1990, Brenner 1991].) But such criticisms of the market principle were not heard, on the whole. Two factors seem to account for this deafness: first, the notorious inefficiencies of the Soviet-type command economy, which could not satisfy basic material needs, particularly when measured by Western standards of living; and second, the continuing apparent success of the West. During the last years of communism, the achievements of Thatcherism in reviving the British economy were much heralded and had a great impact on the thinking of political counter-elites as well as on Communist elites. This facilitated the "round table talks" on economic matters in Poland and Hungary, which offered a ready pattern for the economic choices after the collapse of communism (Comisso 1992). Critical accounts of Thatcherism (e.g., Wells 1991) were not then available, and even if they had been, would probably have had only a minor impact, given the context.

By the 1980s the principle of centrally planned distribution had lost its ideological appeal in the more isolated republics of the former Soviet Union and in Rumania, Bulgaria, and even Albania. The strategies of the 1970s–borrowing from the West to shore up failing economies and maintain consumption levels–had sucked most of the command economies into a debt trap. The dilemma was clear: the market principle appeared as the only real alternative, but this could not be implemented without political liberalization and democratization. This precondition, however, would de-legitimize the cardinal axiom of the Communist system–the leading role of the Communist party–and thus undermine that system (Adamski *et al.* 1991).

The political collapse of the Communist regimes in Central and Eastern Europe thus opened the door for the application of the market principle. Offe poses the issue as follows:

> Post-communist political economies face three problems of transformation: property must be privatized, prices must be liberalized, or "marketized," and the state budget is to be stabilized in order to relieve strong inflationary pressures. Corresponding to these transformations, and in fact motivating them, are three cost considerations: privatization is mandated by the consideration that it will reduce transaction costs . . .; but stabilization, if strictly pursued, does not economize on cost, but leads to *increases* of costs of a special kind, namely "transition costs" (e.g., the social costs of the closing down of unprofitable enterprises, or of cuts in social expenditures), thus generating political resistance to marketization and privatization. (Offe 1992: 1)

Such measures were put in motion in nearly all the new democracies of Central and Eastern Europe, though with varying speed and thoroughness. But, as implementation proceeded, the reforms began to confront obstacles, to which we now turn.

Constraints Inherited from the Command Economy

Some observers have argued that the exit from the Communist system did not produce a new system but rather a sort of "non-system"–a mix of contradictions between remnants of the old system and elements of a new logic for collective action. This resulted in an institutional vacuum, blurred social identity, fluctuating rules of economic life, and, above all, extreme uncertainty (Csanadi and Bunce 1992). Such a portrait is too extreme, because many ingredients of the old system survived its apparent death: "The existence of parallel structures (however contradictory and fragmentary) in the informal and inter-firm networks means that instead of an institutional vacuum we find routines and practices, organizational forms and social ties, that can become assets, resources, and the basis for credible commitments and coordinated actions" (Stark 1992: 79). It is almost impossible to eradicate workable everyday routines, no matter how pervasive are efforts for radical reform and transformation.

What were the main psychological and structural constraints on the implementation of the market principle in the post-Communist societies? In the economic sphere, one fundamental contradiction stands out: *liberal market rules were imposed from above on the institutional structure of a command economy*. The logic of the liberal capitalist economy is that economic units *are* autonomous, not that they are *ordered* to be autonomous. The very process of imposition compromises their true autonomy. That contradiction actually resulted in an unrecognized, mixed system which was dysfunctional for the construction of a true market economy.

A second contradiction has already been mentioned: *between efficiency and justice*. Within the framework of the social-democratic approach, the old economy cannot simply be scrapped wholesale but must be dismantled gradually according to principles of "social justice," which means taking into account considerations of equity in distributing social costs in the transformational process. Within this context the unqualified application of principles of economic efficiency appears heartless and illegitimate. At the same time, any effort to protect group interests slows down the economic transformation and prolongs the crisis. But again, if these group interests are ignored, political resistance to change develops, and this in turn slows down economic transformation and strengthens the hand of populist parties.

Two further contradictions follow from that between efficiency and justice. The first is between society and economy and can be expressed as *the structure-formation function of a market economy* versus *an etatist structure*. The older command economy involved a framework of socialist enterprises functioning within a context of central planning. This generated a series of networks of formal and informal group ties and interests among the enterprises (Narojek 1985). In principle, these group interests can be overcome by the introduction of a new principle of market organization and the development of a new set of "middle-class" interests. But this process does not happen automatically. As Domański has described it:

> In the emerging market society, the middle class could maintain the economic and political stability of the new socio-economic order. Up to now, neither the intelligentsia, nor other non-manual workers or small proprietors, have performed such a function. In regard to economics, these groups did not develop the orientations needed to encourage individual achievements, competition, and other attitudes relevant for the effective operation of a market economy. In regard to politics, the decomposition of the social status among the intelligentsia prompted social tensions rather than the stability of the social system. (Domański 1991: 63)

In a word, both time and political work are required to develop new social structures and their associated classes.

Moreover, the development of market-appropriate class interests is made difficult by the persistent political interests of the "old," etatist group interests. The waves of strikes and street rallies against liberal market-reform measures in many post-Communist countries reflected such resistance, which can in this limited sense be regarded as "reactionary."

Neither the neo-liberal model nor the social-democratic model resolves this contraction. The former, not being well informed by the principles of political sociology, assumes the creation of market structures and market groups (classes such as owners, workers, managers, etc.) as a more or less nonproblematic outcome of the introduction of the market principle. But this assumption was challenged when big industrial enterprises were threatened with bankruptcy and asserted their interest. In the first two years of the transition, neither expansion nor competition worked effectively on a mass scale. Inflation was kept under control only at the cost of recession and high rates of unemployment.

The social-democratic model assumes that the goals of privatization (efficiency) and the protection of group interests in the social structure (social justice) can move forward at the same time. But in practice the relentless pursuit of privatization threatens existing groups' positions and mobilizes them against change, and the protection of group interests undermines the march toward privatization.

Closely related is the contradiction between *a post-socialist mentality* and *a spirit of free enterprise* (discussed by many, including Kolarska-Bobińska 1992, Koralewicz and Ziólkowski 1991, Mokrzycki 1991, Sztompka 1991, and Wnuk-Lipiński 1990). A population living under communism for half a century cannot be expected to know, or even learn quickly, the rules of the game of a market economy. What is appreciated is the glitter of material prosperity; what is not appreciated is greater inequality, unemployment, personal risk, and the pains of choice that accompany personal freedom. The unpleasant confrontation with these market-based realities often stimulates a selective nostalgia for the "old, secure times" of the Communist regimes and a selective forgetting of the political terrors embedded in those regimes. At the same time, some adapt too well perhaps to the new capitalist realities. These are the entrepreneurs who built quick fortunes from the legal gaps involved in transition or simply violated the law. The post-Communist period has witnessed some scapegoating of these dynamic entrepreneurs, and their presence has introduced yet another sour element into the transition process.

Despite the negative aspects of the transition to market-based structures and practices, surveys in the early 1990s reveal a positive correlation between the property status of a given enterprise and the mood of its employees. One study found that in newly privatized enterprises the morale of employees is generally higher (in part because uncertainty about the future is reduced) than among those employed in state enterprises (Jarosz 1993). Another study specified the range of positive outcomes of the first stage of market reforms in post-Communist countries: the disappearance of shortages as a result of price liberalization; wider choice, higher dollar wages, and better access to imported goods; better access to foreign know-how; improved incentives; improved quality and composition of products; and a better credit rating for the countries (Gomulka 1993).

Group Interests, Democracy, and the Market

One remarkable feature of the transition from the command economy to a market economy is that it has proceeded, by and large, under democratic procedures. This has entailed three kinds of political and social consequences:

First, changes must take place in the context of the expected responses of the populations affected. This is extraordinary, because of the "total" character of the changes involved–from one politico-economic system to another. By contrast, the innovations of Reagan and Thatcher were incremental modifications of existing, ongoing systems.

Second, if the political responses of the population are to be taken into account, state policies must be constrained so that the changes will continue to enjoy the support of the majority of the population.

Third, among the group interests to be contended with are those inherited from the command economy. As indicated, market innovations often pose fundamental threats to those interests, and their opposition tends to slow reforms. This, in its turn, inhibits the growth of the economy, which undermines popular acceptance of the need to sacrifice in the interests of the future. The vicious circle is completed when the whole process leads to the expression of short-term interests and gives support to those who wish to stop change or return to the *status quo ante*. Most countries have not fallen into this vicious circle, but the victory of post-Communist forces in Lithuania and the continuing vitality of hard-line

Communist thinking among Russian elites demonstrate that it is a real, not simply a theoretical, possibility.

At the risk of oversimplification, we may say that two essential political factors, both articulated in the democratic procedure, are at work in the transition to a market economy: values and interests. Values are judgments enabling people to distinguish "right" from "wrong" behavior and situations, whereas "interests" are judgments enabling people to distinguish what is "advantageous" or "disadvantageous" for them. (The content of both values and interests are, of course, the result of a complex combination of personal backgrounds, structural position in society, influence by others, etc.) Different combinations of these factors yield different probabilities for level of political behavior. We represent these schematically in table 9.1.

Table 9.1 Expectancy of political behavior according to value-related and interest-related definitions of the situation

	Interest-related definitions	
	"advantageous"	*"disadvantageous"*
Value-related definitions	*expectancy of political behaviour*	
"right"	high	medium
"wrong"	medium	low

We might suggest four general possibilities for predicting levels of political behavior that arise from the "political rationality" inherent in table 9.1.

- If some kind of political action is evaluated by the actor as both "right" and "advantageous," the probability of that action is correspondingly high.
- If such action is seen as "right" but at the same time "disadvantageous"–that is, it entails a sacrifice of interest–the political actor will be in a state of conflict and will be likely to act only if the expected pain from abandoning the "right" line of action outweighs the expected disadvantages.
- If a line of action is thought to be "advantageous" but at the same time "wrong," then the advantages must outweigh the moral pain incurred in undertaking wrong actions if political action is to occur.
- If some line of action is regarded as both "wrong" and "disadvantageous," it is unlikely that any political action will occur.

To apply this rough scheme to the real world, in Poland the initial rejection of the Communist system in the 1989 election was based on the conviction of the majority that it was both "right" and "advantageous" to do so. This was so because the Communist system had been experienced as politically oppressive (wrong) and because the adoption of an alternative market system would bring about substantial improvements in the standard of living (advantage). By the fall of 1988, 80 percent of the adult Polish population accepted the market principle as appropriate for the Polish economy. In the fall of 1990, nearly a year after the initiation of the Balcerowicz program of conversion, 80 percent still approved the idea of the market principle, but some seeds of ambivalence were appearing; 67 percent now favored a full employment policy and 66 percent supported the idea of state-controlled prices (Kolarska-Bobińska 1991).

As time went on, the bitter side of the transition began to be experienced. It became apparent that many commodities and services were unwanted, consumer purchasing power was low, productivity was low in industry and agriculture, the quality of products was inferior (compared to those importable from the West), the banking system was inadequate, interest rates were too high, and tax collection was inefficient.

As a result of these and other problems, the gross domestic product declined significantly in all post-Communist countries (see table 9.2). Unemployment, virtually unknown (at least in open form) under the Communist regimes, escalated. In Poland it rose from 1.5 percent in early 1990 to 13.6 percent at the end of 1992. The corresponding figures for Hungary were 1.7 percent to 10 percent, and the 1992 unemployment figures for Bulgaria and Rumania were 12 percent and 9 percent respectively (Central Statistical Office 1992, Central Office of Planning 1992, Körösenyi 1992). Needless to say, the increase in social frustration was correspondingly great. Furthermore, as often happens after the "honeymoon" phase of revolutionary change, the "interest" factor began to overshadow the "value" factor, and people began to regard the transition more in terms of its presumed advantages or disadvantages.

The definition of interests may emerge from the old economic order, or may be associated with the new market system. With respect to the former,

Table 9.2 Gross domestic product, 1991–2 (estimated)

Country	1989	1990	1991	1992
			(1988 = 100)	
Bulgaria	100	88	68	64
Czecholsovakia	101	101	85	78
East Germany	98	84	58	60
Hungary	98	95	87	82
Poland	100	89	82	82
Rumania	92	78	67	60
Former Soviet Union	102	98	88	70

Source: Gomulka 1993.

some defined their group interest in terms of the "old, secure times" of the command economy. Most preferred to accept the new system as "right" but wished simultaneously to safeguard their security interests by reducing its uncertainty by state intervention (full employment, price control, etc.) (Csanadi and Bunce 1992). Still others felt so strongly that the market principle was "right" that they were willing to undergo temporary disadvantages (Przeworski 1991). These sentiments, moreover, were class-related: the higher the level of education and occupational status, the lower the perceived threat of the market principle (Białecki 1991, Kolarska-Bobińska 1991, Morawski 1991).

It is plausible to hypothesize further that the weaker the belief in the foreseeable success of market reform, the more salient become short-term group interests. Conversely, the stronger the faith in the success of the market principle, the more likely people are to accept temporary sacrifices in consumption and other areas. These ranges of opinions translate into political terms, of course, and political forces for or against the transition to market capitalism are mobilized through the press and other means available under the democratic process. The more this political conflict paralyzes political leadership, moreover, the slower the transition and the longer the period of political and economic instability.

Inequalities, Efficiency, and Social Justice

One of the most pervasive sociological principles is that any change in the social structuring of institutional activities is invariably accompanied by a corresponding change in the distribution of resources and rewards. The social structuring of the market is a prime example of this. In particular, the introduction of the competitive market principle simultaneously introduces a new normative basis for stratification and a new principle for the distribution of income, wealth, goods, and services. Distribution, in its turn, raises questions of social justice. For any given society, definitions of social justice will be influenced by the prevailing value system (or systems) and by the particular structural position of different groups in the society. Those definitions of social justice also equip those who believe in them with bases for expressing *dissatisfactions* if they feel that their canons of social justice are being violated.

Three definitions of social justice may be identified for purposes of the following discussion:

- equal opportunity, which does not imply an equality of final distribution, but does imply a minimization of barriers to access to positions, resources, and rewards;
- outputs proportional to inputs, which also need not result in complete equality, but does contain a principle of equity;

- equal results, which, when taken in the extreme, completely obliterates the differential distribution of resources and rewards.

These principles work themselves out in both the social and the economic spheres, and we will consider these in order.

Social inequality　In the social sphere we may distinguish two ways of generating inequalities: first, the ways in which individuals gain access to different social positions in society; second, the rewards attached to the different positions. In a market economy the first principle is worked out through the mechanism of a "free" labor market, and the second through the mechanisms of supply and demand. The administered or command economy relies on different mechanisms. Political criteria typically enter into the assignment of positions, and this, of course, constitutes a violation of the principle of equal opportunity. Further, from the standpoint of those who adhere to the social-justice principle of economic opportunity, such a distributional system is illegitimate, and, ultimately, the whole stratification system which it produces may be challenged. This is certainly what happened in Poland during and after the emergence of the Solidarity movement.

Before the development of that opposition, however, the stratification system generated by the Communist social order had been able to sustain sufficient legitimization to function adequately. Some have argued that it never really gained legitimacy in the eyes of the people but that people consented to it because they had no alternative (Rychard 1987). Be that as it may, as a matter of practice people lived with it and cooperated with it according to principles imposed from above, and this proved enough for it to function for several decades.

The Communist system of allocating positions and rewards produced a distinctive pattern. One of the bases for inequality, private property, virtually ceased to exist. Others, at least in the first decade of the Communist order, were downplayed–for example, social origin, gender, and education. Still others, especially political affliation, were highlighted in the assignment of positions and rewards. During the first period of Communist rule, upward mobility showed some increase, especially for the working class and the peasantry (Kolosi and Wnuk-Lipiński 1983). In addition, the early impact of the Communist order was one of leveling inequalities. The price paid for this, however, was a serious limitation on certain types of freedom:

> Egalitarianism seems to require a political system in which the state is able continually to hold in check those social and occupational groups which, by virtue of their skills or education or personal attributes, might otherwise attempt to stake claims to a disproportionate share of society's rewards. The most effective way of holding such groups in check is by denying them the right to organize politically, or in other words, to undermine social equality. (Parkin 1971: 183)

Viewed on a large scale, the social policy of the Communist era in Poland was aimed at achieving equality of condition ("results") rather than equality of opportunity. But because of various economic constraints, the leveling became one of equalizing downward: low salaries and low quality of commodities and services (cheap food, housing and transport, free education, free health care, etc.). Nearly all resources were under state control, and their redistribution followed the distinctive political priorities of the ruling elite–priorities such as economic stabilization of the system, forced industrialization, reproduction of manpower, full employment, social security, and social peace. This produced a system of domestic policies aimed at the reconstruction of society.

That reconstruction foundered for two reasons: first, it produced an extremely inefficient economy, and second, it imposed other forms of inequalities, particularly with respect to opportunity, on the system. Studies have revealed that equality of opportunity was seriously compromised in the educational system (Najduchowska and Wnuk-Lipiński 1987) and that serious gender inequities persisted within occupational categories (Reszke 1987) and in different branches of the national economy (Domański 1987). Ultimately, however, the most serious erosion of legitimacy rested on the fact that membership in the Communist party was so closely associated with positions of privilege (Pohoski 1983, Wnuk-Lipiński 1987).

Surveys conducted in Poland after 1990 indicated substantial changes in social inequality under the implementation of the market principle. Most obviously, membership in the Communist party was no longer a market asset. However, in the initial stages of the transition, many holders of top positions in the party "nomenclatura" succeeded in converting their privileged political positions into economic assets. Differential levels of rewards according to type of enterprise have also appeared. Private employers offer higher wages and better conditions than state employers. And the risk of unemployment for females is higher than that for males (Reszke 1991).

Economic inequality   Income inequalities are an evident source of inequality in the economic sphere. In the Communist economy this was only one of several factors. Money is not the only way of gaining access to scarce goods and services (as it is in a market economy). Equally important means are holding a privileged position in the distribution process, having access to informal (even "black market") channels where personal influence can be exchanged for goods, services, or money ("corruption"), withholding goods and services for one's own consumption (especially in rural areas), and access to earnings in convertible ("hard") currency (Wnuk-Lipiński 1989a).

The social policy of minimizing income as the source of inequalities was not so much a matter of incentives as an instrument to level standards of living for employees and their families. In practice, this tended to result in an equality of poverty rather than an equality of affluence. Income inequalities among occupational groups in Poland were reduced, and the ratios were held relatively stable over time. Taking professional salaries in 1988 as the base (= 100), the wage level for private owners outside agriculture was 120 (122 in 1980), for individual farmers 98 (100 in 1980), and for workers in industry 75 (87 in 1980) (Wnuk-Lipiński 1989b).

Communist society thus involved a trade-off between individuals' and groups' economic freedom and greater centralization of economic power and greater equality of economic conditions. In the end, this strategy resulted in both greater equality and reduced efficiency; that was the formula that produced "leveling downward." The crisis engendered was a double one: a decline in average economic well-being for the population and a failure to attain true equality of conditions, because of the informal and political sources of unequal access. The latter were generally regarded as corrupt–and consequently as violations of the norms of social justice– and contributed significantly to the de-legitimization of the entire communist system.

Once again, transition to the market principle has introduced new sources and new patterns of inequality. Even when moderated by lingering state intervention, the free market has led to a greater inequality of incomes and to more extreme differences in standard of living. The state's redistributive function is diminished, and personal income is emerging as the most decisive determinant of level of consumption. Unemployment, disguised under communism, is now an evident and permanent feature of economic life. Poverty, also hidden under communism, is now more socially visible, as is great wealth.

Many surveys in the 1970s and 1980s (e.g., Nowak 1979, Kolarska and Rychard 1983) indicated that egalitarian attitudes were widespread in Poland. Some interpreted these attitudes as a kind of adaptation to the Communist social order (Rychard 1987). Others argued that those attitudes referred more to the principles of centralized distribution than to the outcomes of that distribution. Such interpretations regard egalitarianism as a kind of "second-best" accommodation to the fact that the Communist system did not, in fact, leave any room for the emergence and differential gratification of different groups' interests. This interpretation notwith-standing, it remains the case that many egalitarian attitudes have carried over to the present and constitute an obstacle to the full development of a more liberal market economy.

The key question for post-Communist society is: will people be willing to live in a freer and more efficient economic system at the cost of less equality? That trade-off is precisely the opposite of the one that communism proposed. The question will admit of no simple answer, because the political spectrum will continue to show a great array of groups taking different positions in relation to that central question. Moreover, the new system brings the prospect of greater individualization and responsibility for life and a correspondingly higher level of risk and uncertainty. To some this may prove a greater burden than they wish to bear, and, as a result, the new system lives with the prospect that people may want to "escape" from their "freedom" by returning to some kind of populist-authoritarian political and social regime.

Summary: Toward a Global Market

The collapse of the Soviet-type system in Central and Eastern Europe simultaneously created a sense of relief and a social vacuum. This vacuum is gradually being filled by the introduction, on a modified basis, of well-established Western market solutions. The various countries are proceeding with varying degrees of boldness (or caution) in this transition. But sooner or later, confrontation with profound "marketization" will have to be faced head-on. Furthermore, a straightforward return to some type of Communist command economy seems beyond consideration. The bitterness of historical memories of that system appear to rule out of bounds such a retrogressive experiment.

We may be reasonably confident that the future will bring three general lines of change in the post-Communist societies:

- further implementation of the market principle in the *economies* of those societies;
- further development of *institutional* arrangements (in the areas of industrial relations, law, and civil society) and *organizational forms* (such as voluntary organizations) that are compatible with the principles of the market and political democracy;
- further integration into world markets and the world economy.

The general movement, then, will continue to be toward the West and toward the world. The period of bipolar ideological and political rivalry appears to have given way to a world that exists as a vast, competitive economic arena for nations and groups of nations, marked by organizations and institutions that cross and penetrate the boundaries of political entities organized along national lines.

References

Adamski, W., Rychard, A. and Wnuk-Lipiński, E. (eds) 1991: *Polacy '90–Konflikty i zmiana*, (Poles '90–Conflicts and Change). Warsaw: Polish Academy of Sciences.

Balcerowicz, L. 1993: "Najpierw demokracja, potem kapitalizm" ("First Democracy, then Capitalism"). *Gazeta Wyborcza*, 25: 11.

Białecki, I. 1991: "Pracownicze interesy i orientacje polityczne" ("Interest of Laborers and their Political Orientations"), in Adamski, W. *et al.* (eds), *Polacy '90*, 123–35.

Brenner, Y. 1991: *The Rise and Fall of Capitalism*. Aldershot: Edward Elgar Publishing.

Central Office of Planning 1992: "Wstepna ocena sytuacji spoleczno-gospodarczej w 1992 roku" ("A Tentative Evaluation of the Socioeconomic Situation in 1992"). Warsaw: mimeograph.

Central Statistical Office 1992: *Rocznik Statystyczny 1992* (Statistical Yearbook 1992). Warsaw: Central Statistical Office.

Comisso, E. 1992: "Political Coalitions, Economic Choices," in G. Szoboszlai (ed.), *Democracy and Political Transformation*, Budapest: Hungarian Political Sciences Association, 122–37.

Csanadi, M. and Bunce, V. 1992: "A Systematic Analysis of a Non-System: Post-Communism in Eastern Europe." *Sisyphus – Sociological Studies*, 1: 55–75.

Domański, H. 1987: *Wpływ segmentacji rynku pracy na formowanie się struktury społecznej* ("Influence of Labor Market Segmentation on the Formation of a Social Structure"). Warsaw: Ossonlineum.

Domański, H. 1991: "Structural Constraints on the Formation of the Middle Class." *Sisyphus–Sociological Studies*, 7: 59–64.

Gomulka, S. 1993: "Economic and Political Constraints during Transition." Mimeograph.

Hausner, J. 1992: *Populistyczne zagrozenie w procesie tranformacji spoleczeństwa socjalistycznego* (Populist Threat in the Process of the Transformation of Socialist Society). Warsaw: Friedrich Ebert Stiftung.

Hayek, F. 1979: *The Road to Serfdom*. London: Routledge and Kegan Paul.

Jänicke, M. 1990: *State Failure: The Impotence of Politics in Industrial Society*. Cambridge: Polity Press.

Jarosz, M. 1993: *Prywatyzacja: Szanse i zagrozenia* (Privatization: Opportunities and Threats). Warsaw: Institute of Political Studies.

Jowitt, K. 1993: "Nowy światowy nielad" ("New World Disorder"). *Gazeta Wyborcza*, 49: 12–15.

Kolarska, L. and Rychard, A. 1983: "Interesy polityczne i ekonomiczne" ("Political and Economic Interests"), in W. Morawski (ed.), *Demokracja i gospodarka*, Warsaw: Warsaw University Press, 427–60.

Kolarska-Bobińska, L. 1991: "Ustrój ekonomyczny a interesy grupowe" ("The Economic Order and Group Interests", in Adamski *et al.* (eds), *Polacy '90*, 61–80.

Kolarska-Bobińska, L. 1992: "Social Interests and their Political Representation: Poland during Transition." Warsaw: mimeograph.

Kolosi, T. and Wnuk-Lipiński, E. (eds) 1983: *Equality and Inequality under Socialism: Poland and Hungary Compared*. London: Sage Publications.

Koralewicz, J. and Ziólkowski, M. 1991: *Mentalność Polaków* (The Mentality of Poles). Warsaw: Institute of Psychology.

Körösenyi, A. 1992: "Demobilization and Gradualism: The Hungarian Transition." Budapest: mimeograph.

Lewis, P. 1992: "Superpower Rivalry and the End of the Cold War" in A. McGrew and P. Lewis *et al.*, *Global Politics*, Cambridge: Polity Press, 31–44.

Mokrzycki, E. 1991: "Dziedzictwo realnego socjalizmu a demokracja zachodnia" ("The Legacy of Real Socialism and Western Democracy"). Warsaw: mimeograph.

Morawski, W. 1991: "Przemiany ekonomiczne a społeczeństwo obywatelskie" ("Economic Changes and Civil Society") in R. Gortat (ed.), *Społeczeństwo uczestniczace–Gospodarka rynkown–sprawiedliwość społeczna* (Participating Society–Market Economy–Social Justice), Warsaw: Warsaw University and Institute of Political Studies.

Najduchowska, H. and Wnuk-Lipiński, E. 1987: "Nierównosci społeczne w dostępie do wyksztalcenia" ("Social Inequalities in Access to Education"), in E. Wnuk-Lipiński (ed.), *VII Ogólnopolski Zjazd Socjologiczny–Materialy* (vii All-Polish

Sociological Congress–Proceedings), Warsaw: Polskie Towarzystwo Socjologiczne, 357–70.

Narojek, W. 1985: "Pluralizm polityczny i planowanie" ("Political Pluralism and Planning"). Warsaw: IFIS PAN: mimeograph.

Nowak, S. 1979: "System wartości społeczeństwa polskiego" ('The Value System of Polish Society'). *Studia Socjologiczne*, 4: 155–73.

Offe, C. 1992: "The Politics of Social Policy in East European Transitions. Antecedents, Agents, and Agenda of Reforms." Bremen: Zentrum für Sozialpolitik: mimeograph.

Parkin, F. 1971: *Class Inequality and Political Order*. London: MacGibbon and Kee.

Pohoski, M. 1983: "Ruchliwość społeczńa a nierównosci społeczne" ("Social Mobility and Social Inequalities"). *Kultura i Społeczeństwo*, 27: 135–64.

Przeworski, A. 1991: "Political Dynamics of Economic Reforms: East and South," in G. Szoboszlai (ed.), *Democracy and Political Transition*, 21–74.

Reszke, I. 1987: "Zróżnicowanie rynku pracy w Polsce jako źródlo nierówności między mężczyznami i kobietami" ("Differentiation of the Labor Market in Poland as a Source of Inequalities between Men and Women"), in Wnuk-Lipiński (ed.), *VII Ogólnopolski Zjazd Socjologiczny–Materialy*, 327–56.

Reszke, I. 1991: "Problemy bezrobocia kobiet" ("The Problems of Female Unemployment"). *Studia Socjologiczne*, 3–4: 81–91.

Romanow, Z. 1992: "Rola mechanizmu rynkowego w kształtowaniu procesów gospodarczych w dziejach katolickiej myśli społeczno-ekonomicznej" ("The Role of the Market Mechanism in Shaping Economic Processes in Contemporary Catholic Socioeconomic Doctrine"), in *Ruch Prawniczy, Ekonomiczny i Socjologiczny*, 54: 115–28.

Rychard, A. 1987: *Władza i interesy w gospodarce* (Power and Interests in an Economy). Warsaw: Warsaw University, pamphlet.

Stark, D. 1992: "From System Identity to Organizational Diversity: Analysing Social Change in Eastern Europe." *Sisyphus – Sociological Studies*, 1: 77–86.

Sztompka, P. 1991: "Dilemmas of the Great Transition." Radziejowice: mimeograph.

Wells, J. 1991: "Britain in the 1990s: The Legacy of Thatcherism," in J. Cornwall (ed.), *The Capitalist Economies: Prospects for the 1990s*, Aldershot: Edward Elgar Publishing, 171–200.

Wnuk-Lipiński, E. (ed.) 1987: *Neirównosci i upośledzenia w świadomości spolecznej* (Inequalities and Deprivations in Social Consciousness). Warsaw: Institute of Philosophy and Sociology, Polish Academy of Sciences.

Wnuk-Lipiński, E. 1989a: "Inequalities and Social Crisis." *Sisyphus–Sociological Studies*, 5: 103–14.

Wnuk-Lipiński, E. 1989b: "Nierówności, deprywacje i przywileje jako podłoze konfliktów społecznych" ("Inequalities, Deprivations and Privileges as a Foundation of Social Conflicts") in *Polacy '88–Dynamika konfliktu a szanse reform* (Poles '88– The Dynamics of Conflict and Reform Opportunities), Warsaw: CPBP, 18–80.

Wnuk-Lipiński, E. 1990: "Freedom or Equality: An Old Dilemma in a New Context," in P. Ploszajski (ed.), *Philosophy of Social Choice*, Warsaw: Institute of Philosophy and Sociology Publishers, 317–31.

10

Work, Commitment, and Alienation

The advance of industrialization in the world over the past two and a quarter centuries has occasioned fundamental changes in the character of human work (see chapters 6 and 11). From the standpoint of the expenditure of energy, this has meant above all the shift of expenditure of human and animal energy to alternative, more powerful, and more efficient forms (hydroelectric, fossil fuel, and nuclear). From the psychological and social–in a word, human–standpoints, the changes have been equally profound, though often not as clear as the transformations of energy. The title of this chapter identifies, first, the core phenomenon of concern of this chapter–work or labor–and then positive and negative orientations toward it.

Significantly, the concepts of alienation and commitment can be traced directly to the works of Karl Marx and Max Weber, whose works on the significant preconditions for, and consequences of, the development of capitalism have framed most of the major debates about that economic system. We refer in particular to Marx's conception of alienated labor and Weber's conception of commitment to work. Both those conceptions are products of the individualistic traditions within which Marx and Weber worked. Since the time of their writings, other, more collectivist forms of industrialization have served to complicate the views of Marx and Weber and to spur major debates regarding their general validity. The collectivist efforts on the part of the former Soviet Union and Eastern European countries were unsuccessful, proving–among other things–incapable of creating a work ethic compatible with sustained economic growth. The collectivist efforts on the part of Japan and the newly industrialized countries in Asia have raised fundamental questions about the psychological and social character of commitment to work.

This chapter is based on a contribution by Dimitrina Dimitrova.

Marx, Weber, and Early Capitalism

The major foci of the classics of economic sociology, which include the works of both Marx and Weber, are the relations between economy and society, the role of labor in the development of society, and the meaning of work for the individual (Martinelli and Smelser 1990). In their treatment of early capitalism, Marx and Weber stressed different aspects, and for these reasons their approaches are typically regarded as alternatives if not opposed. The major differences can be put succinctly as follows:

- Re subject of study: Marx stressed the objective conditions for the development of capitalism, laying special stress on conflict, whereas Weber analyzed the role of culture, religious values in particular, in the origin of capitalism. Examination of the totality of their respective works, however, reveals that neither had a monocausal–material or cultural–explanation, but both emphasized the mutual interaction between economic fores and a broad set of social factors (Israel 1971, Furnham 1990).
- Re nature of theoretical reflection: Marx falls in the positivist tradition of Western social science, which stresses the objectivity of things and the possibility of scientific laws, whereas Weber acknowledges the necessary and legitimate role of value preferences and value commitments on the part of the investigator in selecting topics for analysis and in formulating conclusions about the causes and consequences of phenomena.
- Re methods of analysis: Marx's method was mainly one of materialist dialectics, whereas Weber relied on understanding (*verstehen*) and the generation and extraction of ideal types from the complex historical process.

Within his materialistic framework Marx regarded labor as an activity through which an individual reveals his species being. His starting point is that the human being, by contrast with animals, has the capacity for transforming nature and bringing it under his own power. Through labor man both creates the material base of social life and develops his own nature. This idea goes back to the Renaissance concept of *homo faber*. Under conditions of capitalism, in which the means of production are controlled by a small number of owners, however, labor is converted into a means of subsistence. In his early work Marx treated labor as a sphere of dehumanization under capitalism. "Work is external to the worker; it is not part of his nature; consequently he does not fulfill himself in his work, but denies himself" (Marx 1964 [1844]: 124–5). Marx identified four aspects of alienated labor: alienation of the direct producer from the products of his or her labor, alienation from the work process, alienation from others, and alienation from oneself. In his discussions of the nature of communism, Marx argued that human emancipation is realized in the shift from the realm of necessity to the realm of freedom, and in the latter the objective conditions giving rise to alienated labor are eliminated.

Because of the bifurcation of society into a class of owners and a class of laborers, commonly-shared values are impossible. Bourgeois culture and proletarian culture are characterized by differences rooted in their opposed class interests. Bourgeois culture is dominated by the individualistic values which underpin its dominant ideology, whereas proletarian class culture derives ultimately from the formation of class consciousness and the building of solidarity on the basis of common interests. By extension, de-alienation of workers' labor is possible only through a reversion to man's species being through joint, collective activity.

What Marx understandably could not have foreseen in the context of nineteenth-century conditions was that under certain conditions collective mobilization might eventuate not in emancipation but in a mechanism of collective enslavement of the individual through the enforcement of the collective will. Under some forms of socialism a *nomenclatura* developed to absolutize its power position and create conditions for its own perpetuation, while legitimizing this in the name of collectivist values. For the developed capitalist West, Marx's stress on economically based classes also requires historical modification in the late twentieth century. While class remains a powerful dimension in contemporary society, welfare capitalism has tended to mute class conflict and generate new conflicts based on the distribution of public goods, with empirical evidence of cross-class political alliances (see Joppke 1987).

Weber directed his attention mainly to the origins of capitalism and the historical conditions underlying its development in the West. In this process the conception of rationalization–the progressive introduction and elaboration of rational thinking and action in every sector of society– played a central role. In fact, Weber's conception of capitalism was specifically one of *rational* bourgeois capitalism, which implies the systematic, methodical organization of the factors of production in the interests of production.

For Weber, however, the rationalization of economic activity under capitalism did not arise autonomously, that is, of its own accord. In his economic sociology he laid out a number of institutional and political conditions (Weber 1968: I, 161–4), but in his comparative writings on religion he singled out a certain elective affinity between the values and beliefs of ascetic Protestantism and the rationalization of economic activity (Weber 1958 [1904–5]). According to Weber's now familiar formulation, the Calvinist doctrine of predestination constituted a source of profound existential anxiety over individuals' likelihood of salvation and prompted a search for external signs of election. Among what were seen as signs of grace were evidence of hard work, conceived as a moral duty, and the worldly success that accompanied it. Among the specific manifestations of this were sustained labor, its methodological organization, and the saving and reinvesting of money–all simultaneously signs of virtue and important ingredients in developing and sustaining capitalism.

In his own work Weber introduced a number of important qualifications and elaborations of his principal thesis.

- While his thesis clearly involves a rejection of materialism, he insisted that he did not wish to fall into the contrary error of a "one-sided spiritualistic causal interpretation of culture and of history" (Weber 1958 [1904–5]: 183).
- Weber identified a number of tendencies that worked to undermine the specifics of the original Protestant work ethic. Among these were the waning of religious faith, excessive individualism, the growth of hedonism, the institutional minimization of risk taking, and the desacralization of property (see Ditz 1980).
- As if to counter those tendencies, Weber argued–in his famous "iron cage" formulation–that modern capitalism "needs [Protestantism's] support no longer" (Weber 1958 [1904–5]: 182). Capitalism was now being sustained by "technical and economic conditions of machine production which today determine the lives of all the individuals who are born into this mechanism" (ibid. 181).
- Perhaps as a result of the last two factors, commitment to work under capitalism was becoming a thing of "purely mundane passions" (ibid. 182). Elsewhere Weber was to speak of human "disenchantment" associated with the march of scientific and material progress, in which life comes to lack meanings "that go beyond the purely practical and technical" (Weber 1948 [1922]: 139).

The last point suggests a certain irony in the Marxian and Weberian conceptions of work. Marx, starting from the standpoint of *alienation* of workers from the whole labor process, envisioned an emancipation from that situation with the revolutionary onset of communism and the end of private property; under such conditions a positive commitment to work was possible and would occur. Weber, starting from the standpoint of an active *commitment* to work, envisioned in the end his own version of alienation under capitalism, with those who worked becoming more mechanical, more dehumanized, and more disenchanted.

But ultimately it was the process of history, rather than the niceties of logical irony, that brought about the breakdown of the classical formulations of both Marx and Weber. Experiments in abolishing private property in the name of Communist values certainly did not eliminate dehumanizing conditions of work; nor did they result in the emancipation of the individual. The social rights granted under Communist regimes were in the end undermined by the complete failure of the system to grant political rights (see chapters 5 and 9). In the West–according to Bell's (1976) diagnosis at least–the development of entrepreneurship under capitalism engendered mobility and freedom from collective ties. However, the complex system of entitlements that has grown up in late capitalism constitutes a new system of collective ties that inhibits, if it does not contradict, freedom. And in one capitalist country after another–the United Kingdom, the United States, Germany (see Kalberg 1992), and perhaps even Japan–the early capitalist work ethic, however generated, appears to have weakened and thus kept the issues of commitment and alienation alive. In the end, then, although the validity of both Marx's and Weber's diagnoses and predictions has proved historically questionable, the issues themselves have remained timeless and at the center of the organization of work in all contemporary economies.

Work, Commitment, and Integration

Orientations to Work under Mass Production

According to one line of thinking, it was not capitalist ownership of the means of production as such that promoted alienation, but rather the *specific* organizational form of capitalist work known as mass production. The end of the nineteenth century in the United States, it is argued, marked an eclipse of the classical, individual capitalist entrepreneur and the rise of large organizational capitalism. Not only was the scope of corporate control enlarged through horizontal and vertical integration and, later, diversification; organizations themselves grew in size and complexity, both of which required new and better modes of coordination and control (Didrichsen 1977). As a consequence of these changes, the power of the foreman to hire and fire was undermined (Nelson 1988), and workers' discretion and decision making on the shop floor was diminished.

The system of principles that came to describe (and justify) work processes under this new form of corporate capitalism is known as Taylorism, named after their principal theorist, Frederick Taylor (Taylor 1967 [1911]; see also chapter 11). Taylor's concept of scientific management meant the systematic application of knowledge to the production process, so that efficiency could be maximized and irregularities of the production process minimized. The system's main practitioner, the automobile-manufacturer Henry Ford, perfected assembly-line mass production as a system of standardization, reduction of production costs despite increased wages, and vastly increased efficiency (Ford 1968).

Fordism as a productive system carried several implications. First, it called for market stability and predictability, especially as regards labor (Chandler 1988). Initially, this expressed itself in an active hostility toward labor unions, but in the longer run it led to the intervention of the state as a facilitator and guarantor of labor–management agreements. Second, the new system of production, combined with and partially responsible for the rapid economic growth of the United States, permitted an increase in workers' and others' level of income and a rise in the standard of living. Third, however, and most important for the topic of this chapter, the mechanization of production often produced a pattern of de-skilling, monotonous routine, and social isolation, all of which are key components of alienation by any definition.

It should come as no surprise that the attention of American social scientists turned increasingly to questions of quality of work in the decades following the triumph of the mass production principle. The ''human relations" approach, associated with the work of Roethlisberger and Dickson (1939) and Mayo (1945), though not guided by any specific conceptualization of worker alienation, nevertheless studied such alienation in effect, as these researchers concentrated on the determinants of worker morale and workers' resistance to authority and recommended management strategies to counter the effect of diminished morale and its impact on worker efficiency.

Other studies focused more directly on workers' outlooks. Chinoy's (1955) study of automobile workers stressed both a decline in the importance of the work ethic and a shift in workers' goals, both occasioned by the meaninglessness and fragmentation of work typical of the assembly line. Chinoy pointed to a contradiction between traditional beliefs in the personal achievement of the "self-directed man" and the realities of the factory system, which builds in structural barriers to occupational advancement. Under these circumstances workers turned their interest more in the direction of job security and incremental increases of income *within* their jobs, identification with the ambition of their children, and consumerism and hedonism generally (see also Rodgers 1978).

Blauner's (1964) comparative study of several industries focused directly on alienation. Building on Seeman's (1959) efforts to classify the components of alienation from work, Blauner specified its several ingredients: *powerlessness*, which arises when workers do not control the means of production or the work situation; *meaninglessness*, which arises when workers contribute only in small measure to the final product; *isolation*, which arises when a worker does not belong to an effective social unit on the job; and *self-estrangement*, which arises when work becomes simply a means to make a living rather than a path toward individual self-fulfillment. Blauner assumed further that different types of industry give rise to different levels of alienation, because they have different technologies, different divisions of labor, and different bureaucratic structures. On the basis of this reasoning, he studied worker alienation in four industries differing from one another along these dimensions: automobile production, textile production, automated chemical production, and printing.

As might be expected, auto workers scored highest on alienation, printers lowest. On the assembly line, auto workers had little control over their conditions of work, little relief from monotony, little responsibility for the final product, little personal interaction on the job, and little involvement in a cohesive occupational community. By contrast, printers, practitioners of one of the surviving crafts, set their own pace of work, saw the results of their labor, worked in a more intimate social setting, and belonged to an occupational community. Textile workers showed an intermediate level of alienation. As loom-tenders they were subject to the same constraints as auto workers; they were tightly supervised, their pace of work was set for them, and they had almost as little control over the final product. The particular setting of the workers studied, however, was a small southern town in the United States, with a traditional, homogeneous, and relatively stable social life, all of which probably counterbalanced the effects of the work situation. In a more urbanized setting, Blauner argued, these community ties would probably be weaker, and the level of alienation would, accordingly, approach that of the auto workers.

Interestingly, the level of alienation among operators in the chemical refinery was only slightly higher than that among the printers. Though the operators did not determine the rate of continuous flow of production, they were responsible for monitoring it. They were often members of a team, in which each member made a definite contribution to the total work process, and they had some freedom to vary their style of work. They were not likely to be closely supervised by managers. This latter finding suggested that some of the most advanced, automated systems of production might constitute more benign settings than those of mass production.

Preoccupation with worker alienation came to a head in 1973 with a report entitled *Work in America* (1973), sponsored and published by the Department of Health, Education, and Welfare, which documented the high levels of worker dissatisfaction with meaningless, repetitive, dull work, as well as their efforts to achieve greater autonomy, recognition, and opportunities to develop their skills. Some interpreters tied these findings to a generational argument. The children of the 1950s–the "baby boomers"–it was maintained, were experiencing higher aspirations for autonomy, self-esteem, and independence because of their experience of affluence and their higher levels of education. (This reverses the argument that alienation makes for a displacement of workers' attitudes toward consumerism.) The logic of the argument is that workers accustomed to greater material comfort and exposed to the materialism of the mass media (Gatewood and Carroll 1979) are less willing to endure dehumanized work situations (Davis 1971). Surveys conducted at the time (e.g., Yankelovich 1972) still reported high commitment to work on the part of three-quarters of young Americans, though he did find a weakening of traditional attitudes toward authority.

Partly as a response to the preoccupation with alienation, a number of more constructive theories and recommendations directed toward the greater humanization of work also appeared. Among these was the vision of work as "self-actualizing" (Maslow 1954, McGregor 1957, Herzberg 1966). The basic assumption was that people aspire to utilize their abilities in and through work. In Maslow's scheme, needs are organized in hierarchies ranging from lower (physiological) to higher (self-actualization). When needs at the lower levels are satisfied through material affluence, values relating to self-actualization become more salient in work satisfaction. This approach resembles the human relations approach of the mid-twentieth century in at least two respects: first, its ultimate concern is with productivity, but the main determinants of productivity are now social and "human," not the coerciveness and economic incentives associated with scientific management; second, the human needs involved are security, recognition, autonomy, achievement, challenge, and participation. The argument proceeds further by asserting that if the organization (i.e., management) satisfies such needs, people will respond by contributing to the attainment of organizational goals (Tausky, 1978).

The idea of a universal hierarchy of needs has received little empirical support. A group of researchers focusing on the "central life interests" of workers (Dubin *et al.* 1975) found that white-collar workers find higher levels of satisfaction in the work itself than do blue-collar workers; but this finding is not itself a direct confirmation of the notion of a hierarchy of needs. The idea of the universality of needs has also been challenged on psychological grounds, with Grint (1991) observing that needs and expectations are socially constructed, not internally given or determined by objective work circumstances. Furthermore, the empirical connection between job satisfaction and job performance remains uncertain (Kelly 1980, 1982). In the last analysis, attuning job conditions to workers' "higher needs" involves high levels of investment with unknown levels of payoff for the organization; as a result, managers are often reluctant to make such investments.

Post-Industrialism and the Changing Work Ethic

Whatever the precise defining characteristics of "post-industrialism"–if any–the last third of the twentieth century has witnessed the acceleration of changes in production systems. Under conditions of increased international competition, technological change, and diversified markets, the new password is "flexibility" (see chapters 11 and 18). Involving a clear rejection of the notion of standardized process that was at the center of Taylorism (Friedman 1988), the idea of flexible specialization calls for a new set of worker characteristics. Functional flexibility involves the possession of flexible skills on the part of workers, together with a willingness to move freely between tasks and even jobs (Atkinson, 1985). Similarly, the new flexibility ideology calls for an adaptive, cooperative style of management–employee relations (Fox 1974).

With respect to the orientation of workers under new conditions of flexible specialization, the argument continues, workers themselves should be both predictable and dependable, so that they will be willing to put more effort into increasing the company's competitiveness (Child 1984). Correspondingly, the emphasis on fixed "needs" of workers has given way to a psychology called "expectancy theory." This, in effect, is a return to utilitarian/instrumental theory, in that it stresses specific rewards to be offered for work efforts. It is important in this connection to determine how employees evaluate the potential outcomes of job experiences (Vroom 1964, Porter and Lawler 1968).

This post-industrial framework stresses maximizing commitment to the organization, by contrast with earlier emphases on increasing the satisfaction of work personnel. (The influence of the Japanese system's collective commitment to organizations is apparent.) In this connection, some researchers have turned to a new kind of tension or contradiction: that between commitment to an occupation and commitment to an organization. This is certainly an issue for professionals in organizations (Patchen 1970, Sheldon 1971). This tension is relevant to the issue of flexibility; more particularly, occupational commitment, characteristic of Anglo-Saxon traditions, is considered to be an obstacle to flexibility (Child 1984). In spite of educational expenditures, high salaries, and guarantees of organizational security–all high-cost items–flexible commitment to the organization is regarded as efficient and conducive to increased participation in the decision-making process.

Some writers have taken an optimistic view of the future of work in this kind of post-industrial setting. Toffler (1980), for example, paints a cheerful picture of the future worker as a person who accepts responsibility, who can handle ever larger tasks, and who can adapt swiftly to new circumstances. Such workers are complex in their abilities and proud of their distinctive capabilities. Toffler argues that flexibility is a virtue both for managers, who offer a set of rewards among which employees can choose, and for employees, who have multiple possibilities in their relationships with corporations.

Such optimism is not shared by all. Littler (1985), for example, indicates that the accumulated evidence shows no decline in people's attachment to work. However, certain structural problems in contemporary economies have appeared: in particular, new distributions of work and power. Littler argues that "New social divisions are opening up around work. The rift between the employed and unemployed is the starkest. But within the world of work there are also new divisions. There is growing evidence that sub-contracting and the use of temporary and part-time workers are erecting a new feudalism" (Littler 1985: 203). Among those suffering most in the process are low-paid women workers, in both developed and less developed countries (see chapter 18). Insofar as this is true, the new flexible specialization has not brought an end to dehumanization but only changed its face. Kern and Schuman (1990) suggest that there is a new polarization associated with the new wave of rationalization, depending on whether workers are fully a part of it. Those who develop new skills and knowledge may perform work that is self-actualizing; those who are excluded, however, may continue to suffer underemployment, uncertainty when not employed, and drudgery and monotony as well as uncertainty when employed.

Speculations regarding the fate of the Protestant work ethic continue into the post-industrial era but fall as far short of closure as earlier. Some (Levitan and Johnson 1983) have maintained that the desire to obtain and participate in a job is high. Rosow (1978) has even suggested that commitment to work is on the increase. One basis for his argument is that other, nonwork social involvements have declined through the continuing processes of social mobility, secularization, a decline in marriage rates and an increase in divorce rates. Though an interesting response to the intensified concern with alienation in the 1970s, Rosow's thesis has not been demonstrated, and it certainly does not take global economic changes into account. In a related diagnosis, Yankelovich (1972) did not take a definite stand with respect to work commitment, but he did express alarm at the increasing commitment to private goals. He described the new ethic as one of self-fulfillment, as opposed to the earlier ethic of self-denial. Moreover, the new commitment creates a moral and social absurdity. It gives moral sanction to desires that contribute nothing to the collective well-being of society. It contains no principle for synchronizing the requirements of society and the goals of the individual and fails to discriminate between socially valuable desires and socially destructive ones. In the end, this privatization and self-centeredness of individual goals may work perversely against the goals of organized societies (Yankelovich 1981; see also Bellah *et al.* 1985).

Labor Process, Conflict, and Alienation

Monopoly Capitalism and Alienation

Much of the research and thinking reviewed up to this point, dealing as it does with individual self-realization, does not have any direct theoretical link with Marx's objective, materialist theory of alienation. But another line of research on the subject stands directly in that tradition. According to this, class conflict persists, and though exploitation takes new forms, objective alienation continues to be among its inevitable consequences.

Braverman's (1974) work on monopoly capital is perhaps the most influential contribution to this tradition. Consistent with the Marxist tradition, Braverman focused on the objective aspects of the labor process and management control. Starting from the notion of craft work that combines knowledge and skills, control of work and autonomy, Braverman argued that in relation to that model modern work has been degraded in the evolution toward monopoly capitalism. The key developments are the uncoupling of the labor process from the skills of the worker and the separation of the conception from the execution and control over the labor process. Technologies serve the interests of management; their main effect is to fragment and de-skill labor. Managers gain in that they maintain a cheap work force and a high level of productivity, but the consequence for workers is that they are further deprived of control and become alienated from the labor process.

One criticism of Braverman's approach is an empirical one: namely, that advancing technology has the effect of eliminating many low-skill jobs (e.g., in mining and construction) and replacing them with jobs demanding more technical skill. Other lines of criticism of the neo-Marxist approach are theoretical: that the approach is too rooted in objective conditions, is too closely linked with fixed ideological presuppositions, and does not take into account the subjective interpretations that individuals give to their experiences of alienation (Seeman 1959). While not denying the importance of objective conditions, Seeman designated his approach a socio-psychological one and set himself the task of delineating the phenomenon as the individual experiences it. He broke down alienation into a number of separable aspects: powerlessness, meaninglessness, normlessness, isolation, and self-estrangement. Seeman's work has gone far in separating the idea of alienation from the specific Marxist tradition and giving it an independent analytic status (Ludz 1973).

Blauner's (1964) research, summarized earlier, can be regarded as occupying a kind of middle ground between the objectivist and the psychological approaches to alienation. On the one hand, his stress on technology roots his approach in objective structural conditions. On the other, he is willing to admit the operation of other factors (e.g., traditional community organization) as contributing to alienation. Furthermore, he regards it as a variable phenomenon, to be measured psychologically (through survey responses, interview results, etc.), rather than as an extrapolation from posited conditions or stages of capitalist development. Finally, he breaks with Marx in suggesting that alienation is not necessarily a cumulative feature of capitalism, since some of the most advanced technologies (e.g., automated, continuous work flow) seem to be less alienating than traditional assembly-line methods of production.

Responding to the same line of theoretical criticism, others in the Marxist tradition have attempted to bridge the double gap between theory and empirical research on the one hand and between objectivist and subjectivist definitions of alienation on the other. Archibald *et al.* (1981) acknowledged the overlap between positivist and phenomenological definitions and tried to overcome the resulting measurement difficulties by devising a number of behavioral indicators of alienation. Applying these, they found different levels of alienation in a comparative American–Canadian sample, with property-owners registering lower scores on alienation than those who owned no property.

The conflict between the Marxist/objectivist and the non-Marxist/subjectivist approaches to alienation has not been resolved. Schacht (1981) has attempted to assign two separate meanings to the concept of alienation: one a purely descriptive-analytical (neutral) construct, the other an interpretative-evaluative construct that can serve as a basis for moral and humanistic criticism of the dominant values and institutions of capitalist society. Ideological accusations flow in both directions. The Marxian definition of alienation is clearly rooted in the moral-political framework of that system of thought, and Marxists are quick to point out that the subjective emphasis connotes a position of ideological conservatism, in that it is not oriented to the elimination of unfavorable conditions but rather to the adaptation of individuals to these conditions. Braverman (1974) argued that the psychological approach, insofar as it was incorporated into Blauner's study, constitutes a tacit agreement with managers on the part of sociologists that work is indeed degraded and the labor process necessary and inevitable. This leaves sociology in the position, Braverman argued, of joining with management in focusing not on the nature of the labor process but on the manner in which workers adjust to it.

Central Planning and Alienation: The Waning of the Work Ethic?

As part of the ideology of Marxism, worker alienation as a phenomenon is expected to disappear, whether immediately or slowly, under conditions of socialism or communism. The theoretical basis for this rests on the assumption that, with the transformation of the relations of production and the abolition of private ownership, an emancipation of the proletariat from exploitation will be achieved. Commitment to this theory involves an expectation–and sometimes a claim–that because these features of capitalism are the root causes of worker alienation, this alienation will itself be eliminated and conditions of creative labor will replace it. In a word, public ownership transforms labor under socialism into the social labor of free producers, and the socialist relations of production contribute to the development of collaboration and mutual aid.

The evident persistence of worker dissatisfaction under those regimes in the former Soviet Union and Eastern Europe in the twentieth century, to say nothing of the failures of industrialization itself under them, calls for a reconceptualization of labor relations under socialism. Such a reconceptualization may throw some light on the reasons for the failure and may aid understanding of some of the barriers confronting the development of market economies in those regions (see chapter 9).

One reading of the idea of alienation under socialist regimes concerns the ideological service it provided for those regimes. On the one hand, its disappearance as the result of the abolition of private ownership was taken for granted, and this became one of several bases of self-congratulation and propaganda for the regimes (Ludz 1973). As part of the dominant ideology of socialist regimes, it became the basis for revealing the continuing shortcomings of bourgeois capitalism, and thus served as one kind of prop–a denial of self-criticism and an instrument for criticism of others–for the socialist ruling elite in the party–state apparatus.

It is correct to say that private property was virtually abolished in many of the socialist countries. At the same time an enormous amount of economic power was concentrated in the hands of the party and the bureaucracy because that apparatus continued to maintain complete control over the *distribution* of resources, a control that accomplished much the same effects as ownership, because it deprived the direct economic producers of control over the work environment. Thus the stage was set for a new, but not entirely different, kind of alienation from that posited under conditions of capitalism.

Burawoy, a Marxist himself, suggested (1985) a reconsideration of the socialist thesis that labor relations had reached a state of nonconflict under that system of government. Within the Marxist tradition he analyzed the process of production under socialism and illuminated its essentially conflictual character. Under state socialism, he argued, the processes of reproduction and expropriation are separated. Unpaid labor became transparent. The exploiters and the exploited were revealed as the class of redistributors and its agents on the one side and the direct producers on the other. Under these conditions workers no longer had a clear-cut material interest in the success of the firm. As a result, they had to be coerced or bribed into rendering surplus product. The state was present at the point of production simultaneously as exploiter and oppressor, appropriator of surplus and regulator of production. It requires little imagination to appreciate that such a system would score very low on productivity, because of having to rely so heavily on moment-to-moment monitoring and control, and very high on alienation, because of the enormous inroads made on the freedom of the workers.

Central planning appears to contain a logic that ends in coercion. To be effective, planning requires an extremely complex system of intelligence, to provide knowledge of who produces what, who provides to whom, and who receives from whom, at every single moment. Adequate planning, in short, requires administered predictability. Human resources are no exception to this rule. In principle, planners required complete knowledge of workers' whereabouts and control of their movement from place to place. This necessity helps to explain the draconian measures of legislation against absenteeism and turnover that characterized socialist systems; they were prompted by the necessity to control the work force in the interests of the state employer.

Obedience and discipline were also indispensable conditions for the functioning of planned and administered systems. Under these conditions, the individual worker confronted limited opportunities for achievement and advancement, because of the enormous numbers of formal regulations that controlled changes in job situation, to say nothing of the motivational premium placed on keeping the job one had. Promotions were dependent in large part on considerations of political loyalty and nepotism. Through the centralized system of wage determination, performance was essentially divorced from wages received. With such a top-heavy mode of coordination and with an absence of effective sanctions for work, much of the work force came to be underutilized. The inefficiencies of the system and the erosion of motivation had to be compensated for by methods of coercion, because few other motivating sanctions were available. This coercion was carried out by managers of enterprises, by enterprise-based party units, and by the trade unions, which had themselves been coerced into operating, in effect, as an extension of the interests of the state employer.

Given these circumstances, it seems hardly surprising that Lenin (1972 [1918]) himself should have admired the fit between the Taylor system of scientific management and the power of the Soviets. Both were mechanisms designed specifically to control and make work conditions predictable and by so doing to increase productivity. The outcome of the specifically socialist methods of control, however, was a fragmented and uncoordinated division of labor and massive amounts of routine work. The failure of technological progress in the former Soviet Union resulted from many factors, but among them were the extreme centralization of enterprise profits and the continuing low cost of labor, a guaranteed market for produce, plus, perhaps most important, a virtually complete absence of incentives for individual initiative.

In the end, such a system could not fail to generate opposition on the part of workers, despite extreme efforts to control the mechanisms (notably trade unions) for the expression of opposition. The form of opposition, moreover, was dictated by the structure of the controls that were built into the system. Burawoy has captured the essence of the struggle:

> Enterprise struggles are immediately struggles against the state, because the factor apparatuses are also apparatuses of the state and because the state is the transparent appropriator of the surplus as well as the redistributor of wages and services and the regulator of prices. Moreover, as long as direct producers are not systematically joined to a collective societal interest, their struggles are only limited by the forces of repression or the distribution of concessions. (Burawoy 1985: 116)

Under conditions of such thoroughgoing political domination, circumstances dictated that any opposition, whether direct or indirect, had to be political in the last analysis.

What forms did worker resistance take under such conditions? Because of the pervasiveness of state control and because of the danger of political repression at all times, resistance tended to take on a secretive, indirect, but nonetheless often effective form: concealing one's work capacity, poor performance, working to rules, absenteeism and malingering, worker turnover, sabotage of machinery and the work process, and theft (Burawoy 1985). The effectiveness of such resistance was seen in the significant role it played in determining the very low levels of productivity in Eastern European socialist countries. The effect was considerable and was one of the factors in the long-term failure of those regimes.

Also, because of the omnipresence of political controls, opposition could not take public form through unions or political parties. Despite this, the Eastern countries developed the kind of class conflict that Marx envisioned in capitalist countries: a thoroughgoing hostility to the ruling classes that found expression in small, solidary groups initially, but then, when the opportunity presented itself, as in Poland in the early 1980s, burst forth as fully developed class conflict. This development of "classical" Marxian class conflict in systems posited on its disappearance in the name of Marxist principles is one of the great ironies of modern history.

When the socialist regimes of Eastern Europe came crashing down in the revolutions of 1989, those countries initiated a headlong rush to institute both political democracy and a restructuring of the economy along the lines of markets and private property. Progress along these lines has been halting, however, and in some quarters a certain nostalgia for the security of state responsibility and direction has reappeared (see chapter 9). While the long-term prospects for sustained economic growth are more favorable, those regions in transition reveal a picture that is not favorable from the standpoint of gross national product, unemployment, and the distribution of income.

From the perspective of work, it might be suggested that one of the obstacles to the resumption of growth might be found in the legacy of discipline and passive resistance inherited from the years of socialist regimes. Collectivism nurtured values that are antipathetic to those that are essential for dynamism in a market setting–the values of entrepreneurship and commitment to work. The inherited paternalism, the culture of dependence upon institutions, the pervasive distrust–all worked toward a social personality characterized by passivity and lack of initiative. Much of the entrepreneurship that has appeared has been of the "pre-capitalist" kind identified by Weber–private, acquisitive, often operating on the edge of legality and morality, but not systematic or organizationally based. Thus the victory of worker passivity and indirect resistance under socialism may have been perverse in one sense; for that passivity, combined with the East's embrace of Western consumerism, may prove a liability in forging the combination of commitment, discipline, and entrepreneurship that appear to be necessary for the economic development of Eastern Europe.

A Concluding Remark

One lesson that might be drawn from these pages is that the contemporary world has not really hit upon the right formula for the organization and motivation of work under industrial conditions. Virtually all efforts to secure commitment have failed in the long run to stem the rise of significant levels of alienation. This is certainly true of the moral and punitive discipline of early capitalism, the heavy control of scientific management in capitalist countries, and the oppressive system of centralized political control in socialist countries. The diverse movements and experiments that have underscored the "human" dimension of work–the human relations and self-development approaches, worker participation, Asian notions of corporate belonging–appear to have demonstrated that no enduring system of organization of work can survive without the component of membership in a meaningful and rewarding social group. Yet, the best formula for the social organization of work has not emerged, either. One can safely conclude that work and its social organization continue to constitute an arena of life that remains in great need of human inventiveness.

References

Archibald, P., Owen, A. and Gartrell, J. 1981: "Propertylessness and Alienation: Reopening a Shut Case," in R. F. Geyer and D. Schweitzer (eds), *Alienation: Problems of Meaning, Theory, and Method*, London: Routledge and Kegan Paul, 149–74.

Atkinson, J. 1985: "Flexibility: Planning for an Uncertain Future." *Manpower Policy and Practice*, 1: 26–9.

Bell, D. 1976: *The Cultural Contradiction of Capitalism*. New York: Basic Books.

Bellah, R. N., Madsen R., Sullivan, W. M., Swidler, A. and Tipton, S. M. 1985: *Habits of the Heart: Individualism and Commitment in American Life*. Berkeley, Calif.: University of California Press.

Blauner, R. 1964: *Alienation and Freedom*. Chicago: Phoenix Books.

Braverman, H. 1974: *Labor and Monopoly Capital: The Degradation of Work in the Twentieth Century*. New York: Monthly Review Press.

Burawoy, M. 1985: *The Politics of Production*. London: Verso.

Chandler, A., jr. 1988: "The United States: Seedbed of Managerial Capitalism," in F. Hearn, (ed.), *The Transformation of Industrial Organization*, Belmont, Calif.: Wadsworth, 34–45.

Child, J. 1984: *Organization: A Guide to Problems and Practice*. London: Paul Chapman.

Chinoy, E. 1955: *Automobile Workers and the American Dream*. Garden City, N.Y.: Doubleday.

Dahrendorf, R. 1959: *Class and Class Conflict in Industrial Society*. Stanford, Calif.: Stanford University Press.

Davis, L. 1971: "The Coming Crisis for Production Management: Technology and Organization." *International Journal of Production Research*, 9: 65–82.

Didrichsen, J. 1977: "The Development of Diversified and Conglomerate Firms in the United States, 1920–1970," in E. Perkins, (ed.), *Men and Organization: The American Economy in the Twentieth Century*, New York: G. Putnam's Sons, 38–50.

Ditz, G. 1980: "The Protestant Ethic and the Market Economy." *Kyklos*, 33: 623–56.

Dubin, R., Champoux, J. and Porter, L. 1975: "Central Life Interests and Organizational Commitment of Blue-Collar and Clerical Workers." *Administrative Science Quarterly*, 20: 411–21.

Ford, H. 1968: "Mass Production," in C. Walker (ed.), *Technology, Industry, and Man: The Age of Acceleration*. New York: McGraw-Hill, 51–6.

Fox, A. 1974: *Man Mismanagement*. London: Hutchinson.

Friedman, D. 1988: "Beyond the Age of Ford: Features of Flexible-System Production," in Hearn (ed.), *Transformation of Industrial Organization*, 254–65.

Furnham, A. 1990: *The Protestant Work Ethic: The Psychology of Work-Related Beliefs and Behaviours*. London: Routledge.

Gatewood, R. and Carroll, A. 1979: "The Interaction of the Social Environment and Task Specialization on Worker Attitudes," in R. Huseman. and A. Carroll (eds),

Readings in Organizational Behavior: Dimensions of Management Action, Boston: Allyn and Bacon, 187–91.

Grint, K. 1991: *The Sociology of Work*. Cambridge: Polity Press.

Herzberg, F. 1966: *Work and the Nature of Man*. New York: World Publishing Co.

Israel, J. 1971: *Alienation: From Marx to Modern Sociology*. Boston: Allyn and Bacon.

Joppke, C. 1987: "Collective Consumption and the Rise of New Social Actors." *Berkeley Journal of Sociology*, 32: 237–60.

Kalberg, S. 1992: "Culture and the Locus of Work in Contemporary Western Germany: A Weberian Configurational Analysis," in R. Münch and N. J. Smelser (eds), *Theory of Culture*. Berkeley, Calif.: University of California Press, 324–65.

Kelly, J. 1980: "The Cost of Job Redesign: A Preliminary Analysis." *Industrial Relations Journal*, 11: 22–34.

Kelly, J. 1982: *Scientific Management, Job Redesign and Work Performance*. New York: Academic Press.

Kern, H. and Schuman, M. 1990: *The End of the Division of Labor?* Sofia: Profisdat.

Lenin, V. 1972 [1918]: "The Immediate Tasks of the Soviet Government," in *On the Development of Heavy Industry and Electrification*, Moscow: Progress, 23–38.

Levitan, S. and Johnson, C. 1983: "The Survival of Work," in J. Barbash, R. Lampman, S. Levitan and G. Tyler (eds), *The Work Ethic: A Critical Analysis*, Madison: IRRA, 1–25.

Littler, C. (ed.) 1985: *The Experience of Work*. Aldershot: Gower.

Ludz, P. 1973: "Alienation as a Concept in the Social Sciences." *Current Sociology*, 21: 9–39.

McGregor, D. 1957: "The Human Side of Enterprise." *Management Review*, 46: 22–8, 88–92.

Martinelli, A. and Smelser, N.J. 1990: "Economic Sociology: Historical Threads and Analytical Issues," in A. Martinelli and N. J. Smelser (eds), *Economy and Society: Overviews in Economic Sociology*. London: Sage Publications, 1–49.

Marx, K. 1964 [1844]: *Early Writings*. New York: McGraw-Hill.

Maslow, A. 1954: *Motivation and Personality*. New York: Harper Brothers.

Mayo, E. 1945: *The Social Problems of an Industrial Civilization*. Boston: Graduate School of Business Administration, Harvard University.

Nelson, D. 1988: "The Foreman's Empire," in Hearn (ed.), *Transformation of Industrial Organization*, 20–33.

Patchen, M. 1970: *Participation, Achievement, and Involvement on the Job*. Englewood Cliffs, N.J.: Prentice-Hall.

Porter, L. and Lawler, E. 1968: *Managerial Attitudes and Performance*. Homewood, Ill.: R. D. Irwin.

Rodgers, D. 1978: *The Work Ethic in Industrial America 1850–1920*. Chicago: University of Chicago Press.

Roethlisberger, F. J. and Dickson, W. J. 1939: *Management and the Worker*. Cambridge, Mass.: Harvard University Press.

Rosow, J. M. 1974: *The Worker and the Job: Coping with Change*, Englewood Cliffs, N.J.: Prentice Hall.

Schacht, R. 1981: "Economic Alienation: With and Without Tears," in Geyer and Schweitzer (eds), *Alienation: Problems of Meaning, Theory, and Method*, 36–67.

Seeman, M. 1959: "On the Meaning of Alienation." *American Sociological Review*, 24: 783–91.

Sheldon, M. 1971: "Investments and Involvements as Mechanisms Producing Commitment to the Organization." *Administrative Science Quarterly*, 16: 143–50.

Tausky, C. 1978: *Work Organizations: Major Theoretical Perspectives*. Itasca, Ill.: F. E. Peacock.

Taylor, F. 1967 [1911]: *The Principles of Scientific Management*. New York: Harper and Row.

Thibault, A. 1981: "Studying Alienation without Alienating People: A Challenge for Sociology," in Geyer and Schweitzer (eds), *Alienation: Problems of Meaning, Theory, and Method*, 275–83.

Toffler, A. 1980: *The Third Wave*. New York: William Morrow.

Vroom, V. 1964: *Work and Motivation*. New York: Wiley.

Weber, M. 1948 [1922]: "Science as a Vocation," in H. H. Gerth and C. W. Mills (eds), *From Max Weber: Essays in Sociology*, London: Routlege and Kegan Paul, 129–56.

Weber, M. 1958 [1904–5]: *The Protestant Ethic and the Spirit of Capitalism*. New York: Scribner's.

Weber, M. 1968: *Economy and Society: An Outline of Interpretive Sociology*, ed. G. Roth and C. Wittich. 3 vols. New York: Bedminster Press.

Work in America: Report of a Special Task Force to the Secretary of Health, Education, and Welfare. Washington, D.C.: US Government Printing Office, 1973.

Yankelovich, D. 1972: *The Changing Values on Campus: Political and Personal Attitudes of Today's College Students*. New York: Washington Square Press.

Yankelovich, D. 1981: *New Rules, Searching for Self-Fulfillment in a World Turned Upside Down*. New York: Random House.

11

Technology, Production, Consumption, and the Environment

One of the most enduring cultural heritages of the Judeo-Christian tradition is dualistic thinking. It continues to pervade ordinary discourse and social science frameworks–good and evil, right and wrong, spirit and flesh (or mind and body), individual and society (Durkheim), ideal and material interests (Weber), *Gemeinschaft* and *Gesellschaft* (Toennies), and oppressors and oppressed (Marx). Not all the consequences of this dualistic mode of thinking are felicitous, however. Such thinking suggests separable, real worlds, between which distinct lines can be drawn, and in many cases worlds that are fundamentally opposed or contradictory. In practice, however, the more we come to understand the world, the more we see these distinctions as relatively contingent and the "separate" sides as interpenetrating. So, while our heritage and language force us to use the distinctions, it is necessary to appreciate their essential unreality.

The same observation can be made with respect to the distinction between man and nature. In no productive way can such a distinction be maintained as an absolute one. To begin with, it is evident that humanity is a part of nature, systemically involved with nature's continuity, its evolution, and its (and humanity's own) possible ruination. It is impossible to conceive of any distinctively human contrivance – for example, a social institution such as a school–without simultaneously conceiving of a

This chapter is based on a contribution by György Széll. I have also profited from an essay by Johannes Berger, "The Economy and the Environment," prepared for publication in Smelser and Swedberg, forthcoming, 1994.

distribution of organisms that populate it and the range of resources (including physical space) that are part of its existence.

The sociology of the environment (or the study of society and environment) is an endeavor that underscores the interrelatedness and intermeshing of those somewhat mythical entities, man and nature. Of relatively recent invention, the subject has been forced upon us, as it were, by the complaints of nature–complaints of its spoliation, its exhaustion, its destruction–as human civilization has reached unprecedented magnitude in the twentieth century. The new enterprise is understandably engaged in a certain groping for identity, but it is already clear that it is inherently interdisciplinary, involving simultaneously the study of science and technology, economics, cultural attitudes, power relations, and social institutions, since all are intimately related to the environmental balance.

In this chapter we approach the problem by considering the relations among technology, production, and consumption, with an eye always on the relations of this complex of social forces to the human environment.

Historical Considerations

Looking back to the origins of human society, we recognize that two of the most fundamental defining characteristics of the rise of human association are language and technology. Gehlen, the anthropologist, has gone so far as to designate human beings as "animals with tools" (1957). And tools are inseparable from production and consumption. If work is the interrelation between man and nature, as Karl Marx argued, work is equally well conceived as the contrived activities of socially associated humans (society) using their natural setting (environment) to survive and prosper. These relations go back to the beginning of history, and an account of them would include the remarkable technologies of Sumerian, Egyptian, and Chinese civilizations. For purposes of this chapter, however, we will limit consideration to modern developments, which are essential to the understanding of the development of sociology itself. In this discussion we follow the main lines of analysis laid down in the works of Mumford (1967), Giedion (1948), and Bernal (1969).

Among the most common terms used to designate the formation and character of modern societies are "industrial," "capitalist," and "bourgeois." They are overlapping, but each suggests a somewhat different facet of those societies. At the same time, it must be recognized that these terms are themselves products of those very kinds of societies. A kind of dialectic is at work: as new economic, political, social, and cultural structures have emerged, actors within them and thinkers about them have had to invent new terms and concepts to describe them and, perhaps, to overcome or destroy the older structures. "Revolution" is one such term, but consider also "class," "interest," "political party", "industry", "liberty", "equality," "fraternity," "solidarity," "wage," "machine," and "cooperative" (noun)– all of which are simultaneously descriptive and directive in implication.

The social sciences–and sociology in particular–are part of this dialectic between structural change and conceptualization. The end of a cyclical vision of human nature and human activities was closely associated with the end of religious ideologies linked to feudal and aristocratic systems of dominance. New ideologies with a "religious" character–democracy, nationalism, socialism, anarchism–gradually evolved as ways of understanding and shaping the world. The development of sociology, which typically advertised itself as science, not ideology, was part and parcel of this process. Although these changes in world view evolved over long periods of time, their rise was also punctuated by dramatic and revolutionary events, of which the French Revolution was the most conspicuous.

To narrow it down to the theme of this chapter, the eighteenth-century Physiocrats (notably Quesney and von Thunen) were the first to develop a theory that linked economic activities to the preservation of nature. The source of the wealth of nations was to be found not in labor but in nature. This theme reappears in contemporary ecological debates, in which it is asserted that nature is the only value-producing source (Immler 1985). But the main drift of the Enlightenment went in another direction. It followed the Kantian dictum that enlightenment frees humanity from self-inflicted coercion. Most of that impulse was directed toward the obliteration of coercive religious, political, and class institutions inherited from earlier ages. With respect to the economy, however, enlightenment meant liberation from natural, economic, and social constraints. Nature was something to be overcome and controlled. Landes captured the spirit in the title of his history of technological change and industrial development from 1750: *The Unbound Prometheus* (1968).

The modern Japanese mode of production has been advertised as "The Machine that Changed the World" (Womack *et al.* 1990), but the latter is an equally apt designation for the technological revolution at the end of the eighteenth century, which ushered in the spinning jenny, the steam engine, and the railway. Technology also revolutionized warfare and colonialism; improvements in navigation, arms, vessels, weapons, and vehicles were a necessary condition for European imperialism.

For national societies the new system of technology and production was simultaneously an economic engine for amassing profits and a means for exercising internal (class) and external (world) dominance. In his critique of capitalism, Marx recognized this truth by building in distinctions among the "production process," the "mode of production," and the "social relations of production," to designate the technological, the historical relations, and the relations among groups, respectively. That multi-sided complex, furthermore, contained, in Marx's work, a dynamic for fundamental, irreversible change.

What were the interrelations between technology, production, consumption, and the environment in this new system? They were manifested in the division of labor (or work organization), which is the effect of the concrete combination of labor, technology, and capital in the workplace, whether this be a factory or a service-dispensing bureaucracy. Pre-modern societies had a division of labor, and manufacturing started as early as the twelfth century in Italy, but craftsmanship dominated until modern times.

The central precondition for the development of wage labor was the emancipation of work from feudal ties, which permitted in turn the forging of *individual contracts* for labor. But while labor contracts could now be free formally, they were not in fact free and equal. The industrial entrepreneur emerged as the dominant force in the capital–labor equation. The history of trade unions underscores this inequality. For a long time the dominance of industrialists was assured by the prohibition and persecution of trade unions, and the development of those organizations was a manifestation of the efforts of workers to protect their interests and prevent manufacturers from pressing their wages to the subsistence minimum. The influence of trade unions, in its turn, spilled over into the political arena, as the labor movement became the focus of class conflict and as trade unions became the major moving force in the development of Labor and Socialist parties in Western economies in the late nineteenth century.

It has been argued that the development of mass production techniques around the beginning of the twentieth century was at least in part a strategy on the part of management to regain control of the production process–a control that had been challenged by the rise of trade unions (Braverman 1974). Piore and Sabel (1984) treat this period of the rise of the trade unions as "the first great divide" in modern industrial history. It marked the divide between craft production and mass production. The latter was based on techniques associated with the names of Frederick Winslow Taylor and Henry Ford; indeed, the methods they devised now receive their names: Taylorism and Fordism. Taylor provided a rationale for the new method under the head "scientific management." Taylor advanced four principles of this new system:

- to create a real science of management;
- to choose workers on a systematic basis;
- to educate workers on a scientific basis and to train them on a permanent basis;
- to build cooperative relations between management and workers, thus rendering trade unions unnecessary (Taylor 1967 [1911]).

The corresponding results were to be created:

- an accumulation of knowledge through management, which is the essence of modern management;
- the separation of planning from execution; planning decisions, previously made on the shop floor, were to be prepared in a separate work office;

- the forging of a new link between performance and income, with wages and salaries increasing by 60 percent and output sometimes tripling;
- preparation, in advance and by management, of the work load for each worker.

Henry Ford, the inventor of the assembly line, took some of Taylor's ideas even further. Under this system, management could control the pace and output of work by increasing or decreasing the speed of the line. Ford doubled the average wages of his workers and thus achieved a double revolution. First, he reduced turnover in his work force. Second, he made it possible for workers to buy their own products, particularly in light of the fact that the price of cars was reduced by half; that is to say, his methods led not only to a revolution in productivity but also to a revolution in consumption. The influence of Taylorism and Fordism was enormous, appearing even in Lenin's socialist ideas about production (Széll 1988), and these methods are still vital in many industrial settings, although they are perhaps being eclipsed by a second industrial divide ("flexible specialization"), according to Piore and Sabel (1984).

With the new system of mass production, however, came new forms of opposition, even sabotage, and new ways to deal with this began to appear in the literature on management and the social sciences. Mayo (1945) described the informal group in the work process, noted how it sometimes took control of the pace of production, and proposed a kind of "human relations" approach to deal with issues of morale and worker cooperation. New forms of presumably less alienating work organization have appeared since the 1950s: job rotation, job enlargement, job enrichment, and semi-autonomous work groups (Heller *et al.* 1989–93). Opposition to the increased intensification of work continued, however, partly expressed in the refusal of young educated workers in the 1950s to take positions having a "three-D" (dirty, dangerous, and difficult) component. The quality of working life, the humanization of work, and the identity of the workplace have also become salient issues in industrial relations. Scholars in England and Norway have developed the notion of socio-technical systems, which takes into account the social side of the production process; systems of this sort have been implemented by some Scandinavian companies, notably in the Swedish Volvo factory at Kalmar.

The most recent innovations in the efficient control of production have been developed in Japan. Traditional Western production rested on several operations: development of a product through research and development (R & D), design of the appropriate technology, production of the item at a workplace, and marketing of the product through a marketing organization. The Japanese have scrapped this traditional approach to production by developing what has been called "lean production" (Womack *et al.* 1990)–also known as Toyotism or Ohnism (after the name of its chief exponent, Taiichi Ohno). On close examination, the slimming of production turns out to be not primarily a matter of machines but rather a matter of the organization of human effort. The watchwords of the system–quality circles, total quality control, just-in-time, zero-defect group, and corporate identity–indicate its human dimension. It has been suggested further that Japanese culture, with its stress on benign hierarchy and informal social controls, is a particularly fruitful breeding ground for this kind of system. At the same time, these principles have been adopted successfully as transplants in some American and European industries; and there is no reason to believe that this new principle of organization cannot migrate from Japan, much as Western technology and industrial organization migrated *to* that country in an earlier era.

The Environmental Dimension

So much for a sketch of some of the dynamics that have led to unprecedented advances in technology, production, and consumption in the past two centuries. Taken together, these advances have revolutionized the human condition. Carried out under the ideological umbrellas of science and progress, this revolution has been regarded mainly in positive terms–that is, in terms of the increase in the material welfare of humanity. The darker sides of that development have been portrayed up to the present mainly in terms of social injustice, the exploitation of one class of human beings by another, and the alienation of those who work from the means of production, the products of their labor, and themselves. More recently, another dark side has become apparent; this might be called the alienation of humanity from nature. It could even be argued that this growing divergence between the logic of the technological-economic aspect of human existence and the logic of survival in the human environment will become the major contradiction of the twenty-first century, replacing others in terms of urgency.

Environmental crises have always occured in human history – natural disasters such as floods, earthquakes, storms, famines, and plagues, as well as man-made disasters such as the destruction of forests, diversion of rivers, burning of plains, and exhaustion of lands. All these shrink by comparison with the contemporary threats to the environment, however, because the latter are so much greater in both *scope* and *systematic organization* of the exploitative process.

The worsening of humanity's environmental situation that is traceable to human economic activities has been well documented in the reports of international agencies. A recent OECD report (1991a) detailed grave problems in the areas of atmospheric pollution, waste, noise, soil degradation, pressures on forests, and threats to wildlife. At the same time, the report noted that "OECD countries have made progress in dealing with a number of the most urgent problems of the last two decades" (OECD 1991a: 283), singling out the reduction of urban air pollution and pollution of waterways and lakes. Oddly, the report did not mention two of the most urgent problems which are now at the center of the discussion of environmental perils: global warming (the greenhouse effect), which stands to wreak havoc on the coastal regions of the world through a rise in sea level and create a massive shift in rainfall patterns and global vegetation zones, and the depletion of the ozone layer, which, if destroyed, would permit the penetration of solar ultraviolet radiation to the earth's surface, which would damage both plants and people.

If one considers predictions that have appeared over the past several decades, one can find ample cause for gloom. In the early 1970s the Club of Rome (Meadows *et al.* 1972) predicted the exhaustion of critical resources by the next century. The Worldwatch Institute in Washington, D.C., is most pessimistic about the impending effects of global warming, the ozone hole, and acid rain. Goodland and colleagues (1991) project the end of civilization in several decades, because of the choking effects of humanity's waste and rubbish. The German economist, Leipert (1989), estimates that three-quarters of the growth in national product is now devoted to compensating for environmentally related threats, rather than improving the quality of life; within five to ten years we will be standing still, destroying as much of our livelihood as we sustain, instead of creating new value. The late Norbert Muller (1989–91) foresaw the destruction of our global economic, social, political, and cultural system around the year 2030 or 2040, unless we change our production, consumption, and life-style patterns radically.

Discounting elements of carelessness, inexactness, hysteria, and drama in some of the predictions, it is nevertheless clear that the prospect of global ruination is upon us, and it is essential to pinpoint the reasons. The OECD report traced the crisis to two basic causes: inefficiency of environmental policies and the interdependency between the state of the economy and the state of the environment. This diagnosis is fair enough as far as it goes, but especially in relation to the latter cause, the relations between the economy and the environment are not linear, and appreciation of the "economy" side of the equation must take into account that direct economic factors are multiple and stand in systematic relation to one another. Furthermore, "behind" the immediate economic causes are a whole range of social, political, and cultural factors that condition those causes. Among these are the organization of much of the world's economic life according to a capitalist economic system that thrives only with growth; patterns of intra-national and international inequality, which promote economic exploitation as well as differential patterns of waste and pollution; and materialist attitudes that pervade the whole culture of modernity, in both developed and developing countries. This interconnectedness can be represented graphically, as in table 11.1.

Regarding the "direct" causes of environmental spoliation and destruction, we mention four–technology, growth of production, population, and consumption.

Table 11.1 Society and Nature: Some Interrelationships

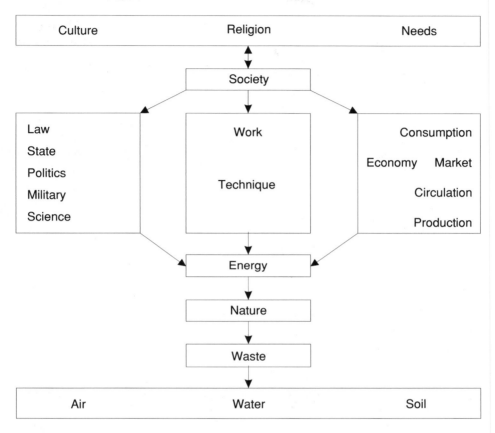

Source: Adapted from Széll, 1991, p. 11.

Technology   As indicated earlier, technology–or the application of scientific principles to production–is probably the greatest single engine of economic reorganization and advance, and, thereby, among the chief villains with respect to environmental damage. But technological impacts are highly variable. Consider only the production of energy; its generation by solar, thermal, wind, and water sources is relatively clean, whereas the use of coal and petroleum is polluting, and that of nuclear power is productive of enormous radioactive risk and poisonous waste. Two of the great technological bases of the Industrial Revolution–the replacement of human energy by energy derived from internal combustion and fossil fuels and the chemical decomposition and recombination of natural substances–seem to be the most destructive of the natural environment (Landes 1968).

Because of the variable effects of technology on the environment, it is possible to regard it as either a foe or a friend of environmental efforts. On the one hand, fossil fuel, chemical, and nuclear technologies share a large part of the blame for the world's current environmental problems. On the other hand, it is via the technological route that the much pollution, toxicity, and radioactive risk can be minimized. That route includes the invention of new technologies that can counteract their effects (e.g., smog control devices) and the development of new, more benign technologies that will replace the offending ones (e.g., solar-powered automobiles).

Economic growth Closely linked with wealth, the rate and volume of economic growth multiplies the effects of technology. It may be the case that world economic growth is such that it will simply reach the limits that are possible, given the finite supply of the world's resources. Those who are less apprehensive about this outcome point out that the limits themselves are variable, and are less likely to be reached if substitution, new technologies, and changes in cultural attitudes can be realized. But whereas the nature of the ultimate limits is uncertain, the known rate of growth and the probable rate of near-future growth are more clearly known. The rates of growth of Western economies and Japan were higher between 1950 and 1973 than at any previous period in history. By the 1970s, the rates of growth of socialist and developing countries had passed those of the West, but by the 1980s the Western countries had taken the lead again.

Regarding the world as a whole, the World Bank (1992) has estimated that the world's real economic product will rise from around $20 trillion in 1990 to $69 trillion in the year 2030. The increase of polluting, toxifying, and resource-exhausting effects is not known precisely, because the exact technological mix is not known. It is also true that the countries with the highest levels of economic development produce the highest levels of pollution–for example, the emissions of carbon dioxide in high-income countries are approximately three times higher than those in low- and middle-income countries (World Bank 1992)–and an absolute increase will necessarily mean some kind of corresponding increase in environmental damage.

Population In 1650 the population of the earth was about 500 million; by 1850 this figure had passed the one billion mark. At present the world's population is about 5.3 billion and is growing by about 100 million per year. The World Bank (1992) estimates that between 1990 and 2030 the world's population will grow by about another 3.7 billion to a total of 8 billion, a rate of growth that is greater than in any previous generation. More than nine-tenths of this growth will occur in the developing countries, which in all likelihood will continue to be the poorest. The European experience suggests that increased economic growth leads to lower rates of population growth, whereas the continuing rate of population increase in the developing countries suggests the continuing relevance of the Malthusian principle. It is difficult to pass judgment on the current population debate as between these two principles; but from the standpoint of the environment, it is clear that every person that is born and survives in the world is a consumer of resources, products, and energy and, for that reason, that his or her presence on the earth is directly relevant to the environmental question.

Consumption   The economic growth (the production of wealth) and the growth of human population, taken together, make it inevitable that consumption will rise. Consumption, moreover, is directly linked to the exhaustion of the world's resources and to environmental damage. Even if consumption patterns are shifting more toward services in the aggregate, the absolute consumption of polluting products (automobiles, certain types of plastics) continues to increase as well. In the last analysis, whatever the relative contribution of producers and consumers to environmental damage, it remains the case that those countries that are high on both counts are also high on environmental damage. "OECD countries represent only 16 percent of the world's population . . . but they also account for about 72 percent of world gross product, 78 percent of all road vehicles and 50 percent of global energy use," (OECD 1991a: 13). Europe and North America account for 80 percent of the world's emissions of sulphur dioxide, nitrogen oxides, carbon monoxide, and hydrocarbons, which are the causes of acid rain and oxidant smog. One is not cheered, moreover, by the knowledge that the developed countries aspire to continue to improve their standards of living and that the developing countries aspire (at least) to reach the levels of the West.

The impacts of technology, economic growth, population, and consumption are distinguishable in their effects, but, taken together, they reveal the interrelatedness of even those four factors. They are all part of an economic *system*, each part of which has depended in complex ways on the others. A second systemic feature is that economies–the most direct links with the environment–are embedded systematically in *societies*, which give them the stamp of cultural legitimacy and provide their institutional infrastructure. By virtue of those connections, society is as heavily implicated in the problems of the environment as the economy, even though the social implications are often more indirect. We now turn to a number of questions that are central to the sociology of the environment.

Sociological Dimensions of Environmentalism

The first observation to be made is one ventured at the outset of this chapter: namely, that sociology of the environment is a field groping for its own identity. There are some subfields of sociology that are rooted in humanity's environmental realities – demography, social geography, social ecology, urban sociology (see chapter 1)–but many of these have existed outside "mainstream" sociology, and, in any event, they provide few guides for understanding the contemporary nature and magnitude of the environmental problems facing the world.

Part of the explanation for the neglect of environmental problems in sociology is historical. One of the major themes in the rise and consolidation of sociology has been its negative dialogue with individualistic, utilitarian economics. Sociology has represented the reassertion of the *collective* dimension of social life and, more particularly, has been critical of unregulated economic activity with regard to its social injustices (inequality, oppression, poverty), the social problems generated in an unregulated industrial-urban society, and the impoverishment of cultural values in a society based on individualistic materialism. In a word, sociology has been concerned with the *social* rather than the *natural* costs of capitalist industrial society. The concern of economists with environmentally damaging externalities is of relatively recent vintage (see Hardin 1968), and the focus of sociologists on waste and environmental damage has been late in developing as well. Both have been captives–even when critical–of the individualistic and material world view that engulfed Western society as a whole in the late eighteenth and nineteenth centuries.

With regard to the research on the sociology of the environment that has developed, what have been the foci? In a 1989 survey covering 359 European projects and 13 country reports, Gabrovska and colleagues (1989) reported the following areas of research:

- ethics, concepts, and methods of environmental research;
- description of environmental problems, impact of environmental pollution;
- environmental law and legislation;
- environmental policy;
- environmental management;
- environmental awareness, behavior, movements, and environmental delinquency;
- environmental education;
- environment and information.

In assessing this survey, Széll noted that it revealed a number of core topics and a certain continuity, but at the same time "a lack of imagination" (Széll 1992). If so, this should be attributed mainly to the condition of being a field seeking its bearings. Under such conditions, a field often displays a strong preoccupation with ethics, methodology, and practical applications. All of this is a sign, moreover, that concern with the relations between environment and society as a scholarly exercise is still undifferentiated, in large part, from the environmental "movement" itself. But despite the analytic nebulousness of the study of environment and society, we may note a number of emerging sociological foci.

Stratification and Environmental Issues

The first challenge for a sociology of stratification is to draw insights from the analysis of rank and class in society that relate to the environment. And within that assignment, the first task is to analyze the class dimensions of consumption. It is clear that in the upper reaches of the stratification systems of Western societies–and probably all societies–consumption of energy is unusually high, as manifested in the use of large automobiles, multiple automobiles, summer homes and retreats, and international leisure travel. Naturally enough, consumption drops off as income decreases, largely because of the inability to afford it, but the environmentally fatal factor is that individuals and groups lower down the income scale *aspire*, through the dynamics of fashion and striving for status, to participate in those forms of expenditure that are relatively wasteful and polluting. The environmental dimensions of products other than energy also merit close study and analysis.

The stratification system also yields interesting differences with respect to environmental consciousness. Though environmental concern is found in all strata of societies, it tends to be more concentrated in the upper and middle classes. This regularity has been noted by students of the "new social movements" (Eyerman 1992), which include the anti-nuclear, animal rights, and environmental protection movements. Hostility to environmental concerns clusters in lower income and rural groups (e.g., the "Pick-up Truck and Rifle" group in the United States). The reasons for this differential distribution are not clear, but class analysis might suggest at least one line of explanation. Environmental protection, involves, above all, the imposition of cleanup costs (often in the form of taxes) and increased costs for industrial production (most often passed on in the form of higher prices on products). Environmental concern thus might be regarded as a kind of luxury affordable (like George Bernard Shaw's middle-class morality) only by the better-off classes in the society.

Stratification is a relevant dimension at the international level as well. It was highlighted dramatically at the Earth Summit, an international meeting of heads of governments held in Rio de Janeiro in the summer of 1992. While important as a consciousness-raising event for the entire world, the summit was a failure in at least one respect: it was characterized by international wrangling, the expression of national interests, and mutual pointing of fingers (mainly in a northward and southward direction). Then President George Bush of the United States reflected the problem most dramatically, with his near-refusal to attend and his public assertion of the interests of American workers, but the entire aura of the meeting was somewhat acrimonious. In effect, the sense of global seriousness of the environmental situation was a victim, in part at least, of the parochial interests of nations.

The actual global situation is very complex and does not permit any simple assignment of blame or responsibility. As indicated earlier, economically more advanced nations clearly produce a higher proportion of environmental damage, if for no other reason than their sheer volume of consumption of resources and the associated waste. At the same time, and for good reasons, the movement for environmental protection and the implementation of environmental regulations are most advanced in the developed West. Furthermore, some of the most damaging specific polluting *practices* are found in the newly developing and less developed countries and in the former Communist and Socialist regimes of the Soviet Union and Eastern Europe. Again, however, much of the pollution and toxicity of the less developed countries can be attributed to the presence of international capitalism in these countries through the multinationals, whose corporate headquarters are based in developed Western societies. Yet the governments of the developing societies often cooperate, as it were, with international capital by doing little to control the polluting and toxifying effects of enterprises in their countries. The environmental problem, in short, is a global problem, with little to be gained by a simple assignment of blame.

The kind of class analysis mentioned in connection with environmental efforts *within* countries might be applied at the international level as well. The international economic arena is the site, above all, of a struggle, with the developed nations interested in maintaining their economic hegemony and the less developed nations struggling for short-term survival and long-term parity. Given this competitive struggle, neither class of nations is interested in assuming the additional costs involved in environmental protection and cleanup. But Western societies, simultaneously the worst environmental offenders and the richest, are better able to afford the more enlightened policies that are found in those societies.

The State-Economy Complex in the Culture of Modernity

Eisenstadt (1992) has put forcefully the argument that the culture of "modernity" is now so widespread as to constitute a "new civilization." By this he does not mean simply that Western ideas have spread and that all developing societies aspire to be like the West (as argued in some strands of modernization theory in the 1950s and 1960s). The culture of modernity is always adapted to the traditions and circumstances of different nations. However, it does include a drive for economic growth and an improvement in standard of living, a commitment to mobilize the relevant sectors of the populations to that end, and an effort to construct an institutional infrastructure to achieve both those ends. Such goals must be worked out, as indicated, in the context of the international economy, so a competitive dimension is always present in implementing the culture of modernity.

The state governments and elites of virtually all nations of the world are committed to the implementation of this culture of modernity. This does not bode well for the environmental future of the world, for three reasons. First, it sets the entire world on a spiral of further economic modernization, which is, generally speaking, a major systemic factor in the deterioration of the world's environment. Second, because most environmental problems are not individual-actor but rather national or *system* concerns (or public externalities, to use the economists' term), the state as the concretization of "the public" is the favored candidate to take leadership in environmental reform. But the commitment to the culture of modernity pushes states in the contrary direction of the most effective and competitive roads to economic growth. Third, because most environmental problems are global in character, the internationally competitive stance in which most nations are placed by virtue of their commitment to the culture of modernity means that individual nations are not predisposed to cooperate with other nations in a collective assault on environmental problems. This line of reasoning points to the evident fact that long-term solutions of environmental problems rest on fundamental and global cultural changes.

Risk

Some additional work has been done along the lines of sketching the dominant characteristics of developed societies and tracing their implications for the environment. The work on risk in society is an example. At the theoretical level, Luhmann (1991) has argued that modern societies are characterized by a shift from danger to risk. Pre-modern societies were basically confronted with dangers–floods, famines, storms, and so forth– that were fundamentally beyond their control. Modern societies have learned to control these kinds of dangers to a significant degree (though not completely) through the development of transportation systems, storage facilities, and modern medicine. At the same time, these modern societies have constructed a technical and institutional order in which risk, including fatal risk, is built into social life. Along the same lines, Perrow (1984) has provided an analysis of high-risk systems (the best, but not the only, example is nuclear power), which have the characteristics of great technological complexity and "tight coupling," such that one technological failure spreads quickly to other areas. Despite all precautions, a certain minimal occurrence of accidents is inevitable in high-risk systems. In a related line of argument, Beck (1986) has argued that the distributional (class) conflicts of industrial society have been superseded by distinctive features of the distribution of risks in those societies (including risks of damage to the environment). While institutionalized risks are to some degree subject to measurement and control by scientific means, this is so only to an extent, and a degree of uncertainty always remains. In consequence, many conflicts in modern society are between expert personnel (who are often in "control" of risk situations and tend to underestimate risks) and potential risk victims (who feel powerless and tend to overestimate risks). In any event, the phenomenon of risk and its societal consequences is a promising line of inquiry in the sociology of the environment.

Social Movements

One facet of the sociology of the environment is the fact that much environmental concern takes the form of organized social movements, mostly national in character, which take environmental threats as the reason for their existence. Sometimes these are movements directed at specific targets–the movement against the use of nuclear energy, the animal rights movement, and specific movements protesting water pollution, air pollution, smoking (especially against secondary effects), and so on. Green parties are also based ultimately on environmental concerns, although they have become multi-issue in character and tend to participate more "inside" the political arena as political parties, rather than outside as social movements or political lobbies. Many other movements–such as the women's movement and the peace movement–have aims that are not primarily environmental in character but include such concerns (such as the environmental dangers emanating from radioactive nuclear arsenals). In addition, environmental movements may generate public hostility, which on occasion may take the form of an organized counter-movement. The Small Automobile Party in Switzerland, for example, had its origins as a kind of anti-green force but in the course of its development acquired other ingredients, such as an anti-immigrant ideology.

Environmental social movements are to be understood in the first instance as constituting a social force pitted against the threat of environmental degradation. In addition, they are like all other social movements in that they demand explanation in terms of their structural origins, their composition, their ideologies, their strategies and tactics, and their fate in relation to countermovements, state governments, and other agencies to which they typically orient their efforts. Sociologists are uniquely qualified to undertake analyses of these aspects of social movements. (In surveying research on environmental problems, Széll [1992] found most research to be interdisciplinary and that "for genuine sociological topics there is not much besides environmental movements.") One fascinating question is why pro-environmental mobilization into social movements is so relatively weak throughout the world, given the seriousness of the diverse threats to the world's environment. Adequate answers to this question are not available, but one suggestion may be found in that very direness: the thought that environmental destruction, exhaustion, and spoliation may be experienced as so overwhelming as to seem to lie beyond individual control and even beyond collective mobilization. From the point of view of participation, this may create a "no-rider" effect (parallel to the economists' "free-rider" effect), stemming from widespread feelings of helplessness, an effect that weakens the mobilizing power and effectiveness of environmental social movements.

One recent social movement study of interest is Joppke's (1993) comparative analysis of the movements against the peaceful use of nuclear energy in the United States and West Germany. Among Joppke's findings was the assimilation of the ideologies and strategies of the two movements to the political styles of the two countries, the American movement being more local, specific, and instrumental in goals, the German more state-oriented and philosophical. Both movements experienced internal splits but different ones: the American between public interest and direct action wings, the German between moderate citizen initiatives and radical anti-statist groups. Thus the nation and its culture exercise their influence in the arena of pro-environment movements, just as they do in the international conflicts over responsibility for environmental damage and its prevention and control.

Concluding Comment

The world's environmental situation and understanding and control thereof may well be in the process of gaining the dubious honor of parity with domestic instability and international war as threats to the human situation. Being of recent origin and being as complex in its causes and ramifications as it is, the world's environmental situation now defies systematic understanding and control more than these other threats. As such, it poses a special challenge to the study of environment and society, young as it is and peripheral as its subject matter has been to the history of the social sciences. This challenge is to redirect the tools of sociological analysis to the understanding of the special implications of different social organizations and societies for environmental destruction and its control.

References

Beck, U. 1986: *Risikogesellschaftr. Auf dem Weg eine ander Moderne*. Frankfurt: Suhrkamp.

Berger, J. 1994: "The Economy and the Environment." Forthcoming in N. J. Smelser and R. Swedberg (eds), *Handbook of Economic Sociology*, Princeton, N. J.: Princeton University Press and Russell Sage Foundation.

Bernal, J. D. 1969: *Science in History*, 4th edn. London: C. A. Watts.

Braverman, H. 1974: *Labor and Monopoly Capital*. New York: Monthly Review Press.

Eisenstadt, S. N. 1992: "A Reappraisal of Theories of Social Change and Modernization," in H. Haferkamp and N. J. Smelser (eds), *Social Change and Modernity*, Berkeley, Calif.: University of California Press, 412–29.

Eyerman, R. 1992: "Modernity and Social Movements," in Haferkamp and Smelser (eds), *Social Change and Modernity*, 37–54.

Gabrovska, S., Schwefel, E. and Marks, A. 1989: *Environment and Society. A Documentation of Current Research 1986–1988*. Vienna: European Coordination

Center for Research and Documentation in Social Sciences and Sofia: Scientific Information Center of the Bulgarian Academy of Sciences.

Gehlen, A. 1957: *Die Seele im technischen Zeitalter. Sozialpsychologische Probleme in der industriellen Gesellschaft*. Reinbek: Rowohlt.

Giedion, S. 1948: *Mechanization Takes Command*. Oxford: Oxford University Press.

Goodland, J., Daly, N., Elserafy, S., and Von Droste B. (eds) 1991: *Environmentally Sustainable Economic Development: Building on Brundtland*. Paris: UNESCO.

Hardin, G. 1968: "The Tragedy of the Commons." *Science*, 162: 1243–7.

Heller, F., Pusic, E., Reynaud, J.-D., Strauss, G. and Wilpert, B. (eds): 1989–93: *International Handbook of Participation in Organizations. For the Study of Organizational Cooperation and Self-management*. 3 vols. Oxford: Oxford University Press.

Immler, H. 1985: *Natur in der okonomischen Theorie*. Opladen: Westdeutscher Verlag.

Joppke, C. 1993: *Mobilizing against Nuclear Energy: A Comparison of Germany and the United States*. Berkeley, Calif.: University of California Press.

Landes, D. 1968: *The Unbound Prometheus. Technological Change and Industrial Development in Western Europe from 1750 to the Present*. Cambridge: Cambridge University Press.

Leipert, C. 1989: *Die heimlichen Kosten des Fortschritts*. Frankfurt: S. Fischer.

Luhmann, N. 1991: *Soziologie des Risikos*. Berlin: de Gruyter.

Mayo, E. 1945: *The Social Problems of an Industrial Civilization*. Cambridge, Mass.: Harvard University Press.

Meadows, D., Zahn, E. and Milling, P. 1972: *The Limits to Growth*. New York: Universe Books.

Muller, N. 1989–91: *Civilization Dynamics: Fundamentals of a Model Oriented Description*. 2 vols. Aldershot: Avebury.

Mumford, L. 1967: *The Myth of the Machine*. New York: Harcourt, Brace, Jovanovich.

OECD, 1991a: *Environmental Policy: How to Apply Economic Instruments*. Paris Cedex: OECD Publications.

OECD, 1991b: *The State of the Environment*. Paris Cedex: OECD Publications.

Perrow, C. 1984: *Normal Accidents: Living with High-Risk Technologies*. New York: Basic Books.

Piore, M. J. and Sabel, C. F. 1984: *The Second Industrial Divide: Possibilities for Prosperity*. New York: Basic Books.

Széll, G. 1988: *Participation, Worker's Control and Self-Management*. London: Sage Publications. (*Current Sociology*, 36.)

Széll, G. 1991: " 'Environment and Society' or 'Environmental Sociology'? In Search of a Paradigm." Presidential Address to the Thematic Group on "Environment and Society" of the International Sociological Association. Osnabrück: Universität Osnabrück.

Széll, G. (ed.) 1992: *Concise Encyclopaedia of Participation and Co-Management*. Berlin and New York: de Gruyter.

Taylor, F. W. 1967 [1911]: *The Principles of Scientific Management*. New York: Harper and Row.

Womack, P., Jones, D. T. and Roos, D. 1990: *The Machine that Changed the World*. New York: Rawson Associates.

World Bank, 1992: *World Development Report 1992. Development and the Environment*. Oxford: Oxford University Press.

12

Population in Its Social Context

Whether regarded as a set of groups or as all of humankind, population is the biological substrate, the vehicle for all human society. It is evident, furthermore, that the size, composition, reproduction, mortality, and movements of population groups are interdependent on–that is, are simultaneously cause and effect of–the formation of humans into organized society. Yet the field of demography (the study of populations) is ambivalent on this score of interdependency. On the one hand, demographers seek to locate formal relations among variables such as fertility and population growth and, if possible, to express them in mathematical terms. On the other hand, they are also aware of the inherently interdisciplinary character of their field, which links it to economic processes such as the distribution of wealth and sociological concerns such as family arrangements, stratification systems, and the social policies of nation-states. Demography is also centrally involved in the study of environmental issues (see chapter 11). The interplay of demographic and sociological forces will be a recurrent theme in this chapter.

Historically speaking, scholarly, scientific concern with population issues is a relatively recent development. Its inception is usually identified with the mathematical work of John Graunt in the seventeenth century and the socioeconomic concerns articulated by Thomas Malthus in the eighteenth. But administrative and practical concerns with population go back further. Population records were maintained for imperial Rome during the early Christian era and for ancient China in roughly the same period. The establishment of a decennial census in the early history of the United States was explicitly linked with the need to determine voting districts on the basis of numbers in the young democracy. Current

This chapter is based on a contribution of Sudha Shreeniwas.

preoccupation with population issues is closely linked to the spectacular rates of growth of human populations in the twentieth century, particularly as these relate to questions of poverty and the world's environmental crises. Figure 12.1 shows the contours of long-term changes in human population numbers and growth rates. It indicates that while an upswing in rates of growth can be seen in the mid-eighteenth century, the Malthusian potential for human populations to increase by geometric progression is fully visible only in the twentieth century.

According to Coale's (1974) analysis, the history of human population growth in the common era can be divided into two periods:

- a long era of very slow growth from A.D. 1 to 1750, during which the period required for a doubling of the world's population was approximately 1,200 years; it is presumed that similar patterns prevailed before A.D. 1, though documentation is very scanty for the earlier periods;
- a short period of rapid growth from about 1750 to the present, during which the doubling time of the world's population was 34.7 years.

The mathematics of the recent growth are staggering. The average annual growth rate of the population from A.D. 1 to 1750 was approximately 0.36 per 1,000, as contrasted with the current rate of 20 per 1,000. The latter rate is the highest in history and evidently cannot continue indefinitely. If it should, the world's population would grow over the next 700 years to a density of one person for each square foot of space on the earth's surface, a result clearly incompatible with the sustenance of human life on earth.

The world's current population situation is a matter of concern to both scholars and the general public. Because of the evident importance of population growth, scholarship has focused mainly on fertility and mortality, the principal determinants of that growth. Migration, or shifts of groups from one area to another, is also a major topic of investigation. In the nineteenth century sociologists were little concerned with issues of population size and growth, concentrating instead on social institutions and social integration and disorganization, as well as societal evolution. In the twentieth century, however, more sociologists have turned to demographic issues. The main bases for this growth of interest have been the emergence of social problems–including urban crowding, the emptying out of rural areas, and poverty–associated with demographic change, the failure of many efforts on the part of states to formulate and implement population policies, and the evident importance of institutional (e.g., family) and cultural (e.g., religious) factors in the determination of demographic behavior. More recently, sociological demographers have entered into new areas of inquiry, such as those of gender and reproduction rights, social conflict arising from migration of groups, and the epidemiology of diseases such as AIDS (see chapter 3). Needless to say, most sociological/demographic research is directly related to both policy and moral concerns in society.

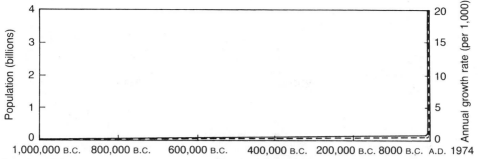

Overview of the human population, from the emergence of man about a million years ago to the present, emphasizing the dichotomous nature of man's history. On this scale the size of the population (*solid line*) and the annual rate of increase (*dashed line*) are seen to have been constant for almost the entire period and then to have risen almost vertically in recent years.

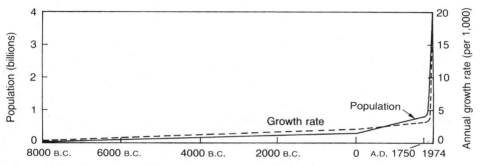

The introduction of agriculture some 10,000 years ago marks the beginning of a period that represents about 1 percent of the period illustrated above. Even in this much briefer time span, however, the rate of population increase was modest until a few centuries ago, when it started to rise very rapidly.

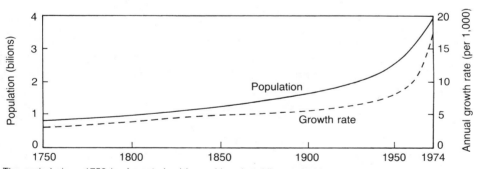

The period since 1750 is characterized by rapid and rapidly accelerating growth in the size of the world population. This period represents only about 0.02 percent of man's history, yet 80 percent of the increase in the population has occured in it. Moreover within this period, the rate of increase has climbed most dramatically in very recent times, doubling in the past 25 years.

Figure 12.1 Overview of human population history, from the emergence of man about a million years ago to the present (*top*). On this scale, the size of the population (*solid line*) and the annual rate of increase (*broken line*) are seen to have been constant for almost the entire period and then to have risen almost vertically in recent years. The introduction of agriculture some 10,000 years ago marks the beginning of a period (*middle*) that represents about 1 percent of the period illustrated at the top. But even in this much briefer time span, the rate of population increase was modest until a few centuries ago, when it started to rise very rapidly. The period since 1750 (*bottom*) is characterized by rapid and rapidly accelerating growth in the size of the world population. It represents only about 0.02 percent of man's history, yet 80 percent of the increase in population has occurred in it, climbing most dramatically in very recent times and doubling in the past 25 years. *Source*: Coale 1974: 16

This chapter is organized into three parts: first, fertility and mortality patterns as major factors in the growth and composition of population; second, some issues concerning marriage, the family, and gender; and third, migration processes.

Fertility

The Demographic Transition

The principal account of the population history of the developed regions is known "as the demographic transition". It is linked to a distinctive theory of economic and social development. The argument goes as follows. Traditional societies are marked by high birth and death rates, resulting in low rates of population growth. The "transition" itself is one of declining death rates but continuing high birth rates, a combination which produces very rapid rates in growth. The transition comes to an end with a decline in fertility rates and continued low mortality rates, with population growth rates becoming low or in some cases negative. Consistent with the theory, most developed nations now have low fertility and mortality rates. Many of the newly industrialized nations in eastern and southeastern Asia have recently completed the transition, though the timing and extent of the process have shown great variation. Other less developed and developing nations can presumably be located somewhere in the transition phase.

The two most interesting aspects of the theory of the demographic transition are the causes of the declines in mortality and fertility rates, respectively. There appears to be a consensus that various improvements associated with increased economic growth and productivity–improved diet, hygiene, and sanitation and better medical services and disease control–are responsible for declines in mortality.

Explanations of the decline in birth rates are less well established, but the dominant ones are rooted in a theory of the societal change that accompanies the process of modernization. This process, the argument goes, involves the transformation of a largely agrarian, nonmonetized, illiterate, stable society into an urban, industrialized, formally educated, constantly changing one. Changes in work and schooling patterns render the bearing and raising of large numbers of children economically unfeasible, because the latter do not produce family income and have to be supported during long periods of schooling before entering the work force. Furthermore, increasing opportunities for women outside the home (mainly in the work force) lower their propensity to bear and rear children. All these forces combine to produce lower birth rates.

However, this account of the demographic transition as an aspect of a presumably universal process of modernization has some evident short-comings. First, the late nineteenth-century demographic transition in the developed countries did not uniformly accompany economic development but preceded it in some cases; furthermore, some of the current demographic changes in the less developed areas of the world are occurring in the absence of prior economic development. Second, some of the developed countries have experienced fertility rates that are far below replacement level, resulting in negative growth rates. Thus we have two puzzles as regards fertility behavior: persisting high fertility in the developing regions and excessively low fertility in some developed countries.

Persisting High Fertility in Developing Areas

Asia and sub-Saharan Africa continue to experience very high fertility rates. The total fertility rate (TFR, or number of children born to an average woman during her reproductive span) in India is now 4.2, contributing to an annual population growth rate of 2.2 percent, on a population base of approximately 850 million. (The figure represents a drop from more than 6 in the 1960s but is still very high.) Pakistan, Bangladesh, and Nepal also have very high TFRs. Similarly, in Africa, most nations currently show TFRs of 4–6 children per woman. UN projections made in 1984 reveal a world population increase of 800 million people per decade from 1985 through 2005, with 90 percent of the increase occurring in the less developed regions, especially Asia and Africa. Why high fertility persists in these regions, while it has fallen in countries such as Sri Lanka, constitutes a demographic and sociological riddle.

China, the demographic giant of the world, has attained much lower fertility rates than India. By 1984 its TFR had dropped to about 2.3, and it now fluctuates somewhat around that level. This implies a fertility rate close to replacement level in the long run. (In most societies, replacement of population calls for about 2.1 births per couple or per woman.) However, because of past high fertility, China has a large proportion of women currently of childbearing age, with the result that absolute numbers of children born continue to be large. China's current population of 1.1 billion is thus expected to climb to approximately 1.57 billion before stabilizing.

Interpretations of these sustained increases in population vary. On the optimistic side, some scholars and policymakers argue that population pressures in these countries will spur technological innovations that will enable societies to cope with these numbers and make progress in their efforts to overcome poverty and improve standards of living. (Defenders of this position point to historical examples in the West.) The pessimistic–and more widely held–interpretation is that world population increases will overwhelm technological efforts to contend with them and will continue to have a negative impact on resources, environment, and the quality of life (see chapter 11).

The major question requiring explantion, however, remains why fertility rates have remained high in some developing areas while falling in others.

Empirical studies have revealed that the main reasons why people want and have children vary across cultures and socioeconomic strata; among the reasons given are that children provide psychological or spiritual satisfaction or that they will provide economic support for parents in their old age. Any adequate explanation of fertility behavior, however, must include both an account of these reasons and an account of the cultural and institutional characteristics underlying them.

Researchers seeking explanations for fertility change have expressed dissatisfaction with accounts given or implied by the theory of demographic transition; that is, those tying fertility behavior to macro-economic developmental forces. The Princeton European Fertility Project has questioned the link between economic developmental factors and demographic behavior in the historical experience of Europe, and this link also seems tenuous in contemporary developing countries. An alternative explanation emerging from the project is a cultural one: that the transition to lower fertility occurred in areas sharing a culture or language, not necessarily in regions experiencing industrialization or modernization. This in turn has led to the argument that controlled fertility involves a behavioral innovation that is diffused most rapidly among groups that can communicate among themselves and whose culture or world view is not antagonistic to such an innovation (Cleland and Wilson 1987). This cultural line of thinking has received support from studies in Thailand, which trace its decline in fertility (in the 1970s, when the country was less developed than it is today) to a religious tradition that was not inimical to family planning and a social climate in which women's status and autonomy were relatively high (Knodel *et al.* 1984). Other scholars have argued that declines in fertility in developing regions are associated with the spread of Western ideologies, including a mass consumption culture and the notion of individualistic family relationships.

Other lines of explanation derive from reasoning that attempts to specify economic reasons why such behavioral innovations as restricting the number of children might arise in the first place. The main argument is that decisions to bear children depend on parents' weighing of the costs and benefits of children versus the costs or inconveniences of controlling fertility. The aggregated results of these decisions constitute the demand side for children in a society. The supply side is a function of the biological capacity to bear children, plus any practices that might affect this capacity (e.g., abstinence, contraception) (see Bulatao and Lee 1987). Such an emphasis points to population policies that would affect individuals' decisions, policies such as a well-designed family welfare and planning program.

In a related line of reasoning, Coale (1991) identified three conditions for the transition to controlled fertility: first, the society must perceive it as advantageous; second, the means (e.g., contraception) must be available; and third, these means must be morally and practically acceptable to its members. Caldwell (1982) argued that as long as the flow of services and benefits between generations is greater from children to parents, high fertility will persist. If the flow is in the other direction–as, for example, when the costs of formal schooling are significant–parents will devise ways to have fewer children.

What are the kinds of costs and benefits that come into play in fertility behavior? The broadest factors in the equation are cultural. Research in many regions of sub-Saharan Africa (Caldwell *et al.* 1993) reveals that the family structure is predicated on the need for several children to perpetuate the lineage or clan. In these societies women also derive their sense of identity through motherhood. Predictably, the majority of them disapprove of any efforts to curtail childbearing.

Within these broad cultural contours, more particular costs and benefits are relevant. For example, in some African societies, couples who bear children often send them to relatives or friends who may be able to provide them with greater benefits than the natural parents can (Bledsoe 1990). Later in their lives these parents may take in others' children for care. This spreading of the burdens of child-rearing through a wider circle of kin and others lowers the costs of children, in effect. In addition, it is often perceived that bearing *many* children constitutes a hedge against economic and emotional insecurity of parents in their older years.

In some South Asian countries many couples have a preference for more than one surviving son, a preference that has obvious implications for high fertility. Sons are important for family labor and for the support of parents in old age. Indian kinship traditions mandate that daughters leave the home and require a dowry for marriage and that only sons can carry on the family name. Uncertain prospects of child survival also contribute to the desire for many sons. As for women, they tend to define their identity in terms of their roles as mothers and to lack autonomy in making decisions, including reproductive decisions, that affect their lives. Thus the economic value of children, the low status of women, and the preference for sons conspire to produce both high fertility and high female child mortality in many regions of South Asia (Dyson and Moore 1983, Miller 1981).

Such are some of the microeconomic and cultural institutional factors that have come to supplement, if not replace, the macroeconomic explanations contained in demographic transition theory.

Very Low Fertility in Developed Societies

For the past two or three decades, many industrialized nations of the world–the United States, Australia, New Zealand, Japan, and a number of Northern and Western European countries–have been experiencing unprecedentedly low rates of population growth, associated mainly with extremely low fertility rates. Table 12.1 shows the TFRs of 34 nations in this category. In 1965 only East Germany and Rumania were experiencing

Table 12.1 Levels and trends, total fertility rates, 1965–1989, of low-fertility regions

Major area, region and country or area	1965	1970	1975	1980	1985	1986	1987	1988	1989
Asia									
Hong Kong	4.93	3.31	2.75	2.06	1.47	1.35	1.29	1.36	–
Japan	2.15	2.10	1.93	1.74	1.74	1.69	1.67	1.64	1.57
Republic of Korea	4.67	4.07	3.23	2.70	1.68[a]	1.55	–	–	–
Singapore	4.62	3.10	2.11	1.74	1.62	1.48	1.65	1.98	–
Europe									
Eastern Europe									
Bulgaria	2.08	2.18	2.24	2.06	1.98	2.02	1.95	–	–
Czechoslovakia	2.37	2.07	2.46	2.15	2.06	2.02	1.98	2.02	1.95
German Democratic Republic	2.45	2.17	1.55	1.97	1.76	1.72	1.75	1.67	1.80
Hungary	1.81	1.97	2.38	1.93	1.83	1.83	1.81	1.79	–
Poland	2.52	2.23	2.27	2.28	2.33	2.22	2.15	–	–
Rumania	1.91	2.85	2.62	2.45	2.26	2.40	2.39	2.31	2.20
Northern Europe									
Denmark	2.61	1.95	1.92	1.54	1.45	1.48	1.50	1.56	1.62
Finland	2.47	1.83	1.69	1.63	1.64	1.60	1.59	1.59	–
Ireland	4.03	3.87	3.40	3.23	2.50	2.44	2.32	2.17	2.11
Norway	2.93	2.51	1.99	1.73	1.68	1.71	1.74	1.84	–
Sweden	2.41	1.94	1.78	1.68	1.73	1.79	1.84	1.96	2.02
United Kingdom	2.84	2.41	1.78	1.87	1.79	1.77	1.82	1.84	1.85
Southern Europe									
Greece	2.25	2.40	2.32	2.23	1.68	1.62	1.52	1.52	1.50
Italy	2.60	2.38	2.17	1.64	1.41	1.34	1.32	1.34	1.29
Portugal	3.07	2.62	2.59	2.06	1.70	1.63	1.56	1.53	–
Spain	2.96	2.85	2.79	2.18	1.63	1.54	–	1.38	1.30
Yugoslavia	2.70	2.29	2.28	2.14	2.04	2.01	2.00	1.98	–
Western Europe									
Austria	2.70	2.29	1.82	1.65	1.48	1.46	1.44	1.46	1.46
Belgium	2.60	2.25	1.74	1.69	1.51	1.55	1.55	1.56	1.58
France	2.81	2.47	1.94	1.95	1.83	1.84	1.82	1.83	1.81
Germany, Federal Republic of	2.51	1.99	1.45	1.45	1.29	1.35	1.38	1.40	1.39
Luxembourg	2.43	1.96	1.52	1.50	1.40	1.44	1.41	1.54	1.52
Netherlands	3.03	2.58	1.67	1.60	1.51	1.55	1.56	1.55	1.55
Switzerland	2.61	2.12	1.62	1.55	1.52	1.53	1.52	1.58	–
North America									
Canada	3.07	2.26	1.82	1.71	1.63	1.63	1.62	–	–
United States of America	2.91	2.47	1.77	1.83	1.84	1.83	1.86	1.93	–
Oceania									
Australia	2.96	2.86	2.22	1.92	1.89	1.87	1.85	1.84	–
New Zealand	3.56	3.16	2.33	2.05	1.93	2.02	2.03	2.09	2.10
Soviet Union	2.46[b]	2.39[c]	2.39[d]	2.25[c]	2.46[f]	2.53[g]	2.53	2.45	–

[a] Refers to 1984. [b] Refers to 1965–66. [c] Refers to 1969–70. [d] Refers to 1975–76. [e] Refers to 1980–1. [f] Refers to 1985–6. [g] Refers to 1986–7.

Source: United Nations, *Patterns of Fertility in Low Fertility Settings.* New York: United Nations, p. 7, table 1.

below-replacement fertility rates (TFRs of less than 2.1). By 1988 only Rumania, Ireland, and the Soviet Union still had above-replacement fertility (the Rumanian upswing may have resulted from a strong governmental pro-natalist policy). All other nations, though fluctuating, exhibited an overall downward trend. According to Bourgeois-Pichat (1986) north central Italy reached a TFR of 1.28 in 1983, the lowest ever recorded for a human population.

These developments have set off reactions of alarm, even fears of extinction, based on "population implosion" of these regions. Such reactions are associated with fears that these nations may be swamped by migrants from high-fertility regions, which raise more direct fears of immigrants taking jobs away from natives, as well as the aggravation of already serious ethnic conflicts. Other apprehensions include fear of the "dependency burden," which increases as populations gain larger proportions of persons of old age, a burden which in turn raises serious questions about taxation policy and old-age security schemes. At the same time, attempts to reverse the pattern through pro-natalist policies seem possible only by authoritarian means, which infringe on individual liberties, especially of women, or by incentive systems that governments soon discover become very costly.

While most accounts of declining fertility still reside in the moderniza-tion paradigm, some scholars have developed different views, though these are not always directly opposed to modernization. Taking a long-term perspective, Davis (1986) noted that while below-replacement fertility is unprecedented, low fertility itself is not unknown in early history. Extrapolating from the reproductive patterns of twentieth-century hunting-and-gathering populations (such as the Dobe !Kung and some groups in Australia), he argued that women in such groups typically have such a low body fat proportion as to inhibit ovulation. Davis also ventured the functionalist argument that the presence and care of many dependent children constitutes a liability in such societies, in light of the fact that care-givers (typically mothers) were gatherers of food. The development of settled agriculture, by contrast, encouraged higher fertility, because of improved food supplies, and necessitated it, because of increased labor requirements. In modern times, sociocultural, technological, and organiza-tional changes have provided the main evolutionary advantage, and, as a result, it is no longer necessary to rely on the highest possible fertility to balance death rates.

Other scholars have concentrated more specifically on the twentieth century. In doing so, they often rely on a demographic distinction between two types of determinants of fertility behavior and rates:

- Proximate determinants (Bongaarts 1982), behavioral and biological determi-nants that impinge directly on fertility. These include exposure to the likelihood of conception, conception itself, gestation, and childbirth. Factors affecting low fertility would be the development of effective contraception, a rising age at first marriage and bearing the first child, increasing proportions of women not marrying, and increasing rates of divorce.

● More remote determinants, which lie in the broader social transformations that influence low fertility. These would include the progress of industrialization as it affects family organization and the costs and benefits of childbearing, changes in women's roles and status, and changes in societal values such as the rise of a philosophy of individualism and cultural conceptions of parenthood and childhood.

Demographers tend to agree that contemporary marriage patterns are the primary cause of most societies' low fertility rates. Although nonmarital sexual activity and out-of-wedlock births have both risen, total fertility itself has fallen. The logic behind this is that if people are unwilling to commit themselves to marriage, they are also likely to be less willing to commit themselves to parenthood; for example, in the United States in 1965 (the peak year of nonmarital fertility), the TFR for unmarried women was only 0.71. But there is a need to focus directly on the characteristics of marriage as well, since in many societies with low fertility (Japan, Hong Kong, Singapore, and Korea), only a small proportion of adults are unmarried.

Evidently, total time spent in marriage is an important determinant of fertility. Between 1960 and 1985, the proportion of women between 20 and 24 in the United States who remained unmarried rose from 30 to 50 percent and the percentage of such women between 25 and 29 rose from 10 to 20 percent (Westoff 1986). (The "baby boom" between the mid-1940s and the early 1960s was the result of a kind of historical "blip" in these trends, as women married earlier and in higher proportions.) The very high rates of divorce also influence time spent in marriage. Divorces in the United States rose from 11 to 23 per 1,000 married couples between 1968 and 1981; the corresponding figures for Denmark were 5 to 12 per 1,000 (see also chapter 19). Taken together, marriage postponement and marriage dissolution rates conspire to make the time spent in marriage unprecedentedly low.

The greater availability of means to lower fertility is also a major consideration. The pill was introduced in the 1960s, and most countries experiencing low fertility rates have also seen a switch to more effective methods of contraception (chemical means rather than barrier methods such as condoms). In addition, the 1970s witnessed the legalization of abortion in many nations of the world.

In the discussion of high fertility in less developed countries we noted two important factors: the economic cost of children and the status of women. Both factors operate in industrialized nations as well. In many countries the costs of preschool and school-age child care for working women are high, given the level of women's wages (Presser 1986). Education and health-care costs for children are considerable; children do not work, as a rule; and parents have come to rely less on children in their older years as formal old-age security systems have become institutionalized. In addition, the vastly increasing participation of women in the labor force is a hallmark of advanced industrialized societies. This circumstance has given women viable alternatives for self-definition beyond being wives and mothering a family. In Melbourne in 1967, 78 percent of married women between 18 and 34 agreed with the statement that "whatever career a woman may have, her most important role in life is that of becoming a mother"; in 1982 only 46 percent agreed. In 1962, 84 percent of a cohort of Detroit mothers agreed that "almost all married women who can, ought to have children," compared to a figure of only 43 percent in 1983 (Preston 1986b).

Preston (1986a) insists that arguments based on changes in economic organization, women's status, and contraceptive technology do not tell the whole story. Fertility in many regions of Europe declined historically irrespective of economic development; furthermore, fertility declines in the twentieth century have spread across all socioeconomic strata. Preston suggested as another factor fundamental changes in ideas and values that spread through regions that shared cultural characteristics. Among these was the elaboration of the idea of "responsible parenthood." This idea goes back several centuries, and is found in expectations that people not marry until they can support a family properly. Its twentieth-century manifestation, however, stresses the rearing of "high-quality," physically and emotionally healthy, well-educated children; the corresponding expectation is that parents should have fewer children so that they can be better parents.

An interesting special case is that of Japan, where fertility decline has been steep and has occurred at a lower level of economic development. According to Kono (1986), factors important in Europe and America, such as the spread of feminism or individualist philosophies, were not strong in Japan. On the contrary, women's participation in the labor force has always been low and varies over the life course to accommodate child-raising. In Japan, the perception of acute shortages of resources, including land and housing, and a strong, competitive emphasis on formal educational qualifications has made raising children an expensive and tension-filled experience. Kono also mentioned the "conformist" nature of Japanese society, which encouraged the spread of the small family norm among all classes.

Mortality

The demographic transition theory, summarized above, posits declining mortality rates in periods of industrial development, associated with improved hygiene and sanitation and medical discoveries and innovations. Originally, towns and cities had higher mortality rates because of crowded, unsanitary conditions; correspondingly, most of the innovations were developed and implemented in urban areas, with rural areas lagging behind. Mortality has by now reached low levels–albeit with significant variations–in all the more developed countries. The experience of developing regions has been somewhat different. In them economic development did not accompany or precede declines in mortality; instead, health technologies were generally transferred from the more developed regions, first to urban regions.

Another facet of the worldwide decline in mortality is that termed the "epidemiological transition" (Omran, 1982). This refers to a shift from the prevalence of infectious diseases that earlier characterized morbidity to the predominance of degenerative diseases. Initially, a decline in mortality depends on the control of infectious diseases. As more of the population survives to older ages, however, a higher proportion die from degenerative diseases, such as heart disease and cancer. Another seemingly paradoxical feature of the epidemiological transition is that as mortality declines, morbidity rises. This is explained, however, by the fact that in the past high mortality culled out the weaker members of society. Now, such individuals survive longer but tend to remain ill or hospitalized for longer periods, which drives up morbidity rates. Also, degenerative diseases tend to have a longer course of development before death than infectious ones, a circumstance which also contributes to increased morbidity.

Social scientists have come increasingly to appreciate that, beyond biological factors, behavior plays a central role as a determinant of mortality and morbidity. The established relationship between smoking and many kinds of cancer is the most obvious example. In many cases these behavioral factors are in turn affected by socioeconomic factors such as sex, class, and ethnicity. For example, the leading cause of death for white males aged 20–4 in the United States is vehicular accidents; for black males in the same age-group, homicide is number one. In the remainder of this section we consider two kinds of mortality that are clearly behavior-related: female mortality and AIDS.

The "Missing Women" of Asia

As a general rule, a normal population tends toward a sex ratio slightly in favor of females. There is a global pattern of male dominant sex ratio at birth (approximately 106 males to every 100 females born). However, mortality is typically higher for males than for females in every age-group, with the result that at a certain point females come to predominate. The overall sex ratio of a population depends on the age at which this "crossover" occurs and the proportion of the population above and below that age (Coale 1991). The sex ratio may also be affected by sex-specific migration patterns–for example, males from less developed countries migrating to find jobs in more developed countries. However, a persistent and abnormally high male sex ratio usually implies that large numbers of women are "missing," either because they have died or because they have not been counted for various reasons. At the present time, China, South Asia (India and Pakistan), and some regions of Western Asia exhibit abnormally high male sex ratios.

China   In China, the sex ratio at birth, according to the 1990 census, was the expected 106 to 100. However, among those aged 0–4, the ratio is 110.4 to 100. Johansson and Nygren (1991) have demonstrated that the death rate in China reveals an excess of female deaths as compared to the normal global figure of approximately 130 male deaths to 100 female deaths before the age of 1. The trend in China now accounts for approximately four deaths per 1,000 live-born girls, and appears to be increasing over time. Accordingly, the sex ratio among surviving children in China is also more male-dominant than that of other societies.

In the search for explanations, it must first be noted that traditionally Chinese culture favored sons. They were necessary for carrying on the family name in the patriarchal and patrilineal Confucian family tradition. Daughters "married out" and became part of their husbands' families. In addition, sons were expected to care for their parents in old age. This cultural pattern has persisted through vast social and cultural changes. Especially under conditions of declining mortality, families act to ensure that children who are born are male. The pressure to keep fertility low results in a family-building strategy that focuses on the birth and survival of male children.

Demographers have observed that current demographic trends in China–especially fertility declines–have been affected more strongly by government policies than by forces of modernization (Bongaarts and Greenhalgh 1985, Wolf 1986). Early attempts at control began in the 1950s, and family planning programs had been established in urban areas by 1963. The 1970s witnessed governmental campaigns whose slogan was "Later, longer, fewer'–that is, delayed marriage, longer intervals between births, and a total of two children per woman. During this period the TFR plunged from 5.7 to 2.7 and is now about 2.3. A one-child policy was promulgated in 1979, though its enforcement, especially in rural areas, was sporadic. In 1984 the difficulties of uniform enforcement were tacitly recognized in a policy known as Document 7, which permitted certain categories of persons a second child–for example, rural residents after a few years' wait (in recognition of their need for familial labor) and some groups where the first child was a daughter. In this way, the preference for sons was incorporated into government policy, even though the official position of the government was to discourage the idea.

The combination of strict governmental fertility controls and a continuing pattern of preference for males has intensified the problem of the "missing girls of China." Estimates of the total number of such girls range from 60 million (Coale 1991) to 100 million (Sen 1989). Approximately half the "missing" girls may have been adopted by other families, while misreporting and excess female mortality probably account for the rest (Johansson and Nygren 1991). In any event, the problem is growing in significance and raises issues of population composition, the role of the state in population policy, gender stratification, and human rights.

India   The figures for India show an increasing male sex ratio over time, as follows:

1901	104.8
1921	105.8
1941	105.7
1961	106.2
1981	106.9
1991	107.2

Regional patterns are striking; northern India exhibits ratios that are higher than the national average, whereas in southern India sex ratios are more equitable. The state of Kerala, India's demographic showpiece, is the only one in which female-dominant sex ratios have been the norm, even when male outmigration is discounted.

Like China, India has cultural traditions that place a high value on sons, to carry on the family name and support parents in old age and because of the dowry expenses for daughters who marry. Development in India appears to have aggravated gender inequalities. Males, who receive higher education than females, have more opportunities to participate in the increasingly urban-based economy than females. Ideas about the seclusion of women and traditional attitudes which see women as workers within the home also discourage families from sending girls to school. All this tends to drive up the value of men in Indian society. In fact, the higher rates of excess female mortality are found in districts with higher levels of development, as measured by conventional indicators. Observers have long noted fatal neglect of female children, female feticide (associated with the introduction of the technology of amniocentesis), and sometimes outright female infanticide in the north; and scattered reports of female infanticide in poor and isolated communities are now appearing in south India.

Even increased education for women appears to have an adverse effect on the infant mortality of females. DasGupta (1987) has shown that in agrarian Punjab, a society with marked son-preference and gender stratification, increasing maternal education and lowered fertility raises mortality among daughters, especially among later births. Mothers who have some education and who wish to control their fertility still feel the need to bear sons rather than daughters, it appears. The preference for sons shows up in birth-order figures as well. In Bangladesh, later-born girls have a greater risk of dying if they have older sisters, while all girls are at greater risk than boys. Only if there are already several sons in the family do boys exhibit greater chances of mortality (Muhuri and Menken 1993).

Behavioral Factors in AIDS

The global AIDS conference in Berlin revealed a grim statistic: 14 million cases of HIV infection worldwide and the number growing. In Western countries the AIDS phenomenon appears to be approaching the Black Death of medieval Europe in the public imagination. Among the reasons for this are the irreversibility of the course of the disease, its prevalence among the young, and its apparent resistance to both prevention and cure— the latter especially disturbing in societies which have taken for granted that, in time, technology can conquer all infectious diseases.

AIDS is clearly related to behavioral and attitudinal issues. Certain groups are infected at higher rates than others; people have to be made aware that they are ill or at risk before they will seek treatment; and their understanding of the disease and its characteristics determines in part their choice of treatment. Because of this social and psychological context, AIDS lends itself to study by the social science specialties of medical sociology, medical anthropology, and epidemiology, as well as by biological medicine. Yet, studies of the behavioral and social factors are only very preliminary at present, and for that reason only tentative findings can be presented.

One pertinent issue is the assignment of blame. The history of disease has shown that with certain maladies the victim is held morally responsible for his or her plight. Leprosy and the venereal diseases are the clearest examples; even disorders of the urethra and the colon are sometimes considered as falling in this category. Another recent example is SIDS (Sudden Infant Death Syndrome); when physicians make this diagnosis, it often carries an element of suspicion (e.g., of smothering the child) with it. It has also been found that such suspicion is more often directed at classes and ethnic groups that are low in the socioeconomic pecking order (see Rutrough 1991).

AIDS falls into the class of disorders for which the victims are seen as morally culpable. A common public perception is that AIDS is contracted on account of membership in certain stigmatized *groups* (e.g., gay men or intravenous drug-abusers) rather than as a result of risky *behavior*. Such a perception hampers efforts to curb the spread of infection, since the majority of people, not being members of such groups, tend to believe themselves not to be at risk, because they do not belong to categories they perceive as deviant. Such perceptions persist even in the face of the fact that heterosexual married women now constitute an at-risk group for HIV infection.

This identification of the disease with certain groups is evident worldwide. In Southeast and South Asia, which now experience full-fledged epidemics of AIDS, the disease was initially perceived as one affecting only homosexual foreigners. This perception has faded; but the dominant perception now is that the disease affects mainly individuals who perform sex for payment, a perception that ignores the salient fact that men who visit them and return to their wives play a crucial role in spreading the disease. The perception of the disease as group-related also influences treatment personnel, who may find it easier to target groups than to treat the phenomenon as society-wide in its significance.

Decision-making regarding the use of condoms   The decision to use or not to use condoms not only expresses a contraceptive and prophylactic concern but also reflects the relationship between partners. Power is often involved. For example, in both developed and developing regions, prostitutes are often in no position to insist that their customers use them. Married couples may choose not to use this protective device, since they may be using other forms of birth control more suited to a supposedly monogamous relationship, albeit one in which one partner may be involved in an extramarital relationship that he or she wishes to conceal.

In developing regions particularly, the use of condoms for birth control frequently overshadows their use for disease control. In both India and Thailand, condom use is promoted as a means of birth control, and contraception is commonly regarded as synonymous with condom use. Among prostitutes, condom use is low, partly because of their reluctance to push customers to use a device that will reduce their pleasure and partly because family planning is not an issue in the relationship. Among married couples in India the use of contraceptives is infrequent, largely because sterilization is the most popular technique of birth control. Two further, relevant considerations stem from women's low level of power in the family: first, they are expected to accept and "understand" male infidelity, and second, communication between couples on family planning is generally low if not nonexistent. All these family factors tend to discourage the use of condoms as a means of disease prevention and, for that reason, to limit their use in protecting against AIDS and other sexually communicated diseases.

The social context of AIDS in Africa   Sexual practices involving multiple partners are also directly relevant to the spread of AIDS. Marriage institutions and attitudes toward sexuality are important in determining the number of partners, and nowhere is this relationship more clearly demonstrated than in sub-Saharan Africa. This region is, according to some calculations, the area of the world most afflicted by AIDS. In 1991, almost 75 percent of all HIV-positive persons resided in that region, as did five-sixths of sero-positive women and children (Caldwell *et al.* 1993). In contrast to North American and European patterns, AIDS in Africa is transmitted mainly through heterosexual intercourse, and family and gender structures in those societies are implicated in the patterns of intercourse in several ways.

First, though there is a wide organizational variety of family systems in western and southern Africa, many are based on lineage-based descent groups and involve polygyny (multiple wives). Agricultural organization is labor-intensive, and economic and social strength depend on high fertility, so fertility control is regarded as unhealthy and antisocial. Furthermore, women often have little control over fertility decisions, because the typical decision-making unit involves a wider circle of kin in which spouses may or may not participate.

Economic systems depending on factors other than agriculture may also involve multiple sexual partners. In western Africa many men migrate to cities for jobs while women remain on the farm as cultivators. Cities such as Dakar and Abidjan have high male sex ratios. Many men, separated from their wives, form temporary or more lasting liaisons with prostitutes. The latter have many partners and serve as nodes of infection. The infection circle is completed when these men return to their wives on a seasonal or cyclical basis.

Women's economic situation may also contribute to the spread of AIDS. Girls often become sexually active at an early age, forming liaisons with older men who assist them with school fees and other expenses. Women often marry men older than themselves, so the rates of widowhood and remarriage are high. Married women also frequently form liaisons with other men who may support them economically, especially when their husbands are away for extended periods. Such considerations led Caldwell and colleagues to observe that "[if] the AIDS epidemic puts a stop to most nonmarital sexual relations, then there will be a relative decline in the economic condition of many women, and a need for alternative sources of income" (1993: 2). Such are some of the contradictions between the imperatives of economic survival and the imperatives of disease control.

Gender stratification is also relevant. Women have no say over their husbands' sexual activities, such as taking another wife or visiting prostitutes. Tradition mandated long periods of post-partum sexual abstinence, but this was primarily seen as the woman's responsibility, and men were considered justified in forming other liaisons during this period (Awusabo-Asare *et al.* 1993). Thus men had "rights" to "promiscuity" which women did not, although the latter often entered into extramarital liaisons out of economic need.

Finally, societal norms and mores regarding sexuality play a role. In contrast to South Asia, sex in much of Africa is perceived as healthy and necessary, especially for men. For women, virginity is associated with sterility or physical or psychological inadequacy. A study among adolescent schoolchildren in Lagos found that half the sample were sexually active, and most of them had more than one partner (Oloko and Omoboloye 1993). Among adults sampled in Calabar (Nigeria), 53 percent of currently married men kept another sexual partner, as did 23 percent of married women. Thirty-four percent of men and 49 percent of women had between one and five sexual partners over their life course (Ogbuabu and Charles 1993).

Efforts to control the AIDS epidemic in Africa meet with another range of obstacles. Campaigns promoting monogamy and inveighing against "promiscuity" tend to be regarded as manifestations of Western cultural imperialism. The experience of shame on the part of those with AIDS often leads them to conceal their affliction. Finally, because the disease has a long latency period and people infected with it often die from "other" diseases, the true incidence and causes of AIDS are often obscured.

Migration

Migration studies have traditionally been inductive in character, with a correspondingly modest level of theorizing. Some economic models have been developed, which, predictably, consider the relations between costs and benefits to migrants. Geographers have developed a number of "gravity models," which treat migration as a function of distance and direction of movement. Sociologists have tended to analyze specific patterns, such as movement from agrarian and capitalist sectors and between core and periphery regions (McGee 1976), or patterns of circular mobility, where movers shuttle back and forth between destinations (Mabogunje 1972, Hugo 1981), and to focus on characteristics of migrants as well as their family and social networks. Zelinsky (1971) has proposed a typology encompassing all possible types of mobility patterns, ranging from daily or seasonal commuting to long-term changes of residence.

Most contemporary concern with migration has focused on population movements to Western Europe. Over the longer haul, European experience with in-migration is different from that of other major immigrant nations such as Australia and the United States. During the past 20 years, Western Europe has switched from exporting humans to importing them. Even Italy, traditionally an out-migrating nation, now experiences in-migration from Africa and Eastern Europe (Pacini 1991). Figure 12.2 presents the numbers of immigrants and asylum-seekers in various European nations, Australia, Canada, and the United States.

Much of the migration to Western Europe has to do with the demand for labor which the domestic population cannot or will not perform. This demand has created very rapid increases in foreign in-migration. Shortages of this type are expected to continue even though the European Community labor force overall is estimated to contract by 5.5 percent during the next three decades (Ghosh 1991). These "pull" factors are matched by "push" factors from southern countries experiencing a surplus

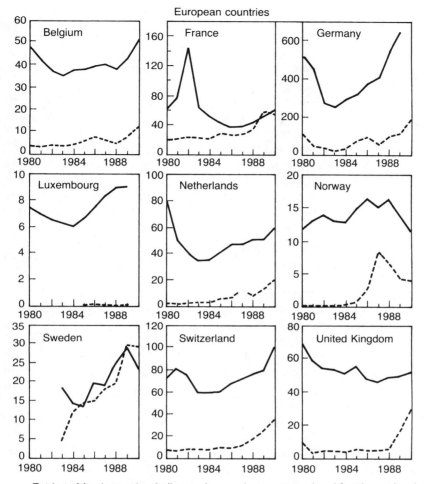

European countries

Entries of foreigners (excluding asylum-seekers, seasonal and frontier workers)
---- Entries of asylum-seekers

Non-European countries

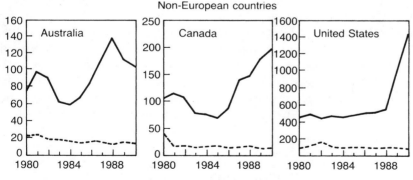

—— Entries of permanent settlers (excluding refugees)
---- Registered refugees

Figure 12.2 Immigrants and asylum-seekers or refugees in 12 OECD countries, 1980–90 (thousands). For the nine European countries shown, the solid line shows the entries of foreigners excluding asylum-seekers and seasonal and frontier workers, the broken line entries of asylum-seekers. For the three non-European countries, the solid line shows entries of permanent settlers excluding refugees, the broken line registered refugees. *Source*: **OECD.**

of working-age population coupled with lower levels of economic development.

In addition, Austria, Germany, the Netherlands, and Sweden have witnessed an acceleration of immigrant flows resulting from the arrival of workers' families and asylum-seekers. Much of this flow has resulted from the restructuring of Eastern Europe which started in 1989 and the lifting of emigration restrictions in former Eastern-bloc countries. Germany is the main destination for asylum-seekers, who come from Poland, the Balkans, and Rumania (among them many Gypsies). In addition, ever-increasing numbers of ethnic Germans–nearly 400,000 in 1990 and again in 1991 (Manfrass 1992)–arrive from the former Soviet Union, Poland, and Rumania. Connected with these influxes, Germany has experienced considerable political protest against foreigners from right-wing, "nativist" sources and is currently debating restrictions on its hitherto generous asylum laws.

France has also experienced political complications arising from immigration. In light of long and friendly relations with Rumania, France granted asylum freely after the 1989–90 revolution; but since that time the government has made efforts to consolidate immigrant and refugee policies, with the understanding that the capacity for absorption had been reached. France's long-term immigration problems stem from immigration of Arabs from its former colonies Algeria and Tunisia, as well as the recent fallout from the Gulf War in areas such as Lebanon. In some confusion about how to stem migration from the South and the East, France has also experienced an intensification of anti-foreign political movements and the rise of extreme right-wing parties that have gained greater political support than the neo-Nazi youth groups in Germany.

Issues of absorption and assimilation of immigrant groups go beyond economic considerations. The ethnically different immigrants are posing a challenge to the relatively homogeneous populations of these nations. It appears that the concept of a multicultural society, as experienced in the United States, Canada, and Australia, is becoming increasingly relevant to European societies. At the same time, these societies have limited historical experience and know-how of receiving and accommodating people with religious, cultural, and ethnic characteristics that diverge sharply from their own. It is inconceivable that ethnic absorption and conflict will not be on the political agendas of Europe for decades to come (see chapter 4).

Conclusion

As indicated at the beginning of this chapter, demography is a discipline with a strong positivist tradition, stressing the measurement and quantification of core variables such as births, deaths, sexual unions, and to a lesser extent the movement of persons from place to place.

Measurement, quantitative analysis, and mathematical modeling have reached high levels of sophistication.

By the same token, demography has tended to eschew systematic sociological theory, relying instead on a variety of loosely formulated functionalist theories of modernization. The importance of institutional and cultural variables for demographic processes has been generally recognized, but these variables have not traditionally been incorporated theoretically into the somewhat restricted models of formal demography. As this chapter illustrates, however, both demographers and general sociologists are making progress in the effort to forge connections with one another's subject matter, with substantial connecting links being built along the dimensions of gender, family, socioeconomic and racial-ethnic stratification, and state policy. Because of the evident importance of these dimensions for the understanding of demographic processes, there seems little doubt that this kind of interdisciplinary cross-fertilization will grow in the coming decades.

References

Awusabo-Asare, K., Anarfi, J. and Agyeman, D. 1993: "Women's Control over their Sexuality and the Spread of STD's and HIV/AIDS in Ghana," in J. Caldwell, G. Santow, I. O. Orubuloge, P. Caldwell, and J. Anarfi (eds), *Sexual networking and HIV/AIDS in West Africa*, supplement to *Health Transition Review*, 3: 69–84.

Bledsoe, C. 1990: "The Politics of Children: Fosterage and the Social Management of Fertility among the Mende of Sierra Leone," in W. Handwerker (ed.), *Births and Power: Social Change and the Politics of Reproduction*, Boulder, Colo.: Westview Press, 81–100.

Bongaarts, J. 1982: "Fertility Determinants: Proximate Determinants," in J. Ross (ed.), *International Encyclopedia of Population*, New York: Free Press, I: 275–9.

Bongaarts, J. and Greenhalgh, S. 1985: "An Alternative to the One-Child Policy in China." *Population and Development Review*; 11: 585–618.

Bourgeois-Pichat, J. 1986: "The Unprecedented Shortage of Births in Europe," in K. Davis, M. Bernstam and R. Ricardo-Campbell (eds), *Below Replacement Fertility in Industrial Societies: Causes, Consequences and Politics*, supplement to *Population and Development Review*, 12: 3–25.

Bulatao, R. and Lee, R. (eds) 1987: *Determinants of Fertility in Developing Countries*. 2 vols. New York: Academic Press.

Caldwell, J. C. 1982: *Theory of Fertility Decline*. London: Academic Press.

Caldwell, J. C., Caldwell, P., Ankrah, E. M., Anarfi, J. K., Agyman, D. K., Awusabo-Asare, K. and Orubuloye, I. O. 1993: "African Families and AIDS: Context, Reactions and Potential Interventions," in Caldwell, *et al. Sexual Networking and HIV/AIDS in West Africa*, 1–16.

Cleland, J. and Wilson, C. 1987: "Demand Theories of the Fertility Transition: An Iconoclastic View." *Population Studies*, 41: 5–30.

Coale, A. 1974: "The History of the Human Population." *Scientific American*, issue on the human population, 230: 16–25.

Coale, A. 1991: "Excess Female Mortality and the Balance of the Sexes in the Population: An Estimate of the Number of 'Missing Females'." *Population and Development Review*, 17: 517–23.

DasGupta, M. 1987: "Selective Discrimination against Female Children in Rural Punjab, India." *Population and Development Review*, 13: 77–100.

Davis, K. 1986: "Low Fertility in Evolutionary Perspective," in Davis *et al.* (eds), *Below Replacement Fertility in Industrial Societies*, 48–65..

Dyson, T. and Moore, M. 1983: "On Kinship Structure, Female Autonomy, and Demographic Behavior in India." *Population and Development Review*, 9: 35–9.

Ghosh, B. 1991: "The Immigrant Tide." *European Affairs*, 5: 78–82.

Hugo, G. 1981: "Village–Community Ties, Village Norms, and Ethnic and Social Networks: A Review of the Evidence from The Third World," in G. de Jong and J. R. Gardner (eds), *Migration Decision Making*, New York: Pergamon Press, 186–224.

Johansson, S. and Nygren, O. 1991: "The Missing Girls of China." *Population and Development Review*, 17: 35–52.

Knodel, J., Havanon, N. and Pramual Ratana, A. 1984: "Fertility Transition in Thailand: A Qualitative Analysis. *Population and Development Review*, 10: 297–328.

Kono, S. 1986: "Comment," in Davis, *et al.* (eds), *Below Replacement Fertility in Industrial Societies*, 171–5.

Mabogunje, A. 1972: *Regional Mobility and Resource Development in West Africa*. Montreal: McGill University Press.

McGee, T. 1976. "Rural–Urban Mobility in South and South-East Asia. Different Formulations, Different Answers?" Paper presented at Seminar on Human Migrations sponsored by the Midwest Council of the American Academy of the Arts and Sciences.

Manfrass, K. 1992: "Europe: North-South or East-West Migration?" *International Migration Review*, 26: 389–99.

Miller, B. 1981: *The Endangered Sex*. Ithaca, N.Y.: Cornell University Press.

Muhuri, P. and Menken, J. 1993: "Excess Mortality of Young Girls in Rural Bangladesh: An Investigation into Circumstances of Great Jeopardy." Paper presented at Bay Area Colloquium on Population, University of California, Berkeley.

Ogbuabu, S. and Charles, J. 1993: "Survey of Sexual Networking in Calabar," in Caldwell, *et al.* (eds), *Sexual Networking and HIV/AIDS in West Africa*, 105–20.

Oloko, B. and Omoboloye, A. 1993: "Sexual Networking among some Lagos State Adolescent Yoruba Students," in Caldwell *et al.* (eds), *Sexual Networking and HIV/AIDS in West Africa*, 151–58.

Omran, A. 1982: "Epidemiological Transition," in Ross (ed.), *International Encyclopedia of Population*, I: 172–5.

Pacini, M. 1991: "Introduction." *International Migration Review*, 26: 229–32.

Presser, H. 1986: "Comment," in Davis *et al.* (eds), *Below Replacement Fertility in Industrial Societies*, 196–200.

Preston, S. 1986a: "Changing Values and Falling Birthrates," in Davis *et al.* (eds), *Below Replacement Fertility in Industrial Societies*, 176–95.

Preston, S. 1986b: "The Decline of Fertility in North European Industrialized Countries," in Davis *et al.* (eds), *Below Replacement Fertility in Industrial Societies*, 26–47.

Princeton University Fertility Project 1986: *The Decline in Fertility in Europe: The Revised Proceedings of a Conference on The Princeton European Fertility Project*, A. J. Coale and S. C. Watkins (eds), Princeton University Press.

Rutrough, T. 1991: "Real and Artifactual Trends in Sudden Infant Death Syndrome: 1975–1986." Ph.D. dissertation, University of Michigan, Ann Arbor.

Sen, A. 1989: "More than a 100 Million Women Are Missing." *New York Review of Books*, Dec.: 61–6.

Westoff, C. 1986: "Perspectives on Nuptiality and Fertility," in Davis *et al.* (eds), *Below Replacement Fertility in Industrial Societies:* 155–70.

Wolf, A. 1986: "The Pre-eminent Role of Government Intervention in China's Family Revolution." *Population and Development Review*, 12: 101–16.

Zelinsky, W. 1971: "The Hypothesis of the Mobility Transition." *Geographical Review*, 61: 219–49.

13

The Vicissitudes of Development

The idea of development has risen and fallen in the consciousness of social thinkers during the past two centuries. The nineteenth century was the great century of the idea of progress, and this found expression in theories of social evolution that regarded the rise of societies to the heights of civilization as being determined by internal, linear, immanent forces. By the first two decades of the twentieth century, however, classical evolutionism had become more or less discredited in sociology. "Mainstream" Western sociology experienced a gap in its attention to development and change in the interwar period, though note should be taken of the "international" theory voiced by Lenin (1939 [1917]).

During the several decades following the Second World War, interest was renewed, this time in the phenomenon of "modernization" or "development," properly called. In this formulation, Western scholars stressed the increase in wealth, urbanization, and structural differentiation, the development of a social psychology of "modernity," and the idea that less developed countries would follow the path toward modernization taken earlier by the modern West. These elements reveal that this phase of modernization theory revived some, but not all, of the underlying assumptions of classical evolutionary theory.

The late 1960s and 1970s witnessed a critique of modernization theory from two directions. The first, the main topic of this chapter, came mainly from the Latin American scholars associated with the Economic Commission for Latin America and the dependency theorists, the second from world-system theory, associated in large part with the name of Wallerstein (1974). Both these lines of thinking harkened back to the Leninist formulation, in that they stressed the international, or global,

---

This chapter is based on a contribution by Heinz R. Sonntag.

dimensions of development. Both received criticisms in their turn. The 1980s constituted a somewhat sleepy decade with respect to development theory. No one is quite certain what the 1990s and the decades after will bring, but by now it is firmly established that the developmental history of individual nations and regions is inextricably bound up with world forces and can never again be disassociated from them.

From the standpoint of the history of economic and social theory, most thinking about development has been cloaked in the ideas of economic progress and evolution. Before the great economic crisis of the 1920s and 1930s, capitalism was presented–even by its severest critic, Marx–as developing by itself on the basis of mechanisms of self-regulation. Those societies (mainly non-Western) not experiencing development acknowledged, but were not exempted from, it; rather, they were merely primitive, or "backward," or "folk." Implicit in evolutionary theory–and carrying on to the present in various disguises–was the frankly ethnocentric notion that the West was the mirror in which all nations would recognize themselves sooner or later. Even Weber (1956), who was hardly an evolutionist, did not escape this way of thinking in his discussions of rationality, regarding it as the near-universal hallmark of recent Western history.

In this chapter we take a selective look at the general issues of development from the standpoint of one region of the world in which it has been a central preoccupation for decades: Latin America and the Caribbean. We will proceed in the following way. First, we will examine an important statement about development, including its most important critical questions and answers, namely, the Latin American one. Then we will analyze the most relevant results, both positive and negative, arising from this statement, and discuss the implications of the *crisis* and of the *crisis of the development crisis* which began more than 15 years ago. Finally we will put forward some suggestions about returning to the design and application of development models at the present historical juncture of world development.

Development of ECLA and Dependency Theory

One of the early global concepts of development was born in the Economic Commission for Latin America (ECLA), later known as the Latin America and the Caribbean Economic Commission. This Commission was created in the context of the United Nations, as one of five economic commissions (one for each continent), to help the UN's Socioeconomic Council in its work of promoting economic development.

The first ECLA document was written in 1948 under the supervision of Raul Prebisch, an Argentine economist and chairman of the Central Bank, who developed his country's economic policy between 1935 and 1943. Earlier Prebisch had a reputation as a neoclassical economist, even though he had written some essays dealing with international center–periphery relations. Once the United Nations Secretary-General had accepted the document, Prebisch took over the executive secretaryship of the commission and surrounded himself with a number of young economists from the region. Even at this early date, however, the work of ECLA met with some resistance, mainly from some representatives of the United States who felt that the document revealed communist influence.

The practical antecedents of the ECLA doctrines are to be found in the experiences of the Latin American nations themselves, some of which had reached a level of capitalist development by the end of the nineteenth century, and others of which had started industrializing during and after the crisis of the thirties (Sonntag 1988a). Their intellectual antecedents are to be found in the contributions of North American and European scholars such as Roy Harrod, Evsey Domar, Arthur Lewis, Gunnar Myrdal, and Albert Hirschman.

From these antecedents the authors of ECLA's development theories (summarized in ECLA 1969, Cardoso 1977, Rodriguez 1980, and Menzel 1992) formed a unique synthesis, the main characteristics of which are as follows: Latin American underdevelopment must be understood from a world-systems perspective. The countries of the region were seen as constituting the *periphery* of the world economic system, which was dominated by the *center* (mainly North America and Western Europe). This system had imposed on them a structure of production and export of primary goods (farming and mining products), while manufacturing production was concentrated in the countries of the center. Thus ECLA theory contained a statement of the internal economic deformations produced by those countries' "monoproductive" systems, which yielded inadequate levels of savings, capital formation, and rationality in the deployment of manpower.

The subordinated position of Latin America had long been legitimized by reference to the classical theory of foreign trade, the theory of comparative advantage, whereby it could be argued that the concentration on primary production and export was to the benefit of those countries. Prebisch and his colleagues at ECLA attacked this theory, arguing that international specialization had fallen short of the theory's expectations in two respects: first, the international division of labor had failed to maintain a balance between primary and manufactured goods, undervaluing the former and overvaluing the latter; and second, it did not spread the returns of technical progress equitably, with the lion's share going to those countries that produced manufactured goods.

The deformation of Latin American economies was also seen to have led to a number of other consequences. It had forced Latin American countries to rely on the demand for primary goods, insulated the region from many aspects of world trade (especially during the crisis of the 1930s), and, most important, impeded industrialization, including the use of modern technology, and the transformation of traditional social organizations into capitalist ones. In a word, the international system had blocked the modernization of Latin America.

In retrospect, it can be appreciated that the dominant goal that inspired the ECLA group was a straightforward, almost conventional economic one: to reach the state of development achieved by the developed countries and, more particularly, that of the United States, their leader (Wallerstein 1991a). Linked with this goal, it might be added, was acceptance of the idea of a linear development toward capitalism, an idea inherited from the conception of progress it had evolved from the Enlightenment. (It might also be noted, with only some irony, that the same imagery informed some of the aspirations of the Soviet Union, the major ideological enemy and competitor of the United States in the cold war–see "Khrushchev's prediction that his country would be ahead of the United States by the year 2000" [Wallerstein 1991a: 27]–though the Soviet means were to be socialist planning rather than market strategies.)

At the level of practical programs, ECLA proposed policies were designed

- to diversify the existing productive structure by breaking the monoproductive system;
- to modernize the existing productive structure by incorporating new technology and transforming the social organization of labor;
- to promote industrialization by substituting internal production for importation of manufactured goods, using the already formed internal market and its potential for expansion (Hirschman 1985 [1968]); this is the best known of the economic goals of ECLA, and it has had the most impact in other developing countries.

At a more concrete level, a number of mechanisms were proposed to attain these goals. The first was an augmented role for the state, calling for strategies of intervention that went far beyond the kind of role envisioned by Keynes; this state role would focus on the *programming* of economic progress ("programming" was a euphemistic term, designed to avoid the "communist" connotations of "planning," which was such a bugaboo in the United States at the time). The second related to the necessity of acquiring and utilizing foreign *monetary resources*, at least during the early stages of development, because of the internal lack. The third was *regional integration*, a way of encouraging and rationalizing industrialization, and, as a by-product, of reinforcing a Latin American sociocultural identity, also considered a resource for the developmental process.

From quite early on, however, this vision of the development process came to be regarded as too narrow–that is to say, too economic–in its emphasis. In fact, beginning in the middle 1950s, a group of sociologists and other social scientists (led by José Medina Echavarria) enlarged the development debate by calling attention to problems associated with urbanization (which was extremely rapid, even in that decade), inadequate education, and the marginalization of some segments of the population that were not incorporated into the modern economy in the process of accelerated development. Such discussions suggested immediately the need for social policies to accompany the economic strategies.

Worries of this sort grew from the beginning of the 1960s, when the Commission itself began to wonder "where are the failures" when "in a specific country there has been a sustained development policy oriented, in all its aspects, by a well studied program and . . . this notwithstanding, the growth achieved does not meet the proposed goals" (ECLA 1969: 206; see also Sonntag 1988b). Soon thereafter ECLA ventured a major reformulation, much broader in character than earlier versions. The reformulation contained a kind of ECLA theory of modernization. It stated that the transition from "traditional" to "modern" societies consisted in "a group of steady steps through which value systems, attitudes, behavior, and 'traditional' social classification were overcome . . . to become 'modern,' that is to say: these steps were characterized by rationality according to Max Weber" (Sonntag 1988b: 30). Since that time ECLA has spoken about "dual" societies, or societies of "structural heterogeneity" (resulting from the coexistence of "traditional" and "modern" elements within them). The Commission stated on the basis of its assumption that the transition to modernization could take place in a planned way through a series of structural reforms in the areas of agriculture, education, and public administration. (Another ironic note: the program of the Alliance for Progress, developed under the administration of John F. Kennedy, showed a remarkable similarity to the ECLA vision; indeed, the Kennedy administration appeared actively to borrow from them via the influence of W. W. Rostow, a member of the Kennedy team [Rostow 1960].)

ECLA's theory and recommendations became much more than a "trade mark of Latin American thought about the economy" (Cardoso 1977: 9). In the 1950s and 1960s they had repercussions throughout the underdeveloped world, especially in Asia and Africa (see, e.g., Lee 1992). In the same decade ECLA forged a kind of intellectual and policy link among a number of groups and classes in Latin America and the Caribbean. This influence created what amounted to a "development euphoria" for a season and mobilized a variety of political leaders and social classes around certain development policies. During that season "Eclaism" became in effect a developmental ideology for the less developed countries. This ideology was rendered congenial to its holders by two additional means: first, it was advanced as polemically critical of both neoclassical economic theory and the dominant modernization theory espoused by sociologists and political scientists from the dominant center; and second, it held the countries of the center, especially the United States, responsible in a global way for the deformation of the less developed countries.

The major criticisms of ECLA's theories and strategies came from three sources. The first, already mentioned, comprised policymakers and scholars in the developed countries, partly in defense of their own theories of the world economy and its development and partly out of imagined fears of left or even communist elements in the ECLA critique and program.

The second line of criticism, interestingly, came from that very quarter—orthodox Marxist communism. Marxist parties became established in the region around the time of the Bolshevik Revolution, and all of them were incorporated into the III International (COMINTERN). Marxists denounced Eclaism as a new manifestation of imperialist strategies which would eventuate in the continued domination and exploitation of the countries of Latin America and the Caribbean.

The Marxist characterization of Latin American countries rested on a certain "dualism" which they saw in them, a dualism traceable to the coexistence of feudal and capitalist (linked to imperialist) relationships of production. The Marxist strategy was to launch a struggle against both kinds of relationships, hoping to forge an alliance of classes including the peasants, the newly formed proletariat, the petit bourgeoisie, and some representatives of the bourgeoisie itself. The results of this struggle would be the following sequence: a "democratic-bourgeois revolution," the development of local capitalism, the emergence and strengthening of the proletariat, and ultimately a "socialist revolution."

As can be appreciated, the short-term goals of the orthodox Marxist proposals did not differ substantially from those of the ECLA advocates. This circumstance underlies Pedro Paz's characterization of the Marxist position as "leftist Eclaism." The Marxists did not challenge the short-term goals (full capitalism); nor were they against the measures proposed to achieve it, namely, agricultural modernization and industrialization policies. The point of critical difference is found in the Marxists' insistence on the necessity of a final socialist revolution. This difference guaranteed a sustained opposition on the part of the Marxists, despite the similarities in program.

The third line of criticism came from ECLA itself. From the mid-1960s a new set of questions began to be asked, all dealing with the issue of why the developmental process, despite high growth levels, had not been able to correct the deformations of the economy, generate a more equitable distribution of income, and improve the living conditions of the masses. From these concerns developed a new approach to underdevelopment. Cardoso and Faletto suggested an "integral development analysis" (1979: 11), combining the study of social change at the economic level with the analysis of the classes, sectors, and group transformations within the dominating system. They made central a factor implicit in the ECLA analysis, namely, the economic interdependency of the world, and argued that dependency "directly refers to the economic and political system's existence and functioning, showing the links between them in both the countries' internal and external situation" (1979: 24). According to their vision, analysis must proceed by examining how a national economy integrates forces emanating from the international market, the national market, and the classes and groups inside and outside the nation in question.

By the 1970s, then, despite internal differences among Latin American social scientists interested in development, development was regarded as connected with the evolution of the world system; but there was greater hesitation about the possibility of a developmental process from "traditional" to "modern" societies. Further, introduction of the theme of historical specificity meant that, while many could agree on strategy proposals, each society must fashion its own developmental path and developmental strategies, each path being conditioned by the country's specific location in the world economic system.

Achievements and Failures: Development Questioned

Achievements

Without question, the application of the ECLA strategies–carried out with only minor differences in the several countries–changed the face of Latin America and the Caribbean. In the 1940s these societies were dependent mainly on agriculture or mining, with only early (but highly variable) signs of industrialization. By the end of the 1960s, these countries had developed the primary sectors while simultaneously breaking away from their economic dependence on them; their industrial sectors had grown and become more diversified; and a significant service sector–sometimes more developed than seemed justified by the level of industrialization–had also developed. Spurred by these changes, these countries achieved rates of economic growth that surpassed those of the developed ones in many cases. Their international trade also witnessed an extraordinary rate of growth.

It should be acknowledged that these dramatic changes occurred in the context of a favorable international environment that had been developing since the Second World War. The Great Depression had been overcome, and the developed world had survived the war. In fact, it was the renewal of capitalism at an international level that fostered Latin American and other Third World development. Such development was compatible with both the economic and the political agendas of the developed world. It fed into their own economic developmental strategies, including foreign investment, in many cases. And it seemed to be consistent with a special article of faith held in the postwar North America and Europe at the time: that a growing and prosperous Third World would be less vulnerable to Soviet interventions and less tempted to establish socialist or communist regimes.

In addition to economic transformation, Latin American and Caribbean countries witnessed extraordinary changes in the social sector during the

1950s and 1960s. Through a sometimes brutalizing process of urbanization, the relationship between the urban and rural populations was inverted. Education expanded dramatically at all levels, including the university level. Improvements in health and sanitation (provision of drinkable water, elimination of sewer waste) were reflected in marked decreases in infant mortality and endemic diseases and increases in life expectancy.

With respect to stratification, the role of peasants was reduced, and that of the industrial proletariat increased–both in keeping with the demographic transformations of the rural and urban sectors. The middle class expectably grew in numbers and importance and partially assumed the modernizing role that had been assigned to it in the developmental strategy. The structural heterogeneity of the society persisted, largely because inherited rural values, patriarchal labor relations, and family values were slow to change. At the same time, there was a movement toward homogenization, particularly with respect to consumption patterns of the middle classes and workers in the modern sector, with the main differences in consumption resulting from differences in purchasing power among the various groups.

The most problematic ingredients of the remarkable story of development were political. The developmental process did not find expression in democratization of the region's societies, as both modernization theorists to the North and West and many ECLA theorists might have predicted or at least hoped. The political trajectories took a variety of directions:

- A number of countries attained a considerable degree of democratic stability: Chile, Colombia, Costa Rica, Mexico, Uruguay, and Paraguay. Most of these countries also experienced decided economic growth and modernization, and many had established democratic institutions to build upon. In these countries it was possible to create, as a slogan, the Nations' National-Popular Commitment (Portantiero), the existence of which was regarded as inseparable from the aspirations of Eclaism.
- A number of other countries experienced turbulence in the industrialization process and ended up with new authoritarian governments–starting with Brazil in 1964, proceeding through Peru and Panama in 1968, and ending with Ecuador in the early 1970s.
- In still other cases patrimonial-type authoritarian regimes persisted, openly in Paraguay, Nicaragua, and Haiti and more disguisedly in El Salvador, Guatemala, and Honduras. In Argentina, after Juan Peron's populist dictatorship was overthrown, the polity lived in a permanent crisis that made every regime highly vulnerable to shifts in social forces and political alliances.

In a word, political modernization in Latin America and the Caribbean constituted the most unstable and voluble piece of the developmental puzzle, a circumstance that made life difficult for those who adhered explicitly or implicitly to a notion of parallelism in economic, social, and political development.

Despite the thorns of political instability and lack of democratic development that stuck in the side of many of the Latin American and Caribbean countries, the developmental story of those decades had many successful aspects. At the same time, the doctrines and practices contained in the ECLA vision included a number of elements making for weakness, if not failure, of that paradigm, considered as a model of development.

Weaknesses

First, the theory lacked a clear definition of the concept of development itself. What theory there was seemed to have been adopted from the traditions of developed Western societies; it focused on building a modern productive system, economic autoregulation (even taking into account the state's interventions), and the satisfaction of people's material needs. It takes no stretch of the imagination to see the parallels between these goals and those that lay at the core of eighteenth- and nineteenth-century notions of development, which also stressed material progress above all. ECLA thinkers appeared to give little thought to the place of their countries in the world system or to the historical traditions or sociocultural identity of the peoples affected by the developmental process. In retrospect, the ECLA mission appeared to focus rather narrowly on modernization, without reflecting on its consequences and implications. In its defense, however, it should be pointed out that this kind of mindlessness about the effects of developmental processes also characterized other models, including the Soviet model, which forced modernization at a blind and ruthless pace (see Menzel 1992), even though it had available a model of a socialist utopia as a larger orienting context for developmental goals.

A second weakness, already mentioned, has to do with the specification of mechanisms whereby economic modernization (which dominated ECLA's first documents–see Sonntag 1988b) might be translated into social and political institutions that would ultimately guide it. It is true that some thought was subsequently given to these issues. But in general, as in the approach of some North American and European political scientists, it was tacitly assumed that political development (i.e., the differentiation of a democratic political sphere) would develop in parallel with economic development. However, the theory never reached its goal with respect to specifying patterns of social and political modernization.

Third, the ECLA theorists came to consider too late the importance of scientific and technological innovations in the developmental process. Those who designed and applied the theory tacitly accepted the technology of the central, developed countries and believed that development would take place through this acceptance. This assumption resulted, in practice, in a technological dependency (similar to the economic dependency to which the theorists *were* sensitive). The accompanying mentality appeared to close off thinking about creating a scientific and technological basis distinctive to the Third World, even if this meant no more than the creative adaptation of the imported technologies. It is true that recognition of their technological dependency began to develop in the late 1960s, but in many respects this was too late; the scientific and technological hegemony of the central countries had already solidified.

Fourth, the ECLA development theory fell short in terms of its own definitions and goals. The several steps leading to import substitution were fully realized in hardly any of the countries (Hirschman 1985 [1968]). In addition, income redistribution, a fundamental goal of the early formulations, was never realized. The rapid economic development of Latin America and the Caribbean took place in a context of very great inequalities in income–worse, in fact, than in other regions of the Third World. During the 1970s and 1980s, in the 13 countries of Southeast Asia, the per capita income of the top fifth of the population averaged 8.5 times that of the bottom fifth. In Latin America the corresponding figure was 16.7 (Menzel 1992). This led the authors of the ECLA documents to acknowledge both the concentrating and the excluding character of economic growth in the region.

Fifth, the theory revealed a curious ingenuousness about how the world economic system works. The early documents emphasized the necessity of attracting foreign capital, and more recent papers stressed the need for the less developed countries to enter the global system ("equal productive transformation"–ECLA 1990). Both positions rested on the assumption that the central countries would collaborate by providing investments or financial aid and by cutting back on their protective strategies and opening their doors to imports (including manufactured goods) from Third World countries. But the reality has proved otherwise. Throughout the rebuilding of the 1950s, the consolidation during the 1960s, the crisis of the 1970s and 1980s, and the transformation of the early 1990s, the cooperation and contribution of the central, developed countries have not been unqualified but have always been granted–as might have been expected–in ways consistent with their own interests. Nor is it surprising that efforts in the 1970s to construct a new international economic order, depending on cooperative contributions from countries of the North, foundered and ultimately failed.

Sixth, the theory contained a similar naiveté about the commitment of various social groups to the developmental program. Following its dominant image of the central countries' capitalism, ECLA thinkers assumed that the nation-state would be a principal force in fostering development, even though it recognized, in theory, limitations on the powers of the states by virtue of being part of the periphery. The easy assumption was that all groups, sectors, and social classes would subjugate their particular interests to those of the nation, regardless of their place in the economic–class–political structure and regardless of their distinctive cultural identities. The underlying assumption was that because everyone stood to benefit, they would be equally interested and supportive of the state in its developmental efforts. In retrospect, it appears that the theorists may have bought into a theme developed by Western end-of-ideology theorists, that of social consensus among classes and groups on the virtues and value of capitalism as an economic system (see chapter 6). And indeed, for much of the 1950s and 1960s, the region developed a "euphoria of development."

After a season, however, the developmental process itself generated different transformations of the societies' interested groups and classes. The local bourgeoisie, increasingly linked to multinational corporations, began to abandon supportive political coalitions. The middle classes began looking more toward satisfying their own interests and maintaining their privileges, particularly with respect to consumption. The working classes experienced a series of differentiations and polarizations according to their place in the productive system and began to develop groups that were later to be called "informal classes." In the aggregate, these developments constituted a mélange of conflicting political allegiances, rendered political support of the state more fragile, and made the state's interventionist strategies weaker and more tentative.

Seventh and finally, there was an international failure. The pattern of development envisioned was that the primary exporting sector would procure sufficient foreign currency to import machinery and organizational know-how to spur on the process of industrialization. In practice, the supply of foreign currencies was never sufficient. The almost inevitable result was the necessity of falling back on the central, developed countries for help in securing foreign currencies–for developmental assistance from the North in the 1950s, loans from multinational organizations in the 1960s, and loans from private commercial banks in the 1970s. The equally inevitable result was a vicious circle of foreign indebtedness–yet another form of dependency–which finally exploded in the credit crisis of the 1980s.

As with all idealized theories and plans of development, the weaknesses of the ECLA approach became evident in its application, and the net results of its expected transformative powers fell short of the theoretically generated expectations.

Development in Times of Crisis

At the beginning of the 1970s the world economic system entered a phase of crisis followed by a long period of uncertain transition. The causes and manifestations of the crisis were numerous. But the main point is that the world economy did not continue to run along the comfortable rails on which it had traveled during the previous two decades. The prolonged crisis also became a matter of intense preoccupation among politicians, business people, and scholars. As it advanced, "it became a more and more common topic of conversation":

There are only a few who seem to doubt that, in relation to the splendid years of the economic expansion of the postwar decades–that many proclaimed, then, would be eternal–today, a majority of people live less well than before and, what is even more important, they live with the fear that the immediate future forebodes worse happenings. (Amin *et al.* (1983: 9)

The multiple causes and facets of the crisis beginning in the 1970s cannot be detailed here. Suffice it to say that it involved the slow decline and subsequent disappearance of the international monetary system and the stagnation of the productive process. The period since then has witnessed a series of global technologies, productive organizations, and distribution systems that have led many to speak of the end of Fordism as a principle of regulation and accumulation (see chapter 11). In addition, the march of globalization–whether measured by production, finance and credit, trade, or the movement of persons–continued apace.

The last third of the century has seen the consolidation of a new pattern of competition in the world. Three great economic powers have emerged: the United States and Canada, the European Common Market, and Japan and the newly industrializing countries (NICs) in Southeast Asia. Although the "Big Seven" have made efforts since 1977–mainly in annual summit conferences–to agree on economic policies to fight the crisis and to balance economic flows, differences have persisted and have sometimes erupted into commercial wars. Under these circumstances it is somewhat difficult to describe the international system in the 1990s as an "order" at all.

The theme of the environment has also taken center stage in the last third of the century. Beginning with the dire reports issuing from the Club of Rome, attention has been fixed on the perils of growth with respect to ecological imbalances and, more generally, the exhaustion, spoilation, and destruction of resources (see chapter 11). To this preoccupation should be added the emergence of a general souring of the commitment to capitalist economic development and its accompanying values–extreme individualism, materialism, and techno-instrumental rationality–though political leaders and critics alike are hard pressed to articulate alternatives.

Finally, beginning with the velvet revolutions of 1989, the Communist–Socialist bloc has dissolved as an ideological system and at least temporarily as an economic and military force. All the nations affected have deserted the Soviet model of a centrally planned economy, a one-party and authoritarian political system, and the shrill ideology of communism. Initially their disposition was to redirect themselves uncritically toward a market economy–and most have done so–but by now doubts and ambivalence about that system have also developed in those countries (see chapter 9).

It is difficult to summarize this vast range of developments except as the onset of disorganization. In the words of Amin:

The world system is in crisis. It is a general crisis of the accumulation model in the sense that the majority of eastern social formations (ex–"socialists") and southern ones (Third and Fourth Worlds) are incapable of securing a broad reproduction, and at times even a simple reproduction (as in the African "fourth world" case). In view of the economic aspects, there is a capital deficit. In the developed countries the crisis of accumulation assumes the inverse complementary form, that is, in classical economic terms. The appearance of a surplus in the offering of savings over the demand caused by productive investment. This surplus is then invested in a forward escape into financial speculation, which creates a situation without precedents. (Amin 1991: 6)

What has happened to the "development of the developing countries" in all this?

In Latin America and the Caribbean the majority of societies have continued on their course, though at a decelerated rate of industrialization. Transnational companies have expanded their role in the process, either independently or in association with local capital. Many segments of the population have become marginalized because the industrial sector has been unable to absorb them. Coalitions supporting the development policies have dissolved, and in some cases fledgling democracies have collapsed: Bolivia in 1971, Uruguay in 1973, Argentina in 1976, and Honduras, Guatemala, and El Salvador in the same period. The trap of international indebtedness has also increased because of declining export sales and because of the international banking community's willingness to grant loans to less developed countries from the glut of petro-dollars they accumulated following the price increases of oil beginning in 1973. There has been a clear fading of the "euphoria of development" as societies in the region have stayed their course through inertia rather than commitment to a shared project. Internal social and political conflict bred by stagnation have also increased.

Other parts of the Third World have suffered even more dramatic changes. Africa has drifted steadily towards becoming a Fourth World, lacking more and more the perspective of development and moving further and further away from the kinds of expectations held out by the austerity- and development-minded International Monetary Fund. Some Asian countries also seem to have drifted in the African direction.

By contrast, a group of small countries has continued the developmental march. These are the "gang of four," (South Korea, Taiwan, Singapore, and Hong Kong). Taking advantage of their locations and the availability of capital, these countries have directed their industrialization processes toward foreign markets through exporting industrial assets. Aided by, and dependent on, developed countries at the beginning, they soon became dynamic enough to sustain high rates of economic growth and trade. They accomplished this through strategies of low salaries and wages, flexible authoritarianism, and active state intervention (reminiscent of the Japanese pattern in the late nineteenth and early twentieth centuries). These countries have moved into textiles, automobiles, steel, and electronic products, while the developed countries have shifted toward biotechnology, microprocessors, and advanced forms of energy.

In the 1980s, termed by the World Bank the "lost decade" for Latin America, the processes evident in the 1970s were accelerated in this region. Foreign indebtedness underwent a crisis that aggravated the developmental difficulties (Sonntag 1988a). Between 1981 and 1992, 187.2 billion US dollars were transferred from the Latin American and Caribbean region to "service the debt" to the developed countries' private banking system, while the debt itself continued to increase: from US$367 billion in 1984 to US$416 in 1989 and US$451 billion in 1992, all without new loans. The internal gross product per capita dropped 8.3 percent between 1980 and 1989, and the urban minimum salary dropped from an index of 100 in 1980 to 78.4 in 1989 (ECLA 1989, 1992). Each of the societies in the region experienced marked increases in unemployment, corresponding increases in the informal economy, and patterns of multiple job seeking and employment of multiple members of families. Expectably, social indices such as health, education, housing, and access to minimum urban services declined.

Under such conditions, most people in the Third World appear to have lost all developmental perspective. Many societies show signs of internal disintegration and loss of social cohesion, and some have warned of a new "social apartheid" (Sonntag 1988a). Popular rebellions against deteriorating conditions are occurring in many parts of the Third World. All this can only threaten prospects for democracy. Many Latin American, Caribbean, Asian, and African societies experienced at one time a "euphoria of democracy," which substituted temporarily for the fading "euphoria of development," but this too is losing strength and consistency.

There are clear indications, then, that the Third World has lost out in the process of stagnation and crisis that set in during the 1970s. The number of candidates for membership in the Fourth World is increasing. Trade patterns appear to be concentrating more within the US/Canada–Japan/NIC–European Common Market, with a concomitant loss for the Third World. The developed world, flush from "victory" over the Soviet and related socialist models, is already wondering what kind of victory it was. At the same time, the collapse of the Soviet bloc has meant the disappearance of perhaps the only articulated alternative to the capitalist model. Is it too much to say that we have reached the point where there is no viable concept of development left, except perhaps for the surviving capitalist one which has encountered both practical difficulties and ideological disaffection in the last third of the century?

Open Questions about Development

The subject of economic development has not suffered from a complete lack of attention during the long period of crisis at the center and stagnation at the periphery. International organizations such as the World Bank, the International Labor Office, UNESCO, UNICEF, the Food and Agriculture Organization, and the World Health Organization have produced documents relating to poverty, education, children, and the family, but by and large their proposals have been reactive rather than visionary in character and in any event have not been widely applied.

One idea that gained some currency among Third World thinkers in the 1970s and 1980s–one supported by Amin (1974)–is the concept of autonomous, or self-centered, development. It involves *disconnecting* Third World countries from the international system. The argument stems, as many others have, from the concept of dependency. If dependency continues to be a cause of lack of development, the only real solution is for Third World Countries to retreat from the international division of labor, restructure their own resources, rely on their own creativity (rather than imitation), and adopt a pattern of South–South cooperation with other Third World countries. This proposal clearly calls for a radical transformation of present arrangements but invites questions about itself as a feasible alternative.

An almost completely contrary proposal has been laid on the table by the International Monetary Fund, among others. It is a neoclassical kind of program, which argues that the developing countries must become incorporated *fully* in the international market by developing nontraditional exports and opening their markets to goods produced in the developed and semi-peripheral countries, up to the point at which exchange rates become stabilized, internal economies are deregulated, productivity is improved, and government expenditures are diminished. While consistent in its adherence to neo-liberalism, the proposal has drawn heavy critical fire. It has been pointed out, for instance, that the idea that market forces really operate in the international arena is utopian (Sachs 1993), largely because of the monopolistic ingredients of the world economy–ingredients that appear to guarantee the continued accrual of wealth to the central countries by the applications through such policies. Critics have also noted that the neo-liberal policies of Thatcher and Reagan did not in any way ease the problems of poverty, income distribution, and unemployment in the United States and the United Kingdom and can scarcely be expected to be any more helpful in the disadvantaged countries.

ECLA itself has recently (1990) put forward a proposal, but it appears mainly to echo the past. It accepts some of the strategies of the neo-liberals (orientation of economies toward nontraditional exports, reduction of government intervention in the economy, etc.). It also states that the process of development takes place in equal conditions in all countries. The

ECLA proposals call for a new consensus to promote development, a consensus dependent on a decentralization of government and a mobilization of the population. Yet these proposals have been subjected to a range of criticisms, relating mainly to their possibility and feasibility, given the current economic, political, and social circumstances facing the less developed countries.

The world economy thus seems plagued by a central dilemma. On the one hand, the international system continues to "work" in the sense of continuing the long historical process of capital accumulation (Wallerstein 1991b). At the same time, it has succeeded in generating (a) a crisis in the developed countries with respect to the system of market capitalism and its accompanying cultural system, a crisis reflected both in its own performance and in criticisms from environmentalists and others; (b) a commitment to market principles in the former Communist bloc, the prospects for which are mixed at best; (c) a deterioration of the international system, leading to the increased marginalization of Third World countries and the consignment of many of them to Fourth World status. The dilemma is that the system is both working and not working at the same time; moreover, it seems to constitute a prison house of assumptions out of which it is almost imossible to break.

This being the case, it seems necessary, in conclusion, to pose a series of radical questions that apply to all regions of the world, questions that must be responded to if we are to emerge from this dilemma:

- Can traditional views, based ultimately on material progress, continue to be the major cultural molds in which the goals of economic activity are cast?
- In view of the crisis with regard to many Western values, may it not be necessary to elaborate new systems of values and norms with respect to the organization of society and the place of the individuals in it?
- What mechanisms are required to insure that the application of knowledge to the economy does not simply give rise to another phase of "modernization" as traditionally defined?
- Is it possible to invent collective modes of social organization that do not end up in sociocultural alienation of the population?

Translated into more concrete terms, the questions raise fundamental issues regarding the autonomy and independence of societies, the national and international role of the state, the role of markets in societies and the world, and the future of globalism. The answers to these questions are nowhere apparent, either in the abstract or the concrete, but it seems inevitable that radical questioning and radical reformulations be on the developmental agenda in the decades to come.

References

Amin, S. 1974: "Accumulation and Development: A Theoretical Model." *Review of African Political Economy*, 1: 1–24.

Amin, S. 1991: *La Nouvelle Mondialisation capitaliste: l'empire du chaos*. Dakar: Third World Forum.

Amin, S., Arrighi, G., Frank, A.G. and Wallerstein, I. 1983: *Dinámica de la crisis global*. Mexico: Siglo XXI Editions.

Cardoso, F. H. 1977: "La originalidad de la copie: la CEPAL y la idea del desarrollo." *Revista de la CEPAL*, Sigundo Semestre, 7–48.

Cardoso, F. H. and Faletto, E. 1979: *Dependency and Development in Latin America*. Berkeley, Calif.: University of California Press.

Economic Commission for Latin America 1969: *El pensamiento de la CEPAL*. Santiago de Chile: Ed. Universitaria.

Economic Commission for Latin America 1989: *Balance preliminar de la economía de América Latina y el Caribe*. Santiago de Chile: United Nations.

Economic Commission for Latin America 1990: *Transformación productiva con equidad*. Santiago de Chile: United Nations.

Economic Commission for Latin America 1992: *Balance preliminar de la economía de América Latina y el Caribe*. Santiago de Chile: United Nations.

Hirschman, A. O. 1985 [1968]: *A Basis for Hope: Essays on Development*. Boulder, Colo.: Westview Press.

Lee, R. M. 1992: "Modernity, Anti-Modernity, and Post-Modernity in Malaysia." *International Sociology*, 7: 153–71.

Lenin, V. I. 1939 [1917]: *Imperialism: The Highest Stage of Capitalism*. New York: International Publishers.

Menzel, U. 1992: *Das Ende der Dritten Welt und das Scheitern der grossen Theorie*. Frankfurt: Suhrkamp.

Rodriguez, O. 1980: *La Teoría del subdesarrollo de la CEPAL*. Mexico: Siglo XXI Ed.

Rostow, W. W. 1960: *The States of Economic Growth*. Cambridge, Mass.: Harvard University Press.

Sachs, I. 1993: *The Challenges Facing the Countries in Transition and the Experience of Late Peripheral Capitalism*. Paris: Maison des sciences de l'homme, (mimeograph).

Sonntag, H. R. 1988a: "Las Consecuencias sociales y políticas de la deuda: ¿Hacia un nuevo 'apartheid'?" *Capítulos SELA*, No. 19.

Sonntag, H. R. 1988b: *Duda-certeze-crisis: La evolución de las ciencias sociales de América Latina*. Caracas: Nueva Sociedad–UNESCO.

Wallerstein, I. 1974: *The Modern World-System, Vol. I: Capitalist Agriculture and the Origins of the European World Economy*. New York: Academic Press.

Wallerstein, I. 1991a: "Desarrollo: ¿Cinosura o illusión?" *Estudios del Desarrollo*, 1: 12–37.

Wallerstein, I. 1991b: *Geopolitics and Geoculture: Essays on the Changing World-System*. Cambridge: Cambridge University Press and Paris: Maison des sciences de l'homme.

Weber, M. 1956: *Wirtschaft und Gesellschaft*. Tübingen: Mohr.

Part IV

Institutional and Cultural Processes

14

The Urban Complex in a World Economy

Over the past two decades, both cities and the way we study them–that is, urban sociology–have changed radically. The main empirical transformations of cities are the following:

- Seventeen of the world's largest 20 cities are in the developing countries; virtually all these cities suffer from physical decay and an inadequate infrastructure for their populations.
- Both suburbanization and metropolitanization have proceeded apace in all countries.
- Poor, homeless, and unemployed people concentrate in major cities in both developing and developed countries.
- Major cities have experienced a decline in manufacturing industries and a growth of service industries and jobs.

A new urban configuration also appears to be developing. It includes new or more salient inequalities within and among cities at the global, national, and regional levels–inequalities linked with new economic trends. This changes our understanding of the notions of center and periphery. In addition, some urban systems are becoming internationalized as they serve firms, industries, and economies that are increasingly transnational. This development raises questions about the relations between cities and their hinterlands and challenges the received wisdom that cities promote the territorial integration of regional and national economies.

In urban sociology we observe the development of two new literatures. The first consists of descriptive studies of cities, especially mega-cities, and includes a characterization of some of the trends noted (Hardoy 1975, Linn 1983, Stren and White 1989; for an overview, see Dogan and Kasarda 1988). The second consists of theoretical and empirical works on the impact of

---

This chapter is based on a contribution by Saskia Sassen.

economic globalization on national urban systems and on the socio-economic structure of cities; much of this literature concentrates on "world" or "global" cities (Friedmann 1986, Prigge 1991, Sassen 1991, Savitch 1988), often with emphasis on the special role of multinational corporations and banks. To include cities in the study of economic internationalization, moreover, breaks with a more or less exclusive focus on corporations, economies, and governments themselves to focus on the concrete, situated activities of those agencies. It also focuses on place, which underscores vividly the actual locus of interaction of global, national, and local processes.

These two major sets of trends–empirical and scholarly–have succeeded in "bringing the city back into" the social sciences. Cities are recognized as strategic sites for empirical study and theoretical work on processes such as globalization, international migration, the emergence of producer services and finance, and poverty (Fainstein *et al.* 1992, Abu-Lughod 1980, Beneria 1989, Harvey 1985, Kowarick *et al.* 1991, Lomnitz 1985, Mione 1991, Perez-Sainz 1992). Cities have also come to the forefront in some policy arenas. For example, the World Bank has produced studies that focus on the relationship between urban economic productivity and macroeconomic performance (World Bank 1991). In addition, cities shape their own policies to gain advantages in the competitive global markets for foreign investment, headquarters, international institutions, tourism, and conventions (Kunzmann and Wegener 1991, Logan and Molotch 1987).

The topic of the modern city is a vast one, and so is the literature relevant to it. From that expanse we select several changes that are especially salient in the modern urban complex, realizing that this selection omits cities that may not have partaken in these changes and cities where the pattern is one of economic stagnation and poverty (Perez-Sainz 1992, Vidal and Viard 1990). The three topics are:

- new inter-urban inequalities, a topic which includes the impact of modern economic trends on "balanced urban systems";
- the emergent global urban system, a hierarchy among cities that serve as post-industrial production sites and marketplaces for global capital;
- new urban forms and social alignments, which lead us to question whether the conventional concept of "city" is still adequate to encompass phenomena as diverse as the conventional city, the mega-cities of the Third World, and the spatial base of global cities, which in many cases is a regional grid rather than a conventional city.

New Inter-Urban Inequalities

The effects of economic globalization are evident in both balanced and primate urban systems, of which Europe and Latin America, respectively, provide good examples. Both regions have experienced sharp changes.

Among these are the emergence of complex, articulated hierarchies at the transnational and global levels and the increased peripheralization of those cities and areas that are outside the hierarchies.

Impact on Balanced Urban Systems: The Case of Europe

In Europe we observe several tendencies. First, several sub-European regional systems have emerged (Kunzmann and Wegener 1991, CEMAT 1988). Second, several adjacent nations (Austria, Denmark, Greece) have strengthened their role in an emerging European urban system (Hall and Hay 1980, Belil *et al*. 1989). Third, several of the major European cities are part of the global as well as the various regional urban systems.

As a result of these trends, traditional urban networks within European nations are experiencing corresponding changes (Roncayolo, 1990). Once dominant cities are diminishing in importance, while cities in border regions or transportation hubs are on the rise. New European global cities are capturing some of the demand for specialized services and international business functions that previously went to national capitals and major provincial cities. At the same time, some of the older industrial cities, such as Lille in France and Glasgow in Scotland, have rebounded and become parts of new networks. In many cases this has led to changing definitions of center and periphery and an increased isolation of previously involved cities.

Among the "losers" in the modern urban drama are cities in peripheral regions and old port cities, which have become increasingly detached from the major European urban systems (van den Berg *et al*. 1982, Siebel 1984, Parkinson *et al*. 1989). Others have lost politico-economic functions and are unlikely to regain them. Among these are small and medium-sized cities in peripheral areas that were dependent on coal or steel industries (Hausserman and Siebel 1987, van den Berg *et al*. 1982). Not only will these decline in productive importance, but because of their scarred or otherwise unattractive urban environments, they have little chance of becoming tourist centers. Also under threat are cities that have been important as production or control centers in national defense systems– victims of the end of the cold war, as it were (Markusen 1985, Castells 1989). Ports that have not modernized their infrastructures will also fall behind the large, modernized port cities in Europe.

Kunzmann and Wegener (1991) attribute the dominance of the large cities in good part to their competitiveness in drawing high-tech and service industries linked to European and non-European investment. The importance of these cities will be consolidated by the further development of infrastructures for high-speed transport and communication, which will connect the major and specialized centers essential to the advanced economic system (Masser *et al*. 1990, Belil *et al*. 1989). For example, Lille's strategic location in the center of Western Europe has strengthened it as a transportation and communications hub, and the development of a massive infrastructure for this project has replaced the dying industrial base of the city.

Other cities, previously peripheral, may emerge as strategically located centers in a single European market if they can expand their traditional hinterlands. Examples are Aachen, Strasbourg, Nice, Liège, and Arnhem. The spread of the Western European economy to Central and Eastern European countries should revitalize many cities that were inter-regional centers before the Second World War but declined as such during the cold war. Among these are Hamburg, Copenhagen, and Nuremberg. The traditionally grand cities of Central Europe–Vienna and Berlin–are emerging as international business platforms for the whole of Central Europe. As part of the same pattern, major Eastern European cities such as Budapest, Prague, and Warsaw may regain some of their prewar prominence. Take Budapest in particular: by the late 1980s it had emerged as the leading international business center for Eastern Europe. Western European and non-European firms seeking business in Eastern Europe located in Budapest to launch their operations. It has since emerged as a glamorous, Western-looking international business and cultural enclave which offers hotels, restaurants, business services, and an arena of "action" for the young, that are yet to develop in other major East European cities.

Immigration is another important shaping factor in the fate of many European cities (Balbo and Manconi 1990, Brown 1984, Canevari 1991, Cohen 1987, Tribalat *et al.* 1991). The traditional "gateway" cities into Europe will continue to be the conduit for the growing flows of immigrants from Eastern Europe, the Middle East, and Africa (Pugliese 1983, Prader 1992, Blaschke 1991). Some of the old port cities–Marseilles, Palermo, Naples–are already experiencing a decline because of the increasing costs associated with these flows (Mingione 1991). While many of the immigrants passing through these ports will move on to more dynamic centers, some will stop there. This means a heavier burden on their infrastructures and services, which will further peripheralize them in relation to the other leading urban centers. Smaller gateway cities such as Thessaloniki and Trieste do not seem to be as overwhelmed by the immigrant flows as yet. In contrast to the ports of entry, some of Europe's global cities, notably Paris and Frankfurt, are final destinations for many immigrants and employ many of them (Gillette and Sayad 1988, Blaschke 1991). As emerging global cities, Berlin and Vienna are recapturing their roles as preferred destinations for immigrants (Fassmann and Munz 1992, Blaschke 1991, Prader 1992).

In sum, there is now emerging a multiple and overlapping set of geographies of centrality and marginality in contemporary Europe. We see a central urban hierarchy that includes Paris, London, Frankfurt, Amsterdam, and Zurich. These cities maintain a vast network of connections among themselves, and all are implicated in the global economy as well. Other regional centers are financial/cultural/service capitals but focus on the European region and do not have the global significance of Paris, Frankfurt, or London. Dividing lines between east and west and between north and south can also be drawn. Some cities and regions in Eastern Europe will assume central importance, while others, such as Rumania, former Yugoslavia, and Albania, will become increasingly marginalized. In southern Europe Madrid, Barcelona, and Milan are emerging as giants in the urban hierarchy, while Naples, Rome, and probably Athens remain more stable.

Impact on Primate Systems

Many regions of the world have long been characterized by urban primacy: Latin America, the Caribbean, large parts of Asia, and, to some extent, Africa (Dogan and Kasarda 1988, Hardoy 1975, Linn 1983, Abreu *et al.* 1989). These are the areas which contain most of the world's mega-cities, as table 14.1 indicates. Not only are these cities huge by population count; they also account for very significant shares of the gross national product

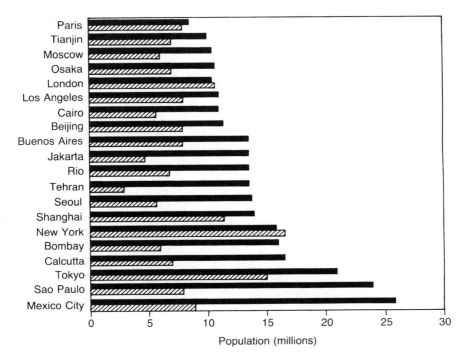

Figure 14.1 Population of twenty large agglomerations, in 1970 (*shaded*) and projected for the year 2000 (*solid*). From UN, *The Prospects of World Urbanization*, 1987.

Table 14.1 Some indicators of the estimated economic importance of urban areas

Urban area	Year	Population	Employment	Public revenues	Public expenditures	Output measure (%)
Brazil						
Greater São Paolo	1970	8.6	"	"	"	36.0 of NDP
						48.0 of net industrial product
China						
Shanghai	1980	1.2	"	"	"	12.5 of gross industrial product
						70.0 of commercial and banking transactions
Dominican Republic						
Santo Domingo	1981	24.0				56.0 of industrial growth
Ecuador						
Guayaquil[a]		13.0	"	"	"	30.0 of GDP
Haiti						
all urban	1976	24.2	15.6			57.6 of national income
Port-au-Prince	"	15.0	7.7	47.2	82.7[b]	38.7 of national income
other urban	"	9.2	7.9	"	"	18.9 of national income
India						
All urban	1970/1	19.9	17.7[c]	"	"	38.9 of NDP
Kenya						
all urban	1976	11.9	"	"	"	30.3 of income
Nairobi	"	5.2	"	"	"	20.0 of income
other urban	"	6.7	"	"	"	10.3 of income
Mexico						
all urban	1970	60.0			(29.0)[d]	79.7 of personal income
Federal district	"	14.2				33.6 of personal income
Pakistan						
Karachi	1974/5	6.1				16.1 of GDP
Peru						
Lima	1980	28.0				43.0 of GDP
Philippines						
Metro Manila	1970	12.0	"	45.0		25.0 of GDP
Thailand						
Metro Bangkok	1972	10.9	14.0[e]	"	30.5[f]	37.4 of GDP
Turkey						
all urban	1981	47.0	42.0			70.0 of GNP
Tunisia						
Tunis	1975	16.0	17.2	"	"	

[a] Guayas Province, [b] Current expenditures only, [c] Workers, [d] Federal public investment only, [e] 1970 data, [f] 1969 data

Source: Friedrich Kahnert, "Improving Urban Employment and Labor Productivity." World Bank Discussion Paper no. 10, May 1987.

of their countries (see table 14.1). What is less well appreciated is that alongside the growth of mega-cities in some countries, there is also a trend toward a deceleration in urban primacy in others.

A basic economic trend in many developing countries has been a shift away from strategies of import substitution toward strategies of export promotion. Import substitution tended to concentrate industrial development in a few locations with the requisite infrastructure and services and to draw migrants from the rural countryside. All this worked toward fostering further growth and consolidation of the primate cities.

Trends toward export development have been promoted in part by the expansion of world markets for commodities and direct foreign investment by multinational corporations. These activities, in turn, have stimulated new growth poles in the affected countries (Portes and Lungo 1992a, 1992b, Landell-Mills *et al.* 1989). Some of this development has been in or around the primate cities themselves, but some has drawn migrants to other regions. The advance of suburbanization and metropolitanization has also decentralized the population of primate cities and raised its density in nearby regions. Finally, the spread of tourism to the hinterland regions–for example, in Jamaica–has also contributed to the declining pace of primacy.

Some suggest that the slowing of primacy may be the result of a kind of exhaustion (Hardoy and Satterthwaite 1989, Kowarick *et al.* 1991). That is to say, the huge primary cities may be reaching the limit in their capacity to absorb people. For potential migrants this means that the margin of economic gain to be realized by emigrating is less. Two major sets of forces seem to be at work simultaneously. On the one hand, "modernization" tends to disintegrate rural economies, in large part through the expansion of large-scale commercial agriculture (Walters 1985, Edel 1986, Roberts 1976, PREALC 1970). This widens the "incentive gap" between rural and urban locations and contributes to growth of urban primacy through migration. On the other hand, some have suggested that the economic crises of the 1980s, along with austerity programs, have slowed the increase in primacy (World Bank 1991, Kowarick *et al.* 1991, Portes and Lungo 1992a, 1992b). These economic difficulties have contributed to increased unemployment and to an incapacity on the part of the informal sector to absorb the unemployed (Perez-Sainz 1992, Beneria 1989, Nabuco *et al.* 1991, Stren and White 1989).

Other economic factors have also contributed to the deceleration of the dominance of primary cities. As indicated, export industries and tourism appear to have had the net effect of moving economic activities and population away from primary cities. In addition, multinational corporations have relocated some of their coordination and planning away from primate cities to major international business centers in developed countries. The ultimate contours of urbanization that will result from these diverse and sometimes contrary pressures are difficult to predict, but

Table 14.2 Select stock exchanges: market size, 1990

| Stock exchange | Market value stocks | (US$ million) bonds | Listed companies | | Members firms |
			Domestic	Foreign	
New York	2,692,123	1,610,175	1,678	96	516
Tokyo	2,821,660	978,895	1,627	125	124
UK (mostly London)	858,165	576,291	1,946	613	410
Frankfurt	341,030	645,382	389	354	214
Paris	304,388	481,073	443	226	44
Zurich	163,416	158,487	182	240	27
Toronto	241,925	–	1,127	66	71
Amsterdam	148,553	166,308	260	238	152
Milan	148,766	588,757	220	–	113
Australia	108,628	46,433	1,085	37	90
Hong Kong	83,279	656	284	15	686
Singapore	34,268	98,698	150	22	26
Taiwan	98,854	6,551	199	–	373
Korea	110,301	71,353	699	–	25

Source: Tokyo Stock Exchange 1992 Fact Book (Tokyo: International Affairs Department, Tokyo Stock Exchange), April 1992.

it would be an error simply to extrapolate the dramatic growth and dominance of the primary cities into the future.

Elements of a Global Hierarchy

From the standpoint of the world's major cities, two fundamental processes are at the center of the current economic scene: the simultaneous geographical *dispersion* and *integration* of economic activities. This double effect seems paradoxical at first sight. However, if economic activities are decentralized through branches, subsidiaries, changes, and subcontracting to smaller firms and even to industrial home-workers, then the necessity of coordinating these dispersed activities calls for an expanded system of control and management. In any event, cities–some of which already have long histories of world trade and banking activities–now operate as command points in the organization of the world economy. They are marketplaces for the leading industries, especially those providing financing and specialized services to firms and those providing research and development.

As investment and finance have become increasingly internationalized, several cities have emerged as world centers for finance and international markets. These are New York, London, and Tokyo, and more recently Paris and Frankfurt. Tables 14.3 and 14.4 show the degree of concentration in investment and banking, respectively. This vast concentration, as well as the equally vast economic influence that these cities wield, raises the possibility of a qualitatively new type of urbanization, a new type of city. Scholars of urban life have come to speak of a *"Weltstadt"* or "world city" (Friedmann and Wolff 1982, Hall 1966) or, more recently, a "global city" (Sassen 1991) to denote this development. Among these cities are–in addition to the five mentioned–Amsterdam, Zurich, Los Angeles, Hong Kong, Singapore, São Paulo, and Sidney. The likely future, moreover, is that with the continuation of the twin economic trends of dispersion and integration, these and perhaps some other cities will strengthen and consolidate their position as centers of strategic planning, coordination, and specialized servicing functions, both globally and regionally. Many cities will be overshadowed by the supercities on the global scene but will gain new regional-level functions. National capitals may not always win in this competition, as is evidenced by the dominance of Milan, Amsterdam, Sidney, and São Paulo, none of which is a national capital (Kunzmann and Wegener 1991, Rimmer 1986, Sassen 1991, Kowarick *et al.* 1991).

Such cities will lead the way in the formation of a new urban economy. Many of them have long been centers for business and finance. What are new–mainly since the late 1970s–are the *structure* of the business and finance sectors, the *magnitude* of these sectors, and the relative *weight* of these cities in the world and regional economies (Hall and Hay 1980,

Table 14.3 USA, Japan, and UK: share of world's 100 largest banks, 1991

Country	Number of banks	Assets (US$ million)	Capital (US$ million)
Japan	27	6,572,416	975,192
USA	7	913,009	104,726
UK	5	791,652	56,750
Subtotal	39	8,277,077	1,136,668
All other countries	61	7,866,276	1,263,771
Total	100	16,143,353	2,400,439

Source: *Wall Street Journal*, World Business, Thursday, 24 September, 1992, R27.

Masser *et al.* 1990, van den Berg *et al.* 1982, Santoso 1991, Smith and Feagin 1987). What factors have contributed to these changes?

The answer to this question is found in large part in the economic and political-economic contexts of business and financial life (Sassen 1991, Machimura 1992, Stanback and Noyelle 1982). In an earlier period a few large corporate headquarters dominated a market characterized by low inflation, moderate but predictable growth rates, and high levels of regulation. In the 1970s the growing use of the Euromarket and the Third World debt crisis, along with high inflation, undermined that pattern. By the mid-1980s the number of firms constituting the core of the business and financial sector had grown considerably. These new firms accounted for most of the growth in the private office sector and a large volume of the business transactions. In the 1980s the reorganization of the financial industry was dramatic, ushering in less regulation, more diversification, more competition, a loss in market share by the large commercial banks, and a great increase in the volume of international transactions. By the late 1980s these trends had become evident in a number of cities in developing countries: São Paulo, Bangkok, Taipei, and Mexico City.

Size is only a weak predictor of a city's power in the world economy. Some of the world's largest cities have no headquarters of major world-class firms or banks. Among the ten most populous cities in the world, half have only one or no headquarters of world-class firms–for example, Calcutta, Bombay, Tehran–while in the other half, numbers of head-quarters range from 14 in Los Angeles to 64 in New York City. Tokyo, London, and Paris have disproportionate concentrations of headquarters in the manufacturing, commercial, financial, and producer-services sectors, even though they rank third, fourteenth, and eighteenth, respectively, in size among world cities (see figure 14.1). These few cities have a disproportionate share of the headquarters of the large industrial transnational corporations which account for 70–80 percent of the world trade in market economies.

Several variables determine what kinds of headquarters concentrate in international financial and business centers:

- How we measure firms makes a difference. Size of revenue is not always the most telling measure. Some of the largest firms in the world are still manufacturing enterprises, and many of these do not need to be located in an international business center, since their markets are mainly national. In the 1960s and 1970s many firms moved their major headquarters out of New York City. But if we measure share of total revenue represented by international sales, fully 40 percent of US firms with half their revenue from international sales still have their headquarters in New York City.
- The character of the national urban system is a factor. If an urban center has high primacy, it will have a high concentration of headquarters (though not necessarily of world-class firms) no matter what measure one uses.
- The specific economic histories and business traditions of any given country affect the pattern of concentration.
- Some headquarters may be associated with a certain economic phase. For example, unlike New York, Tokyo has been gaining all types of headquarters, while two other major Japanese centers–Osaka and Nagoya–are actually losing headquarters to Tokyo. This development appears to be related to the increasing internationalization of the Japanese economy and the associated increase in central command and servicing functions (Sassen 1991).

One way of measuring concentration is to look at producer services. These include financial and legal services, innovation and development, design, administration, transport, communication, advertising, security, and storage services that are bought by firms. They are available to many kinds of industries and serve as a key component in all international transactions. Tables 14.2, 14.3, and 14.4 reveal the concentration, by city, of three kinds of producer services–stock exchanges, banks, and securities firms.

Concentration has grown in recent years in some of the specialized services with strong world-market orientation, largely because of the advantages that come with increasing size. This kind of concentration is especially evident in advertising and accounting firms. For example, the multinational advertising firm can offer global advertising to a specific segment of potential customers on a worldwide basis (Noyelle and Dutka 1988, Delaunay and Gadrey 1987). By the mid-1980s, the world's five

Table 14.4 US, Japan, and UK: twenty-five largest securities firms, 1991

	Number of firms	Assets (US$ million)	Capital (US$ million)
Japan	10	171,913	61,871
USA	11	340,558	52,430
UK	2	44,574	3,039
Subtotal	23	557,045	117,340
All other countries	2	6,578	5,221
Total	25	563,623	122,561

Source: *Wall Street Journal*, World Business, Thursday, 24 September, 1992, R27.

largest advertising firms controlled 38 percent of the Western European market and more than half the Latin American and Pacific Area markets. Concentration brings special advantages in the world market to specialized service firms. US and UK law firms in New York and London, for example, have linkages to financial institutions in those cities, and this gives them a competitive edge over other firms (Noyelle and Dutka 1988, Thrift 1987) they can do business for firms from many different countries. The larger specialized service firms also subcontract in specialized markets, and this means that small independent firms can find niches in the major business and financial centers (Parkinson *et al.* 1989, Sassen 1991, Stanback and Noyelle 1982).

What is the impact of the globalization of major industries–from automobile manufacturing to finance–on national urban systems? This question is often clouded, because, with rare exceptions (Walters 1985, Chase-Dunn 1985), students of cities operate under the probably outmoded assumption that urban systems are coterminous with nation-states. Often they are not. One nation-state may encompass several urban systems, and a given urban system may encompass several nation-states. The multiplicity of linkages among global cities, moreover, has not been fully appreciated in the literature. In addition to having traditional "central-place" functions (Hall 1966, Friedmann and Wolff, 1982), the major cities maintain worldwide transaction connections. The hourly interactions among New York, London, and Tokyo, for example, suggest that these cities constitute an ongoing system among themselves. Furthermore, their relations are more than simply competitive; they constitute important coordinating nodes for the regions they represent. In addition, cities such as Detroit, Liverpool, Manchester, the Ruhr cities, and now Nagoya and Osaka are affected by the decentralization and dispersion of their major industries domestically and internationally. As argued by Sassen (1991), the recent growth in service industries can be accounted for in part by this very process of decentralization. The specialized services concentrated in business and financial centers–international legal and accounting services, management consulting, financial services–are one key element in the management of a manufacturing system.

These shifts also alter the relations between global cities and cities that were once leading industrial centers, though the details of this process are less than fully understood. Does globalization bring about a new triangulation, for instance, such that New York now plays a role in Detroit's fortunes that it did not play when Detroit was the country's leading automobile manufacturing center and when world automobile production and ownership was concentrated in the United States? And do major but not *the* major cities–Chicago, Osaka, and Manchester, for example–lose ground as financial centers? In fact, Chicago and Osaka continue to be major financial centers, but there is evidence that they have lost some share of the financial markets and may be in the process of strengthening their service functions by way of compensation (Sassen

1991). How has the decline of its regional economic system affected Chicago? It remains the hub of a massive agro-industrial complex, but that may be changing too. And has manufacturing decentralization altered the economic base of smaller cities in the national urban hierarchy? It may be the case that cities such as Denver and Atlanta are emerging as regional financial and service sub-centers–lesser versions, as it were, of what New York, London, Paris, Frankfurt, Tokyo, Sidney, and São Paulo are on a national and global scale (Rodriguez and Feagin 1986).

New Urban Forms and Social Alignments

It is inevitable that economic and geographical shifts of the magnitude we have considered will ramify in drastic ways for the internal structure of cities. The question is how. How are the great changes in manufacturing, services, and finance related to *other* components of the large city's urban economy and social structure? And what are their consequences for the general socioeconomic condition of residents of the cities? We know that in an earlier era, when large-scale, standardized manufacturing was the dominant industry in developed countries–and in some developing countries such as Argentina and Chile–this economic pattern produced an expanded middle class. Increases in real wages for large sectors of the work force were facilitated by strong unionization and the central role of household consumption in the industrial complex. Our knowledge about the social-structural and class ramifications when the economy is dominated by services is less clear, and this is even more true when these services are increasingly geared to international markets (Gershuny and Miles 1983, Giarini 1987, Sassen 1991).

Recent research reveals sharp increases in socioeconomic and spatial inequalities within major cities in the developed world (Harrison and Bluestone 1988, Wilson 1987, Deere *et al.* 1990, Scott 1988). One line of interpretation posits that this is a transformation in the geography of center and periphery, rather than a simple quantitative increase in inequality. As such, it signals that peripheralization processes are occurring inside areas once conceived of as "core" areas whether at the global, regional, or urban level. In addition to the sharpening of peripheralization processes, centrality has become sharper at all three levels.

Three distinct patterns are now emerging in the major cities and their sourrounding regions in the developed countries:

- In the 1980s there was a growing density of workplaces in the traditional urban centers. This was associated with growth in leading industrial sectors and their ancillary enterprises. This type of concentration was also seen in the more dynamic cities in the developing world–Bangkok, Taipei, São Paulo, Mexico City, and Buenos Aires.

- Accompanying this central city growth was the appearance of dense nodes of business and commercial activity in the cities' broader regions (Abella 1991, Perez-Sainz 1992, Nabuco *et al.* 1991). These took the form of suburban office complexes, "edge" cities, and "exopoles." This pattern has not yet emerged in the developing countries, except in the export-oriented areas of growth noted above. Further, it is to be distinguished from the seemingly endless metropolitanization of the region around cities that have evolved into mega-cities over the last 20 years. The underlying pattern in developed countries consists in the revitalization of the center and the vitalization of regional nodes. It is more than simple suburbanization or dispersal of population. These nodes tend to be more integrated, through "digital highways," and thus may display more "systemness" than earlier urban hinterland patterns.
- An almost inevitable corollary of the first two developments is a third: what falls *outside* the world-oriented market system becomes more marginalized and localized. This is expressed in increasing economic disadvantages, more visible poverty, and withering of political, social, and cultural life (Brosnan and Wilkinson 1987, Cohen 1987, Fernandez-Kelly and Garcia 1989, Sennett 1992).

A related, more political question also emerges. Does the old central city, which is still the largest and densest element in the new pattern, still command the power and strategic importance it once did? Does it still exert a kind of gravitational pull over its region? From the transnational perspective, the urban "center" is vastly expanded. It is no longer possible to regard the new central area as simply the central place in an agglomeration of populations. With the expansion of global city functions, the centers have also expanded, but their space–time relations with the expanded region have been altered qualitatively as well.

One aspect of this qualitative change is the changing significance of the traditional perimeter of the city. Previously mainly residential, this perimeter is now in the process of realizing new types of industrial and commercial development (Castells 1989, Sassen 1991, Daniels 1985, Gershuny and Miles 1983, Gregory and Urry 1985). It is the "Route 128" complex that Boston experienced–a ring of light industry and commercial and office space–around the urban center. This is a genuine reconcentration of economic activity on the urban periphery, a process that results from an aggregate of decisions by transnational and national firms to locate or relocate there. It is clear that this new vitalization of the urban perimeters constitutes a pattern qualitatively different from the processes of residential suburbanization and metropolitanization noted earlier.

The United States and Western Europe may be experiencing some divergence in this pattern of world-city formation. In the former, major cities such as New York and Chicago have large urban centers which have been rebuilt several times in their histories. This stems from the general American urban pattern of neglect of infrastructures and their consequently short life until obsolescence. This pattern more or less forces American cities to rebuild their centers periodically, and each time this is done according to the requirements of the current urban economy. In

Europe, urban centers have been far more protected and have rarely experienced significant expanses of abandoned space (the wartime decimation of European cities through bombing and other military activities constitutes a grim exception to this rule). In such cities the expansion of workplaces necessarily takes place outside the old center. Perhaps the most extreme example of this is La Défense, a massive industrial development located outside old Paris through deliberate governmental policy and planning. Another example is the expansion of office space into the large and little used area of London's Docklands, as a way of accommodating the rapidly growing demand for office space in central London. Similar projects for "recentralizing the periphery" appeared in the 1980s in several major cities in Europe, North America, and Japan.

As a result of all this, what was once suburban fringe, urban perimeter, or urban periphery has now become a site for dynamic commercial and industrial development. This does not mean that the periphery has disappeared; rather, its definition and locus have changed. In some cases peripheralization loses its strictly geographical connotation. For example, the major cities of the developed countries sometimes experience new forms of marginalization of land within blocks of some of the most expensive commercial land in the world. This new form of inner city metamorphosis can be observed in major American and European cities and in Tokyo (KUPI 1981, Komori 1983). This "peripheralization within the center" has had social-structural manifestations as well (Sassen-Koob 1980, Brosnan and Wilkinson 1987, Portes and Sassen-Koob 1987). It has led to the failure of firms and the degradation of nonprofessional workers in leading industries. The process seems to be more radical than the well-known "segmentation" of labor markets.

Normally financial and other services are thought of as entailing the application of expertise. If we regard service outputs as part of a production process, however, the actual division of labor that goes into those outputs is more easily grasped. Actually, the array of jobs involved–both high-paying and low-paying–is considerable. The elaboration and execution of a financial instrument, for example, requires inputs from law, accounting, and advertising. In addition, the realization of the product requires a variety of workers not usually thought of as part of the information economy–secretaries, maintenance workers, and cleaners. The latter are no less components of the advanced service economy than the professionals who are thought of as being central to it. Thus the firms implicated in the new transnational hierarchies (and the cities in which they are located) inevitably produce a new kind of proletarianization, a world of low-paid workers, mainly service rather than manual, who are conceived as–but are not–irrelevant in an advanced information economy.

The new growth at the world cities' perimeters has also produced new kinds of political crises. New forms of violence arise in the immigrant ghettos, emanating both from and against the new immigrants. New movements for law and order emerge, only to be countered by a reassertion of the importance of civil liberties. Exurbanites clamor for control over growth and more vigorous measures to protect the environment. Traditional forms of urban government may find themselves outmoded as well (Cardew *et al.* 1982, Logan and Molotch 1987, Clavel 1986, Preteceille 1986, Siebel 1984). Regional modes of regulation tend to be based on the old center–suburb model of cities and find themselves unable to deal adequately with "intraperipheral" conflicts–that is, conflicts among different types of constituencies at the urban perimeter or urban region.

The case of Frankfurt is an instructive example in this regard. It is a city that cannot function without its neighboring cities and towns; at the same time, its particular urban region could not have evolved without the specific forms of globally related growth that have taken place in Frankfurt's center. Keil and Ronneberger (1992) have suggested that the ideological motivation underlying politicians' efforts to strengthen the region was a desire to strengthen Frankfurt's position in the global inter-urban competition. Those efforts also mark the emergence of a new kind of solidarity: regional common interests that may be mobilized in the interest of promoting the region in competition with other world regions. Such phenomena introduce regional conflict and solidarity more immediately in the global world–a dimension that takes its place alongside class and racial-ethnic conflict and integration as part of the political kaleidoscope of "post-industrial" world society.

Cities differ in the degree to which they have been brought into the "regional dialogue." In New York City and São Paulo, for example, "city" discourse still appears to dominate. The challenge to these cities is how to come to terms with the relations between the center and the "inner city peripherals" or the squatters at their outskirts. In multiracial cities, the "culture of multiculturalism" seems to be one way of dealing with the new diversity. Perhaps a genuine "regional" discourse will begin to emerge in time, but as of now the region is still subordinated to a preoccupation with suburbanization, a concept that suggests an escape-cum-dependence relation with the city's center rather than a meaningful dialogue with it. Yet, with the emergence of new conflicts within the center, within the periphery, and between the two, the "city" dialogue will become more infused with, and perhaps ultimately subordinated to, a regional dialogue that will include political, social, and cultural themes.

References

Abella, M. I. 1991: "Structural Change and Labour Migration within the Asian Region." *Regional Development Dialogue*, 12: 3–21.

Abreu, A., Cocco, M., Despradel, C., Michael, E. G. and Peguero, A. 1989: *La Zonas Francas Industriales: El Exito de una Politica Economica*. Santo Domingo: Centro de Orientacion Economica.

Abu-Lughod, J. L. 1980: *Rabat: Urban Apartheid in Morocco.* Princeton, N. J.: Princeton University Press.

Balbo, L., and Manconi, L. 1990: *I Razzismi Possibili.* Milan: Feltrinelli.

Belil, M., Alemany, J., Borja, J., and Serra, O. N. A. 1989: *Ciudades del Mundo.* 5 vols. Paris: United Nations and Ajuntament de Barcelona.

Beneria, L. 1989: "Subcontracting and Employment Dynamics in Mexico City," in A. Portes M. Castells, and L. Benton (eds.), *The Informal Economy: Studies in Advanced and Less Developed Countries,* Baltimore: Johns Hopkins University Press, 173–88.

Blaschke, J. 1991: "International Migration and East–West Migration: Political and Economic Paradoxes." *Migration: A European Journal of International Migration and East–West Migration,* 11–12: 5–21.

Brosnan, P. and Wilkinson, F. 1987: *Cheap Labour: Britain's False Economy.* London: Low Pay Unit.

Brown, C. 1984: *Black and White Britain.* London: Heinemann.

Canevari, A. 1991: "Immigrati Prima Accoglienza: E Dopo?" *Dis T Rassegna di Studi e Ricerche del Dipartimento di Scienze del Territorio del Politecnico di Milano,* 9: 53–60.

Cardew, R. V., Langdale, J. V., and Rich, D. C. (eds), 1982: *Why Cities Change: Urban Development and Economic Change in Sidney.* Sidney: Allen and Unwin.

Castells, M. 1989: *The Informational City.* Oxford: Blackwell.

CEMAT 1988: *Draft European Regional Planning Strategy,* 2 vols. Luxembourg: CEMAT.

Chase-Dunn, C. K. 1985: "The System of World Cities, A.D. 800–1975," in M. Timberlake (ed.), *Urbanization in the World Economy.* Orlando, Fla.: Academic Press, 269–92.

Clavel, P. 1986: *The Progressive City.* New Brunswick, N.J.: Rutgers University Press.

Cohen, R. 1987: *The New Helots: Migrants in the International Division of Labour.* Brookfield, Vt.: Gower Publishing Co.

Daniels, P. W. 1985: *Service Industries: A Geographical Appraisal.* London: Methuen.

Deere, C. D., Antrobus, P., Bolles, L., Melendez, E., Phillips, P., Rivera, M., and Safa, H. 1990: *In the Shadows of the Sun: Caribbean Development Alternatives and U.S. Policy.* Boulder, Colo.: Westview Press.

Delauney, J. C. and Gadrey, J. 1987: *Les Enjeux de la société de service.* Paris: Presses de la fondation des sciences politiques.

Dogan, M. and Kasarda, J. D. (eds), 1988: *A World of Giant Cities.* Newbury Park, Calif.: Sage Publications.

Edel, M. 1986: "Capitalism, Accumulation and the Explanation of Urban Phenomena," in M. Dear and A. Scott (eds), *Urbanization and Urban Planning in Capitalist Society,* New York: Methuen, 19–44

Fainstein, S. S., Gordon, I.,and Harloe, M. 1992: *Divided Cities: New York and London in the Contemporary World.* Oxford: Blackwell.

Fassmann, H. and Munz, R. 1992. "Einwanderungsland Osterreich: Gastarbeitter – Fluchtlinge - Immigraten" ("Austria, a Country of Immigration"). *Migration: A European Journal of International Migration and Ethnic Relations,* 13: 33–64.

Fernandez-Kelly, M. P. and Garcia, A. M. 1989: "Informalization at the Core: Hispanic Women, Homework, and the Advanced Capitalist State," in Portes *et al.* (eds), *The Informal Economy,* 247–54.

Friedmann, J. 1986. "The World City Hypothesis." *Development and Change,* 17: 69–84.

Friedmann, J. and Wolff, G. 1982: "World City Formation: An Agenda for Research and Action." *International Journal of Urban and Regional Research,* 6: 309–44.

Gershuny, J. and Miles, I. 1983: *The New Service Economy: The Transformation of Employment in Industrial Societies.* New York: Praeger.

Giarini, O. (ed.) 1987: *La Flexibilité du travail en Europe.* Paris: La Decouverte.

Gillette, A. and Sayad, A. 1988:*L'Immigration Algérienne en France*, 2nd edn. Paris: Éditions Entente.

Gregory, D., and Urry, J. (eds) 1985: *Social Relations and Spatial Structures*. London: Macmillan.

Hall, P. 1966: *The World Cities*. New York: McGraw-Hill.

Hall, P. and Hay, D. 1980: *Growth Centers in the European Urban System*. London: Heinemann Educational Books.

Hardoy, J. E. 1975: *Urbanization in Latin America*. Garden City, N.Y.: Anchor Books.

Hardoy, J. E. and Satterthwaite, D. 1989: *Squatter Citizen: Life in the Urban Third World*. London: Earthscan Publications.

Harrison, B. and Bluestone, B. 1988: *The Great U-Turn*. New York: Basic Books.

Harvey, D. 1985. *The Urbanization of Capital*. Oxford: Blackwell.

Hausserman, H., and Siebel, W. 1987: *Neue Urbanität*. Frankfurt: Suhrkamp.

Keil, R., and Ronneberger, K. 1992: "The City Turned Inside Out: Internationalization and Urbanization on Frankfurt's Northern Fringe." Paper presented at a conference of Research Committee 19, International Sociological Association, Los Angeles, April 24–6. Forthcoming in H. Hitz (ed.) *Financial Metropoles and Restructuring: Zurich and Frankfurt*. Zurich: Rotpunkt.

Komori, S. 1983: "Inner City in Japanese Context." *City Planning Review*, 125: 11–17.

Kowarick, L., Campos, A. M., and De Mello, M. C. 1991. "Os Percursos de Desigualdada," in R. Rolnik, L. Kowarick and N. Somekh (eds), *São Paolo: Crise e Mudanca*, Sao Paulo: Brasiliense, 49–68.

Kunzmann, K. R. and Wegener, M. 1991: *The Pattern of Urbanisation in Western Europe 1960–1990*. Report for the Directorate General XVI of the Commission of the European Communities as part of the study "Urbanisation and the Function of Cities in the European Community." Dortmund: Institut für Raumplanung.

KUPI 1981: *Policy for Revitalization of Inner City*. Kobe: Kobe Urban Problems Institute.

Landell-Mills, P., Agarwala, R., and Please, S. 1989: *Sub-Saharan Africa: From Crisis to Sustainable Growth*. Washington D.C.: World Bank.

Linn, J. F. 1983: *Cities in the Developing World: Policies for their Equitable and Efficient Growth*. New York: Oxford University Press.

Logan, J. R. and Molotch, H. 1987: *Urban Fortunes: The Political Economy of Place*. Berkeley, Calif.: University of California Press.

Lomnitz, L., 1985: "Mechanisms of Articulation between Shantytown Settlers and the Urban System." *Urban Anthropology*, 7: 185–205.

Machimura, T. 1992: "The Urban Restructuring Process in the 1980s: Transforming Tokyo into a World City." *International Journal of Urban and Regional Research*, 16: 114–28.

Markusen, A. 1985: *Profit Cycles, Oligopoly, and Regional Development*. Cambridge, Mass.: MIT Press.

Masser, I., Sviden, O. and Wegener, M. 1990: "Europe 2020: Long-Term Scenarios of Transport and Communications in Europe." Unpublished paper prepared for the European Science Foundation.

Mingione, E. 1991: *Fragmented Societies: A Sociology of Economic Life beyond the Market Paradigm*. Oxford: Blackwell.

Mione, A. 1991: "Legittimita ed Efficacia del Progetto Urbano." *Dis T Rassegna di Studi e Ricerche del Dipartimento di Scienze del Territorio del Politecnico di Milano*, 9: 137–50.

Nabuco, M. R., Machado, A. F. and Pires, J. 1991: "Estrategias de vida e sobrevivencia na industria de confeccoes de Belo Horizonte." Belo Horizonte: Cedeplar/UFMG.

Noyelle, T. T. and Dutka, A. B. 1988: *International Trade in Business Services: Accounting, Advertising, Law and Management Consulting*. Cambridge, Mass.: Harvard University Press.

Parkinson, M., Foley, B. and Judd, D.R. (eds) 1989: *Regenerating the Cities: The U.K. Crisis and the U.S. Experience*. Glenview, Ill.: Scott Foresman.

Perez-Sainz, J. P. 1992: *Informalidad Urbana en America Latina: Enfogues, Problematicas e Interrogantes*. Caracas: Editorial Nueva Sociedad.

Portes, A. and Lungo, M. (eds) 1992a: *Urbanizacion en Centroamerica*. San José, Costa Rica: Facultad Latinoamericana de Ciencias Sociales.

Portes, A. and Lungo, M. (eds) 1992b: *Urbanizacion en el Caribe*. San José, Costa Rica: Facultad Latinoamericana de Ciencias Sociales.

Portes, A. and Sassen-Koob, S. 1987: "Making it Underground: Comparative Material on the Informal Sector in Western Market Economies." *American Journal of Sociology*, 93: 30–61.

Prader, T. (ed.) 1992: *Modern Sklaven: Asyl und Migrations politik in Osterreich*. Vienna: Promedia.

PREALC, 1987: *Ajuste y Deuda Social: Un Enfoque Estructural*. Santiago de Chile: International Labour Office.

Preteceille, E. 1986: "Collective Consumption, Urban Segregation, and Social Classes." *Environment and Planning D: Society and Space*, 4: 145–54.

Prigge, W. 1991: "Zweite Moderne: Modernisierung und stadtische Kultur in Frankfurt," in F.-O. Brauerhoch (ed.), *Frankfurt am Main: Stadt, Soziologie und Kultur*, Frankfurt: Vervuet, 97–105.

Pugliese, E. 1983: "Aspetti dell' Economia Informale a Napoli." *Inchiesta*.

Rimmer, P. J. 1986: "Japan's World Cities, Tokyo, Osaka, Nagoya or Tokaido Megalopolis?" *Development and Change*, 17: 121–58.

Roberts, B. 1976: *Cities of Peasants*. London: Edward Arnold.

Rodriguez, N. P. and Feagin, J. R. 1986: "Urban Specialization in the World System." *Urban Affairs Quarterly*, 22: 187–220.

Roncayolo, M. 1990: *L'Imaginaire de Marseille*. Marseille: Chambre de commerce et d'industrie de Marseille.

Santoso, O. L. D. 1991: "The Role of Surakarta Area in the Industrial Transformation and Development of Central Java." *Regional Development Dialogue*, 13: 69–82.

Sassen, S. 1991: *The Global City: New York, London, Tokyo*. Princeton, N.J.: Princeton University Press.

Sassen-Koob, S. 1980: "Immigrants and Minority Workers in the Organization of the Labor Process." *Journal of Ethnic Studies*, 8: 1–34.

Savitch, H. 1988: *Post-Industrial Cities*. Princeton, N.J.: Princeton University Press.

Scott, A. J. 1988: *Metropolis: From the Division of Labor to Urban Form*. Berkeley, Calif.: University of California Press.

Sennett, R. 1992: *The Conscience of the Eye*. New York: Norton.

Siebel, W. 1984: *Kresenphänomene der Stadtenwicklung arch + d*. 75–76: 67–70.

Smith, M. P. and Feagin, J. R. 1987: *The Capitalist City: Global Restructuring and Territorial Development*. London: Sage Publications.

Stanback, T. M. and Noyelle, T. T. 1982: *Cities in Transition: Changing Job Structures in Atlanta, Denver, Buffalo, Phoenix, Columbus (Ohio), Nashville, Charlotte*. Totowa, N.J.: Allanheld, Osmun.

Stren, R. E. and White, R. R. 1989: *African Cities in Crisis: Managing Rapid Urban Growth*. Boulder, Colo.: Westview Press.

Thrift, N. 1987: "The Fixers: The Urban Geography of International Commercial Capital," in J. Henderson and M. Castells (eds), *Global Restructuring and Territorial Development*, London: Sage Publications, 203–33.

Tribalat, M., Garson, J.-P., Moulier-Boutang, Y. and Silberman, R. 1991: *Cent ans d'immigration, Étrangers d'hier français d'aujourd'hui*. Paris: Presses universitaires de France.

Van Den Berg, L., Drewett, R., Klassen, L. H., Rossi, A. and Vijvergerg, C. H. T. 1982: *Urban Europe: A Study of Growth and Decline*. Oxford: Pergamon.

Vidal, S. and Viard, J., 1990: *Le Deuxième Sud, Marseille ou le présent incertain*. Arles: Éditions Actes Sud, Cahiers Pierre-Baptiste.

Walters, P. B. 1985: "Systems of Cities and Urban Primacy: Problems of Definition and Measurement," in M. Timberlake (ed.), *Urbanization in the World Economy*, 63–85.

Wilson, W. J. 1987: *The Truly Disadvantaged: The Inner City, the Underclass and Public Policy*. Chicago: University of Chicago Press.

World Bank 1991: *Urban Policy and Economic Development: An Agenda for the 1990s*. Washington, D.C.: World Bank.

15

Culture and the Integration of National Societies

"The primary good that we distribute to one another is membership in some human community," wrote Walzer (1981: 1), a political theorist. In a similar spirit, Shils, a sociologist, observed that "membership in a political society is a necessity of man's nature" (1975 [1961]: 7). But which human community? Which political society? At this moment, when we are flooded with news of transnational institutions, of border cultures, of the disintegration of states–the former Soviet Union, the former Yugoslavia, the former Czechoslovakia, and perhaps more to come–and of subcultures and sub-nationalism, and multiculturalism, the question becomes both more complex and more salient. Furthermore, the question is both substantive and methodological. The fluidity of world boundaries is real, and the customary practice in the social sciences of taking the nation-state as the basic unit of analysis is no longer always pertinent. Agnew has criticized the major founders of the field–Marx, Durkheim, and Weber–as "methodological nationalists," all of whom accepted "state boundaries as co-extensive with those of the 'societies' or 'economies' they were interested in studying" (1989: 19).

The error of classical theory, however, was not that it *used* the nation-state as the unit of analysis but that it failed to treat it as a *problematic* social construction (Tiryakian and Nevitte 1985). The nation-state is properly regarded as the dominant human societal type in the world over the past two centuries. The central question to be addressed in this chapter is the

This chapter is based on a contribution by Michael Schudson.

role that culture plays in establishing social membership in the nation-state.

Human societies, whether nation-states or not, persist over time, held together by the following types of mechanisms:

- Territorial integration, which holds people together by their contiguity in space and a shared attachment to place.
- Kinship integration, or the rules of blood, marriage, and adoption. Within kinship, the incest taboo has also been treated as an integrative mechanism; by forcing sexual passions outside the family, the taboo fashions sexual, marital, economic, political, and emotional links to other groups, thereby reducing the potential for conflict.
- Economic integration, which binds people together through exchange and markets.
- Political integration, or the bringing together of people who may be separated territorially or culturally under a central government. When a regime unifies people not only through a system of justice, an administrative apparatus for taxation, and a common center of political allegiance but also through recruitment of citizen armies, political integration may be especially powerful. When a polity is organized along republican lines, accepting popular sovereignty at least in theory and establishing representative institutions, membership in the society is organized as citizenship.
- Cultural integration, which binds people together through a shared belief in a system of values, norms, language, symbols, rituals, and stories–in a word, culture. The most important and widely disseminated cultures have been organized religions, which have sometimes even threatened the sovereignty of the nation-state. Alternatively, a culture may take the form of a kind of "civil religion," either in a mode of national self-worship (represented in extreme form in Nazi Germany) or as a set of ethical principles that go beyond the state and hold it to account (Bellah 1970 [1967]). This chapter focuses on culture as an integrating force.

Culture and Integration

Culture is, paradoxically, both the most visible and the most problematic force for social integration. It is visible because the modern nation-state self-consciously uses language policy, formal education, collective rituals, and mass media for purposes of integrating citizens and securing their loyalty. In modern thought, the idea of integration through cultural symbols goes back at least to Montesquieu. He argued that social homogeneity was essential if citizens are to develop the sense of fraternity required by a republic. Citizens in a republic should be socialized by a patriotic civic education, frequent public rituals, censorship of dissent, and, ideally, a single religion. In their experiment in social integration, the leaders of the French Revolution were intent on harnessing song, story, and schooling–even the calendar and the measurement of space–to mold new citizens and build the new republic. Many Americans in the late eighteenth and early nineteenth centuries, the era of nation building, regarded the nation as essentially Protestant and often identified with northern European or even English ancestry (Smith 1988).

Even so, culture is neither a sole condition nor a sufficient condition for national integration. Switzerland, with local cantons and diversity of language, persists, even though "the Swiss have little emotional investment in the nation" (Bendix 1992: 78). Italy has been integrated by clientelist personal relations between the central government and local notables in the absence of a strong national myth or standard national culture (Tarrow 1977). Furthermore, the content of nationalist sentiments varies greatly from society to society.

Even more, culture may not be the central integrative mechanism for modern societies. Many sociologists and historians do not take it to be so. A scholar of modern China notes, for example, that since 1949 the folk culture of the villages has come under the influence of the culture of the Communist party, but that the greatest gains in cultural uniformity came "not in the ideological propaganda drenchings of Mao's later years, but during the first national land reform and early collectivization efforts of the 1950s" (Shue 1988: 65). Shils (1975 [1961]) observed, more generally, that economic and political integration, rather than cultural forces, have borne the primary responsibility for the integration of the masses into the modern state. Culture is best regarded, then, not as a monolithic unifier of society but as a set of overarching values, beliefs, symbols, and modes of thought with a recognizable pattern which, even if coherent in its own terms, does not necessarily give rise to integration at the societal level.

Societies are thus integrated in several different ways. They may be coherent *orders*, meaning that political control is effectively exercised. They may be *coordinated*, meaning that people of different roles, interests, and values interact harmoniously through various formal and informal mechanisms. Or they may be *communities*, with shared allegiance to a common set of beliefs and values. All these types rely on some level of common cultural understanding and communication, but political order relies on organization and force, coordination on market, exchange, and face-to-face interaction, and community on social relations oriented to common cultural practices, roles, and symbols.

But if culture is not the sole or sufficient condition for the integration of nation-states, it is still essential. Nationalism, Gupta writes, "attempts to create a new kind of spatial and mythopoetic metanarrative" (1992: 71). He and others look to literary or narrative theory to understand the meaning of nationalism and the nation-state. It follows from this line of reasoning that all societies are fictive in a special sense. Personal identification with any group of people depends on an imaginative leap. Cultural cues may lead people to identify themselves with co-religionists, co-residents, co-workers, co-citizens, co-ethnics, or kinsmen. Each of these identifications is part of creating an "imagined community," in Anderson's (1983) words. A sense of community is always *rooted*, in concrete, observable social life. But what features of it? The contribution of the imagination is to deliver one or several of these possible groupings to the individual as primary bases for personal identity and allegiance.

Theories of Culture and the Nation-State

Theories differ with respect to the link between culture and the nation-state. For Durkheim, society's moral unity is rooted in face-to-face experiences around common, sacred symbols of the group in moments of "collective effervescence." These ritual moments and their memories energize members of the society and contribute to social cohesion. The root of solidarity lies in this moment of ecstatic submission to the higher authority of the whole group and is sustained by the authority vested in cultural symbols and practices. In his early work Durkheim thought that this model fitted simple societies best, because modern societies are complex and diversified and must rely on differentiation and interdependence for integration. Later he changed his mind and argued that collective beliefs and rites–and the moral and emotional tone they carry–are essential in all societies (Lukes 1985).

Shils, like Durkheim, stressed the conceptual nature of cultural integration. In addition, he saw a perpetual ground for tension and conflict that is not present in Durkheim. This lies in the important distinction between center and periphery:

> Society has a center. There is a central zone in the structure of society. This central zone impinges in various ways on those who live within the ecological domain in which the society exists. Membership in the society, in more than the ecological sense of being located in a bounded territory and of adapting to an environment affected or made up by other persons located in the same territory, is constituted by relationship to this central zone. (Shils 1975 [1961]: 3)

This center is the locus of the values and beliefs that govern the society and has a sacred quality. It is also symbolized in persons, roles, and activities that embody those qualities.

While Shils's view is a "consensual" one on the surface, the notion of a center and a periphery captures enduring cultural *divisions* in the nation-state that even extreme nationalism can overcome only temporarily. While oriented to, and even in communion with, the sacredness of the center, those on the periphery are forever reminded of just how far from the center they are. Before the rise of the nation-state, Shils wrote, most people lived *"outside* society"; only with their incorporation into it could they experience their remoteness from the center as "a perpetual injury to themselves" (Shils 1975 [1961]: 13). In Durkheim's model, all members of a society unite around the same sacred collective representations; in Shils's view, tension and anxiety regarding one's closeness or distance from the center are intrinsic and omnipresent.

Until very recently, the concept of "integration" has been regarded as somewhat old-fashioned. It was very likely the victim of the deep and persistent criticisms of the sociology of Talcott Parsons and the assault on "modernization" theory in the 1960s and 1970s, both of which seemed to slight social conflict generally and to treat ethnic loyalties and primordial ties as transient in the march of economic development. The notion of integration–insofar as it survives–has taken on a more frankly negative, political meaning. It refers to the process whereby powerful nations incorporate peripheral nations but keep them subordinate in the world system or, within nations, to the process whereby elites incorporate but keep subordinate regions or disfavored ethnic and racial groups. Notions of the collective consciousness or sacred centers, even the "melting pot"– melting, that is, into a common culture–have given way to theories of hegemony or internal colonialism (Blauner 1972, Hechter 1975).

In this development the work of Gramsci (1971) has been especially influential. In his view, the center is not so much a set of common, sacred values as a dominant class that promotes a world view to the population at large, a world view that serves its own interests at the expense of others. When cultural hegemony operates effectively, this world view is accepted by subordinate groups as "natural," and they conspire in their own subordination, accepting beliefs and values that justify the unequal distribution of power and rewards in society.

Anderson developed an argument that supplements Gramsci's position. He sees the nation as an "imagined community," because its members never know or even hear of more than a fraction of its members, yet they conceive of themselves as co-members of that overriding social unit. The imagined entity is "always conceived as a deep, horizontal comradeship," and this helps explain the willingness of millions to die for this imagined object, the nation (Anderson 1983: 15–16). The nature of this fictive entity was caught vividly by Greenfeld, who noted that nationalism "locates the source of individual identity within a 'people,' which is seen as the bearer of sovereignty, the central object of loyalty, and the basis of collective solidarity" (Greenfeld 1992: 3).

In the end, cultural or normative integration, though difficult to measure, is at the center of the definition of the nation, even though its full "sharedness" may be inauthentic. Frequently the claims made for national symbolic sharing, claims of ancient heritage, long-standing tradition, or ethnic or family unity are instrumental inventions, even forgeries. They may arise from central administrations seeking to build or solidify their rule or from middle-class longings for power and meaning (nineteenth-century romantic nationalist movements or Arabist national- ism of the twentieth century) or from movements of resistance, especially in anti-colonial struggles (Hobsbawm 1983, Khoury 1991).

Culture may be over- or under-inclusive vis-à-vis the nation-state. With respect to the former, it may serve not only national societies but also imperial, global, and transnational entities (see chapter 8). The Olympic games, for example, evoke participation in a global–if competitive–culture. The spread of Western science, Marxian thought, and the Koran in national educational systems affirm allegiances beyond the national society. The spread of blue jeans, soccer, and rock music establishes tastes and longings that spill over national boundaries. Some of the most recent developments in media technology also have potential for circumventing the authority of dominant, state, or nationally centralized media; among these are computer bulletin boards, cable television, video cassette recorders, and hand-held video cameras or "camcorders." So do the new forms of satellite-assisted transmission of broadcast signals. A minister in the French government recently warned of "Coca-Cola" satellites and the invasion of American television programming by satellite broadcasting (Palmer 1987). Regional hegemonic powers may spread their influence culturally as well; Egypt, especially in Nasser's day, exported its culture, as well as its political influence, to the Arab nations through radio and films (Hourani 1991).

Mass media and other symbolic systems may also be under-inclusive, integrating groups smaller than the nation. Traditions of regional music and art and sub-national languages and cultures may prove disintegrative to the national society, as with ethnic conflicts in the former Soviet Union or Yugoslavia or Sri Lanka, the persistent battles over language in Canada, or continuing strife among religious groups in Northern Ireland and India.

The success of nation-states in overcoming localisms depends on the kind and level of means they have at hand–transportation, communication, formal organization and bureaucracy, and political ideology, especially the idea of the sovereignty of the people. Understanding culture as a force for integration or definition of membership requires looking at these concrete mechanisms for the objectification, transmission, and distribution of culture. To these mechanisms we now turn.

Language, Print, and Schooling

The medium of print has been linked with the national integration of mass populations through political participation. Anderson has made this point forcefully. For him, the nation-state is a product of "print capitalism," or the interaction between capitalism, print technology, and "the fatality of human linguistic diversity." Print capitalism consolidated the diverse spoken languages of early modern Europe into a smaller number of widely available written languages distributed through books and pamphlets. This "laid the bases for national consciousness" by creating an assemblage of readers connected with one another through their common texts. It provided "a new fixity to language" that advanced the fiction of the antiquity of a given language, culture, and nation (Anderson 1983: 46–47). The assemblage of readers was a creation of the technology of print, but it required a market as well. In eighteenth-century Europe, the print marketplace produced two highly successful new literary forms, the novel and the newspaper, both of which proved to be engines for symbolizing nationhood. Both generated new forms of simultaneity (Anderson: the novel is "a complex gloss upon the word 'meanwhile' "(1983)). The newspaper's diverse items are united by their having happened, become known, or become relevant at the same time. Newspaper reading created an extraordinary mass ceremony: the almost precisely simultaneous consumption ("imagining") of the "newspaper-as-fiction" (Anderson 1983: 39). People, often in private, read their newspapers "knowing" that thousands or even millions of others were doing the same thing at the same time.

Since early newspapers were the media of political and economic elites, they both helped to secure a sense of identity with their place of publication and linked locals to larger worlds through news of markets and affairs of state. Small-town newspapers in nineteenth-century America fostered involvement in local public life while also connecting townspeople to the nation by promoting the "highly prized ideal of citizen awareness–defined by the speech, accuracy, regularity, and currency of one's knowledge about the world" (Gilmore 1989: 112). The newspaper press, more widely circulated in the United States than in Europe, helped to make even rural citizens more actively oriented to the nation-state than their European counterparts.

In Europe regularly published sheets of news began in the early 1600s in the Netherlands and England, but in France and Germany the newspaper developed more slowly and primarily as an instrument of government. In the 1700s, however, as representative political institutions assumed more importance in England and its American colonies, political communication became more oriented to the public. By the mid-1700s, pamphlets and newspapers in the colonies were increasingly directed to all voters, not just to legislatures and elites, were printed by the thousands, and were read aloud at the polls. Their language also began to change toward a more accessible, "republican" style (Schudson 1989).

The development of newspapers in the United States and Europe coincided with the emergence of political parties and the drive to extend voting privileges. As it expanded, the franchise gave more people a stake in political life and a motive to inform themselves about it. Political parties in England and the United States shifted from instruments of elite rule to mass-based organs of political communication, and the newspapers they sponsored were an integral part of this shift. Parties and social movements mobilized citizens for political participation. In the United States in the nineteenth century and in much of the rest of the world up to the end of the Second World War, newspapers were primarily organs of political parties, and this was a key aspect of their integrative force.

Intellectuals mediated the contribution of print capitalism to "fixity" in language, especially in nineteenth-century Europe. In 1800 the Ukrainian language was regarded as a "language of yokels." But in 1864, with the founding of the University of Kharkov, intellectuals produced a boom in Ukrainian literature. A Ukrainian grammar was published in 1819, and in 1846 an intellectual established the first Ukrainian nationalist organization. Norwegians had long shared a written language with the Danes, but Norwegian nationalism proper appeared with the publication of a Norwegian grammar in 1848 and a dictionary in 1850. In Finland, the language of government was Swedish in the eighteenth century, and except among peasants it was the language of private life as well. But early nineteenth-century intellectuals, inspired by a romantic nationalism, pledged themselves to learn Finnish. Finnish folklorists partly rediscovered and partly invented national Finnish "epics" like the Kalevala. By 1900 Finnish-language schools were well established, and Finnish-speaking secondary school students outnumbered those speaking Swedish. While serious scholars came to recognize that the Kalevala was a pastiche of folk stories assembled into an epic narration by folklorist Elias Lonnrot, the schools, the mass media, and most Finns continued until well after the Second World War to regard the Kalevala as the sacred center of their ancient heritage.

Language itself is the key to all this. It is the fundamental human mass medium, the medium through which all other media speak. No other medium is so deeply rooted, so insistently the basis for political aspirations, or so much a source of resistance to the efforts of states to use the media for hegemonic control. A language is a highly charged cultural object. "The use of language not only permits acts of communion about particular objects, such as sacred objects or central objects; it is also an act of communication in itself" (Shils 1975: 76). Language, moreover, has been a central implement in the formation of nation units.

In and of itself, language does not contain explicit political directives. But in the modern era the state has played a central role in putting language to use for social integration. Concretely this takes place in the realm of formal education. To this day, in elementary schools around the world, language instruction (usually in the national or official language) consumes about one-third of instructional hours (Benavot *et al.* 1991). Nationally mandated, language-centered education is coterminous with the meaning of a nation-state. "The monopoly of legitimated education is now more important, more central than the monopoly of legitimate violence" (Gellner 1983: 34).

France provides a prototype of European nineteenth-century experience as well as a prelude to what was to happen later the world over. A law of 1833 required every commune to maintain an elementary school; 15 years later the number of schools in France had doubled. In 1881 education was made free, and in 1882 compulsory. In 1863 at least one-fifth of France's population could not speak official "French"; it was a second language for many students. In 1880 a report in Brittany recommended "Frenchifying" the peninsula through schooling, which would "truly unify the peninsula with the rest of France and complete the historical annexation always ready to dissolve" (quoted in Weber 1976: 313). The imposition of French also imposed local hardships. Students who spoke Breton rather than French at school were punished or shamed. They were taught a new patriotism as well as a new language. They learned that the "fatherland" was not where they lived but "something vast and intangible called France," and their instruction in French language, history, and geography was part of imagining the nation (McDonald 1989, Weber 1976).

In the early nineteenth-century United States, Noah Webster's textbooks were meant to instill a common language across the country and a common knowledge across regions. Webster wrote that in his spelling book he tried "to destroy the provincial prejudices that originate in the trifling differences of dialect and produce reciprocal ridicule, to promote the interest of literature and harmony of the United States." The Illinois Superintendent of Schools recommended Webster's dictionary for the schools in 1855 because it would help "procure that purity and uniformity of language so much to be desired. It will operate as a bond of national brotherhood" (Kaestle 1983: 99).

Third World states today "hold the school institution as sacred; they regard it as being *the* organizational mechanism for delivering mass opportunity, economic growth, and national integration" (Fuller and Rubinson 1992: 4). As the training ground for tomorrow's citizens, education emphasizes the transmission of a national culture, national symbols, and a national language. It is, as such, "an institutional agency for creating national uniformities among the heterogeneous status and class groupings in society" (Ramirez and Rubinson 1979: 79). Perhaps the most dramatic instance of this is found in Indonesia, where a commercial version of the Malay language has become an instrument for the national integration of a vast dispersion of islands and cultures. Singapore offers another interesting twist, in which English as the "official" language is taught in all schools, but three "national" languages–Mandarin, Malay, and Tamil–are also taught as a way of squaring linguistic unity with ethnic diversity.

Educational systems thus play a central role in creating the idea of a nation, through a process of socialization which is highly purposive, self-conscious, and focused on individuals as citizens. In at least two senses, however, a certain deception is involved. First, while typically presented as an egalitarian institution promoting social mobility, schooling operates to legitimize inegalitarian outcomes in economic and political positions. In addition, while it fosters an emotional attachment to primordial folk symbols and values, it simultaneously imposes a high national culture from the center on the relatively isolated folk cultures of the periphery. To put it succinctly, the nation-state is successfully Gramscian only when it presents itself to the people as fully Durkheimian.

World Consumer Culture and National Societies

Both the state and political parties have been cited as agencies of cultural forms of integration. So is the economy, through meanings attached to material goods. Consumer goods are sources of practical utility, of course. But at the same time they are symbolic structures that command attention and evoke allegiance from the fact that they have been shared. This view of consumer culture regards goods as elements in cultural classification schemes that people use to "construct an intelligible discourse" (Douglas and Isherwood 1979).

This discourse has been increasingly a national one over the past two centuries. Boorstin has described the emergence of what he called "consumption communities" in nineteenth-century United States. Through these, people came to recognize their connections and their distinctions from other people in the language of the goods they consumed. In 1800, four-fifths of men's and boys' clothing was made domestically in the United States; a century later almost all of it was made outside the home. Fashion became a signal system by which people could be located as *avant-garde, au courant,* or *passé* (Schudson 1984). Regarding "Middletown" in the 1920s, the Lynds (1929) saw that changes in employment patterns and the increasing use of the automobile, along with exposure to a wider world through movies and other mass media, tended to displace mothers and grandmothers in favor of women's magazines as tutors of consumption. In the Lynds' metaphor, the mass media created a democratization of envy.

Consumer goods may also be an instrument of the center in colonizing the periphery. In highland Ecuador, leavened white bread, symbolizing metropolitan culture, has increasingly been substituted for barley gruel, the traditional staple of the early morning meal. Weismantel, a student of the area's culinary practices, observes that the people "are constantly bombarded from within and without by images of their cultural practices as being backwards and wrong." While national integration is easy to recognize when schoolchildren are taught to salute the Ecuadorian flag, it is equally present "when his mother hesitates over what foods to serve her family, fearful that there is something inadequate in a meal of homegrown foods unembellished by purchased foodstuffs or condiments" (Weismantel 1989: 88). The situation, Weismantel notes, brings to mind Samuel Johnson's disparagement of the porridges of peripheral Scotland.

Nationalization does not always mean standardization. English-language cookbooks of Indian cuisine are common in India. The new aspirations and tastes for foods in the middle-class home have paralleled other aspects of societal integration; new cuisine, both national and regional, is a standard feature at food stands in train stations, railroad dining cars, student hostels, restaurants, and army barracks (a standard-ized colonial military cuisine has survived even after independence). Appadurai noted that "the idea of national Indian cuisine is now taken for granted," but it includes not only "India-wide" principles of cookery but also regional variety (Appadurai 1988). In the Indian case the dialectic is between regional and national. Elsewhere we observe a dialectic between national and international. The social status of consumer goods is, in part, an international language, with Russian teenagers wearing blue jeans and Japanese youths sporting jackets with American college insignia.

Persistence and Transformation of the Durkheimian Collective Experience

Rituals are key elements in the symbolic affirmation of key values. "Without rites and symbols," Kertzer writes, "there are no nations" (1988: 179). Rituals may be integrative or disintegrative–or a balance of both–in their impact. The Chinese Communists regarded local and religious rituals as an impediment to their own efforts of political transformation and integration. In the first years after the 1949 revolution, the state confiscated ancestral halls and temples and turned them into schools, offices, and factories. Later, trees marking neighborhood shrines were sacrificed to backyard furnaces. In the Cultural Revolution, temples were destroyed, while community participation in burial, birth, wedding, funeral, and memorial rites to ancestors was stamped out or confined to households. After the liberalization of state policy, even Communist cadres have restored their domestic altars, and ceremonial funerals and weddings have returned to their traditional extravagance (Siu 1989). The Bolshevik Revolution in Russia also expanded the role of state ritual. Agitation to promote common understandings among the masses was carried out during festivals on May Day and the anniversary of the revolution. Heroic statues were erected, and the cult of Lenin was developed even before his death. In Nazi Germany Hitler self-consciously incorporated symbols (the swastika) and German folk traditions, invented patriotic holidays, and staged mass rallies and festivals in his effort to create allegiance to the Third Reich (Mosse 1973).

Just as all cultures have a myth of origin, so the nation-state seems to require a history. In fact, it often devotes considerable resources to fashioning one. "No matter how culturally artificial or historically serendipitous the new national entity, it must be endowed with a sacred unity and made to seem a natural social unit" (Kertzer 1988: 179). Indonesian political leaders, for example, speak of 350 years of Indonesia's suffering under colonial rule, despite the fact that "the whole notion of Indonesia is a twentieth-century invention," and much of what is now Indonesia came under colonial rule only at the end of the nineteenth century. The rewriting of history in the service of collective identity is a theme of growing interest in several of the social sciences.

Elections may be the single most central ritual in modern democracies. Their actual role in affecting policy is not fully understood, but they are clearly central as a ritual in legitimizing state power and reaffirming the connections of individuals to state and society (Ginsberg 1986). The same may be said for other national events such as Watergate–which became something of a symbol for the reaffirmation of national political integrity (Alexander 1984, Schudson 1992)–and even commemorative activities around such divisive events as the Vietnam War, about which there is no established social consensus (Wagner-Pacifici and Schwartz 1991).

Broadcasting and Collective Identity

In most nations broadcasting has emerged under the control or regulation of the state. And legislation establishing broadcast systems has identified national, integrative, and participatory goals for the society. In Canada, for instance, broadcasting began as an effort to assert cultural autonomy in relation to the United States. It was also begun, however, as a federal rather than a regional agency, in an effort to shore up Canadian national feeling (Raboy 1985). In seeking to renew its license in 1980, the Canadian Broadcasting Corporation suggested that the CBS is really all about "the creation of a national consciousness." Its self-designated goal is to express the "Canadian identity" and to become "a living institution in Canada, a symbol of Canadian nationhood, a central constituent in the cement which binds this country together" (quoted in Ericson *et al.* 1987: 28).

Some cultural critics have perhaps claimed too much for the broadcast media when they suggest that it is the church of modern societies or that people learn their values from television rather than from parents or guardians at home. Meyrowitz has argued that television "de-territorializes" personal identity. "[The] traditionally interlocking components of 'place' have been split apart by electronic media" (1985: 308). He contends that "electric messages on television, telephone, and radio democratize and homogenize places by allowing people to experience and interact with others in spite of physical isolation." Electronic media "begin to override group identities based on 'co-presence,' and they create many new forms of access and 'association' that have nothing to do with physical location" (ibid.: 144).

This extreme view must be qualified in two ways. First, some of the effects attributed to the electronic media predate them. Personal identification with the nation, a vast assemblage of people one has never met, surely predates the electronic media. It has been argued convincingly that even in tribal societies the power of territoriality as a concrete unifying mechanism has been exaggerated. Most tribal societies that anthropologists have studied were neither pristine nor autonomous but have been defined as such in large degree by their encounters with imperial powers and their agents. "People have undoubtedly always been more mobile and identities less fixed than the static and typologizing approaches of classical anthropology would suggest" (Gupta and Ferguson, 1992: 8–9).

Second, people are not simply transformed by the media; they typically use new technologies to reinforce old social habits. The telephone, which, in theory, freed people from dependence on locality, is used above all to call nearby friends and neighbors (Fischer 1992). Similarly, the cosmopolitanism made possible by national and international broadcasting is selectively perceived and interpreted in a way that is consistent with preexisting attitudes and beliefs (see chapter 8).

At the same time, the media play a large role in inventing and perpetuating rituals. Dayan and Katz (1992) have studied the live broadcasting of "media events," including John F. Kennedy's funeral, Anwar Sadat's visit to Jerusalem, the royal wedding of Charles and Diana, and the televised revolutions in Eastern Europe in 1989–90. In such instances news broadcasters break with any pretense at objectivity and become open cheerleaders for the nation. Reporting becomes reverent or celebrative. This enables broadcasters and their organizations to "[repledge] their allegiances to the central values of the commonwealth" (Dayan and Katz 1992: 193).

Audiences of these "media events" often behave in the same way. An Indian student described how her family prepared to watch the Gandhi funeral on television; they washed and dressed "as if we were going to be physically present at the scene. My mother insisted that we wear long clothes and cover our heads as a mark of respect." People drew together, crossing family and class boundaries, to watch (Dayan and Katz 1992: 123). Both solemn and festive media events in the United States (the landing on the moon, political inaugurations, championship sporting events) are often occasions for group viewing. The media provides the audience with a ceremonial sense of community and direct communication with the societal "center," despite their dispersion.

Broadcasting, like schooling, also accommodates itself to linguistic and cultural differences within states. After Zambia's independence in 1964, a "tribal balancing" policy was developed for the radio in that country which has some 73 ethnic groups speaking 15 to 20 languages. In 1967, broadcasting was in English, Bemba, and Nyanja. In the mid-1970s, Kaonde, Lozi, Lunda, Luvale, and Tonga also received broadcasting time. Then in 1988, in a sharp reversal of policy, all Zambian languages were eliminated from the general radio service. As of 1990, Radio 1 and Radio 4 broadcast in English only. On Radio 2 seven Zambian languages received equal time, though prime time went to languages representing the largest groups of people. English, the national language and the language of government and higher education, is the only language that is "ethnically neutral"–as in Singapore–because it is native to none of the indigenous ethnic groups and thus excites less competition among them (Spitulnik

1992). English also links Zambia to the world's political-economic system. In Kenya, Tanzania, and Uganda it was possible to establish an African language, Swahili, as the national language, because there were few native Swahili speakers and they did not represent a political bloc dangerous to other ethnic groups (Mazrui and Tidy 1984).

Even as nations are disintegrating, the national media may operate as a counterforce. In 1988 Mickiewicz described Soviet television as "a powerful force for integration" and "a national medium attempting to forge a national consciousness and a national culture." In addition, she recognized ethnicity as a powerful centrifugal force, but argued that the mass media were slowly overcoming it. In Azerbaijan, for instance, Azeri and Russian language programs were given equal time, but the national programs had superior production values and provided content that made them better for language learning. She judged the popular Azeri language programs to be ineffective in transmitting ethnic culture. She concluded: "In the Soviet Union, as everywhere else, differences and traditions are slowly eroding as national television usurps the role of keeper of the heritage" (Mickiewicz 1988: 207).

Quite evidently, historical events have proved that statement wrong. Yet, while acknowledging this, we should continue to recognize the complex role of the national media. Certainly Soviet television reinforced nationalization, even if in such a way that it may have simultaneously reinforced resentment on the periphery of that empire. Some scholars perceived its ultimate weakness. In 1977 a number of British experts on Eastern Europe argued consistently that there was a growing gulf between the official media's messages of national pride and unity and the public apathy and cynicism with which these messages were regularly greeted (Gray 1977).

Perhaps, in the end, the integrative power of broadcasting may lie in the medium more than the message. In India, for instance, the government television monopoly and its highly partisan news reporting appeared to have little impact in the 1989 elections. "By 1989 voters had experienced a decade and a half of heavily biased broadcasts on All India Radio which had frequently failed to persuade them to re-elect incumbents. Most of them plainly concluded that the still more partisan reports on television should be treated with similar skepticism" (Manor 1992: 116). Nevertheless, television appears to have notable institutional effects in places where political parties have weakened. In the United States, television appears to have grown as a central political mechanism at the expense of parties (Polsby, 1983). Within parties and within candidacies, public relations, polling, and advising experts with no territorial constituency have prospered at the expense of party bosses with local followings (Curran 1991). In Scandinavian countries, television is now the most important source of political information during campaigns. In the first television-centered elections, the political parties controlled television time, but increasingly the broadcast media have become independent actors, while the print media have moved from partisanship to neutrality. The result is that the mass media have changed "from an effective campaign channel to an independent actor in election campaigns, having a strong influence on what issues are actually discussed." In France, television has been "the principal ground of party struggles" since 1965 and an important ingredient in the greater nationalization of French politics (Charlot and Charlot 1992).

Resistance to Hegemony and the Center

Typically the mass media are regarded as a powerful integrative force—positively, insofar as they assimilate peoples to a common culture, and negatively, insofar as they strip them of their folk cultures and embrace them within the hegemonic culture represented by society's elites at the center. Either way, the assumption is that as the media become more powerful, they make people more homogeneous and docile. This assumption, moreover, applies to both authoritarian and liberal regimes. Habermas, for example, emphasizes the "refeudalization" of the media after an emancipatory moment of a "bourgeois public sphere" in late eighteenth-and early nineteenth-century Europe (Habermas 1989).

This assumption of a quiescent audience has been thrown into doubt during the past decade, as studies have documented that different audiences interpret the same cultural materials in different ways (Liebes and Katz 1990, Radway 1984). The accompanying assertion that people regain significant control over the interpretation of mass media messages is reinforced by the evident integrative problems of the former Soviet Union, the former Yugoslavia, and the former Czechoslovakia, not to mention the ethnic, linguistic, religious, and cultural divisions elsewhere in the world.

State-sponsored rituals, while propagandistic and integrative in intent, are subject to subversion. Students involved in the Tienanmen Square uprising of 1989 made their protests public during the funeral procession of Hu Yaobang, thus converting this state-prescribed function into a moment of protest. Such funerals had long been occasions for the wealthy and powerful to display and reinforce the social order symbolically. But the very sacredness of such occasions provides both an invitation and an opportunity for dissidents, as happened also in 1976, after the death of Zhou Enlai, when thousands of Chinese in Beijing used the occasion to criticize the Gang of Four (Esherick and Wasserstrom 1990).

When this kind of criticism develops, we witness political theater rather than political ritual. Theater, Esherick and Wasserstrom write, has "a critical power never possessed by ritual: it can expose the follies of tradition (or the follies of abandoning tradition), mock social elites, or reveal the pain and suffering of everyday life" (1990: 840). Whereas ritual symbolism confirms the political or social order, theater subverts it. During the years before the velvet revolution of 1989 in Poland and Hungary, holidays and anniversary celebrations and the mass gatherings they occasioned frequently provided an opportunity for statements of protest.

Conclusion

In our internationalized world, cultures flow in, out, around, and through state borders; within states, centers radiate to peripheries and peripheries influence centers (see chapters 8 and 14). Noting the flow of culture in the contemporary world system, Hannerz referred to Paris, London, Brussels, and Miami as culturally "among the major Third World Cities" (Hannerz 1987: 549). He argued that "the world system, rather than creating massive homogeneity on a global scale, is replacing one diversity with another; and the new diversity is based relatively more on interrelations and less on autonomy" (ibid.: 555).

The nation-state is still dominant, but in a world that is reconstituting itself. The nations of Europe, for instance, have had their own institutions of communication challenged by transnational institutions in the service of a "European community." The Commission of the European Communities envisioned a role for European television in defending both the cultural identity and economic power of Europe against American and Japanese rivals. In a paper called "Television without Frontiers," the Commission argued that "[information] is a decisive, perhaps the most decisive factor in European unification," basing this claim on a further one that only through common information and common culture will Europeans come to seek and achieve a new European identity (quoted in Schlesinger 1991: 139). Nation-states are likewise threatened from above by the internationalism of the multinational corporation and from below by sub-national forces– ethnic, racial, linguistic, regional. So Gupta's question is a key one. We should ask "why the hegemonic representation of spatial identity in the world continues to be that of the naturalized border of nation-states" (1992: 75). The question poses a profound challenge not only to sociology but to all the social sciences that have developed with the nation-state at the center of their disciplinary stage.

References

Agnew, J. A. 1989: "The Devaluation of Place in Social Science," in J. A. Agnew and J. S. Duncan (eds), *The Power of Place*, Boston: Unwin Hyman, 9–29.

Alexander, J. 1984: "Three Models of Culture and Social System: An Analysis of the Watergate Crisis." *Sociological Theory*, 2:. 290–314.

Anderson, B. 1983: *Imagined Communities: Reflections on the Origin and Spread of Nationalism*. London: Verso.

Appadurai, A. 1988: "How to Make a National Cuisine: Cookbooks in Contemporary India." *Comparative Studies in Society and History*. 30: 1–24.

Bellah, R. N. 1970 [1967]: "Civil Religion in America," in *Beyond Belief*, New York: Harper and Row, 168–89.

Benavot, A., Cha, Y.-K., Kames, D., Meyer, J. W. and Wong, S.-Y. 1991: "Knowledge for the Masses: World Models and National Curricula, 1920–1986." *American Sociological Review*, 56: 85–100.

Bendix, R. 1992: "National Sentiment in the Enactment and Discourse of Swiss Political Ritual." *American Ethnologist*, 190: 68–90.

Blauner, R. 1972: *Racial Oppression in America*. New York: Harper and Row.

Boorstin, D. 1973: *The Americans: The Democratic Experience*. New York: Random House.

Charlot, J. and Charlot, M. 1992: "France," in D. Butler and A. Ranney (eds), *Electioneering: A Comparative Study of Continuity and Change*, Oxford: Clarendon Press, 133–55.

Curran, J. 1991: "Rethinking the Media as a Public Sphere, " in P. Dahlgren and C. Sparks (eds), *Communication and Citizenship*, London: Routledge, 27–57.

Dayan, D. and Katz, E. 1992: *Media Events: The Live Broadcasting of History*. Cambridge, Mass.: Harvard University Press.

Douglas, M. and Isherwood, B. 1979: *The World of Goods*. New York: Basic Books.

Ericson, R. V., Baranek, P. M. and Chan, J. B. L. 1987: *Visualizing Deviance: A Study of News Organization*. Toronto: University of Toronto Press.

Esherick, J. and Wasserstrom, J. 1990: "Acting Out Democracy: Political Theater in Modern China." *Journal of Asian Studies*, 49: 835–66.

Essaiasson, P. 1992: "Scandinavia," in Butler and Ranney (eds), *Electioneering*, 202–21.

Fischer, C. 1992: *America Calling*. Berkeley, Calif.: University of California Press.

Fuller, B. and Rubinson, R. (eds) 1992: *The Political Construction of Education*. New York: Praeger.

Gellner, E. 1983: *Nations and Nationalism*. Ithaca, N.Y.: Cornell University Press.

Gilmore, W. J. 1989: *Reading Becomes a Necessity of Life*. Knoxville, Tenn.: University of Tennessee Press.

Ginsberg, B. 1986: *The Captive Public*. New York: Basic Books.

Gramsci, A. 1971: *Selections from the Prison Notebooks*. London: Lawrence and Wishart.

Gray, J. 1977: "Conclusions," in A. G. Brown and J. Gray (eds), *Political Culture and Political Change in Communist States*, New York: Holmes and Meier, 253–72.

Greenfeld, L. 1992: *Nationalism: Five Roads to Modernity*. Cambridge, Mass.: Harvard University Press.

Gupta, A. 1992: "The Song of the Unaligned World: Transnational Identities and the Reinscription of Space in Late Capitalism." *Cultural Anthropology*, 6: 63–79.

Gupta, A. and Ferguson, J. 1992: "Beyond 'Culture': Space, Identity and the Politics of Difference." *Cultural Anthropology*, 7: 6–23.

Habermas, J. 1989: *The Structural Transformation of the Public Sphere: An Inquiry into a Category of Bourgeois Society*. Cambridge, Mass.: MIT Press.

Hannerz, U. 1987: "The World in Creolisation." *Africa*, 57: 546–59.

Hechter, M. 1975: *Internal Colonialism*. Berkeley, Calif.: University of California Press.

Hobsbawm, E. J. 1983: "Mass-Producing Traditions: Europe, 1870–1914," in E. Hobsbawm and T. Ranger (eds), *The Invention of Tradition*, Cambridge: Cambridge University Press, 263–307.

Hourani, A. 1991: *A History of the Arab Peoples*. Cambridge, Mass.: Harvard University Press.

Kaestle, C. F. 1983: *Pillars of the Republic: Common Schools and American Society, 1780–1860*. New York: Hill and Wang.

Kertzer, D. 1988: *Ritual, Politics, and Power*. New Haven, Conn.: Yale University Press.

Khoury, P. S. 1991: "Continuity and Change in Syrian Political Life: The Nineteenth and Twentieth Centuries." *American Historical Review*, 96: 1374–95.

Liebes, T. and Katz, E. 1990: *The Export of Meaning: Cross-Cultural Readings of Dallas*. New York: Oxford University Press.

Lukes, S. 1985: *Durkheim: His Life and Work*. Stanford, Calif.: Stanford University Press.

Lynd, R. and Lynd, H. 1929: *Middletown*. New York: Harcourt, Brace.

McDonald, M. 1989: *"We Are Not French!" Language, Culture and Identity in Brittany*. London: Routledge.

Manor R, J. 1992: "India," in Butler and Ranney (eds), *Electioneering*, 110–32.

Mazrui, A. and Tidy, M. 1984: *Nationalism and New States in Africa*. Nairobi: Heinemann.

Meyrowitz, J. 1985: *No Sense of Place: The Impact of Electronic Media on Social Behavior*. New York: Oxford University Press.

Mickiewicz, E. 1988: *Split Signals: Television and Politics in the Soviet Union*. New York: Oxford University Press.

Mosse, G. 1973: "Mass Politics in the Political Liturgy of Nationalism," in E. Kamenka (ed.), *Nationalism: The Nature and Evolution of an Idea,*. New York: St Martin's Press.

Palmer, M. 1987: "Media and Communications Policy under the Socialists, 1981–86: Failing to Grasp the Political Nettle?" in G. Ross and J. Howorth (eds), *Contemporary France: A Review of Interdisciplinary Studies*, London: Frances Pinter, 130–55.

Polsby, N. 1983: *Consequences of Party Reform*. New York: Oxford University Press.

Raboy M. 1985: "Public Television, the National Question and the Preservation of the Canadian State," in P. Drummond and R. Paterson (eds), *Television in Transition*. London: BFI Publishing, 64–86.

Radway, J. 1984: *Reading the Romance*. Chapel Hill, N.C.: University of North Carolina Press.

Ramirez, F. O. and Rubinson, R. 1979: "Creating Members: The Political Incorporation and Expansion of Public Education," in J. W. Meyer and M. T. Hannan (eds), *National Development and the World System*, Chicago: University of Chicago Press, 72–82.

Schlesinger, P. 1991: *Media, State and Nation: Political Violence and Collective Identities*. London: Sage Publications.

Schudson, M. 1984: *Advertising, the Uneasy Persuasion*. New York: Basic Books.

Schudson, M. 1989: "Toward a Comparative History of Political Communication." *Comparative Social Research*, 11: 151–63.

Schudson, M. 1992: *Watergate in American Memory*. New York: Basic Books.

Shils, E. A. 1975 [1961]: "Center and Periphery," in *Center and Periphery: Essays in Macrosociology*, Chicago: University of Chicago Press, 3–16.

Shils, E. A. 1975: "The Integration of Society," in *Center and Periphery*, 48–90.

Shue, V. 1988: *The Reach of the State: Sketches of the Chinese Body Politic*. Stanford, Calif.: Stanford University Press.

Siu, H. F. 1989: "Recycling Rituals: Politics and Popular Culture in Contemporary Rural China," in P. Link, R. Madsen and P. Pickowicz (eds), *Unofficial China: Popular Culture and Thought in the People's Republic*, Boulder, Colo.: Westview Press, 121–37.

Smith, R. M. 1988: "The 'American' Creed and American Identity: The Limits of Liberal Citizenship in the United States." *Western Political Quarterly*, 41: 225–51.

Spitulnik, D. 1992: "Radio Time Sharing and the Negotiation of Linguistic Pluralism in Zambia." *Pragmatics*, 2: 335–54.

Tarrow, S. 1977: *Between Center and Periphery: Grassroots Politicians in Italy and France*. New Haven, Conn.: Yale University Press.

Tiryakian, E. and Nevitte, N. 1985: "Nationalism and Modernity," in E. Tiryakian and R. Rogowski (eds). *New Nationalisms of the Developed West*, Boston: Allen and Unwin, 87–109.

Wagner-Pacifici, R. and Schwartz, B. 1991: "The Vietnam Veterans Memorial: Commemorating a Difficult Past." *American Journal of Sociology*, 97: 376–421.

Walzer, M. 1981: "The Distribution of Membership," in P. D. Brown and H. Sheu (eds), *Boundaries: National Autonomy and Its Limits*. Totowa, N.J.: Rowman and Littlefield, 1–35.

Weber, E. 1976: *Peasants into Frenchmen*. Stanford, Calif.: Stanford University Press.

Weismantel, M. J. 1989: "The Children Cry for Bread: Hegemony and the Transformation of Consumption," in H. J. Ruiz and B. S. Orlove (eds), *The Social Economy of Consumption*, Lanham, Md.: University Press of America, 85–99.

16

Race, Ethnicity, and Class

The three words constituting the subject matter of this chapter–"race," "ethnicity," and "class"–enjoy wide currency both as categories in the social sciences and as terms in everyday discourse. Each is employed as if it enjoys a common meaning, yet none is used with precision in either arena. For that reason a certain amount of conceptual clarification needs to be undertaken. This exercise will be supplemented by tracing some of the linkages among the three phenomena, both at a general level and with special reference to the situation of the United States, a country with a complex history and contemporary mosaic of racial and ethnic groups.

Race and Racism

Traditional anthropological classifications of races are based on observable physical and biological features such as cephalic index, texture of hair, blood group, and so forth. This is the basis on which the three great human races–Caucasoid, Mongoloid, Negroid–and their subtypes have been classified. It is legitimate to enquire whether in fact such groupings can be appropriately delimited on physical or biological grounds. This is difficult to determine, of course, given the centuries of migration, mixing, and cross-procreation among the identified groups.

The transition from some biological notion of race to its sociological significance actually involves two distinct transitions. The first is a shift in the point of reference. Race as a sociological phenomenon is a culturally and socially constructed and sustained category. As a social and cultural expression, it includes references to physical and biological characteristics

---

This chapter is based on a contribution by T. K. Oommen.

of other groups, but these are significant as mainly *social* categorizing devices, rather than as empirical statements about physique and biology. The second transition–and this leads to racism proper–occurs when another range of beliefs is invoked: for example, that particular races are superior in some way and deserve to dominate other races. With the development of racism, moreover, the issue of whether race has any physical or biological basis recedes more or less completely into the background. Even when the presumed scientific basis for race turns out to be fallacious–as in the distinction between genotype and phenotype (see Montagu 1964)–race remains a *sociologically* relevant variable when it becomes the structural basis for human interaction, stratification, and domination.

The rise and consolidation of racist beliefs are indistinguishable from the historical process that generates them, and such beliefs are reinforced by a selective appeal to that process. The supposed superiority of the "white" race, for example, is buttressed by reference to the high levels of economic development and scientific attainment in certain European and North American countries. Needless to say, such reasoning ignores the facts that (a) for long periods some "whites"–for example, in Latin America–did not enjoy those achievements; (b) certain geographical advantages, not related to race, accompanied white settlement in the New World; and (c) some of the advantages enjoyed by whites have rested on the exploitation of other groups through colonization and other forms of domination. Two other phenomena also cast doubt on the validity of the supposed link: the differential achievements of certain ethnic or religious groups *within* the "white" race (consider, e.g., Weber's Protestant ethic thesis) and the extraordinary technological and economic attainments of "yellow" races in East Asia and related achievements among "brown" and "black" peoples as well as Hindus and Muslims. Racist beliefs do not assimilate such facts readily, however, and they persist as hardy, legitimizing bases for hierarchical arrangements within and among societies.

Racism is also a product in part of contact with other races, often in colonial contexts. Before the sixteenth century "race" and territory were more closely related than they became later–Black Africa, White Europe, Yellow East Asia, Brown South Asia. Subsequently, however, the processes of colonization and both forced and free migration led to the emergence of multiracial societies. Such societies were usually "plural" in the sense that different races lived and interacted economically in the same society but did not legally co-procreate or blend their cultures (Furnivall 1948). In such societies, moreover, "race" and "class" merged as blacks were assigned to slavery, immigrant yellows and browns to indentured labor, and "natives" to agriculture.

With some exceptions–for example, in southeastern Europe, where ethnic distinctions approach the absolutism of racial ones–the story of ethnicity has been somewhat different. Inter-ethnic interactions have always existed within the same geographical regions, where the inhabitants have professed different religious faiths and/or spoken different languages. As a rule, the ethnic division of labor, though evident, has not been as sharp as that between races. At the same time, ethnicity and class have been closely correlated, as in the United States, where religious and cultural groups have clustered to some degree in certain occupations and, as a result, in particular social classes.

Conceptual Clarifications

Basic Terms

Racism, then, is a mix of ideology and practice based on imputed biological differences. It has a cultural element, because in the end it is primarily a socially and culturally constructed phenomenon. The concept of ethnicity is more explicitly cultural in character. Like race, ethnicity does not necessarily entail superiority or inferiority. At the same time, ethnic groups frequently define themselves as superior and perceive the culture of others as inferior. Some authors (e.g., Bacal 1991) have proposed the term "ethnicism" to refer to discrimination based on ethnicity. In current usage, the term has come to have a somewhat positive valence, constituting a basis for identity and "roots" and potentially a viable feature of civil society (see chapters 7 and 15).

The parallelism of terminology is incomplete with respect to race. While *racism* is an identifiable phenomenon, usually described with negative valence, we have no widely used concept such as "racity," a term suggested by T. K. Oommen, which implies the tendency of those identified as belonging to a distinct physical or biological type to provide others of their type with support and sustenance, particularly when confronted by an oppressive force. The phenomenon of racity does exist empirically, however. It is suggested in the slogans "Black pride," "Black power," and "Black is beautiful" among blacks in the United States and in their idealization of the African homeland as a symbol of solidarity and a basis for mobilization into groups, voluntary associations, and caucuses within political parties. Thus "racism" refers to stigmatization and oppression, "racity" to racial solidarity and efforts to cope with racism. But in any event, whatever the terminology, both sides of racial and ethnic existence should be taken into account.

As a sociological category class has more conspicuous–though not exclusive–economic reference. The class systems of modern societies are mainly products of inequalities engendered through industrial (whether capitalist, socialist, or some mix) and urban development. In societies that are still homogeneous with respect to their mix of racial, ethnic, and national groups, classes are likely to be the clearest and most salient bases of inequality, identity, and solidarity. In multiracial or polyethnic societies, however, these dimensions cut across class and produce complicated patterns of segmentation within racial and ethnic groups, thus confounding class as the main organizing basis for social categorization and inequality.

The salience of racial and ethnic dimensions in the class structures of societies is highly variable. Among contemporary societies racial forces intrude in most extreme form in South Africa. At the other end of the continuum is Brazil, where a systematic and partially successful effort has been made to establish "racial democracy," not only by invoking the law but also by encouraging race mixture. The cases of the United States and the United Kingdom are in-between, in the sense that the legal system prohibits discrimination on racial and ethnic grounds, but both institutional and informal discriminatory practices persist.

A Sociological Case for the Distinction between Race and Ethnicity

With the near-universal condemnation of Nazism and other forms of fascism and the disintegration of European colonialism, racism and the legitimacy of speaking of the superiority of certain races have become correspondingly discredited. But the same has not happened with regard to ethnicity: "By contrast [with race] ethnicity has become legitimate–people can openly claim some ethnic identity without lessened esteem, they can even show they are proud of it and, in many cases, actively seek redress from perceived inequalities in terms of such identities, without being officially banned" (Bjorklund 1987: 23). An unanticipated consequence of these developments, perhaps, has been to assimilate race to ethnicity, that is, to treat racial and ethnic groups and practices alike, as many legal proscriptions do.

Social-scientific definitions of ethnicity also tend to blur the distinction between ethnicity and race. Consider Bulmer's recent definition: "An 'ethnic group' is a collectivity within a larger society having real or putative common ancestry, memories of a shared past, and cultural focus on one or more symbolic elements which define the group's identity, such as kinship, religion, language, shared territory, nationality or *physical appearance*" (1986: 54, italics added; see also Montagu 1964). The reference to physical appearance, in particular, illustrates the blurring of the racial and the ethnic.

Although there may be identifiable historical and institutional reasons leading to confounding race and ethnicity, there are very sound *sociological* reasons for maintaining the distinction, largely because it maintains itself in the realities of institutional and cultural life. The following are some of those reasons.

First, the traditional idea of the genetic inferiority of nonwhites in general and blacks in particular survives as a societal belief (Duster 1990). In some instances such beliefs may be "culturalized" (Steinberg 1981); that is, the biologically attributed traits of blacks as ugly, barbarian, dirty, stupid, and aggressive may be put down to their culture, and on that basis blacks may be described as aggressive and criminal, incompetent, laid back, easygoing, "athletic" but not "smart," and so on (Essed 1991). The appearance and consolidation of similar stereotypes of minorities in Europe since their immigration after the Second World War is the most recent example of this process (Barker 1981). However, the shift from biology to culture in the characterization of races–or, perhaps better, the christening of racism as ethnicity (Chesler 1976)–diminishes neither the social force of racism nor the need for its recognition as a distinct phenomenon.

Second, certain stereotypes in particular show a resistance to dissociation from race. One such stereotype, prevalent in the United States, is the notion that blacks are hypersexual, in terms of both their sexual endowments and their sexual behavior. Such stereotypes are harbored by many whites and by some blacks as well, each for their own psychological reasons. In any event, the stereotype has historically been a basis for lynching or jailing blacks in cases of rape or sexual harassment of white women. Such stereotypes persist to this day (Davis 1981). They surfaced dramatically in the confirmation hearings of Clarence Thomas, a black, for the United States Supreme Court, when Thomas was accused of sexual harassment on the basis of testimony by Anita Hill.

Third, the racial mentality persists in social definitions of the "transformability" of peoples. Even when miscegenation is accepted and systematically pursued as a social goal (as in Brazil), the persistence of racial definitions tends toward an elaboration of socially defined physical types (Ianni 1970). The proliferation of "part-black" categories (mulatto, quadroon, octoroon) in state legal definitions in the United States is a similar example of the sticking power of blood ideology. There are, however, some historical instances in which a group has undergone a genuine transition from "racial" to "ethnic"; the Chinese and Japanese, defined as the "yellow peril" in California in the nineteenth century, are now regarded as ethnic groups in California's multicultural setting. But as a general rule, groups originally defined as ethnic can be transformed more easily over periods of time through assimilation, religious conversion, adoption of a new language, or adoption of new life-styles.

Fourth, ethnic groups may exist within groups defined as the same racial type. All those who belong to the same race may not profess the same religion or speak the same tongue. In the United States, West Indian and Haitian "blacks" are generally recognized as culturally different, ethnic-like groups within the black "race." Thus race and ethnic identifications, in their cross-cutting, indicate the social reality of the distinction between the two.

Fifth, Oommen (1989) has distinguished between attributional ethnicity (a membership category) and interactional ethnicity (a social-distance category). These two combine to condition relations among races. For example, the social distance between a white Christian and a black Muslim is typically greater than that between a white Christian and a black Christian, even though all the distinctions involved are attributional in character.

Sixth, the dynamics of group relations show persistent tendencies for a dominant group to assimilate groups in either a racial or an ethnic direction. In the United Kingdom, there exists a phenomenon that might be called "aggregative racism." This is the tendency to group a great variety of peoples–African, Afro-Caribbean, South Asian, and so on–in the category "black." While decipherable as a shorthand, stereotyping device on the part of the dominant white population, the distinction obliterates important differences, including some racism, *among* these groups. As a rule, "yellow" Southeast Asians consider themselves superior to "brown" South Asians, who in turn consider themselves superior to "black" Africans. Two observations are underscored by such aggregative racism: it shows the distinctively *sociological* character of most institutionalized racism–that is, its independence of any biological reality–and it demonstrates the power of racial thinking to obliterate important ethnic and national differences among groups.

Seventh, the realities of race persist in everyday life. The differential expectations of police vis-à-vis blacks in the United States and other countries is well documented. In Eastern Europe and South Asia white and yellow tourists are pursued relentlessly by shopkeepers, without knowledge of their particular affluence. In Western Europe, black and brown customers are ignored or treated with suspicion in shops. That this stereotyped behavior also extends to national and ethnic groups as well– for example, the suspiciousness of Western European immigration officials of those who look "Arab"–does not significantly diminish the need to retain "race" as a dimension as a means to understand the differences in discrimination (both positive and negative) in everyday, informal interaction.

Eighth, the distinctive responses of minorities themselves differ with respect to whether they are identified in racial or ethnic terms. On American university campuses, for example, black students are much more sensitive to the suspected injustices of "racist" faculty and administration than are, for example, foreign students from Germany and France, who are defined as nationally, ethnically, and linguistically different but of the same "dominant" racial group. It is also true, in the contemporary United States, that many ethnic minority groups, including "white ethnics" or "Euro-Americans", frame and present their political demands in categorical terms that resemble the racial claims made by blacks for entitlements (and honored by some government policies) in the civil rights movement. Those facts, however, do not diminish the continuing power of race in conditioning group responses; if anything, they tend to underscore the continuing reality of race as a social construct.

Ethnicity and Nationality Distinguished

Though variable in character, the socially defined marks of race have a certain simplicity in the end because they stem from assigned physical or biological traits. As Bulmer's definition shows, however, ethnicity constitutes more of a mélange, including common ancestry, memories of a shared past, kinship, religion, language, shared territory, or nationality. The last two items suggest that ethnicity has a close kinship with, or can even include in some cases, the idea of "nationality."

Weber, in an early attempt to identify the nature of ethnicity, also invoked a very inclusive definition: "those human groups that entertain a subjective belief in their common descent because of similarities of physical type or of customs or both, or because of memories of colonization and migration; this belief must be important for the propagation of a group; conversely, it does not matter whether or not an objective blood relationship exists" (Weber 1968: I, 389). In the end, Weber concluded that the term "ethnic" is too inclusive to be very helpful sociologically; for if it were disaggregated into all its component parts and influences, it would be "abandoned" as "unsuitable for a really rigorous analysis" (ibid.: I, 395). Weber also gave careful attention to the idea of "nationality," which he found "most vexing, since emotionally charged" as a concept (ibid.). While we would acknowledge, with Weber, that both terms, "ethnic" and "national," carry confused meanings, some consistent distinction between them is in order.

To approach the matter from another angle, while both "ethnic" and "national" share a cultural dimension–Weber preferred to think of "national" as connoting, above all, a common language (ibid.)–they cannot be thought of as the same in every respect. Furthermore, though "nation" connotes some kind of territorial claim more than does ethnicity, "nation" cannot be assimilated properly to the idea of a "state," even though the two have come to be used coterminously (see chapter 7), and some protagonists have thought them identical–see Napoleon's maxim "To each nation a state, in each state one nation." Some definite distinction must be kept between ethnicity, nationhood, and statehood.

Oommen (1994) has argued that a "nation" in the full sense exists when territory and culture coincide; a nation is the homeland of a people who share a common culture. Ethnicity–or at least one principal type of ethnicity–emerges when culture and territory are dissociated. It is thus most often a product of conquest, colonization, and/or immigration. What may be called an "ethnie"–that is, a cultural group without a distinct territory–may stake its claim over a territory from which or into which it has moved. That territory is a nation. Such a claim, moreover, may be moral (Jews' claims to Middle-Eastern land prior to 1948, Palestinians' contemporary claims to the same land) or legal (Israel after 1948, but not Palestinian claims, as of the moment). In the latter case, the nation becomes a state. A state may be multinational, as in the case of the former Soviet

Union. The breakup of that state into multiple states brought nationhood and statehood into a closer relation with one another.

The United States, a nation, is a country of immigrants, so it is understandable that its social life is permeated by ethnic groups and ethnicity. Yet these have been considered in different ways. Glazer and Moynihan presented a "tilted" definition of ethnic groups: "minority and marginal sub-groups at the edges of society–groups expected to assimilate, to disappear, to continue as survivals, exotic or troublesome to major elements of a society" (1975: 5). Needless to say, such a definition tends to raise objections among many ethnic groups because it carries a pejorative ring of marginality and transitoriness. Partly as a result of such objections, more contemporary definitions tend to include all groups, dominant and dominated alike, which carry the appropriate markers of ethnic identity.

Such definitions also create difficulties, however, largely through omission. To label groups as ethnic on the basis of the specificity of their cultures leaves aside the vital distinction between privileged ethnic groups and underprivileged ones. To deal directly with this dimension, Oommen (1989) distinguished between symbolic ethnicity and instrumental ethnicity. The former is essentially a matter of constructing sociocultural boundaries and entails a question of identity. All ethnic groups produce and reproduce their own boundaries, whether or not they are deprived economically (Gans 1979). Instrumental ethnicity relates more to the dimension of inequality and to struggles of an economic and political sort. The distinction is a viable one, even though groups will sometimes employ assertions of their distinctive identity in their instrumental struggles.

Race, Ethnicity and Class: Linkages

Separations, Intersections, and Overlaps

Race, ethnicity, and class can all be represented either as aggregates or as membership groups. It is possible to count, in a census or survey, those in the society that are identified as belonging to certain races or ethnic groups. It is also possible to aggregate classes in a society by relating them to some structural characteristics of the economy–occupational status, ownership of the means of production, access to property. Alternatively, these various aggregates may possess, in varying degree, the attributes of membership. This refers to the social-psychological consciousness of belonging (race consciousness, class consciousness), solidarity, and political mobilizability of the group. As a rule, boundaries between racial groups in society are relatively rigid (because assignment to such groups is usually on an either/or, immutable basis). Boundaries among ethnic groups may also be dichotomous, especially when common ancestry is salient, but other, cultural elements make for a greater possibility of the fusion of boundaries. Class boundaries are usually more fluid than either racial or ethnic boundaries, though class systems vary in this respect (e.g., the class systems of the United Kingdom and the United States).

Because of the prevalence of the categorical language that is typically used to characterize race, ethnicity, and class, it should not be forgotten that they intersect with one another at both the social and the psychological levels. As indicated, a given social class may contain a variety of racial and ethnic groups, and members of specific racial and ethnic groups, while often clustering in one class or another, can be found at different class levels. Racial groups may contain many ethnic groups, and, more rarely, technically defined ethnic groups (e.g., Americans living in France) can contain members of more than one "race." At the individual level, a person's identity includes not one but several dimensions, including one's racial, ethnic, and class membership (e.g., middle-class black Protestant, working-class Polish Catholic).

Among the most important tasks in the comparative study of race, ethnicity, and class is to determine the degree to which the three overlap one another in different societies and at different historical periods. Consider the race–class linkage in Worsley's ideal-type descriptions of two extreme cases, Brazil and South Africa:

> Today in Brazil, the inter-mixture of physical stocks has been so extensive that there is a continuum from the Caucasoid through various degrees of mixed physical appearance to Negroid, and only a minority at either pole. The poles therefore provide reference points, but most people fall into the intermediate area between them. Yet though there are no social groups formally marked off from each other by colour, few blacks are to be found in upper classes, and most blacks are poor. (Worsley 1984: 265)

> The earning-gap began to rise with the establishment of a legal colour bar in the mines in 1926, under which skilled jobs were reserved for Whites. By the time *apartheid* was enacted as law, after the Second World War, the gap had increased from 11.7: 1 before the First World War to 20: 1 by 1969. African miners' wages, in real terms, were probably lower than in 1911, while those of Europeans had increased by 70 percent. (ibid.: 240)

In Brazil there is considerable class inequality by race, but it has developed without benefit of legal and other formal mechanisms of discrimination, whereas in apartheid South Africa much of the economic, legal, and political order stands arrayed to maximize the coincidence of the racial and class dimensions.

It remains only to point out that the linkages between racial and economic stratification have a global significance as well. The deep international division between North and South (or, very approximately, between developed-industrial and developing, or rich and poor) is in rough terms a division between white European-American peoples (with some yellow East Asians) on the one hand and the "black" and "brown" peoples of Africa and Asia on the other. As a result, the tensions between those two great regions of the world are simultaneously economic and racial-ethnic in character. Such a characterization, of course, leaves much of the world stratification system out of account–notably, the former Socialist and Communist societies (which are neither North nor South) and the aggressively developing countries of Latin America (which are South geographically but have Northern ethnic linkages through their Spanish and Portuguese backgrounds). For most nations, the international race–ethnicity–class situation is more a kaleidoscope than a map with clear boundaries.

The Ethnic Economy

As the discussion so far has indicated, the relations between racial, ethnic, and class groups are highly variable with respect to the themes of separation, intersection, and overlap. If one scans the nations of the world, one finds the greatest variation in the class experiences of different racial and ethnic groups. Table 16.1 gives a series of illustrations of this variation, showing the vast possibilities of crisscrossing of racial, ethnic, and class groupings.

One of the "linkage" phenomena among these groupings that has drawn the interest of scholars in recent decades has been termed "the ethnic economy" (Light 1994). It has long been recognized that racial and ethnic groups specialize occupationally and that special minority groups such as Jews, Chinese, Syrians, Indians, and Goans have played special

Table 16.1 Race–ethnicity–class linkages: some illustrative variations

Race/color	Ethnic groups/nationality	Classes
White	Italian Catholics and German Protestants in the USA	Represented in all classes, but German Protestants have more capitalists, and Italian Catholics are more heavily represented in the working class.
Black	Black Muslims in the USA, South African black Protestants, Brazilian mestizo	Few capitalists and a limited middle class, mainly lower class.
Yellow	Japanese Buddhist, Chinese Confucians	Substantial capitalist and middle class among Japanese Buddhists, Chinese Confucians largely working-class.
Brown	Gujarati Hindus, Singhala Buddhists	Gujarati Hindus have a substantial capitalist and middle class; Singhala Buddhists have a limited capitalist class but a considerable middle and working class.

commercial and entrepreneurial roles in various societies (Hagen 1962). The ethnic economy is to be distinguished both from these economic forms and from the idea of an informal economy which exists outside the state-recognized economy and performs important, if quasi-legal functions for the economy as a whole.

The term "ethnic economy," as defined by Bonacich and Modell (1980), refers to an ethnic or immigrant group's self-employed, employers, and co-ethnic employees. It implies a networking along the lines of financial assistance, preferential hiring of co-ethnics, and perhaps preferential selling, though in many cases the ethnic economy maintains linkages with the general market. The ethnic economy is a worldwide phenomenon, not linked to any special type of national economy. Certain groups are more entrepreneurial than others in forming ethnic economies–Arabs, Chinese, Greeks, Jews, Koreans, Pakistanis, for example. Such economies are often built up through the development of "vacancy chains" in an economy, into which entrepreneurs move and which they develop by making use of their own co-ethnics.

Ethnic economies have a certain hardiness, because they frequently provide economic advantages. For one thing, they may provide a source of ready capital, as co-ethnics lend to one another on more favorable terms than could be secured on the open financial market. Common ethnicity may also prove to be a source of employee discipline, as workers, motivated in part by the security and loyalty they feel "among their own," labor diligently and long and in some instances for lower wages than the market might dictate. More intangible, but probably most important, is the element of ethnic solidarity and trust, which is sometimes more important than contractual guarantees in assuring predictability of behavior in the market. Ethnic trust also facilitates the flow of market information to co-ethnics (and inhibits that flow to those outside the ethnic economy). In a word, ethnicity often constitutes a "social capital" (Bourdieu 1979), which may translate into economic advantage. More generally, the ethnic economy leads us to question the traditionally articulated opposition between the principles of *Gesellschaft* and *Gemeinschaft*. It constitutes an ingenious invention that embodies both the values of competitiveness in the market and the values of group solidarity.

The Racial and Ethnic Situation in the United States

As indicated, the United States is one of the most extreme countries in the world from the standpoint of its racial, ethnic, and religious diversity, matched perhaps only by India in this respect. We conclude this chapter with a brief sketch of the history and contemporary situation with respect to the racial and ethnic dimension of that country, including a few selected observations about two groups with very contrasting histories–Jews and blacks.

The first point to be made is that the interplay of racial and ethnic history has taken place within a stratification system that is often thought to lie at the base of what is called "American exceptionalism." It is a system which has traditionally incorporated the central American values of individual-istic achievement and equality of opportunity and the corresponding rejection of *ascribed* group membership, hereditary privilege, and established religion. According to this cultural definition, the main criteria for ranking in the society are occupational achievement and the attainment of wealth. Thus, in principle, the system is culturally tilted against giving high salience to racial, ethnic, religious, and other ascribed or semi-ascribed categories in assigning position in the stratification system; in a word, it is antagonistic to caste as a basis for ranking. This tilt has proved to be a power-ful influence in the American stratification system, where the American dream of "rags to riches" has thrived, where there have been only local echoes of aristocracy, where the vast majority of citizens have regarded themselves as in the middle class, and where class consciousness and conflict have been notably weak by comparison with Europe, as both Marx and Sombart ("Why is there no socialism in the United States?") noted.

In practice, of course, two centuries of American history have demonstrated that ascribed, "racial" characteristics have occupied a very salient place in the history of discrimination in that country. The prime case of this concerns blacks, who were consigned to a status of racial slavery and since emancipation have constituted a racial group suffering continuing privation. Native American Indians have experienced both genocide and enforced isolation on reservations (a form of nonurban ghettoization), and, as indicated, for a time Asians, especially Chinese, were viewed in distinctively racial terms ("the yellow peril"), though since the Second World War the status of Asians has approached more nearly that of a number of ethnic groups. Other ethnic groups have also experienced discrimination on the basis of their being ethnic ("No Irish need apply"). It was, in fact, the fundamental tension between the dictates of the values of universalistic achievement and equality of opportunity and the ascribed racial disadvantages of blacks that constituted the kernel of Myrdal's *An American Dilemma* (1944).

One of the most interesting developments in the last three decades in the United States is the movement called "affirmative action," which applies not only to selected minorities–blacks, Hispanics, native Americans, mainly–but also to women. The logic of this movement is as follows. Certain groups have experienced long, severe histories of discrimination and hardship. Affirmative action refers to removing the remaining legal disabilities for these groups and, in special areas such as jobs and education, assuring that they receive preferential consideration, by way of compensating for history and improving their economic and social status in society. The impact of affirmative action has been considerable; but it has rekindled a lingering ambivalence in the United States, given that country's cultural and social traditions. On the one hand, "affirmative action" introduces the principle of socioeconomic advancement based on ascribed qualities (race, ethnic membership, sex) and thus appears to run counter to the principle of universalistic standards of individual achievement (meritocracy). Many, however, have treated affirmative action as a way of equalizing opportunities that have been unequal in the past by removing structural and informal obstacles. In any event, affirmative action seems to strike a sometimes uneasy compromise between the dimensions of achievement and ascription in American life.

The story of migration has also been one of the most salient features of American history. The first and original "natives" were American Indians, and the first "migrants" were colonists, mainly of English and Scottish-Irish stock. These migrants came quickly to dominate colonial America, and subsequently they came to define themselves as "natives" (and were so designated in "nativistic" movements such as the Know-Nothings and the Ku Klux Klan). The 1820s brought a significant German migration (the "Pennsylvania Dutch" and others who settled in large numbers in New York, Ohio, Wisconsin, and Missouri). Then came the Irish, leaving poverty and famine in Ireland, contributing to the building of the canals and railroads, and swelling the urban populations of New York, Boston, Philadelphia, and Baltimore. The Irish and subsequent southern and eastern European migrants also introduced a deep religious divide–Catholicism versus Protestantism–into the American ethnic pattern.

The decades between the Civil War and the First World War mark the greatest period of immigration into the United States, surpassing even that of recent decades. Germans and Irish continued to come, but the main flood was composed of Scandinavians, Italians, Poles, Russians, East European Jews, Balkan sub-nationalities, Greeks, and Armenians–who, taken together, came to outnumber Anglo-Saxon "natives" in many places. In the same period large numbers of Chinese, Japanese, and Filipinos arrived, contributing to the development of agriculture and the railroads in the American West. Hispanics, mainly from Mexico, had long constituted an old, established group in the Southwest. The vast migrations provoked a number of backlash movements, and in the early 1920s the government imposed a virtual ban on new immigration under a complex quota system. In the meantime the new ethnics became a major political force, because the attainment of citizenship was relatively easy and with citizenship came the vote. They came to constitute a major political base for the famous urban political "machines."

More recent American history has continued the theme of immigration. Migrant Mexican laborers have come by the millions; Puerto Ricans flooded New York City in the decades after the Second World War; Cubans moved into Florida and elsewhere in great numbers after the Castro revolution; and Central and Latin Americans constitute a significant part of the current migration. In addition to Hispanics, Asians have contributed to the new immigration, with large numbers of Chinese, Koreans, Pacific Island peoples, and Southeast Asians, the latter largely political refugees emerging from the Vietnam War period and the political disruptions following it. From the beginning of the twentieth century, blacks (who were originally forced migrants to slavery in Southern agriculture) began a long and continuous internal migration northward and westward, so that they now constitute significant minorities in many states outside the South.

Consistent with the "melting pot" thesis, rates of intermarriage (except white–black) are currently very high in the United States. Contrary to that theory, however, virtually all national-ethnic groups in the United States have retained some degree of consciousness of their origins and their racial and ethnic identity. These groups, taken together, constitute a virtual "majority" in some states (New Mexico and California, e.g.) and, as such, assume major political importance.

Each ethnic group has had a different history of assimilation or nonassimilation into American society, and for each there has been a different kind of movement into, and impact on, the stratification system. It is possible to isolate the following factors to account for those differences:

The motives for coming to the country There have been groups who have been forcibly imported (blacks), those who have come seeking religious freedom (Puritans, Quakers, Protestants from southern Germany), those seeking political refuge (Cubans, some "new" Asian immigrants), those fleeing economic hardship and/or seeking economic opportunity (most Western and Eastern European groups). Those motives have conditioned whether and in what ways these groups have sought to join or remain isolated from their host society in the United States.

The economic opportunities available It might be argued, for example, that the dominance of the American economy by heavy manufacturing growth toward the end of the nineteenth century provided immigrant groups with an opportunity to move sequentially up the skill ladder of industry. Modern conditions, dominated by service occupations and more flexible and temporary hiring patterns, may not be so conducive to the sequential incorporation of groups.

The cultural and economic assets of immigrants It is notable that Jewish immigrants in the late nineteenth century were not of peasant stock, unlike many of their Polish and Italian brethren, had been engaged in urban and often commercial occupations, and were literate. Cuban immigrants, unlike most other Hispanic immigrants, were largely bourgeois in origin, and this has accounted in part for their economic success (and the antagonism of blacks and other groups toward them). The peculiar cultural assets of the Chinese, Japanese, and some "new Asian" groups, as manifested in a kind of collectivist "achievement orientation," have been the basis for corresponding advantages for these groups as well. Among the cultural assets (or deficits) of racial and ethnic groups, moreover, are their distinctive patterns of support networks and solidarity, which, as we have seen, can prove to be market assets.

The degree of cultural "distance" between the immigrating group and the traditionally dominant Anglo-Saxon culture   The English, Scottish, and Welsh were of course closest. German and Scandinavian groups were closer in religion (except for German Catholics) and "national character," but not with respect to language. For the Irish, their close adherence to Catholicism proved to be a distancing factor. The Latin and Hispanic (Italian, Mexican, Latino) groups stood further apart because of cultural, language, and religious traditions. The situation with respect to native Americans is ambiguous. One line of interpretation holds that the brutalities of racism have more or less destroyed that culture, while another line holds that tribal cultures have survived and stand in some kind of accommodating/antagonistic relation to the dominant Anglo culture. All in all, the general rule seems to have been that the closer the original culture stood to the white Anglo-Saxon Protestant culture, the less the group was subjected to disadvantage or oppression, the faster and further they seemed to assimilate, and the less salient they became in the panoply of racial and ethnic groups.

Time of arrival, place of settlement, sociocultural environment of the time   Irish nineteenth-century immigrants settled mainly in Eastern cities in the 1830s, 1840s, and thereafter. These places were thoroughly Anglo and Protestant when they arrived, and during those decades they were subjected to economic and educational discrimination, street riots and informal harassment (as "Micks"). Irish coming to the United States in recent years confront an entirely different environment and accordingly suffer less. The same can be said of the "new" Asian immigrants as compared to the early Chinese immigrants. Germans and Scandinavians, largely isolated in rural areas in the early years, were able to maintain a certain cultural integrity, while those in cities were subjected to more assimilative pressures.

The precise pattern of discrimination that each group experienced   This has taken the most diverse forms, including physical isolation and genocide (e.g., native Americans), job discrimination (all groups, in varying degrees), educational discrimination (e.g., Jews in higher education), legal disabilities (e.g., Chinese), and informal exclusion from neighborhoods, clubs, restaurants, and so on.

The degree to which groups have protested against discrimination   Some groups, such as native Americans, were forced almost completely into passivity until very recently. Some have more or less eagerly assimilated and become "American," perhaps more compulsively than those from Anglo-Saxon backgrounds. Some have stressed simultaneously their

American and their special ethnic status, as the frequent use of hyphen-ization (German-American, Irish-American, Polish-American) underscores. Some have resorted to direct political action, either through political parties (especially the Democratic party), social movements, or direct political action such as street demonstrations.

Each ethnic group's history and current status can be read as a complex combining and recombining of these various factors. And because so many factors are involved, it is erroneous to regard the process of assimilation as some linear path toward "Americanism"–a view that Gans (1992) has called "straight-line" theory. Rather, the process of assimilation is more likely to have been a segmented, partial one, based on a complex combination of group resources and motivations, as well as structural opportunities and obstacles.

Among the scores of groups identifiable in the American racial and ethnic kaleidoscope, the experiences of Jewish Americans and black Americans stand in sharp contrast. As already indicated, the Jews came with a high level of commercial and educational skills, constituting a kind of "social capital." This meant that a significant proportion of Jews entered. skilled jobs (Steinberg 1981). In addition, more became owners or employers than workers, as compared with other ethnic groups (Lestchinsky 1946). Perhaps most important, a high proportion of Jews were self-employed, which may have protected them from a certain amount of discrimination, which was usually a phenomenon of hiring in the workplace. Finally, the arrival of masses of East European and Russian Jews (late nineteenth century) occurred in the context of an already established German-Jewish community, which offered the newcomers political and economic support, even though some class and ethnic tensions developed among Jews as well (Dobkowski 1979).

The Jewish experience in the United States presents something of a paradox. On the one hand, Jews have been "assimilative" insofar as they have moved–as successfully as any immigrant group–into the upper occupational and income reaches. At the same time, they have maintained a strongly ascribed definition of their identity (stemming from the historical, "tribal" self-definition of Jews) and strong intra-ethnic ties in the community and society. A debate in the literature is related to this paradox. Bonacich (1973) has argued that Jews attained a kind of "middleman" minority status in the United States, which brought them economic prosperity but political ambivalence. The Jews were not full "sojourners" but developed an outlook that combined a strong financial interest in the society with a limited political commitment to it. This pattern invited among both capitalists and workers the opposition that develops when sojourners monopolize middleman positions. Waldinger (1986) has contested this thesis by arguing that Jews have wanted to merge into the cultural mainstream and acquire a class status that pushes their ethnicity into the background. Furthermore, Jews have been politically active in the trade union movement, in liberal and radical political movements, and in civil rights (Liebman 1979)–activity which, however, being on the Left, has generated opposition among more conservative members of the wealthier classes whose ranks Jews have entered. In any event, the precise relation of Jews to the American class and sociopolitical order has been one of ambivalence, as two of the contradictory negative stereotypes about them– "assimilative" and "clannish"–would suggest.

The story of blacks contrasts on most counts with that of Jews. Emerging from slavery and reconstruction as a very unskilled group with little land and capital as assets and in the context of continuing, pervasive racial discrimination, blacks were foredoomed to occupy the lower rungs in the economic and class order. Business opportunities were few. In 1971, the assets of black-owned banks constituted less than 0.1 percent of the assets of white-controlled banks. Yet 40 percent of the loans secured by black businessmen were from black banks. This small black economic enclave had three distinguishing features: "First, its enterprises evolved mainly before the Civil Rights era and were constrained to operating in an environment of racial segregation. Second, . . . their clientele was black almost exclusively. Third, these constraints tied the fortunes of entrepreneurs of this segment to the economic, political and social developments of the black community "(Boston 1988: 39).

This limited development did not produce a sizable middle class among blacks, though even in the early 1960s Frazier (1962) could write of a "black bourgeoisie." Effective educational segregation has continued in many localities, despite the constitutional banning of segregated education in 1954. And job discrimination has continued. The development of a sizable black middle class in the United States did not develop primarily through business entrepreneurship or advancement through the private sector so much as through governmental hiring and through professional advancement in the religious sphere, education, social work, and–to a minor but spectacular degree–entertainment and sports. There is no agreement as to the exact size of the black middle class, but it is clear that blacks have bifurcated into a middle-class income group that is relatively comfortable and a much larger "underclass" which remains at the very bottom of the social ladder from an educational and economic point of view. This bifurcation of blacks along class lines led Wilson to observe in 1978, in a controversial formulation, that there had been a "declining significance of race": "Race relations in America have undergone fundamental changes in recent years. So much so that now the life chances of individual blacks have more to do with their economic class position than with their day-to-day encounters with whites" (Wilson 1978: 1). Wilson's formulation proved something of a bombshell, initiating an unfinished dialogue over the relative salience of class and of race and racism, respectively, in American society. Whatever the merits of the altercation, it is clear that the historically unique, disadvantaged place of blacks in American society continues to lie at the center of national concerns and debates about discrimination, poverty, education, and crime.

This is perhaps an American testimony to the more general observation that, in the end, the social construction of race and racism, including the conversion of ethnic definitions to racial ones, constitutes a more intractable social fact than does ethnicity.

References

Bacal, A. 1991: *Ethnicity in the Social Sciences*. Coventry: Centre for Research in Ethnic Relations, University of Warwick.

Barker, M. 1981: *The New Racism*. London: Junction Publications.

Bjorklund, U. 1987: "Ethnicity and the Welfare State." *International Social Science Journal*, 3: 19–30.

Bonacich, E. 1973: "A Theory of Middleman Minorities." *American Sociological Review*, 389: 583–94.

Bonacich, E. and Modell, J. 1980: *The Economic Basis of Ethnic Solidarity*. Berkeley, Calif.: University of California Press.

Boston, T. E. 1988: *Race, Class, and Conservatism*. Boston: Unwin Hyman.

Bourdieu, P. 1979: "Les Trois États du capital culturel." *Actes de la recherche en sciences sociales*, 30: 3–6.

Bulmer, M. 1986: "Race and Ethnicity," in R. G. Burgess (ed.), *Key Variables in Sociological Investigation*, London: Routledge and Kegan Paul, 54–75.

Chesler, M. 1976: "Contemporary Sociological Theories of Racism," in P. Katz (ed.), *Towards Eliminating Racism*, New York: Plenum, 21–71.

Davis, A. Y. 1981: *Women, Race and Class*. New York: Random House.

Dobkowski, M. N. 1979: *The Tarnished Dream*. Westport, Conn.: Greenwood Press.

Duster, T. 1990: *Backdoor to Eugenics*. New York: Routledge and Kegan Paul.

Essed, P. 1991: *Understanding Everyday Racism*. Newbury Park, Calif.: Sage Publications.

Frazier, E. F. 1962: *Black Bourgeoisie*. New York: Collier.

Furnivall, J. S. 1948: *Colonial Policy and Practice: A Comparative Study of Burma and Netherlands India*. Cambridge: Cambridge University Press.

Gans, H. J. 1979: "Symbolic Ethnicity: The Future of Ethnic Groups and Cultures in America." *Ethnic and Racial Studies*, 1: 1–11.

Gans, H. J. 1992: "Second-Generation Decline: Scenarios for the Economic and Ethnic Futures of the Post-1965 American Immigrants." *Ethnic and Racial Studies*, 15: 173–92.

Glazer, N. and Moynihan, D. P. 1975: Introduction to Glazer and Moynihan (eds), *Ethnicity: Theory and Experience*, Cambridge, Mass.: Harvard University Press, 1–26.

Hagen. E. E. 1962: *On the Theory of Social Change: How Economic Growth Begins*. Homewood, Ill: Dorsey.

Ianni, O. 1970: "Research on Race Relations in Brazil," in M. Morner (ed.), *Race and Class in Latin America*, New York: Columbia University Press, 256–78.

Lestchinsky, J. 1946: "The Economic Development of Jews in the United States." *The Jewish People: Past and Present*, 1: 391–406.

Liebman, A. 1979: *Jews and the Left*. New York: Wiley.

Light, I. 1994: "The Ethnic Economy," in N. J. Smelser and R. Swedberg (eds), *Handbook of Economic Sociology*, Princeton, N.J.: Princeton University Press and the Russell Sage Foundation.

Montagu, A. (ed.) 1964: *The Concept of Race*. New York: Free Press.

Myrdal, G. 1944: *An American Dilemma*. New York: Harper and Row.

Oommen, T. K. 1989: "Ethnicity, Immigration and Cultural Pluralism: India and the United States of America," in M. L. Kohn (ed.), *Cross-National Research in Sociology*, Newbury Park, Calif.: Sage Publications, 279–307.

Oommen, T. K. Forthcoming: "State, Nation and Ethnie: The Processual Linkages," in P. Ratcliffe (ed.), *Race, Ethnicity and Nation: International Perspectives on Social Conflict*, London: University College London.

Steinberg, S. 1981: *The Ethnic Myth*. Boston: Beacon Press.

Waldinger, R. 1986: "Immigrant Enterprise: A Critique and a Reformulation." *Theory and Practice*, 15: 249–85.

Weber, M. 1968: *Economy and Society: An Outline of Interpretive Sociology*, ed. G. Roth and C. Wittich, vol. I. New York: Bedminster Press.

Wilson, W. J. 1978: *The Declining Significance of Race*. Chicago: University of Chicago Press.

Worsley, P. 1984: *The Three Worlds: Culture and World Development*. London: Weidenfeld and Nicolson.

17

Religiosity, Religious Secularism, and Secular Religions

Thirty years ago it was in effect a sacred tenet among sociologists of religion that secularization is part and parcel of the modernization process. According to that article of faith, we have seen, and will see, the ending of the sacred (or "religion" as we have known it) or, alternatively and more precisely, its "eclipse" (Acquaviva 1979). Yet the word "eclipse" already reveals an ambiguity that opens the door to a complex, sometimes confused, and certainly interminable debate. It may be possible to identify the onward historical march of secularization at the expense of traditional religions, but this still leaves several questions unanswered:

- Following the astronomical analogy, is the "eclipse" to be regarded as a total or a partial one?
- Is the process of secularization continuous or irregular?
- Does it make sociological sense to suggest the *complete* disappearance of a long-standing feature of social life (religion) and its *total* replacement by another mentality (secularism)?
- If there is some kind of partial eclipse of religion as we have known it and its replacement by secular beliefs, do the latter share some characteristics with the former?
- If the answer to the last question is positive, what becomes of the metaphor "replacement," and has anything fundamental really changed?
- If the process of secularization is not either/or, not a contrast between a religious universe and a secular universe, then how do we conceptualize the resulting complex relations between the religious and the secular?

This chapter is based on a contribution by Roberto Cipriani.

All these questions are alive in the current challenges to, and debates about, the secularization thesis. In this chapter we attempt to throw light on some of them from both theoretical and empirical points of view.

The Complexity of the Religious Phenomenon: Variations on the Theme of Secularization

Eliade

A valuable starting point in studying the sacred is the work of Eliade (1959), much of which derived from Rudolph Otto's essay on the sacred (1923 [1917]), which appeared a few years after Durkheim's classic work on the sociology of religion (1965 [1915]). Eliade's aim was to provide a historical definition of the sacred and to remove the connotations of the "irrational" that seemed to characterize Otto's conception. Eliade stressed that the religious experience was not exclusively a fear of the "totally or radically other," and he set it in a perspective that allows us "to present the phenomenon of the sacred in all its complexity, . . . *in its entirety*" (1959: 10).

He regarded the sacred as "opposed to the profane" and as manifesting a specific phenomenology, hierophany, which covers religious phenomena all the way from "primitive" animism to the divine revelation which characterizes Christianity. It is always the same mysterious act, the manifestation of a reality not belonging to our world through objects that are part of our "natural," "profane" world (ibid.: 11). For him, the normal human condition is that of a total, universal experience of the sacred, whereas secularization, or the experience of the profane ("profanization" or "desacralization"), is a recent historical phenomenon.

What, more specifically, are the religious and sacred attitudes? Eliade used the categories of space and time to characterize the religious, as follows:

> Religious man . . . is always recognizable. Whatever the historical context in which he is placed, *homo religiosus* always believes that there is an absolute reality, *the sacred*, which transcends this world but manifests itself in this world, thereby sanctifying it and making it real. He further believes that life has a sacred origin and that human existence realizes all of its potentialities in proportion as it is religious–that is, participates in reality. (ibid.: 202)

The essential nature of the profane is the negation of transcendence, the denial of an ultimate meaning to existence.

> But it is only in the modern societies of the West that nonreligious man has developed fully. Modern nonreligious man assumes a new existential situation; he regards himself solely as the subject and agent of history, and he refuses all appeal to transcendence. In other words, he accepts no model for

humanity outside the human condition as it can be seen in the various historical situations. Man *makes* himself, and he only makes himself completely in proportion as he desacralizes himself and the world. (ibid.: 203)

While thus setting up a conceptual opposition between the sacred and the secular, Eliade nonetheless identified a dynamic interplay between the two historically. In fact, secularization cannot be understood except as an active, if hostile and rejecting, dialogue with the traditions of the sacred. The choice of "non-religiosity" springs from the preceding *homo religiosus* and his material environment; "[just] as nature is the product of a progressive secularization of the cosmos as the work of God, profane man is the result of a desacralization of human existence" (ibid.: 203–4). Eliade distanced himself from the theorists of "total secularization" in the following way:

Nonreligious man has been formed by opposing his predecessor, by attempting to "empty" himself of all religion and all transhuman meaning. He recognizes himself in proportion as he "frees" and "purifies" himself from the "superstitions" of his ancestors. In other words, profane man cannot help preserving some vestiges of the behavior of religious man, though they are emptied of religious meaning. Do what he will, he is an inheritor. He cannot utterly abolish his past, since he himself is the product of his past. (ibid.: 204)

Thus the profane or a-religious person, "to acquire a world of his own . . . has desacralized the world in which his ancestors lived; but to do so he has been obliged to adopt the opposite of an earlier type of behavior, and that behavior is still emotionally present to him, in one form or another, ready to be reactualized in his deepest being" (ibid.: 204).

Eliade's observation is perhaps a special case of a more general sociocultural principle: that one confronts the greatest difficulty in rebelling against inherited and ingrained cultural patterns in terms other than those set by those patterns. Following Eliade's reasoning, moreover, the supposed contemporary "religious re-awakening" should not be set in total opposition to the "secular," against which it rebels, either.

Luckmann's (1967) notion of an invisible religion, in which various "new subjects" (individualism, familialism, sexuality, etc.) are treated as functional alternatives to religion, is completely consistent with Eliade's conclusion that "nonreligious man *in the pure state* is a comparatively rare phenomenon, even in the most desacralized of modern societies. The majority of the 'irreligious' still behave religiously, even though they are not aware of the fact" (Eliade 1959: 205–6). More recently, Luckmann (1987) has distinguished among "small," "medium," and "large" transcendences. However small, the choice of the word "transcendence" itself betrays the clear and unmistakable presence of the religious impulse.

On many occasions, "secular" rituals and behavior, customs and festivities, myths and ceremonies, more or less explicitly reassert religious contents. For this reason, "the great majority of the irreligious are not liberated from religious behavior, from theologies and mythologies" (Eliade 1959: 205–6).

Eliade's position, up to this point, seems correct and unobjectionable. Try as he did to avoid them, value judgments entered his own analysis from time to time. He characterized a number of "little religions" as "aberrant" (ibid.: 206). He wrote communism off as "religious fanaticism" and "degenerated or camouflaged religious behavior" (ibid.: 206–7). His treatment of nonreligious man reveals another kind of bias; it appears to regard him as having "fallen" in a Judeo-Christian sense. To the extent that this is the case, it constitutes a certain sacrifice of his stated goal of making his analysis of the religious phenomenon as broad and comparative as possible.

Troeltsch

Another great theorist of religious change, Troeltsch, generated a somewhat different view of the process of secularization. He, too, struggled with the problem of how to distance himself from the moral dimension of religious phenomena, but in a different way. Troeltsch made no secret of the fact that he himself was a believing Christian, but–and only apparently paradoxically–this declaration perhaps constituted a way of striving for an objective attitude. He stressed explicitly the distinction between a specifically scientific approach and a more theological orientation and asserted: "My work recognizes no special theological or Christian methods of research" (Troeltsch 1931: I, 21).

In his comprehensive treatment of Christian history, Troeltsch took as a central issue the relations between the ancient ethic of the Christian churches and the new themes emerging in modern societies. In doing so, he focused on the conception of the world and in particular how this evolved into something different from the organic, unitary kingdom of salvation originally envisioned in the Christian church.

His starting-point is the distancing of the Church from "the world": "[The] more the Christian movement closed its ranks and became an organized and unified body, the more it tended to regard the rest of life as the 'world'" (ibid.: 100). Such a stance is understandable as a manifestation of the Church's original condition of *statu nascenti*, an initial self-defensiveness. Even more, that stance included a certain hostility to the world, thus separated; "the world with all its ordinances came to be regarded as a solid and unchangeable mass of evil, a system which could only be accepted or rejected *en bloc*" (ibid.: 101). This position came to constitute a fundamental assumption for the Church, even as Christianity came to constitute the very center of Western civilization, an assumption maintained right up to the present as the Church has continued to discharge its role in the development of morals.

At the same time, Troeltsch noticed a growing mundaneness in the Christian churches, which could be regarded as his recognition of the secularization process. But this increased participation of Christians in the world was nevertheless accompanied by the haunting sense that in participating in the profane world they were submitting to the consequences of sin, even if "in his heart he is still opposed to them" (ibid.). Thus we see a certain continuity with Eliade, that secularization necessarily involves a dialogue with the sacred.

What were the ethical precepts of the Christian world view? Troeltsch summarized them as (a) a conception of the importance of personality and individuality (personalistic theism); (b) the idea of a unifying socialism (derived from extending divine love to every being); (c) the rejection of elitist-selective criteria, as well as exaggeratedly egalitarian ones; (d) charity, as an indispensable attitude for the relief of suffering in the world. Thus the core of Christian value orientations is found in the fact that "the Christian Ethos gives to all social life and aspiration a goal which lies beyond all the relativities of this earthly life, compared with which, indeed, everything else represents merely approximate values" (ibid.: II, 1005).

For Troeltsch, secularization is mainly a reflection of the fact that the Christian churches have had to compromise in order to preserve their centrality in the face of complexity. This process, however, far from replacing the religious outlook, continuously carries on a dialogue with the continuing and vital religious attitude:

> Nowhere does there exist an absolute Christian ethic, which only awaits discovery; all that we can do is to learn to control the world situation in its successive phases just as the earlier Christian ethic did in its own way. There is also no absolute ethical transformation of material nature or human nature; all that does exist is a constant wrestling with the problems which they raise. Thus the Christian ethic of the present day and of the future will also only be an adjustment to the world situation, and it will only desire to achieve that which is practically possible. (ibid.: 1013)

Secularization thus proceeds only in the shadow of the continuity of the religious conscience. Consistent with Troeltsch's analysis, one would also expect this conscience to operate outside the walls of the churches themselves, pervasive as the influence of the religious culture continues to be.

O'Dea

Thomas O'Dea, an American sociologist, has put forward a notion of secularization that is not incompatible with that of Troeltsch, but his analysis of the origins of the process stands in marked contrast. They are *immanent* in the religious viewpoint of the Church. He comments on how the Judeo-Christian conception of God as transcendent desacralized the world; how it prepared the attitude necessary to approach the world as an empirical "It" rather than a sacred "Thou" . . . The evolution of an idea of the world no longer sacred, and one understandable by human reason, means the emergence of a world where *mysteries are replaced by problems*. It is the development of a secularized understanding of man and his situation. (O'Dea 1966: 86)

This reading is continuous with Troeltsch's insofar as it deals with the man–world relationship. The contrast is that for Troeltsch the history of Christianity is about working out new relations with the world while maintaining the integrity of its values, whereas for O'Dea those very values contain the seeds of their own deterioration from a truly religious mentality. For O'Dea, the Church has played a role which is "a varied one, a many-sided one, a contradictory one" (ibid.: 88).

Van der Leeuw

A fourth variant on the relation between the religious phenomenon and the secular is found in the work of another historian, Gerardus van der Leeuw. Himself a militant socialist, hence a "believer" of sorts, he also attempted to avoid presuppositions that might follow from his own convictions. His method was that of *verstehen*, an attempt to grasp the essence of the religious attitude from the study of a vast range of historical situations. He defined religion very generally, regarding it as a manifestation of a relation with the sacred. Beyond that, he was cautious in his definitions, pointing to the essence of religion as action of people in relation to God (van der Leeuw 1963); but the idea of God is quite problematic in his work, excluding any precise classification, for God is treated as a kind of God-element–that is, as embodying a certain kind of extraordinariness of being with the concomitant idea of distance from those who worship.

Van der Leeuw also developed a conception of the sacred and the profane in his idea of a "sacred environment." This is nature in the broadest sense; it is what people and animals inhabit; the "primitive" feels a unity with the environment and does not conceive of it as a separate object; he senses a "potency" in the environment but never arrives at a perception of its separateness from himself.

By implication, secularization involves a differentiation between the individual and "the world" and, by extension, a greater sense of agency in it. In practice, however, even in modern times, there is no full separation. There survives a sense of co-existence with the world, which is, in fact, a "religious conception of the world." There are, however, as many worlds as there are individuals; each considers as the world the environment in which he or she lives. The "primitive mentality" comprehends everything supernatural in a natural way, yet his natural is more supernatural, more mystical, than what we might call the supernatural (see Waardenburg 1978). Contemporaries may differentiate between themselves on the one hand and nature and "the other" on the other, but in the end that "other" is undefinable and completely different and thus religious in character.

In summary, and at the risk of overgeneralizing and compressing real differences in approach, we might observe that the four views of the religious and the secular reviewed here are variations on a theme. That theme is acknowledgement of the historical reality of the secularization process without absolutizing it and of the elements of continuity with the religious mentality, even though the sacred and the profane can be consistently opposed or contrasted in various ways. Another suggestion arising from the four theorists is that the secular mentality involves a more differentiated cultural view of man, nature, and supernature than does the religious mentality and perhaps a qualitatively different kind of differentiation.

The Mechanisms of Secularization

It is difficult to envision any kind of steady historical, to say nothing of an evolutionary, path of secularization, because a number of different mechanisms, both external and internal to religion, have contributed to its development in the West. These mechanisms differ in salience, moreover, and are not correlated with one another in their historical effects. Among the factors that can be considered *external* are the following:

- The rise of science. In one respect, this is the most obvious of factors, because the religious and scientific cosmologies have come into direct conflict with one another from Galileo through Darwin right up to the debates about creationism in the contemporary United States. By and large the churches have adapted along the lines suggested by Troeltsch's analysis–that is, by alternating strategies of fighting, retreating, accommodating, and reasserting. The "struggle" between religion and science is complicated by the fact that some "scientific" ideologies, especially those in the social sciences, have residues of religious values in them, particularly in the moral sphere.
- The growth of capitalism and materialism. The exact role of these economic factors is unclear, but a common interpretation among religious leaders is that of John Wesley (cited in Weber 1958 [1904–5]): namely, that material prosperity fosters a love for "the world" and thus undermines the fundamental hostility to the world stressed by Troeltsch.
- The rise of the secular state. The development of Lutheran and Calvinist Protestantism during and after the Reformation marked, above all, a challenge to the political authority of the Catholic Church. With rare exceptions, however, Protestantism itself did not step in as the basis of theocracies, and by a complex interactive process the secular state began to consolidate an increasing hold on the political processes of society.

- The process of political compromise. Deep conflict *among* religions has persisted to the present, and, in its role as referee in these conflicts, the state has pursued policies that, in effect, "water down" or minimize the presence of religion. In the development of public education in Great Britain in the nineteenth century, for example, the state pursued policies of either "the lowest common denominator" or the outright removal of sectarian materials from religious education in schools, because squabbling denominations could not agree on a proper formula for religious education (Smelser 1991).
- Competition from other moral ideologies, some with an explicit hostility to traditional organized religions–utilitarianism, socialism, and Marxism, to mention the most evident.

A case has also been made for the *internal* evolution of religious beliefs themselves, and an exemplar of this is found in the work of Dietrich Bonhoeffer (1971), a Lutheran whose analysis of socioreligious developments and debates includes a statement on the progress of secularization. In a general statement couched in terms familiar from Troeltsch, which has to do with the secularizing implications of theological liberalism, Bonhoeffer wrote:

> The weakness of liberal theology was that it conceded to the world the right to determine Christ's place in the world; in the conflict between the church and the world it accepted the comparatively easy terms of peace that the world dictated. Its strength was that it did not try to put the clock back, and that it genuinely accepted the battle . . . , even though this ended with its defeat. (1971: 327)

Here one finds a reproof of the self-defeating strategies of "religious socialists" who intend to impose on the world a self-concern "under the aspect of religion."

Bonhoeffer's doubts about the future of Christianity, the Church, and religion are also speculations about the future of secularization. He wonders "whether there is any 'ground' left for the church" and goes on to ask:

> "Christianity" has always been a form–perhaps the true form–of "religion." But if one day it becomes clear that this *a priori* does not exist at all, but was a historically conditioned and transient form of human self-expression, and if therefore man becomes radically religionless . . . what does that mean for "Christianity"? . . . if our final judgment must be that the western form of Christianity, too, was only a preliminary stage to a complete absence of religion, what kind of situation emerges for us, for the church? . . . If religion is only a garment of Christianity–and even this garment has looked very different at different times–then what is a religionless Christianity? (ibid.: 280–1)

The result of Bonhoeffer's thinking, Mancini argued, is that "he has replaced the custom of contesting the world in the name of God by that of contesting God in the name of the world, so laying the bases of secularization and resistance" (1969: 24).

Doubts about the Secularization Thesis

In 1969 an international symposium on "non-belief" was held in Rome. Franco Ferrarotti, the noted Italian theorist, remarked sarcastically that it was the celebration of the "death of God in a five-star hotel" (Ferrarotti 1969: 74). The sarcasm symbolized Ferrarotti's own reservations about the modern secularization of religion. Commenting on the proceedings of the symposium, Parsons argued:

> The concept [of secularization] has in the Western world and especially in religious circles, been widely interpreted to mean a one-way change, namely the sacrifice of religious claims, obligations and commitments, in favor of secular interests. The other possibility, however, should not be forgotten, namely that the secular order may change in the direction of closer approximation of the normative models provided by a religion, or by religion more generally. (Parsons 1971: 216)

One of the editors of a book of debates on the subject, Guizzardi, also expressed a cautionary note by saying that "it is only possible to assert the end of some characteristics and some functions that religion had assumed and made its own" (1971: 113–14). In a later conference in 1975 in Vienna, a number of the same scholars who participated in the Rome symposium proclaimed a reawakening of religion, and from those meetings a new slogan of the moment came forward: "God-woman" (Caporale 1976).

Many of the discussions of secularization (or nonsecularization) in the past two decades have been empirically based; that is, they have relied on figures of church attendance, surveys of religious attitudes, and the like. Yet the latter are subject to controversies regarding their significance in relation to the trends presumably described by them. The first issue of *Rassegna Italiana di Sociologia* underscored some of the difficulties. The editor of the issue, Sciolla, quoted Glock, an empirical researcher of religious behavior, to the following effect: "In reality, we find nothing on the subject that can seriously and systematically justify the hypothesis of secularization," not to mention the "theoretical deficiency of every definition" (Sciolla 1988: 9). She also referred to the "considerable gap between the fundamental theoretical theses and the empirical basis capable of supporting them" (ibid.: 25). She found no agreement on "the possibility of an interconnection between religious attitudes and practices, and secular attitudes and activities" (ibid.). And on the issue of measures of secularization itself, she found it certain that "non-attendance at mass in no way can measure secularity, so neither can the affirmation of its possible decline be on its own adduced to confirm a growing secularization of society" (ibid.: 27).

In light of all the doubts and the apparent irresolvability of the debate about the secularization thesis–at least as formulated in the history of the sociology of religion–the most appropriate attitude appears to be one of skepticism. We might even question whether we have engaged in "the sociological construction of a non-existent phenomenon" by positing a general trend toward secularization. More constructively, it seems wise to move "beyond secularization," that is, to attempt to define the problem of religious change under a new range of concepts and understandings, difficult as it may be to extricate ourselves from the sociological quagmire we have inherited. Such a "liberated" inquiry now seems to be in its beginning stages, and we turn to some of its strands.

From Religion to Secularization and Vice Versa

The soundest conclusion that can be drawn is that religion has never relinquished its role in society and is not likely to do so, especially since it continually reappears beneath the surface of secularization. The decline in participation in formal church life and the emptying-out of the pews has not meant the end of the resort to the sacred, and there is no sensible way to argue that the religious sentiment is headed for final extinction. Similarly, the "march" of secularization cannot be regarded as in any way inevitable, retarded as it is by both the general persistence and the periodic renewal of religiosity in sometimes unexpected forms and places. There seems to be a tacit truce between religiosity and secularization, each being permitted to manifest selective weakening and strengthening but not always at the expense of the other–a continuous and complex mosaic of orthodoxy, heterodoxy, revitalization, and stagnation.

A conspicuous aspect of the contemporary scene is the vitality of the religious impulse in various forms of fundamentalism, involving both non-Western religions (especially Islam) and Christianity. Religious developments in recent years in areas as diverse as the former Soviet Union, Albania, South America, Africa, and China have had repercussions scarcely imaginable a few years ago. In some cases, ancient and nearly forgotten religious forms have surfaced, and formerly religious spaces have been reappropriated following their use by "secular," authoritarian political regimes. In Albania, for example, long-prohibited Catholic rites are reappearing, while, paradoxically, the churches in Poland have experienced an emptying-out after the fall of communism, since a religious "cover" for mass political protest is no longer required.

More generally, the crises of communism and Marxism–secular religious expressions *par excellence*–have given rise to complex religious consequences. On the one hand, there has been a return to mainstream religion as offering the certainties of faith. On the other, there has appeared a less structured searching for new paths, new meanings, and new utopias as a cultural-religious basis for building a new order; indeed, the "market mania" which swept through East European countries before, during, and immediately after the revolutionary events of 1989–90 (see chapter 9) appeared to have almost religious dimensions. In the meantime, some now traditional forms of frankly "secular" religiosity–the gospel of consumerism, individualism, competitiveness, and striving for status–have continued to prosper in the Western post-capitalist world, but not without grave internal doubts and criticism of them as articles of secular faith.

We also observe a species of "religious secularization" in the growth of new religious movements of Asian origin in both Europe and North America, as well as an increase in Christian affiliation in areas previously dominated by Taoism, Confucianism, Buddhism, and Hinduism. These phenomena simultaneously symbolize an increasing complexity in the religious mosaic as one religious faith comes to complement others, but at the same time a weakening–in a kind of "secularization," if you will–of the dominant traditional religion by forcing religious toleration to new levels.

European Islam presents additional complexities. It tends to distance itself from the fundamentalism of the Middle Eastern countries of origin, taking on a more "modern" look–akin to other religions in European societies–and perhaps envisioning for the first time the option of secularization. Islam is adapting itself in different ways in African countries as well. The somewhat monolithic perception of Islamic fundamentalism on the part of some Westerners tends to ignore the fact that "there exists . . . a strong tradition of secular critique of religion [even] in the Middle East" (Abaza and Stauth 1990: 221). There is, in fact, a possibility that "Islamic fundamentalism should be seen to be a result of mass culture, as an Eastern facet of projected Western imagery of 'religious spirituality' " (ibid.: 213). This phenomenon of religious "projection"–that is, the imposition of one's own religious preoccupations in interpreting the religion of others, with the consequence of distorting the latter–is widespread practice. Abaza and Stauth thus warn that "we have to recognize the fact that we live in a global world today, which has already shaped and transformed 'traditional' structures and values. The paradox of Western secularism, namely, that it was brought about by religious fundamentalism, should not lead us to assume a universality of deeply rooted Christian connotations" (ibid.: 226).

Turning to contemporary Buddhism, certain "secularizing" tendencies are observable–for example, the increasing role of the laity in celebrating the rites, which marks, in effect, a secularization in that it erodes a traditionally sacred prerogative of the priests. The dispute between the Japanese Soka Gakkai movement and the Buddhist priesthood also constitutes a threat to Buddhist orthodoxy. At the same time, certain Buddhist ideas, especially that of reincarnation, have shown signs of spreading to some non-Asian areas.

We should not omit to acknowledge, finally, certain religious overtones of both the worldwide environmental movement (see chapter 11) and the idea of globalization (see chapter 8). The terms "global village" and "spaceship earth" have certain universal, communitarian connotations, and the idea of the spread of common, "global," humanitarian values is reminiscent of the symbolism of certain ecumenical religious movements of the past (see the discussions in Robertson and Chirico 1985, Robertson 1987, and Garrett 1992).

The Case of Europe

Recently, seven scholars based in six European countries (France, Italy, Spain, Great Britain, Germany, and Hungary) met to assess the relation between religion and modernity in each (Hervieu-Leger *et al.* 1992). As might be expected, it is difficult to achieve comparability of results, even though some of the scholars ventured some generalizations (Hervieu-Leger, Beckford, both in ibid.).

France   Consider first the French case. Hervieu-Leger stressed the crisis of the parish, perhaps unduly, as she stated outright: "Traditional communities–villages, extended families, parishes and so forth–have dissolved everywhere, and with them too the modalities that constitute individual and collective identities grounded on the continuity of symbols and the repetition of rites" (ibid.: 7). At the same time she pointed out that some traditional modes have not disappeared altogether and that the French populace in general expresses a certain ambivalence toward religious and other kinds of pluralism. Again, however, some secularization attributable to modernity is undeniable:

> The churches, with their offices, experts, commissions, and deliberative assemblies tend increasingly to align themselves more obviously with the functioning of the great bureaucratic organizations. The way they apply the centrally-made decisions and reforms need fear no comparison with the administrative procedures adopted in the profane order. (ibid.: 5)

Catholicism remains as a kind of "unofficial official" religion in France, though there are substantial religious minorities of Jews (500,000–700,000 in number), Protestants (over 900,000), and Muslims (around 3,000,000 adherents, also reflecting the immigration patterns). Catholic religious attendance stood at 12 percent in 1989, though it had been 20 percent three years earlier. Church marriages and baptisms, as well as ordinations to the priesthood, have been declining.

In reflecting on her survey of France, Hervieu-Leger concluded that "rather than making the fall in belief and religious practice seem mechanically derived from the process of secularization, we should . . .

see the latter as a complex process of re-composition in the sphere of faith, and try to bring out the social shifts in which a specific society has helped to influence the direction of the process itself" (ibid.: 182). Thus, even if the proposition that parish life is finished is true, this need not imply the end of faith. There are signs that the Catholic faith is becoming, in places, more a personal than a communal matter–"experiencing the relation of religion to their personal existence" (ibid.: 195). Hervieu-Leger noted the presence of charismatic religious communities, which have a voluntary, experiential, anti-intellectual bent and devote themselves to the personal development and realization of the participants.

United Kingdom Referring to the United Kingdom, Beckford identified the "believing without belonging" model and suggested that the widespread decline in ritual practices is not always accompanied by a crisis of belief (in Hervieu-Leger *et al.* 1992: 486). More generally, he found a combined picture–"[a] combination of continuity and change"–in the United Kingdom. With respect to attendance patterns, practicing Anglicans are exceeded by practicing Catholics. There are increases for Mormons, Seventh Day Adventists, and Jehovah's Witnesses (all "fundamentalist"), whereas traditional bastions of Methodism and nonconformity (Baptists and Presbyterians) show a decline. Middle Eastern and Asian practitioners (Muslims, Hindus, and Sikhs) have increased in numbers, reflecting immigration from those parts of the world.

Beckford believed that the concept of secularization does not account for the changes he observed. He suggested, rather, that "modernity" tends to connect religious change to other aspects of society. Religion tends to become "implicit religion," "common religion," or "customary religion," as well as a kind of fusion of the public and private realms of religion: "some forms of religion do not simply leave the public sphere; in fact, they help re-define the border between public and private" (ibid.: 482).

Hungary Hungary is an especially interesting case–a "gold mine for sociologists" (Tomka, in ibid.: 409)–having experienced, since 1948, what Tomka called pure totalitarianism, goulash communism, and distancing from communism. In general, there is a rediscovery of religion, a decline in numbers of nonbelievers, and an increase in the prestige of the churches, which contrasts with the picture for post-totalitarian Spain. At the same time, Tomka noted that "only part of society and of those defined as religious take part in Sunday services," so that, in fact, "essentially the demand is for religiosity that does not demand commitment" (ibid.: 456, 460). Hungary remains a multi-confessional society, with a Catholic majority and a Protestant minority (divided among Calvinists and Lutherans). With respect to the thesis of secularization, Tomka believed that for Hungary it was probably inappropriate, since the experience of communism may have reinforced religiosity and has certainly deflected secularizing tendencies, at least for the moment (ibid.: 461–2).

Italy In Italy, one finds two things going on side by side. First, there is a minority that identifies with the Church closely and involves itself in religious practices. Second, there is the majority, whose religion might be called "diffused," "scenario," or "implicit" religion and consists in a general belief in God without any strong sense of religious affiliation. The latter can clearly be said to have been influenced by the forces of secularization. Yet, the vitality of the religious structure persists: there is "still a powerful apparatus of parishes and official Catholic bodies which provide educational, welfare and health services" (Beckford, in Hervieu-Leger *et al.* 1992: 497). The Church remains a "great structural, organizational and manpower apparatus with which the institution of religion deploys its actions in society" (Garelli, in Hervieu-Leger *et al.* 1992: 69).

Spain In Spain there are definite signs of secularization. Formal education is entrusted to Catholic schools less and less. In the field of social welfare, there is also competition between Church and State; "Caritas" is the largest Catholic organization in the welfare field, but the Spanish socialist government tends to favor secular welfare agencies. Despite the obvious practical decline, "overall, Spain seems reluctant to give up religious identity, though not in the sense that an increasing number of persons are drawn from the Church, generally taking up a position of indifference. Usually, this process is not accompanied by hostility concerning religion and its clergy" (Giner and Sarasa, in Hervieu-Leger *et al.* 1992: 122). Spain shows few signs of a privatization of religion (usually thought to be a feature of secularization) or an eclipse of religious institutions in civil society, "though there are signs of future development in this sense in Spain" (ibid.: 130).

Germany Germany is a bi-confessional country (Catholic and Protestant, with the latter divided into the older Lutheran and Calvinist denominations and the independent bodies that have arisen in the past century). There is also a scattering of Jewish, Islamic, Buddhist, and Hindu communities. Approximately 8 percent of the population is nonaffiliated; moreover, leaving a church is facilitated "by the fact that in most localities and, naturally, especially in the big cities, non-membership in one of the major churches is no longer [negatively] sanctioned" (Daiber, in Hervieu-Leger *et al.* 1992: 385–6). The result is that, even when a certain church is numerically dominant in a region, a certain "limited pluralism" prevails, which means "the pluralization of existential orientations, and thus also of possible religious options" (ibid.: 389). This is reflected in the doctrinal and behavioral toleration of the different churches.

Even though leaving a church is relatively easy, many who leave do not totally reject their religious affiliation. Daiber asserts, in fact, that "whoever leaves the Evangelical or the Catholic Church may regard themselves, as before, Evangelical or Catholic" (ibid.: 393). This persistence of a certain religiosity in the absence of membership also explains in part why "in Germany, despite the changes of the past decades, the Christian religion is still solidly linked in the life world" (ibid.: 400). It also means, however, that the churches themselves, as institutions, experience some difficulty in reproducing themselves, dependent as they are on individual decisions.

The conclusion to be drawn from this survey of European nations is perhaps best stated by Beckford: "The background reality of secularization should not . . . be denied . . . [but we should not deny, either] the confused and disorienting dynamics of the recent religious change" (in Hervieu-Leger *et al.* 1992: 501–2). Religiosity and secularism seem to stand in a state of mutual adaptation. On the one hand, secularization is in process, though not enough to obliterate traditional religious orientations. But that very secularization seems to stimulate–and even legitimate, in a paradoxical way–the reinvigoration of old religions and the development of new expressions of religious interest, sometimes within the walls of the churches, sometimes outside them. Because these processes of revitalization are often ranged *in opposition to* secular tendencies, moreover, they constitute a resistance to those tendencies, at least in the short run.

Conclusion

In the last analysis, the relations between secularism and religiosity constitute not a dichotomy, but more a continuum–or, better yet, a mosaic. On the one hand, secularism influences traditional religious orientations. One manifestation of this is significant religious change–most would call it loss–at the structural, ceremonial, belief, and behavioral levels. Moreover, churches, both Eastern and Western, both old and new, make use of "secular" methods of influence such as the mass media and popular agitation to sustain or reassert themselves. To select only one of many possible examples of this process, the International Society for Krishna Consciousness clearly rejects "this world" through its distinctive spiritualism; at the same time, it verifies the principle that "innovative movements build upon the very society they repudiate" (A. S. Parsons 1989: 212). Moreover, "at the core of innovative movements, in their fundamental principles and in their most ritualized social practices, we find components of secular society that have not been rejected but elaborated and intensified" (ibid.: 223).

By this process the "rejected secular" becomes an "exploited secular." In still another way, the very negation of the religious may lead to its reappearance and strengthening in a new guise. Bellah cites the case of Japan immediately after the Second World War in this connection. On January 1, 1946, the Emperor announced on the radio that it was an error to believe he was divine. By that action, "State Shinto was disestablished and the shrines were left to fend for themselves with voluntary support"

(Bellah 1987: 90). Thus collapsed–in principle, at least–the whole marriage between Japanese religion and Japanese politics. Yet, almost immediately, a set of symbols with sacred connotations arose and became consolidated to replace the former basis of legitimization. This was "the holy alliance of capital, labor and bureaucracy" which was to become the foundation of *kanri sakai*, or administered society (ibid.: 91). In this way,

> religion and politics have become in important respects privatized and secularized . . . The 1946 Constitution in separating church and state not only disestablished State Shinto but freed all other religions from government control . . . the rewards that were offered were primarily secular and material: psychological and physical well-being; a better job and more money. Religion by and large reinforced the new secular emphasis on material comfort rather than challenging it. (ibid.: 91–2).

More generally, secularization has a paradoxical nature, in that it arises with the intent of desacralization but in fact gives sustenance to both historic and newer religions, which both actively resist its impact, yet adapt themselves in complex ways, including the incorporation of the secular, and survive with modified values and ceremonial symbols.

The mosaic is thus completed by the recognition that religiosity and secularism *simultaneously* oppose one another, complement and borrow from one another, and thus commingle, and set up conditions for revitalizing one another. Religions become secularized, and secular forms continue to manifest religious elements. So do contemporary discussions about the transition to "post-secularization" (Larouche 1991). Discussions of matters such as sex and death in post-secular society do not escape religious preoccupations. We may observe in these discussions–and perhaps in current sociology more generally–the reappearance of a kind of "Other," which is a generalized religious and moral representation of humanity as endangered by its social disorders and conflicts and by external threats to its existence.

References

Abaza, M. and Stauth, G. 1990: "Occidental Reason, Orientalism, Islamic Fundamentalism: A Critique," in M. Albrow and E. King (eds), *Globalization, Knowledge and Society*, London: Sage Publications.

Acquaviva, S. S. 1979: *The Decline of the Sacred in Industrial Society*. Oxford: Blackwell.

Bellah, R. N. 1987: "Legitimation Processes in Politics and Religion." *Current Sociology*, 35: 89–99.

Bonhoeffer, D. 1971: *Letters and Papers from Prison*. London: SCM Press.

Caporale, R. (ed.) 1976: *Vecchi e nuovi dei. Studi e riflession sul senso religiose dei nostri tempi. Dagli atti del Secondo Simposio Internazionale sull Credenza organizzato dalla "Fondazione Giovanni Agnelli" (Vienna, 7–11 gennaio 1975)*. Turin: Editoriale Valentino.

Durkheim, E. 1965 [1915]: *The Elementary Forms of the Religious Life.* New York: Free Press.

Eliade, M. 1959: *The Sacred and the Profane.* New York: Harcourt, Brace.

Ferrarotti, F. 1969: "Morte di Dio in alberghi di lusso." *La Critica Sociologica*, 9: 74.

Garrett, W. R. 1992: "Thinking Religion in the Global Circumstance: A Critique of Roland Robertson's Globalization Theory." *Journal for the Scientific Study of Religion.* 31: 297–303.

Guizzardi, G. 1971: "Dieci anni di dibattito su l'eclissi del sacro nella civiltà industriale," in S. Acquaviva and G. Guizzardi (eds), *Religione e irreligione nell'età postindustriale*, Rome: AVE, 54–114.

Hervieu-Leger, D., Garelli, F., Giner, S., Sarasa, S., Beckford, J. A., Daiber, K.-F. and Tomka, M. 1992: *La religione degli europei: Fede, cultura religiosa e modernità in Francia, Italia, Spagna, Gran Bretagna, Germania e Ungheria.* Turin: Edizioni della Fondazione Giovanni Agnelli.

Larouche, J. M. 1991: "Au nom du sense et de l'alterité, la post-secularisation." *Revue internationale d'action communautaire*, 26: 79–87.

Luckmann, T. 1967: *The Invisible Religion: The Transformation of Symbols in Industrial Society.* New York: Macmillan.

Luckmann, T. 1987: "Social Reconstruction of Transcendence," in *Secularization and Religion: The Persisting Tension. Acts of the XIXth International Conference for the Sociology of Religion*, Lausanne: C.I.S.R., 23–31.

Mancini, I. 1969: "Introduction" to D. Bonhoeffer, *Resistenza e resa*, Milan: Bompiani, 5–48.

O'Dea, T. 1966: *The Sociology of Religion.* Englewood Cliffs, N.J.: Prentice-Hall.

Otto, R. 1923 [1917]: *The Idea of the Holy.* London: Oxford University Press.

Parsons, A. S. 1989: "The Secular Contribution to Religious Innovation: A Case Study of the Unification Church." *Sociological Analysis*, 50: 209–27.

Parsons, T. 1971: "Belief, Unbelief and Disbelief," in R. Caporale and A. Grumelli (eds), *The Culture of Unbelief: Studies and Proceedings from the First International Symposium on Belief Held in Rome, March 22–27, 1969.* Berkeley, Calif.: University of California Press, 207–45.

Robertson, R. 1987: "Globalization and Societal Modernization: A Note on Japan and Japanese Religion." *Sociological Analysis*, 47: 35–42.

Robertson, R. and Chirico, J. 1985: "Humanity, Globalization, and Worldwide Religious Resurgence: A Theoretical Exploration." *Sociological Analysis*, 46: 219–42.

Sciolla, L. 1988: "Dimensione della secolarizzazione." *Rassegna Italiana di Sociologia.* 29/1: 5–36.

Smelser, N. J. 1991: *Social Paralysis and Social Change: British Working-Class Education in the Nineteenth Century.* Berkeley, Calif.: University of California Press.

Troeltsch, E. 1931: *The Social Teaching of the Christian Churches*, 2 vols. New York: Macmillan.

Van der Leeuw, G. 1963: *Religion in Essence and Manifestation.* New York: Harper Torchbooks.

Waardenburg, J. 1978: *Reflections on the Study of Religion, Including an Essay on the Work of Gerardus van der Leeuw.* The Hague: Mouton.

Weber, M. 1958 [1904–5]: *The Protestant Ethic and the Spirit of Capitalism.* New York: Charles Scribner's.

18

Women in Societies

At this late moment in the twentieth century it is uncontested that women's status and roles have been changing rapidly and dramatically throughout the world. On two other questions there is less consensus: first, regarding the benefits and costs to the societies that are experiencing these changes and to the women of various classes within those societies; and second, regarding the concepts and frameworks that can provide the most adequate account of these changes.

With stratification and social change as two of its major foci, the discipline of sociology is clearly central to the understanding of women in society. Sociology has also been enriched by the systematic recognition that gender is a major source of social inequality. In focusing on this, sociologists of gender have both explicitly and implicitly stressed the societal need and impetus for change in women's situations. More broadly, feminist theory has challenged all the social science disciplines to acknowledge the *gendered* nature of social reality (Hess and Ferree 1987).

At the same time sociology, especially American sociology, has tended to focus on single societies (usually those of the developed North). In the 1980s, some feminists and post-structuralist theorists began to criticize both feminist theory and "Western" social science as ethnocentric and inappropriate to the study of Third World peoples (Barrett and McIntosh 1985). For example, some authors have condemned "neo-colonialist" criticisms of cultural practices such as veiling and female circumcision (see Abaza and Stauth 1988, Ertürk 1992). As a modern manifestation of philosophical relativism, post-structuralism rejects universal frameworks

This chapter is based on a contribution by Valentine M. Moghadam.

and seems to suggest that societies are incommensurate and incomparable and can be studied, if at all, only on their own terms.

We suggest that neither generalization from the experience of the West nor cultural relativism constitutes the most appropriate framework for research on, and analysis of, gender. A more fruitful approach would include the concepts of globalism, the state, gender, class, and social movements as a complex of factors that, taken together, go far in explaining *both* stability *and* change in women's positions. Gender hierarchies and changes in the status of women are features of individual societies, but they are also global in nature. For example, industrial development is a global and interactive process, affecting women workers in North and South alike. The women's movement is simultaneously national and worldwide in its manifestations. A global approach both captures the interactions of regions and societies–and groups within them– and fosters comparative study of them.

This chapter has two main parts. The first discusses some theoretical issues in feminist social science and the sociology of gender. In particular, it considers the interaction between feminist theory and general sociological theory, as well as theoretical debates and empirical data pertaining to women's employment, political power, and patriarchy. The second part proposes an explanatory framework for stability and change in the position of women which is applicable, it is hoped, comparatively and globally.

Gender Inequality, Theoretical Debates, and Empirical Trends

In the mid-1980s Stacey and Thorne (1985) argued that feminist theory has had only a weak impact on the central theoretical perspectives in sociology. A *gendered* paradigm, they argued, would lead to an improved understanding of sex segregation in labor markets, male domination in the family, and sexual violence, as well as class structure, the state, social revolution, and feminism. A fully feminist paradigm would give women and gender a central place in all social relations. It would, moreover, pose new and radical questions about women and gender and give a more complex and adequate account of capitalist industrial societies.

Several years later Acker (1989) took up the same theme and sought to explain why sociology had not experienced a feminist revolution and a corresponding paradigm shift. The answer, she argued, lay both in the politics of the organization of the discipline and in the underdevelopment of feminist theory.

> We have not, as yet, been able to suggest new ways of looking at things that are obviously better than the old ways for comprehending a whole range of problems–from how organizations function to how capital accumulation

processes alter class structure. We know a great deal more about how such things affect women, but are only beginning to know how gender is fundamentally involved in the process. (Acker 1989: 72)

She also criticized the focus of gender analysis on women alone, which "[takes] the theorizing from the general to the specific" and "appears to undermine the theorizing about the abstract and the general. Consequently, talking about gender and women can be seen as trivializing serious theoretical questions, or it can be seen as beside the point" (Acker 1989: 74).

To correct these misdirections, Acker suggested that the Marxist framework was a useful theoretical starting point, mainly because of its focus on oppression, which leads directly to questions of class, capitalism, politics, and the state. This recommendation has merit in that it challenges feminist sociologists to theorize the gendered nature of those macro-structures and thus supplements the body of literature dealing with micro-processes and subjective experiences of women in specific social institutions such as the family, the legal system, and the workplace. For example, sociology needs a theory that incorporates both class and gender– in keeping with Mann's declaration (1986: 50) that "stratification is gendered and gender is stratified"–whereas in practice many feminists write as if class and gender are separate, thus deflecting general analysis.

This said, it should also be pointed out that sociology has been more receptive to feminist theory than some other disciplines, notably economics. The field of stratification generally acknowledges gender as a source of inequality, and gender consistently enters as a dimension in the analysis of segmented labor markets. There has been less success at the macroscopic level, however. What is evidently needed is a synthetic framework–borrowing from many strands of sociology, including stratification, gender analysis, Marxist sociology, and global sociology– that would bridge the general and the specific, the macro and the micro, the objective and the subjective, the comparative and the intra-societal. The ingredients of such a framework are laid out later in the chapter.

Assessing and Comparing the Status of Women

What is implied by the notion of "the status of women," and what are its indicators? Addressing this question, Giele (1977) examined seven life options that were originally formulated by Blumberg: whether and whom to marry; termination of such unions; sexual freedom, before and outside marriage; freedom of movement; access to educational opportunities; power within the household; and control over reproduction and family size. Giele compressed several of these options and added two more (political participation and cultural expression). Her resulting list of six– and the corresponding questions posed by each item–is useful as a tool for empirical analysis and appears to be applicable cross-culturally. Here is her agenda:

Political expression   What rights do women possess, formally and otherwise? Can they own property? Can they express dissatisfactions via their own political and social movements?

Work and mobility   How do women fare in the formal labor force? How mobile are they? How are their jobs ranked and paid? What leisure do they enjoy?

Family   What is the age of marriage? Do women choose their partners? Can they divorce them? What is the status of single women and widows? Do women have freedom of movement?

Education   What access do women have? How much can they attain? Is the curriculum open to them comparable to that of men?

Health and control of fertility   What is women's mortality? To what illnesses and stresses are they exposed? What control do they have over their own fertility?

Cultural expression   What images of women and their "place" are prevalent? To what extent do these reflect or determine the reality? What can women accomplish in cultural fields?

Regional Trends

The United Nations (1991) used a similar framework to assess and compare the status of women around the world. It included women, families, and households (including domestic violence); public life and leadership; education and training; health and childbearing; housing, human settlements, and the environment; women's work and the economy. The following trends in women's status and social positions are drawn from its recent report (1991: 1–2):

Latin America and the Caribbean   Women in urban areas made significant gains according to indicators of health, childbearing, and education, as well as in economic, social, and political participation. However, little changed in rural areas, and the deterioration of many Latin American countries in the 1980s undercut gains in the urban areas.

Sub-Saharan Africa   Women's health and education improved somewhat, but they remained far below the minimal acceptable levels in most countries. Fertility remained high, and serious economic decline was undermining even the modest gains that had been achieved. Women's economic and social participation was high in sub-Saharan countries. But, given the great differences between men and most women by most measures at the beginning of the 1970s, their limited progress and the general economic decline resulted in a situation that must be described as grave.

Northern Africa and western Asia   Gains for women were recorded in health and education. Fertility declined slightly but remained high–5.5 children per woman in northern Africa, 5.3 in western Asia. Women lagged far behind in economic and social participation and decision making. Some fundamentalist movements, by insisting on domesticity for women, have stunted the progress of the past two decades. Other movements are more variable and flexible. In Iran, Turkey, and Egypt, for instance, Islamic movements are supported by many educated women (Moghadam 1991a).

Southern Asia   Women's health and education improved somewhat but were still below minimally acceptable levels elsewhere and far below men's levels. Even economic growth has not appeared to improve women's status, apparently because of their low social, political, and economic participation in both urban and rural areas.

Eastern and southeastern Asia   In much of this part of the world, women's standard of living improved steadily in the 1970s and 1980s. Gender inequalities in health, education, and employment were reduced in both urban and rural areas, and fertility declined. However, considerable political and economic inequality persists, largely because women occupy the lowest paid and lowest-status jobs and are excluded from decision making.

Developed Regions   Throughout these regions, women's health is generally good and their fertility low. In other respects, however, the picture is mixed. Women's economic participation is high in northern Europe, North America, Eastern Europe, and the former Soviet Union, though privatization in the last two makes for uncertainty. Their participation is lower in Australia, Japan, New Zealand, and southern Europe. In all countries occupational segregation and discrimination in wages and training contribute to the advantages of men. Only in northern Europe are women well represented in political participation and decision making.

Several questions arise in the interpretation of these trends. What factors explain them? Do they actually constitute an improvement in political, economic, and social status? Or has gender inequality changed only in form, with patriarchy and institutional disadvantage still in evidence? We turn now to some responses to those questions.

How Important are Income, Economic Resources, and Employment?

Interpreters differ with respect to the stability and intransigence of patriarchy. Walby, who defined patriarchy as "a system of social structures and practices in which men dominate, oppress, and exploit women" (1992: 5), suggested that patriarchy in the United Kingdom over the last 150 years works itself out in five arenas: household work, relations in paid work, male violence, sexual relations, and cultural institutions. She argued that the system is highly stable, particularly with respect to women's engagement in paid work.

In a contrasting argument, Chafetz and Blumberg have stressed the impact of macro-level (e.g., economic, political, and stratification systems) changes on micro-levels (intrapsychic phenomena and face-to-face interactions among individuals in primary groups). For Chafetz, the gender division of labor in the family–in which women carry dispropor-tionate responsibility for children and housework and men are universally involved in extra-domestic work–reflects unequal power relations in the larger society and, derivatively, within the family (Chafetz 1984, 1990). She advances two propositions:

- The greater the division of labor concerning work roles to which accrue material resources (i.e., the macro division of labor), the greater the micro power resources available to husbands relative to their wives.
- The greater the micro power resources available to husbands relative to their wives, the more wives defer to, and comply with, the demands of their husbands (Chafetz 1990: 48).

In other words, Chafetz began with the macro-level division of labor that places material resources disproportionately in the hands of men and argued that micro-level processes between husbands and wives reinforce this division of labor.

A similar analysis is found in Blumberg (1984, 1991), who also stressed the economic domain. Though not monocausal, her approach stresses that "the greater women's relative economic power, the greater their control over their own lives" (Blumberg 1991: 120). Thus, as a woman's economic power increases, it is likely that her fertility "will reflect her own perceived utilities and preferences (rather than those of her mate, family, state, and so forth)" (ibid.: 101). Correspondingly, a decline in a woman's indepen-dently controlled resources often leads to a decrease in her relative power position in the household.

Blumberg's work also provides some empirical evidence from develop-ing countries on the micro-level consequences for women when they control income. For one thing, control of incomes enhances women's self-esteem and power within the family. Other research points in the same direction. Chant (1987) found that women in a Mexican industrial town value earning money highly and that extra-domestic work is a source of power and prestige for them. In a subsequent study, she found that many women in Querétaro expressed enjoyment of their new-found freedom to secure a job and gain some economic independence (Chant 1994). Safa (1992), in a study of women in the export-processing zones of the Dominican Republic, found that, despite adverse work conditions, women who worked experienced an increase in bargaining power within the household and more control over their own fertility. Finlay (1989) found that samples of Dominican factory women and housewives differed significantly in levels of consciousness, aspirations, control over decision making, distribution of household tasks, and fertility. Moghadam (1993) found that women in a pharmaceutical plant in Casablanca, Morocco, enjoyed their jobs and would not quit even if the family no longer needed the additional income they earned.

As a rule, the public sector is a more sympathetic employer of women than the private sector. Educated women often choose the public sector because it offers them white-collar conditions, employment security, benefits, and more opportunities for advancement than jobs in the private sector. Public sectors are taking the lead in employing women in many of the developed and developing countries–among them, Finland, Denmark, Mexico, the Philippines, and Sweden (United Nations 1991). In the United States, the "glass ceiling"–the lid on women's advancement–is lower in the private than the public sector.

With respect to fertility in particular, it is now the case the world over that women in gainful employment marry later, begin childbearing later, and have fewer children than do women outside the labor force. Education also plays a role, in that women with more education enter the paid labor force with greater frequency. Conversely, poor, rural, nonliterate, uneducated women manifest higher fertility rates, and these in turn are associated with high rates of infant mortality, maternal mortality, and reproductive health problems. Some studies have suggested that an adverse sex ratio–that is, fewer women than men–may be related to low female labor force participation. The mechanism is that when women are economically inactive as "wives and mothers," their diminished access to resources also diminishes their chances for survival (Blau and Ferber 1992: 41). Skewed population ratios are found in Pakistan, India, Bangladesh, and Iran, countries which show low female labor participation and have official and unofficial ideologies associating women with marriage and motherhood (Moghadam 1991b). In a word, economic activity and literacy appear to be positively related to women's control over their fertility, as well as to their health and life expectancy. Furthermore, considering worldwide developments, the disadvantages of women in terms of access to stable high-income and high-status occupations, while persisting, have decreased over the course of the century. As this has happened, so women have gained greater control over their fertility and health.

Women and Political Activity

Some feminist social scientists apply the term "patriarchal" to all states and use the terms "public patriarchy" or "social patriarchy" to describe welfare states and the former socialist states (Walby 1992; Dolling 1991). According to these social scientists, welfare states have merely changed the form of partiarchy from individual men in institutional positions to the state as father figure. Is this the case? Or do some countries redistribute political power away from concentration among men? And what would be the appropriate indicators of such a change?

A United Nations report (1991) indicates that in a few countries–for example, the Bahamas, Barbados, Finland, and Norway–women in decision-making positions have a strong influence on politics. In other areas, such as northern Africa, eastern Asia, and western Asia, their representation and influence are negligible. Most women in government hold positions in "women's" ministries–education, social welfare, and culture; an exception is Finland, where in 1991 women held the top position in the Central Bank and the ministries of Defense, Justice, and the Environment. In 1986 nearly half the cabinet ministers were women. In 1991 women's political representation in Norway was as follows: in Parliament 35.8 percent; in the General Council of the Confederation of Trade Unions 14 percent; senior civil servants 10.9 percent; university professors 7.2 percent, and leaders of business corporations 3.3 percent; (Skjeie 1991: 89). Before 1989 the parliaments of Eastern Europe and the Soviet Union had about 33 percent women members, but subsequent democratization has reduced that percentage (to 17 percent in Russia, 6 percent in Czechoslovakia, 7 percent in Hungary, 3.5 percent in Rumania in 1991), leading activists to coin the term "male democracies." Those same countries have seen a corresponding elimination of many social services and benefits for women, especially working mothers (see Moghadam 1992).

The United States compares poorly with many other countries in terms of women's political participation. Though granted the suffrage in 1920, by 1987 they held only 5.3 percent of positions in representative government–about the same as Tunisia, Malaysia, Brazil, and Peru (United Nations 1991). However, relatively more women are appointed to government decision-making positions in the United States–though at the cabinet level only in the administrations of Roosevelt and Clinton. Also, the United States is the only industrialized country without a national social insurance program, which in other countries includes policies targeted for women and families.

Participation in the community and social movements has a long history. In the past 20 years, however, there has been a burgeoning of groups headed by, or composed primarily of, women. Throughout the world groups have formed to oppose discriminatory practices, increases in poverty, violence against women, environmental threats, armaments, and the negative effects of economic programs. Many such groups have been formalized as nongovernmental organizations (NGOs) or community-based organizations (CBOs).

Women's mobilization is one salient indicator of change in the status of women. In recent decades this has increased throughout the world, dramatically so in the developing countries. The Indian women's movement is among the most active, having organized campaigns around bride burning, ritual widow immolation, a uniform civil code for all religious communities, and development issues. Many independent women's organizations appeared in the 1980s in the Middle East and North Africa. In Algeria, feminist groups first formed to oppose the government's attempt to institute a conservative family law and later organized against *intégrisme*. In Egypt the Arab Women's Solidarity Association tied the question of women to political, social, economic, and cultural issues. Its opposition to the Gulf War of 1991 led to its banishment by the Egyptian government.

In Turkey, the women's movement gained strength in the 1980s, protesting against practices such as the treatment of women prisoners, male harassment of women in public places, and wife battering. It has also applied pressure on the government to implement fully the UN Convention on the Elimination of All Forms of Discrimination against Women (Moghadam 1993). According to Jaquette, Latin America is experiencing "a new era of women's mobilization, comparable in many ways to the women's emancipation movement of the early twentieth century, but much broader in scope" (1989: 4). In Argentina, Uruguay, Peru, and Chile women have mobilized into women's human rights groups, feminist groups, and organizations of poor urban women (Jaquette 1989).

In the longer run, this kind of mobilization will no doubt eventuate in greater representation in formal political institutions. For the moment, Norway and Finland are the countries where women have made most inroads on this score. But Skjeie (1991) has argued that even this progress may not represent greater gender equality, because women are being integrated into "shrinking institutions"–that is, once powerful organizations that have gradually lost their efficacy–and that only limited progress has been made in powerful institutions such as the state bureaucracy, universities, and especially business corporations. At the same time, Skjeie has provided data showing that the proportion of women on public boards, councils, and committees–state bodies that legislate and maintain social policies that benefit women–has grown from 7 percent in 1967 to 35 percent in 1989. More generally, it should be observed that while *all* states manifest gender inequalities, the differences between the extremes are dramatic. In Saudi Arabia and Kuwait, women do not vote, and political power is held exclusively by elite men, whereas in Norway, Finland, and Barbados, women have gained significant access to political institutions and decision-making bodies.

Stability and Change in the Status of Women: A Macro-Structural Framework

Any adequate framework for explaining the dynamics of women's position needs to be formulated at multiple analytic levels and stress the continuities between gender theory and general sociological theory. One such synthesis combines the fundamental forces of the world economy, the state, gender, class, and social movements in the following way.

The World Economy and Female Labor

One version of the world economy is that of world-systems theory (Wallerstein 1974). Its basic premise is that there exists a capitalist world economy which integrates the societies of the world into a single economic system of core, semi-peripheral, and peripheral nations. According to Wallerstein (1984), over a period of 400 years, successive expansions have transformed the capitalist world economy from a system located primarily in Europe to one that covers the entire globe. In the modern world system, social relationships develop in part along class lines. As Chase-Dunn put it, "The world class structure is composed of capitalists . . . and propertyless workers. This class system also includes small commodity producers who control their own means of production but who do not employ the labor of others, and a growing middle class of skilled and/or professionally certified workers" (Chase-Dunn 1983: 73).

Whatever the merits of the materialist assumptions of world-systems theory and of the core–semi-periphery–periphery schema, it has underscored the new salience of the internationalization of the economy. At the same time, it has included little about the place of gender in world-system stratification. Yet there is reason to believe that world-systems theory can throw light on gender inequalities and their consequences. Ward's (1985) analysis of fertility is an example. One version of modernization theory holds that economic development results in a decline in fertility. But in her study of increasing inequality, Ward found that in peripheral countries, this is not so. The limited number of jobs in the formal sector typically go to men. Similarly, men become the primary workers in commerce, export agriculture, and other parts of the export economy. Women are relegated to the informal service sector of the urban economy and to subsistence agriculture in the countryside. In this way women's labor subsidizes and makes possible the export sector and permits exploitation of the mostly male work force in that sector. Fertility then *increases*, because women's socioeconomic position vis-à-vis men is lower, and they have less control over their fertility, or because children are regarded as necessary for old-age security. By this chain of mechanisms, peripheral status in the world economy may create pressure for high fertility rates.

Women on the semi-periphery and at the core engaged in industrial labor and service jobs have been affected by recent changes of the kind described as global restructuring in different ways. The term "global restructuring" refers to the emergence of what is in effect a global assembly line, in which research and management are centered in developed countries, while assembly-line and processing work is relegated to less developed countries. Restructuring also involves control over increasingly dispersed production sites and decentralized organizations through subcontracting and product differentiation. As Ward suggested:

> The global assembly line approach to production is attractive to transnational corporations . . . and to employers seeking greater access to markets, diffusion of political and economic costs, improved competitive abilities, and product diversity. Within developing countries, restructuring is marked by growth of the service sector and specialization in export industries such as electronics, garments, and pharmaceuticals as a development strategy. Restructuring is also marked by increasing use of female workers in the informal sector. (Ward 1990: 1–2)

Global restructuring entails, above all, a growth in the number of informal-sector workers and women workers. This sector provides an alternative, cheap source of labor that is largely unregulated by labor legislation. Employers can minimize wages, the threat of unionization, and competitive risks and maximize flexibility in hiring, overhead costs, and production processes (Ward 1990). In the United States global restructuring has meant relying on immigrant labor (Portes and Sassen-Koob 1987), especially Hispanic women in the garment and electronics industries of New York and California (Sassen and Fernandez-Kelly, forthcoming). The main advantages for employers in hiring women are low wages, temporary hiring, and reduced membership in unions.

Economic internationalization has led to what Joekes (1987) calls "the globalization of female labor." What affects women most is the relocation of labor-intensive industries from developed to developing countries in the search for cheap labor–mostly young, unmarried, inexperienced women (ILO/INSTRAW 1985). Textiles and clothing were the first to be relocated, followed by food processing, electronics, and pharmaceutical products. Relocation is effected by subcontracting or by setting up subsidiaries with foreign or local capital. The relocation process has affected women mainly in Southeast and East Asia and in Latin America and the Caribbean. The five countries with the largest export-processing zone operations are Hong Kong, South Korea, Puerto Rico, Singapore, and Taiwan, followed by Brazil, Haiti, Malaysia, and Mexico (Joekes and Moayedi 1987). Most jobs in these areas go to women. Joekes (1987) argues that industrialization in the Third World has been as much female-led as export-led. This applies especially to the newly industrializing countries of Southeast and East Asia, which may have experienced growth in part because they have integrated women so massively into industrial production–as did the former socialist countries.

During the 1970s and 1980s, global restructuring has involved several shifts: from import-substitution industrialization to export-led growth, from state ownership to privatization, from government price- and trade-regulation to liberalization, from a stable, organized work force to "flexible labor," from formal employment to the proliferation and expansion of informal sectors. The worldwide economic crises of the 1980s accelerated these shifts. In the United States and the United Kingdom, international declining profits drove capital to accelerate the process of informalization. In the latter, the number of "flexible workers" increased by 16 percent between 1981 and 1985, while permanent jobs *decreased* by 6 percent. Over a similar period nearly one-third of newly created jobs were "temporary" in character (Harvey 1989: 152). Women are those mainly affected by such developments:

> Not only do the new labor market structures make it much easier to exploit the labor power of women on a part-time basis, and so to substitute lower-paid female labor for that of more highly paid and less laid-off core male workers, but the revival of sub-contracting and domestic and family labor systems permits a resurgence of patriarchal practices and homeworking. (Harvey 1989: 153)

By 1990 economic restructuring had also spread to the former socialist countries. This process, too, has a gender dimension. At one time this region of the world had the highest rates of female labor-force participation and the largest female share of paid employment. At present women face unemployment, marginalization from the productive process, and loss of social security benefits such as maternity leaves and child-care facilities. Prior to unification and restructuring, more than 90 percent of women had a secure job by age 23 (Mussall 1991). Under privatization female employees are frequently let go before male employees, and in unprofitable companies child care is one of the first benefits to be cut. In the former Soviet Union, "unemployment has already become a particularly severe prospect for women workers and for ethnic minorities in the various parts of the country" (Standing, 1989: 10). In 1992 it was estimated that 80 percent of unemployed people in Moscow were women (Weir 1992).

If the costs of providing social benefits for women, formerly assumed by the state, are assumed by private employers, this may reduce demand for female labor, limit women's access to full-time employment, and reduce their earnings in the formal sector. From a market point of view, female labor in parts of Eastern Europe is more expensive than male labor–notwithstanding an earnings gap–because of the costs involved in maternity and child-care provisions. One has the impression that the status of female labor in the former socialist countries, while not to be romanticized, was of a different order from the "cheap and expendable female labor" of the industrializing Third World countries. Whatever one's judgment on that score, it is apparent that privatization in that unstable part of the world is creating differential economic hardship for women and may work to strengthen patriarchal notions about men's and women's roles.

Gender and Processes of Social Change

Like the concept of class, the concept of gender refers to a structured relationship of inequality. With respect to economic class, the relationship derives from differential control of the means of production (Marx) or unequal market opportunities (Weber). With respect to gender, the asymmetry stems originally from women's childbearing function and is expressed in the sexual division of labor. As Papanek puts it, "Gender differences based on the social construction of biological sex distinctions are one of the great 'fault lines' of societies–those marks of difference among categories of persons that govern the allocation of power, authority, and resources" (1990: 163). As such, gender pervades the general organization of social inequality.

Gender asymmetry is universal, but its specific structuring and the resulting degree of inequality are variable. It is connected, furthermore, with economic and other institutional structures, including the state. For this reason gender hierarchies are constructed differently in kinship-ordered, agrarian, developing, and advanced industrial settings. The gender system is further influenced by the type of regime and state ideology. States which are Marxist (e.g., the former German Democratic Republic), theocratic (Saudi Arabia), individualistic democratic (the United States), or social democratic (the Nordic countries) manifest different legal arrangements affecting women and different family policies. In addition, gender hierarchies are sustained by processes of socialization and reinforced through distinct institutions, including the labor market, of which occupational sex segregation is an invariable accompaniment.

Though often resistant to change, gender systems are not fixed or immutable. They change when economic and political forces change. We have already indicated, for example, that increased trade, multinational investment, and cross-regional flows of capital and labor have drawn women increasingly into the process of economic internationalization and restructuring. This has had the dual effect of utilizing them as cheap, flexible labor and undermining notions of the exclusively domestic role of women.

The major sources of gender redefinition in the twentieth century appear to be the following:

- the expanded utilization of female labor in national economies, first in the Soviet Union and then, after the Second World War, throughout Western and Eastern Europe, North America, and the modernizing countries of Asia and Latin America;
- the efforts of international bodies, especially the United Nations and its agencies, to make women's involvement in national development more visible and to improve women's legal status;
- the activities of women's movements and feminist researchers and writers in all countries;
- the remarkable progress of women in the Nordic countries of Finland, Norway, and Sweden, where women's participation in the labor force and in political institutions approaches that of men.

Internationalization appears to be undermining some of the most extreme aspects of patriarchal attitudes and practices (restrictions on women's mobility, access to education and employment, choice of spouse, and control over fertility), but gender inequality persists in all countries and has become more extreme in some cases.

Social change affecting women's position is irregular. The expanded role of women in production and their visibility in public life sometimes give rise to backlash movements. Bastions of conservatism persist among men– perhaps most evident in the lower middle class and among the economically insecure. For some women, moreover, the decline in the ideology of men as family providers and women as childbearers is a source of anxiety. This rests in turn on such factors as a fear of decline in the "family wage," from increased unemployment of men, from inflation, and from declining wages, and a fear of women having to work to meet household needs out of economic necessity rather than choice–as well as on persistent cultural traditionalism. In some cases–for example, in the anti- abortion movement in the United States and the Islamic movements of the Middle East–women themselves are drawn into movements that call for the return of women to domestic life and traditional values.

The Articulation of Class and Gender

Despite ambiguities regarding the nature of social class that have arisen in post-industrial society, class continues to operate significantly in shaping cultural practices, patterns of consumption, life-styles, patterns of reproduction, and cultural world views. Milliband put it directly: "[Class divisions] find expression in terms of power, income, wealth, responsi- bility, 'life chances,' style and quality of life, and everything else that makes up the texture of existence" (Milliband 1989: 25). With respect to women in particular, while educational and other changes have increased occupa- tional access and social mobility, class location still determines access to resources, including education.

Generalized theories of patriarchy, which often posit a stable system of subordination of all women by all men, tend to oversimplify differences between the North and the South, between developed and less developed countries, and between different classes and status groups within societies. In fact, the degree of gender disadvantage is strongly conditioned by class. This appears most obviously in the realm of reproduction; educated middle-class and upper-class women tend to have fewer children than peasant or poor women. Upper and upper-middle-class urban women have more choices than lower-middle-class, working-class, urban poor, and peasant women, and thus have greater possibilities for "emancipation." In 1971 Safilios-Rothschild wrote that in developing countries professional and marital roles become compatible for the wealthier classes because of the availability of cheap domestic labor and the extended family network. More generally, class operates to determine what kind of child-care assistance women can secure–cheap immigrant labor, paid day care (both certified and uncertified), adolescent baby-sitters, relatives, or none.

The State and Gender

In all countries the state plays a central role in creating social policies, development strategies, and legislation that determine women's opportunities. Examples are family law, affirmative action, provisions for restrictions on working mothers, education policy, health policy, and population policy. State policies may reinforce customary patriarchal structures and discriminatory practices, undermine them, or have mixed effects. As Pyle (1990) observed, state policy in Ireland appears to rest on a contradictory set of goals: the development of the economy and the expansion of services *and* the maintenance of the "traditional family." Such policies may intensify both role conflicts for women and social conflicts in society. Individual women, for example, may find themselves torn between the economic need or desire to work and a gender ideology that stresses their family roles. With respect to social conflict, a state policy of development, state-sponsored education, and inclusionary policies for women in the state sector may create a "new class" of professionally employed, politically active, articulate women whose presence may constitute a threat to conservative groups.

Modern Egypt provides a ready example of the direct and largely positive effect that state policies can have on women's economic social status. Under the regime of Gamal Abdel Nasser of the 1950s, the public sector of that country expanded significantly through a series of "Egyptianization" decrees (1956–9) which secured government control of foreign-owned assets, including the Suez Canal. In the early 1960s the government adopted a centralized development policy which included a wave of nationalization of Egyptian-owned enterprises in industry, banking, trade, and transport. It simultaneously initiated an employment drive whereby state owners were forced to create significant numbers of new jobs. The administrative apparatus of the state was also expanded rapidly at the central and local government level. At the same time, the government adopted an objective of spreading health and education services in urban and rural areas, with a corresponding growth in these services as well (ILO 1990: 52). The state's guarantee of a job to all high school and university graduates, moreover, encouraged women–including working-class and lower-middle class women–to take advantage of the government's free education policy.

The Nasserist state thus offered political support for the education of women and for their integration into national development. A labor law of 1954 guaranteed equal rights and equal wages and made special provisions for married women and mothers. Later, under Anwar Sadat, these provisions were expanded to facilitate women's participation in the labor market. This law was applied primarily in the public and government sectors, which made jobs in these areas particularly attractive to women. As a result, the state became the most important employer of women (Hoodfar 1991).

Social Movements and Women's Empowerment

Social movements, which are vehicles through which people organize to try to influence social life, both appear with great frequency in times of rapid social change and foster further social change. While the study of social movements has burgeoned in recent decades, their gender aspects have not always been considered explicitly. With few exceptions (Moghadam 1991b, 1993), the gender dynamics of revolutions have not been explicated, even though feminist scholars have documented the importance of "the woman question" in revolutionary discourse, as well as the significant participation of women in social movements. The gender dynamics of women's movements themselves, whether in their nineteenth- and early twentieth-century manifestations or as "new social movements" in the late twentieth century, have been the subject of more research. For example, Jayawardena's study shows a link between feminism and nationalism in parts of Asia (Jayawardena 1986); Rowbotham and Weeks (1977) have established a link between feminism and socialism, and Simon and Danziger (1991) have assessed the impact of women's movements in the United States on both attitudes and institutional change in politics, the workplace, and the family.

The unique contemporary role of women as political subjects and political actors is now commonly acknowledged. As Molyneux put it, it is now necessary to take account of both feminism and "the widespread and growing involvement of women in politics on a global scale, as participants in popular movements together with men, as actors with specific women's demands, and in their own autonomous movements" (quoted in

Rowbotham 1992). West and Blumberg (1990) have attempted to specify the types of women's social protest thus:

- as participants and leaders in organized struggles to attack problems that directly threaten their economic survival and that of their families and children;
- as participants in social protests focused on nationalist or racial/ethnic issues;
- as participants and leaders in movements that address broad humanistic/nurturing issues such as peace, the environment, public education, and so on;
- as activists on behalf of their own rights as women and those of various specific groups of women (battered women, older women, teenage mothers, child brides, and so on).

The worldwide movement has had the effect of highlighting gender oppression, encouraging activists, bringing pressure to bear on elites and governments, fostering changes in legislation and social policy, and consolidating women as new political constituencies in many countries.

Explanation of the unprecedented historical rise of the women's movement is far from complete, but at least two major components have been identified. Chafetz and Dworkin (1986, 1989) explain it in terms of macro-level changes such as urbanization, expanding education and employment for women, and the size of the middle class. Piven (1985) explains it in terms of the convergence of "a moral economy of domesticity" (women's traditional ideas derived from their maternal and domestic roles) and "change in the objective circumstances of women" which has necessitated political activism for greater rights as women, as mothers, as workers, and as citizens.

Conclusion

By way of a concluding remark, nothing seems more appropriate than to underscore the complexity and unevenness of changes in gender inequality in the contemporary world, characteristics which stem from the multiple embeddedness of gender in virtually all society's institutions. Women's social positions have been significantly affected by urbanization, industrialization, and proletarianization, as well as by the expansion of education, legal reforms, and women's movements. In their turn, women, both directly through conscious mobilization and indirectly through their growing presence in the public sphere, have contributed to changes in key societal institutions: the labor market (through increases in female participation and shifts in occupational sex-typing), the political structure (through increased political participation and application of political quotas), and the family (as a result of greater sexual freedom, greater control over fertility, changing family forms, expansion of female-maintained households, more equitable decision making, and cultural pressure on men to involve themselves more equitably in family life).

Any evaluation of these changes, however, must take account of the mixture of facilitating and hindering forces. Female employment has expanded globally, but often under conditions of a decline in the social power of labor, the rise of flexible labor markets, and a deterioration of work conditions. The growing visibility of women and their demands for equality constitute a cultural revolution. But counter-pressures in the form of backlash movements and other developments are also in evidence. While the larger picture suggests that universal education, increased economic participation, and political mobilization of women guarantee a secular trend toward less, rather than more, gender inequality in the long run, this trend is nevertheless subject to punctuations and irregularities.

References

Abaza, M. and Stauth, G. 1988: "Occidental Reason, Orientalism, and Islamic Fundamentalism." *International Sociology*, 3: 343–64.

Acker, J. 1989: "Making Gender Visible," in R. Wallace (ed.), *Feminism and Sociological Theory*, Vol. 4: *Key Issues in Sociological Theory*, Newbury Park, Calif.: Sage Publications, 65–81.

Barrett, M. and McIntosh, M. 1985: "Ethnocentrism and Socialist-Feminist Theory," *Feminist Review*, 10: 23–47.

Blau, F. and Ferber, M. 1992: "Women's Work, Women's Lives: A Comparative Economic Perspective," in H. Kahne and J. Z. Giele (eds), *Women's Work and Women's Lives: The Continuing Struggle Worldwide*, Boulder, Colo.: Westview Press, 28–44.

Blumberg, R. L. 1984: "A General Theory of Gender Stratification," in R. Collins (ed.), *Sociological Theory 1984*, San Francisco: Jossey-Bass, 23–101.

Blumberg, R. L. 1991: "Income under Female versus Male Control: Hypotheses from a Theory of Gender Stratification from the Third World," in Blumberg (ed.), *Gender, Family, and Economy: The Triple Overlap*, Newbury Park, Calif.: Sage Publications, 97–127.

Chafetz, J. S. 1984: *Sex and Advantage: A Comparative, Macrostructural Theory of Sex Stratification*. Totowa, N.J.: Rowman and Allanheld.

Chafetz, J. S. 1990: *Gender Equality: An Integrated Theory of Stability and Change*. Newbury Park, Calif.: Sage Publications.

Chafetz, J. S. and Dworkin, A. G. 1986: *Female Revolt: Women's Movements in World and Historical Perspective*. Totowa, N.J.: Rowman and Allanheld.

Chafetz, J. S. and Dworkin, A. G. 1989: "Action and Reaction: An Integrated, Comparative Perspective on Feminist and Antifeminist Movements," in M. L. Kohn (ed.), *Cross-National Research in Sociology*, Newbury Park, Calif.: Sage Publications, 329–50.

Chant, S. 1987: "Family Structure and Female Labour in Querétaro, Mexico," in J. Momsen and J. Townsend (eds), *Geography and Gender in the Third World*. London: Hutchinson, 277–93.

Chant, S. 1994. "Women and Poverty in Urban Latin America: Mexican and Costa Rican Experiences," in ISSC/UNESCO (eds), *Poverty in the 1990s: The Responses of Urban Women*, Oxford and Paris: Berg/ISSC in cooperation with UNESCO.

Chase-Dunn, C. 1983: "The Kernel of the Capitalist World-Economy: Three Approaches," in W. Thompson (ed.), *Contending Approaches in World-Systems Analysis*, Beverly Hills, Calif.: Sage Publications, 35–78.

Dolling, I. 1991: "Between Hope and Helplessness: Women in the GDR after the 'Turning Point'." *Feminist Review*, 39: 3–15.

Ertürk, Y. 1992: "Convergence and Divergence in the Status of Women: The Cases of Turkey and Saudi Arabia." *International Sociology*, 6: 307–20.

Finlay, B. 1989: *The Women of Azua: Work and Family in the Rural Dominican Republic.* New York: Praeger.

Giele, J. 1977: "Introduction: The Status of Women in Comparative Perspective," in J. Giele and A. Smock (eds), *Women: Roles and Status in Eight Countries*, New York: John Wiley and Sons, 1–31.

Harvey, D. 1989: *The Condition of Postmodernity: An Enquiry into the Origins of Cultural Change.* Oxford: Blackwell.

Hess, B. and Ferree, M. M. 1987: *Analyzing Gender.* Beverly Hills, Calif.: Sage Publications.

Hoodfar, H. 1991: "Return to the Veil: Personal Strategy and Public Participation in Egypt," in N. Redclift and M. T. Sinclair (eds), *Working Women: International Perspectives on Labour and Gender Ideology*, London: Routledge, 104–24.

ILO 1990: *World Labour Report 1989.* Geneva: ILO.

ILO/INSTRAW 1985: *Women in Economic Activity: A Global Statistical Survey, 1950–2000.* Geneva: ILO and Santo Domingo: UN Training and Research Institute for the Advancement of Women.

Jaquette, J. (ed.) 1989: *The Women's Movement in Latin America: Feminism and the Transition to Democracy.* Boston: Unwin Hyman.

Jayawardena, K. 1986: *Feminism and Nationalism in the Third World.* London: Zed.

Joekes, S. 1987: *Women in the World Economy: An INSTRAW Study.* New York: Oxford University Press.

Joekes, S. and Moayedi, R. 1987: *Women and Export Manufacturing: A Review of the Issues and AID Policy.* Washington, D.C.: ICRW.

Mann, M. 1986. "A Crisis in Stratification Theory?" in R. Crompton and M. Mann (eds), *Gender and Stratification.* Cambridge: Polity Press, 40–56.

Milliband, R. 1989: *Divided Societies: Class Struggle in Contemporary Capitalism.* Oxford: Clarendon Press.

Moghadam, V. M. 1991a: "Islamist Movements and Women's Responses in the Middle East." *Gender & History*, 3: 168–86.

Moghadam, V. M. 1991b: "The Reproduction of Gender Inequality in Muslim Societies: A Case Study of Iran in the 1980s." *World Development*, 19: 1335–50.

Moghadam, V. M. (ed.) 1992: *Privatization and Democratization in Eastern Europe and the Soviet Union: The Gender Dimension.* Helsinki: UNU/WIDER Research for Action Series.

Moghadam, V. M. 1993: *Modernizing Women: Gender and Social Change in the Middle East.* Boulder, Colo.: Lynne Rienner Publishers.

Mussall, B. 1991: "Women Are Hurt the Most." *Der Spiegel*, Hamburg, rep. in *World Press Review*, June.

Papanek, H. 1990: "To Each Less Than She Needs, From Each MoreThan She Can Do: Allocations, Entitlements, and Value," in I. Tinker (ed.), *Persistent Inequalities*, New York: Oxford University Press, 162–83.

Piven, F. F. 1985: "Women and the State: Ideology, Power and the Welfare State," in A. S. Rossi (ed.), *Gender and the Life Course*, New York: Aldine Publishing Co., 265–87.

Portes, A. and Sassen-Koob, S. 1987: "Making it Underground: Comparative Material on the Informal Sector in Western Market Economies." *American Journal of Sociology*, 93: 30–61.

Pyle, J. 1990: "Export-Led Development and the Underdevelopment of Women: The Impact of Discriminatory Development Policy in the Republic of Ireland," in K. Ward (ed.), *Women Workers and Global Restructuring*, Ithaca, N.Y.: ILR Press, 85–112.

Rowbotham, S. 1992: *Women in Movement: Feminism and Social Action*. London: Routledge.

Rowbotham, S. and Weeks, J. 1977: *Socialism and the New Life*. London: Pluto.

Safa, H. 1992: "Gender Inequality and Women's Wage Labor: A Theoretical and Empirical Analysis," forthcoming in V. Moghadam (ed.), *Trajectories of Patriarchy and Development: Theoretical and Comparative Studies*.

Safilios-Rothschild, C. 1971: "A Cross-Cultural Examination of Women's Marital, Educational and Occupational Options,' in M. T. S. Mednick, S. S. Tangri and L. W. Hoffman (eds), *Women and Achievement*, New York: John Wiley and Sons, 48–70.

Sassen, S. and Fernandez-Kelly, P. Forthcoming: "Recasting Women in the Global Economy: Internationalization and Changing Definitions of Gender," in E. Acosta-Belen and C. Bose (eds), *Women and Development in the Third World*. Newbury Park, Calif.: Sage Publications.

Simon, R. J. and Danziger, G. 1991: *Women's Movements in America: Their Successes, Disappointments, and Aspirations*. New York: Praeger.

Skjeie, H. 1991: "The Uneven Advance of Norwegian Women." *New Left Review*, 187: 79–102.

Stacey, J. and Thorne, B. 1985: "The Missing Feminist Revolution in Sociology." *Social Problems*, 32: 301–16.

Standing, G. 1989: *Global Feminisation through Flexible Labour*, Working Paper No. 31, Labour Market Analysis and Employment Planning, WEP. Geneva: ILO.

United Nations 1991: *The World's Women 1970–1990: Trends and Statistics*. New York: UN.

Walby, S. 1992: "The 'Declining Significance' or the 'Changing Forms' of Patriarchy?" Paper given at UNU/WIDER Conference, Helsinki. Also in Moghadam (ed.), *Trajectories of Patriarchy and Development*, forthcoming.

Wallerstein, I. 1974: *The Modern World System* vol. I: *Capitalist Agriculture and the Origins of the European World Economy in the Sixteenth Century*. New York: Academic Press.

Wallerstein, I. 1984: "Long Waves as Capitalist Process," *Review*, 4: 559–76.

Ward, K. 1985: "The Social Consequences of the World Economic System: The Economic Status of Women and Fertility." *Review*. 8: 561–93.

Ward, K. 1990: "Introduction and Overview," in Ward (ed.), *Women Workers and Global Restructuring*, 1–22.

Weir, F. 1992: "Russian Working Women a Public Enemy: Interview with Elvira Novikova." *Guardian* (N.Y.), Apr. 15, 12–13.

West, G. and Blumberg, R. L. 1990: "Introduction: Reconstructing Social Protest from a Feminist Perspective," in West and Blumberg (eds), *Women and Social Protest*, New York: Oxford University Press, 1–35.

19

Family and Intimacy

Of all the institutions that constitute sociology's subject matter (see chapter 1), the modern family comes closest to being an exclusive preserve of the discipline. Kinship has been of central concern to anthropologists, but they have traditionally concentrated on its extended forms in simpler societies. Economists consider the "household" as a central unit of analysis but treat it analytically as something empty and abstracted that neverthless behaves like a rational individual. The history of the family is now a concern of social historians, but its arrival on the scene in history has been very recent.

Despite their near-ownership of the family as an institution, sociologists have studied only some aspects of it. Demographers analyze patterns of marriage and divorce, fertility, and family dissolution through death. Sociologists have concentrated on premarital relationships, mate selection, power and decision making in the family, the functional significance of the family in society, the causes and consequences of divorce, the reconstitution of the family into new family-like forms, and, most recently, the family as a locus of the gendering process in society. The study of other aspects of family life is less in evidence. In particular, concern with love and intimacy, while not absent from the sociological literature, is generally marginal, often seen as more properly investigated by social psychologists and psychoanalysts.

In this chapter we will extend a sociological concern to these more "private" aspects of family life, limiting our consideration mainly to the "First World." The starting point of the analysis is that love and intimacy are themselves sociological subjects and sociologically shaped, as Giddens's phrase "the transformation of intimacy" suggests (1992). We regard the family as a variable construct, with all its aspects molded by historically specific political and economic constraints. Marriage itself can

---

This chapter is based on a contribution by Don Edgar and Helen Glezer.

be regarded as a historically specific phenomenon, in that in many societies families have existed without it and that, as an institution, it appears to have evolved as a mechanism for controlling the inheritance of property and the legitimacy of sexual relations all with an eye to the reproduction of society.

In approaching the family thus, it is helpful to make use of the concept of family "career." This term carries two helpful meanings: first, it acknowledges that there has been a historical process of change in the construction of the family's private life; and second, it reflects the increased contingency in people's life patterns, which is a product of the greater role of choice in modern (and post-modern) life, by contrast with earlier, simpler times. The idea of career is preferable to the traditional concept of life cycle, which has connotations of naturalism and inevitability, suggesting that individuals move through a set of fixed or normative stages of development from childhood through adulthood, leaving the parental home, finding a partner, marrying and forming a new family of procreation, thus beginning the cycle anew. The notion of career is closer to the concept of "life course," also used to describe family life (Clausen 1973, 1993). The latter concept implies a diversity of pathways followed by individuals and groups. It is a mapping exercise, tracking life histories through a maze of opportunities and constraints, and suggesting a continuous process of adaptation to varying contingencies.

Aspects of the Contemporary Family Career

The idea of career takes into account the following patterns of change in families' and individuals' histories in modern society:

- The life course is increasingly open to negotiation and construction. Both work and intimacy require training and preparation; they involve deliberately taken decisions and a calculated assessment of the likelihood of achieving certain goals. Longitudinal studies (Moxnes 1991) reveal how family patterns, functions, and relations change over time, constituting a career that is a product of decisions within restraints. This view contrasts with the idea of the life course just "happening" as a series of events. This version of rationality does not contradict the contrasting image of the modern person as confused, alienated, and drifting, without the support of moral guidelines or traditions. Indeed, insofar as the opportunities and constraints throughout life are unstructured, this constitutes a source of confusion and challenge and calls for a greater degree of invention and rational adaptation on the part of individuals.
- The traditional model of courtship, marriage, two-parent family grows increasingly less relevant. More and more children are born and raised in one-parent families, a phenomenon deriving from more childbearing outside marriage and increased rates of divorce. In Western societies sexual intimacy begins earlier, and marriages occur later than in previous times. These trends

mean that many women and men have sexual relationships with a number of partners, and that private life is restricted to intimate relationships with one partner, with kin, and with a few (usually same sex) friends.

- The emphasis in marriage itself is now mainly the quality of the relationship between partners, rather than performance in separated private and public spheres. The high incidence of divorce also means that individuals' expectations increasingly include the possibility of painful endings to closely bonded marital relationships.

- Women have increasingly removed themselves from the private side of family life (mainly, though not exclusively, through wage labor), just as men did during the Industrial Revolution. As a result, women have expanded their range of social contacts (which makes the marital relationship less exclusive and possibly weaker), and intimate relationships within the family, both between partners and with children, have changed.

- Increased longevity also has implications for the life pattern of intimate relationships. In particular, older people (particularly women) face the option of forming new partnerships as their companions die, partnerships which endure for many years in some cases.

The Concept of Intimacy

Intimacy is a feature of the close primary relationships that are typically found in families. Closeness implies mutual understanding, a shared history of special information, the communication of feelings, and rituals that reinforce personal bonds through repetition. Above all, intimacy involves trust and a special kind of secrecy–that is, a tacit understanding that privately disclosed beliefs and feelings will not be revealed publicly in damaging ways. Through intimate interaction families create their own "family culture"–often peculiar to ethnic or class position–which sets off the family as a group of sociological friends who differ from others who are sociological "strangers."

Intimate relationships are most commonly contrasted with the instrumental relations that are found in market exchange and in the authority structures of large formal organizations, in which mutual trust is formalized through law and contractual understandings. This contrast, of course, is part of the long-standing sociological distinction between *Gemeinschaft* (community) and *Gesellschaft* (society). *Gemeinschaft* relations, found in traditional societies, rest on intimate trust, communal alliances, and comradeship built on honor; whereas *Gesellschaft* relations, the hallmark of modern societies, secure their continuity through more abstract mechanisms. In practice, however, the distinction cannot be treated as an absolute one: formal relationships are invariably infused with powerful affects, and personal, trusting relationships always contain an element of calculation and are continuously negotiated and renegotiated.

Much received sociological wisdom regards the relationship between *Gesellschaft* and *Gemeinschaft* as opposed, even inimical. Critics with conservative leanings, such as the Bergers (Berger 1973, Berger and Berger 1983), see the growing institutionalization of the public sphere and the breakdown of civil society and communal ties as detrimental to the quality of personal life. Marxist critics argue that capitalism and consumerism weaken the private sphere, or, in Habermas's (1987) language, that the "technical systems" separate from and overwhelm the "life world." Others have disputed this kind of contrast. Fischer (1982), for example, pointed to a whole world of surviving and new communal life in otherwise formalized urban settings: communal relations in neighborhoods, persisting kinship ties, relations of personal intimacy among peers, including friendship, and relations of sexual intimacy within and outside marriage. These communal–kinship relations may have *changed*, Fischer argued, but they are not necessarily weaker or less significant in contemporary life.

Giddens (1992) provided yet another slant on the intimacy–instrumentality axis. Abstract administrative systems–and the market system in particular–have transformed friendship. To establish trust in the context of these abstract, impersonal systems, individuals must seek out and create relations of loyalty and sincerity. Such ties pervade abstract markets and bureaucracies. Furthermore, they transform the nature of intimacy; in Giddens's words, "as personal trust is not just focused on local and kin networks trust becomes a *project* of opening out to others" (1992: 121, emphasis added). There are no fixed norms for this kind of project, and trust must be won and built through openness, warmth, and self-disclosure.

The modern transformation of intimacy, Giddens argued further, is based on a number of intersections. The first is between *displacement*, or personal estrangement, on the one hand and *re-embedding* of intimacy on the other. Globalized cultural and information systems (see chapter 8) estrange individuals from local settings, but modern transportation and telecommunications recreate locality, kin contacts, and friendships, thus re-embedding the individual in global communities of shared experience. A current academic jest holds that any given scholar interacts more with his or her esteemed colleagues abroad than with his or her (not so esteemed) colleagues in the home department!

A second intersection is that between *intimacy*, or personal trust, and *impersonality*. Modernity has created a world of strangers, but it has also created new environments in which relations of trust and personal ties can be fashioned with people who were once strangers. People can sustain intimate relationships at a distance and can even buy intimacy in counselling and therapy. Relationships of this last type are likely to be fragile, however, because they are fraught with the ambivalence that comes with the omnipresent prospect of the severance of the relationship and the work required to reconstitute and reaffirm another.

The third intersection in the modern world is that between *expertise* and *re-skilling*. In some respects the world of intimacy has been taken over by professionals–psychiatrists and counsellors–but at the same time "lay" people continuously struggle to reappropriate and refashion intimate relationships on their own. Modern life is a struggle to create intimacy through purposiveness in a world that continuously threatens to depersonalize even intimacy into contractual relations. Giddens coined the phrase "modernity as juggernaut" to contrast with the Marxian image of "modernity as monster" and the Weberian image of "modernity as the iron cage of bureaucratic rationality." In terms of the juggernaut image, modernity starts from "the inevitability of living with dangers which are remote from the control not only of individuals but also of large organisations including states" (Giddens 1992: 131). The juggernaut is forever threatening to rush out of human control, but it is also driven and partly controlled by individuals' decisions.

This view of modernity underscores what is new about family life and intimacy: the place of the individual, including his or her self-identity, has become more problematic and contingent. Both private and public life have become more reflexive and open to negotiation; and the lines between private and public, never completely distinct, have become increasingly permeable. Individuals are less likely to be embedded in local, closed communities of kinship and communality; but this does not mean that intimacy has disappeared. Rather, the individual and the family must now construct a private life rather than having it constructed for them. In one important respect this marks an extension of individualism, because so much more of individual life has become discretionary. Nowhere has this development been clearer than in the long-term sociological evolution of love. In arranged marriages, love and sexual intimacy developed within the context of a union fashioned out of kinship, property, and communal considerations. Modern society reverses the two; love has come to precede marriage and the family and to condition all the relationships within them. We now turn to the particulars of that evolution.

Romantic Love and Family Life

The transition from traditional to modern society involved an across-the-board separation of spheres. The Industrial Revolution separated the workplace from the home; the democratic revolution separated politics from kinship and/or aristocratic control; and the civil service separated office from privilege. Each of these splits was accompanied by ideological developments that furthered, explained, and legitimized it. With respect to the family, the splits between workplace and home and between public and private involved new distinctions along gender lines, with women assuming greater responsibility for the home and child rearing. Some of the notable ideological accompaniments of this split were romantic love, the cult of domesticity, the "invention" of motherhood, and changes in the affective relations between parents and among parents and children

(Shorter 1975, Stone 1977, Dally 1982, Badinter 1981). One aspect of these changes was the decline of patriarchy as a daily monitoring system in the domicile. The social definition of children also changed over time, from one of children as young adults to one of children as vulnerable and in need of protection and nurturing (Aries 1962). Along with this came the romanticization of the wife and mother and the division of functions which presented the female role as that of fostering love, subordination in the home, and separation from the public world of wealth and power (Reiger 1985).

While depriving and subordinating women in many respects, these developments also had the ironic effect of endowing women with autonomous power in the home (Mount 1982, Ryan 1981). This subversive aspect was held in check by the historical association between romantic love on the one hand and marriage and motherhood on the other. Men could pursue passionate love through extramarital liaisons but were kept at a certain distance from feminine-controlled intimacy in the home. Romantic love–a specifically Western creation linked with motherhood, childhood, and the family home–elevated intimacy over lust as the basis for enduring sexual relationships and became an important ingredient of individual self-realization.

Giddens has argued that this also transformed the nature of intimacy. It projected a course of future life development bound within the confines of a lifetime marital commitment and validated the individual's identity through the discovery of the other in intimate relationships (Giddens 1992: 41–5). It moved sexuality closer to intimacy and further from reproduction. Love relationships also left more room for negotiation between partners *in the relationship*, which contrasted with the situation of traditional, structured expectations of male and female responsibilities. Earlier definitions of love tended to be instrumental and/or companionate, tied to the mutual practical responsibilities of men and women in running the household. Romantic love has thus been seen as "feminized love" (Cancian 1987, Radway 1984) in the special sense that the separation of work and family gave the fostering of love more exclusively to women.

Romantic love thus had a double effect. It was "an expression of women's power, a contradictory assertion of autonomy in the face of deprivation" (Giddens 1992: 43). Denied a certain kind of sexual activity via the double standard, women were able to develop new domains of intimacy via the ideals of love and motherhood. Women became "specialists of the heart." In one respect men were losers in this development, because they were less able to participate in the warmth, self-disclosure, and mutual support that were called for in the "pure relationship" of love (ibid.: 49–64). Their domination of market, public, and family property and power remained secure, however, until women began to enter the economic and public domains themselves.

Looked at like this, the "phase" of romantic love in the West assumes the status of a way station in the relations between the sexes, a precondition for further changes, rather than a simple system of domination. Again Giddens:

> Intimacy is above all a matter of emotional communication with others and with the self in a context of interpersonal equality. Women have prepared the way for an expansion of the domain of intimacy in their role as the emotional revolutionaries of modernity. Certain psychological dispositions have been the condition and outcome of process, as have also the material changes which have allowed women to stake a claim to equality. (Ibid.: 130)

This leads us to look more closely at the importance of material determinants of the shift in the nature of equality,

> for the sexual division of labour remains substantially intact; at home and at work in most contexts of modern societies men are largely unwilling to release their grip upon the reins of power. Power is harnessed to interests and obviously there are sheerly material considerations which help explain why this is so. However, insofar as male power is based on the compliance of women and the economic and emotional services which women provide, it is under threat. (Ibid.: 131)

Challenging the Division of Labor

The Feminist Critique

One of the main accomplishments of the feminist literature has been to expose the "objectivity" of male and female roles contained in the "Victorian" construction of the family, as well as some sociological constructions of "sex roles" and of the family as a "haven in a heartless world" (Lasch 1977). As Ferree (1990: 867) says, "feminism questions every aspect of this privatized view" of the family and reestablishes the linkages between the family and the political and economic world. Part of this endeavor has been to highlight the diverging, and sometimes conflicting, interests of family members.

In particular, feminist writers generated criticisms of ideal types of sex roles as constructed by Parsons (Parsons, Bales *et al.* 1955), among others, who divided them along "instrumental" (= male, work, authority) and "expressive" (= female, socio-emotional, domestic) axes. Writers such as Connell (1985) and Lopata and Thorne (1978) suggested that such characterizations were reactive defenses against women's advances in education and employment. The view of the family as a protective counterforce against strains generated in the outer world also came under attack, although some writers identified different ways in which families can constitute a resource for women: "Families are also institutions of support and resistance for women as they confront other forms of social oppression providing a cultural grounding for self-esteem as well as networks in which concrete resources can be traded" (Ferree 1990: 868).

Expectedly, the critique of the social construction of maleness and femaleness has occasioned a weakened emphasis on childhood socialization into sex roles and a stronger emphasis on structural opportunities and constraints (Ferree 1990), social categorization, stratification, and power (Reskin 1988). Like so many innovations in sociological thinking, moreover, this critique identified a number of previously taken-for-granted elements of family life and rendered them problematical, thus focusing attention on a range of determinants previously ignored or implicit.

Even the basic concept of "family" has become the object of critical attention. Rapp (1982), for example, distinguished between co-residential households and the term "family," which is an ideological expression dictating who should live together, share income, and perform common tasks. Such an expression, it is argued, is a cultural prescription which legitimizes male dominance and is supported by the ideology of motherhood and homemaking, which justifies self-sacrifice on the part of women.

A more realistic view of the family would include two ingredients: first, a focus on the interaction between family and society: that is, a movement away from a simple focus on family relationships as the basis of women's oppression so as to draw attention to the varying opportunities, structured by race, class, and different economic systems, for women to move beyond the home and establish a position of greater equality, which in its turn has the potential to transform intimate relationships; and second, a focus on interactions within the family. Writers such as Scott (1986) have suggested a change in terminology which also involves a change in approach to family life. She prefers the term "conventional" rather than "traditional" to describe pre-modern family relationships. The former term suggests the historical contingency of "the family" as well as the diversity of gender conventions by class and ethnicity. "Conventional" also underscores the culturally defined nature of supposedly fixed traditions and suggests that those conventions are created, sustained, *and* challengeable. The implications of this line of thinking have been specified by Edgar:

> The dynamic nature of how family units negotiate joint action to produce economies of scale and mutual benefits suggest that the family is not a passive victim of social change, rather the maker of change (Elise Boulding's *familia faber*). It is in the dynamics of family negotiation that the labour market demands for legislation about equal opportunity are forged into a behavioural reality that has lasting impact. (Edgar 1992b: 31)

In short, what has previously been regarded as structure is more profitably regarded as process.

The Dichotomization of Sex Roles

The feminist literature has also brought out the deeper implications of the dichotomy of male provider/female housekeeper. May (1987) characterized Henry Ford's "family wage plan" as a way of allying wives and employers by imposing work discipline. Ferree, drawing on Hareven and Parr, characterized the blue-collar notion of "labor aristocracy" as a construction "of white men with skilled and secure jobs that allowed the ideology of dual spheres to become a working-class ideal" (Ferree 1990: 872). Such constructions became an ideal for both sexes: male property-owners manifested the bourgeois values of citizenship, self-development, and moral responsibility, while mothers created human capital by rearing children and represented the earned social status of the family as volunteers in the public sphere (Daniels 1989, Ostrander 1984). Such considerations led Papanek (1973) to characterize family life as a "two-person career."

This dichotomy was not without its inner problems and contradictions. Some studies have shown that the provider role was often resisted and resented by working-class men, who regarded their wives as "nagging, forcing them to work when they hate it" (Luxton 1980). For women, even when they began entering the labor force in numbers, the supplementary character of their jobs and earnings tended to keep them "in their place." For men the "working wife" presented yet another opportunity–what Ehrenreich (Ehrenreich 1983, Ehrenreich *et al.* 1986) has called the "male flight from commitment" to breadwinning, a phenomenon stereotypically associated with black males but now a more general phenomenon.

Viewed more generally, the contemporary family must be regarded as an institution in continuing transition and conflict. There are still major obstacles to achieving equality in the sharing of paid labor and homemaking; most jobs are built upon assumptions of family support structures that locate women in the private caring sphere (Moen 1989, Goode 1982, Weiss 1987). Household labor continues to find no place in economic calculations of gross national product, a practice that minimizes the reality of the trade-off between wage and family work hours between husbands and wives (Tiano 1987, Ironmonger 1989).

Housework appears to be the area in which resistance to change is most in evidence. Even where wives hold full-time jobs, their share of household work remains disproportionately large (Hochschild and Machung 1989, Glezer *et al.* 1992). Most "family-related" benefits, such as child-care arrangements, are still regarded as benefits for women, rather than flexible structures that might enable both men and women more room for growth in their private lives (Galinsky *et al.* 1991). Despite clear ambiguities and difficulties, however, many families experience little conflict over house-work (Pleck 1985, Komter 1989), which still appears to be sustained by conventional gender expectations. Ferree, however, suggests that in the future it is likely to become the arena of tension in "cracking the boundaries of the family sphere" (1990: 877).

The control of family finances is another core arena for concern, because such control is an important dimension of gender relations. The insight that women who earn an income in their own right have more power in the family goes back at least as far as Engels (1969 [1884]). Class differences are crucial in understanding who controls the purse-strings, and the issue of control becomes especially problematical in families that remain below the poverty line, even when both parents work (Blumberg 1988, Charles and Kerr 1987). In any event, the fluidity of the issue of financial control underscores the general principle that the contemporary family is best described in terms of neither traditional structures nor uncontested male domination, but as a locus of active bargaining, negotiation, and cooperative conflict (Sen 1983).

The Reconstruction of Private Life

We turn now to a number of areas of intimacy, keeping in mind the salience of our two general themes: that intimacy cannot be insulated from its institutional contexts and that, like all aspects of family life, it is characterized by dimensions of power and negotiation as well as affective expression.

Premarital Intimacy

Postponement of marriage has become widespread in the United States. In 1970 the percentage of men aged 20–4 not yet married was 55; in 1988 it was 78. The corresponding increase for women in the same age range was from 36 to 61 percent (US Bureau of the Census 1988). The median age for first marriage is at its highest since the beginning of the twentieth century. It should not be inferred, however, that these trends are a sign of lack of interest in close or committed relationships. There has been a marked increase in the number of couples who cohabit outside marriage–reaching more than 2.5 million in 1988. One third of a 1988 sample of 23–year-olds had cohabited at some time or another, and among those who were married by that age, one-third of the women and two-fifths of the men had cohabited previously (Thornton 1988). A national survey in the same year found that half of a sample aged 19 and older had lived together at some time before their early thirties, and 4 percent of the population were currently cohabiting (Sweet *et al.* 1988, Bumpass and Sweet 1989). Four out of ten cohabiting couples had children present.

Cohabiting couples had more liberal attitudes toward family life and were more likely to have come from a background of parental instability than married couples (Booth and Johnson 1988, Bumpass and Sweet 1989).

Such cohabiting relationships were more unstable than married relationships, with 40 percent dissolving within two years and 23 percent ending in marriage to their partners. Similar patterns of early sexual relations and high rates of cohabitation have also been noted in Norway (Eriksen and Wetlesen 1992). The forces underlying these patterns are not altogether clear, but some demographic research suggests that an overabundance of women weakens their traditional roles, whereas men who thereby have a surplus of partners have less of a commitment to marriage (Glick 1988, Guttentag and Secord 1983).

Cohabiting couples typically do not manifest the "Romeo and Juliet" complex of social disapproval and isolation. Research on social networks indicates that developing intimacy between cohabiting couples depends on the supportive presence of significant others. Couples may develop their own "culture" based on intimacy and mutual self-disclosure, but they do not tend to withdraw from kin in the process (Surra 1985, Milardo *et al.* 1983). Rather, partners are built into networks of kin and others as part of the process of developing intimacy and formalizing the relationship (Milardo *et al.* 1983).

Couples who cohabit and then decide to marry emphasize the dyadic reciprocity of their relationships and the equality of the partnership (Surra and Huston 1987). Moreover,

> relationship-driven commitments were associated with higher levels of subsequent marital happiness. This commitment process was tied to attributions that concern spending time together, getting to know one another and disclosing information to one another–the kinds of inferences that typically were associated with moderate, slower changes in commitment. Relationship-driven commitments more closely match the rational choice process believed to be important for marital success. (Surra 1990: 856).

Findings of this sort suggest that stereotyped models that couples are "made for one another" or that "love conquers all" are less adequate as accounts of the process whereby intimacy develops than models that stress sustained and close interaction, gradual acquisition of information and the building of affects, and continuous though not always conscious negotiation (Murstein 1987).

Young Adult Independence

Research in several countries reveals a shift from marriage as the marker of independence of the young to a more complicated pattern: early departure from home, usually for educational purposes, followed by return and reliance upon parents for economic and emotional support. Start-up costs for housing and employment opportunities for the young are obvious factors influencing this pattern. Young Americans are more likely to leave home to gain a college education than young British or Australians. Australian males are more likely than British to leave home for purposes of establishing their independence and less likely to return than those who have left for educational purposes (Hartley 1992). In general, leaving has become a more gradual, multistage process than before, and is often marked by the ambivalences that arise when adult parents and adult children engaged in sexual relationships live under the same roof.

Marital Intimacy

Marital intimacy follows some of the same principles as intimacy in cohabitation. Successful marital communication seems to involve the ability to disclose or reveal private thoughts and feelings about the self to the partner (Schapp *et al*. 1988, Christensen 1986). Self-report and diary studies on marital interaction indicate that happy couples spend longer periods of time each day together than distressed couples and that there is less discrepancy in affective disclosure between partners (Chelune *et al*. 1984, Davidson *et al*. 1983). Distressed spouses seem to be less accurate at decoding their partners' attempts at communication, and, as a rule, husbands are less able than wives to encode and decode messages and respond accurately to spousal communication (Noller 1984, Sillars and Scott 1983).

Fitzpatrick (1984, 1988) has developed a typology of interactional styles in marriage which vary along the dimensions of ideology, interdependence, and conflict avoidance/expressivity. There are *traditionals*, who hold conventional values about marriage and the family, are very interdependent in the marriage, and readily argue over serious issues; *independents*, who are more liberal in their marital and family values, moderately interdependent, and habituated to conflict; and *separates*, who have ambivalent family values, are not very interdependent, and tend to avoid marital conflict. While suggestive, such a typology overlooks the fact that most marriages do not fall into fixed types but shift continuously in different directions according to the changing goals and identifications of the spouses, changing economic and status fortunes, and accumulated patterns of interaction evolved though past experience in both routine and crisis situations.

Intimacy and Divorce

As a general rule, divorce increases with the industrial development and complexity of societies, though developed countries vary in their adherence to this pattern. In countries such as the United States divorce has become so widespread that in 1989 Martin and Bumpass estimated that three-fourths of all current first marriages in that country would end in divorce. The historical causes for the widespread and long-term trends in increases in divorce rates–and variations in them by social categories–are almost impossible to untangle, but we will mention a number of findings and suggestions reported in the literature:

- The ease or difficulty of legal divorce–for example, the possibility of "no fault" divorce–cannot be related in a linear way to divorce rates, but it clearly has an effect on norms and expectations relating to lifetime obligations (Weitzman 1985).
- Early marriage increases the chances of divorce (Martin and Bumpass 1989), so increases in the age of first marriage should presumably have a dampening effect on divorce rates.
- Economic decline retards divorce, while prosperity increases it (Glick and Lin 1986). This may be a special instance of the larger principle that industrial societies open up alternative sources of financial security, personal services, satisfaction, and leisure for people, beyond the family as an institution (Cherlin and Furstenberg 1988). This has the effect of making the family and family stability less important (Schoen *et al*. 1985).
- A society's sex ratio may make a difference; in particular, a higher proportion of women to men increases the divorce rate because of the availability of alternatives to marriage for men (Guttentag and Secord 1983).
- The effects of women's increasing participation in the labor force on divorce are no doubt complex and multiple. There is evidence that the greater economic independence acquired thereby by women is related to increasing divorce rates (Schoen *et al*. 1985, Cherlin and Furstenburg 1988). Increased female labor force participation is also related to the possibility of new opportunities for better partnerships (Rank 1987, Spitze and South 1985), but other studies show that female employment improves life satisfaction and is related positively to marital stability (Greenstein 1990, Spitze and South 1985).
- Feminist writers have stressed divorce as a way of fulfilling expectations of quality in societies by providing support for women and children outside marriage (Moxnes 1985). The increased tendency for wives to initiate divorce proceedings suggests that an increase in women's autonomy may also be a factor (Hill 1988, Spitze and South 1985). Divorce opens up new opportunities for relationships of intimacy. Many divorced people re-partner but do not remarry, indicating a level of suspicion about legal commitments and a greater emphasis on the quality of relationships. Many women in particular seem to prefer to develop intimate relationships that are more autonomous and/or more equal than they experienced in a marriage.

While these findings and suggestions do not add up to a decisive account of the determinants of divorce, the general picture suggests that more explanatory mileage can be gained by focusing on patterns of constraints and the availability of alternatives and resources, than on "marital happiness" and its relation to divorce (Booth *et al*. 1986, Morgan 1988).

Children and Family Intimacy

The long-standing changes in the social definition of children have implications for intimate relations involving them. Writers from different perspectives have noted the long-term trend away from parental authority, toward a more egalitarian approach, with the corresponding expectation that children have a right to be cared for emotionally. More particularly, psychoanalytically oriented writers (e.g., Reibstein and Richards 1992) have argued that early self-identity and the potential for intimacy are developed first in relation to a pervasively important mother figure. Yet this general truth is clouded by the complexities of the contemporary family situation and raises a number of as yet unanswered questions:

- Can the role of "pervasively important mother figure" be played by others besides mothers? The increased involvement of women in work and other activities outside the home necessarily entails some temporal and possibly emotional distancing from the young child. Can men play a complementary role? Giddens (1992) has predicted that as fathers become more closely involved in the rearing of children and as men face increased demands from their female partners for expression of feelings and more generous self-disclosure, so they, too, will enter the new world of intimacy created by women.
- What are the psychological implications for intimacy with children and children's gender identification in that small, but possibly growing, number of same-sex unions?
- What are the psychological implications of the increasing proportion of parental roles being taken by step-parents, nonmarried mates, and siblings? While large numbers of children are born to single parents, only a small percentage of these are born to mothers without a male partner. Also, far more children live with a brother or sister than is suggested by census data on family size (Jensen 1989, McDonald 1993). Siblings thus become increasingly important to socialization and private relationships in the family home (Edgar 1992b).
- With all these complexities, what becomes of the status of developmental mechanisms once thought to be widespread if not universal? The Oedipus complex, for example, the special Freudian theory relating to conflicts revolving around intimate relations with the mother and authority relations with the father, presupposes a certain model of the family with conventionally gendered parental relations. Will the general decline in authority–not only male authority–call for a fundamental revision of such theories, or will they still apply with different combinations of actors on the familial stage?

One promising approach to the study of parent–child intimacy, as well as adult intimacy, is to regard it as a learning and learned process within the context of new constraints imposed on families and other unions. Social-structural conditions, such as increased autonomy and financial independence for women, as well as increased capacity to control reproduction, impose a new imperative on men to work harder at the construction of intimate relationships. Both mothers and fathers will be called upon to engage in more "love work" because of these new and different demands. This observation is consistent with the general principle guiding our discussion in this chapter, namely, that as social-structural arrangements become less certain and more contingent, so greater demands are placed on the learning, adaptive, and decision-making capacities of the individuals involved in those arrangements.

Some research findings can be related to this concept of learned intimacy. Studies of mothering and child development from a perspective of task-related interaction show some promise. Research by Haavind (1984), for example, appears to show that a mother's intimate knowledge of her child makes it possible to include him or her in social and task-related settings that promote social and cognitive skills, enhance a sense of mastery and self-esteem, and more effectively meet the child's emotional needs for both attachment and separation. There is no reason to believe that fathers cannot enter into this kind of relationship with children as well. Ve (1989) has shown, for example, that daughters' intimacy with mothers does not exclude closeness to fathers or friends. Future research will need to track the changes in processes of learning and "practicing" intimacy as different patterns of parent–child relations emerge.

Intimacy in Old Age

With high divorce rates (the United States close to 50 percent, Australia 35 percent, the United Kingdom 37 percent), it is easy to forget that the remainder (50, 65, and 63 percent, respectively) stay married "for life," and it is a longer lifetime than ever before. As a general rule, marital satisfaction appears to decrease in the middle years and improve in later life, though the mechanisms underlying these changes are not very well understood. In any event, the later years are marked by experiences of companionship and support "through thick and thin" (Gilford 1984), though objective circumstances such as more ample finances and better health make for better quality in the relations among the elderly (Johnson 1985).

Old age is also necessarily marked by high rates of family dissolution, mainly through the death of a spouse but also through divorce. The divorced elderly experience more stigmatization and more limited interactions than elderly widows (Kitson *et al.* 1980), with contacts and friends dropping away, particularly in the case of divorced men, who can become very isolated in old age (Keith 1989). If the adult children of parents divorce, the potential networks of social support alter, and grandparents on the (usually noncustodial) male side may lose close contact with their grandchildren (Cherlin and Furstenberg 1986). Patterns of social support established during marriage often continue after the death of a spouse, with widows more able and more likely to turn for help to friends, children, and relatives than widowers (Kohen 1983). Limited research on remarriage in later years suggests that both sexes are looking for a long-term intimate relationship, with men more likely to focus on the need for intimacy to avoid feelings of loneliness (Brubaker 1990). The thread running through these findings is that, in old age, women's lifelong "relation-orientations" serve them better than men's lifelong "instrumental" and "self-sufficient" orientations.

Generational relations are also salient in the lives of the elderly. On the one hand, there is little evidence that childless elderly couples are less happy or less satisfied in their marriages than those who are parents, though they have fewer social contacts (Lee 1988, Bachrach 1980). For the elderly who have children, an earlier picture of isolation has been modified by more recent research. The so-called sandwich generation (Schlesinger and Schlesinger 1992) can serve as a resource for their children when the latter establish families. Adult women often find themselves squeezed between caring for their own children (or grandchildren) on the one hand and caring for an aging parent on the other (Hagestad 1990). The car and the telephone have served as important resources in maintaining contact between the elderly and their children (McDonald 1993). Finally, in the case of older parents and adult children, there is some evidence of a female "generational solidarity between mother and adult daughter, with the male's place in family closeness still remote and ambiguous" (Eriksen and Wetlesen 1992).

Coda

At the risk of oversimplifying the complex range of issues addressed in this chapter, we might suggest that of all those reviewed, the central issue in the modern West has to do with the refashioning of gender relations. One might even suggest a pervasive contradiction in this regard: on the one hand, we have observed an ongoing, but unfinished, revolution for women, who have entered previously inaccessible spheres (work and the public arena generally). On the other, the "intimacy gap" in the family thereby created has not yet been filled by a corresponding redefinition of men's roles and responsibilities. By virtue of these changes, women's roles, once described as "domestic" and often "empty," now seem both overburdened and ambiguous; and men's role, once described as "responsible breadwinner," now seems both uncertain and curiously lacking. We call this contradiction central largely because whatever changes in gender and gendering arise in future decades are bound to have ramifications in all the areas we have discussed–family structure itself, patterns of sexuality and intimacy, the fortunes of children, and the fate of the elderly.

References

Aries, P. 1962: *Centuries of Childhood: A Social History of Family Life*. London: Cape.

Bachrach, C. A. 1980: "Childlessness and Social Isolation among the Elderly." *Journal of Marriage and the Family*, 42: 627–37.

Badinter, E. 1981: *Myth of Motherhood*. London: Souvenir.

Berger, P. 1973: *The Homeless Mind*. New York: Random House.

Berger, B. and Berger, P. L. 1983: *The War over the Family*. London: Hutchinson.

Blumberg, R. L. 1988: "Income under Female versus Male Control: Hypotheses from a Theory of Gender Stratification and Data from the Third World." *Journal of Family Issues*, 9: 51–84.

Booth, A. and Johnson, D. 1988: "Premarital Cohabitation and Marital Success." *Journal of Family Issues*, 9: 255–72.

Booth, A., Johnson, D., White, L. and Edwards, J. 1986: "Divorce and Marital Instability over the Life Course." *Journal of Family Issues*, 9: 51–84.

Brubaker, T. H. 1990: "Families in Later Life, a Burgeoning Research Area." *Journal of Marriage and the Family*, 52: 959–81.

Bumpass, L. L. and Sweet, J. A. 1989: "National Estimates of Cohabitation." *Demography*, 26: 615–25.

Cancian, F. M. 1987: *Love in America*. Cambridge: Cambridge University Press.

Charles, N. and Kerr, M. 1987: "Just the Way It Is: Gender and Age Differences in Food Consumption," in J. Brannen and G. Wilson (eds), *Give and Take in Families: Studies in Resource Distribution*, Boston: Allen and Unwin, 155–74.

Chelune, G., Waring, E. M., Vosk, B. N., Sultan, F. E. and Ogden, J. K. 1984: "Self-Disclosure and its Relationship to Marital Intimacy." *Journal of Clinical Psychology*, 40: 216–19.

Cherlin, A. J. and Furstenburg, F. 1986: *The New American Grandparent, A Place in the Family, A Life Apart*. New York: Basic Books.

Cherlin, A. J. and Furstenburg, F. 1988: "The Changing European Family." *Journal of Family Issues*, 9: 291–7.

Christensen, E. 1986: *Nordic Intimate Couples with Children*. Copenhagen: Hans Reitzel.

Clausen, J. A. 1973: "The Life Course of Individuals," in M. A. Riley, M. Johnson and A. Foner (eds), *Aging and Society*. New York: Russell Sage Foundation, III, 457–514.

Clausen, J. A. 1993: *American Lives: Looking Back at the Children of the Great Depression*. New York: Free Press.

Connell, R. W. 1985: "Theorizing Gender." *Sociology*, 19: 260–72.

Dally, A. 1982: *Inventing Motherhood*. London: Burnett.

Daniels, A. K. 1989: *Invisible Careers: Women Civic Leaders*. Chicago: University of Chicago Press.

Davidson, B., Balswick, J. and Halverson, C. 1983: "Affective Self-Disclosure and Marital Adjustment: A Test of Equity Theory." *Journal of Marriage and the Family*, 45: 93–102.

Edgar, D. 1992a: "Conceptualising Family Life and Policies." *Family Matters*, 32: 28–37.

Edgar, D. 1992b: "Childhood in its Social Context: The Under-Socialised Child." *Family Matters*, 33: 32–6.

Ehrenreich, B. 1983: *The Hearts of Men: American Dreams and the Flight from Commitment.*. London: Pluto.

Ehrenreich, B., Hess, E. and Jacobs, G. 1986: *Remaking Love: The Feminization of Sex*. London: Fontana.

Engels, F. 1969 [1884]: *The Origin of the Family, Private Property, and the State*. New York: International Publishers.

Eriksen, J. and Wetlesen, T. S. 1992: "Family Theory and Research in Norway: A Review Essay of the 1980s." Unpublished paper prepared for special issue of *Marriage and Family Review*.

Ferree, M. M. 1990: "Beyond Separate Spheres: Feminism and Family Research." *Journal of Marriage and the Family*, 52: 866–84.

Fischer, C. 1982: *To Dwell among Friends*. Berkeley, Calif.: University of California Press.

Fitzpatrick, M. A. 1984: "A Typological Approach to Marital Interaction: Recent Theory and Research," in L. Berkowitz (ed.), *Advances in Experimental Psychology*, vol. 18, New York: Academic Press, 1–47.

Fitzpatrick, M. A. 1988: *Between Husbands and Wives*. Newbury Park, Calif.: Sage Publications.

Galinsky, E., Friedman, D. and Hernandez, C. 1991: *The Corporate Reference Guide to Work and Family Programs*. New York: Families and Work Institute.

Giddens, A. 1990: *The Consequences of Modernity*. Cambridge: Polity Press.

Giddens, A. 1992: *The Transformation of Intimacy: Sexuality, Love and Eroticism in Modern Societies*. Cambridge: Polity Press.

Gilford, R. 1984: "Contrasts in Marital Satisfaction throughout Old Age: An Exchange Theory Analysis." *Journal of Gerontology*, 39: 325–33.

Glezer, H. D., Edgar, D. and Prolisko, A. 1992: "The Importance of Family Background and Early Experiences in Premarital Cohabitation and Marital Dissolution." Paper presented at the International Conference on Family Formation and Dissolution: Perspectives from East and West, Taiwan, May 1992.

Glick, P. C. 1988: "Fifty Years of Family Demography: A Record of Social Change." *Journal of Marriage and the Family*, 50: 861–73.

Glick, P. C. and Lin, S. L. 1986: "Recent Changes in Divorce and Remarriage." *Journal of Marriage and the Family*, 48: 737–47.

Goode, W. J. 1982: "Why Men Resist," in B. Thorne and M. Yalom (eds), *Rethinking the Family: Some Feminist Questions*. New York: Longman, 131–50.

Greenstein, T. N. 1990: "Marital Disruption and the Employment of Married Women." *Journal of Marriage and the Family*, 52: 657–76.

Guttentag, M. and Secord, P. F. 1983: *Too Many Women? The Sex Ratio Question*. Beverly Hills, Calif.: Sage Publications.

Haavind, H. 1984: "Love and Power in Marriage," in H. Holter (ed.), *Patriarchy in a Welfare Society*, Oslo: Norwegian University Press, 136–67.

Habermas, J. 1987: *The Philosophical Discourse of Modernity*. Cambridge: Polity Press.

Hagestad, G. O. 1990: "Changing Societies–Changing Families: International Perspectives on Lives and Relationships," in P. Conrade and V. White (eds), *The Changing Family in an Aging Society: Caregiving Traditions, Trends, Tomorrows?*, Ottawa: Canadian Gerontological Association.

Hareven, T. 1982: *Family Time and Industrial Time*. Cambridge, Mass.: Harvard University Press.

Hartley, R. 1992: "No More than a Phone Call Away, Adult Children and their Parents." *Family Matters*, 32: 38–40.

Hill, M. 1988: "Marital Stability and Spouses' Shared Time." *Journal of Family Issues*, 9: 427–51.

Hochschild, A. with Machung, A. 1989: *The Second Shift*. New York: Viking.

Ironmonger, D. 1989: *Households Work: Productive Activities, Women and Income in the Household Economy*. Sydney: Allen and Unwin.

Jensen, A. M. 1989: "Reproduction in Norway: An Area of Non-Responsibility," in P. Close (ed.), *Family Divisions and Inequalities in Modern Society*, London: Macmillan, 112–27.

Johnson, C. L. 1985: "The Impact of Illness in Later-life Marriages." *Journal of Marriage and the Family*, 47: 165–72.

Johnson, M. P. and Milardo, R. M. 1984: "Network Interference in Pair Relationships: A Social Psychological Recasting of Slater's Theory of Social Regression." *Journal of Marriage and the Family*, 46: 893–9.

Keith, P. M. 1989: *The Unmarried in Later Life*. New York: Praeger.

Kitson, G. H., Lopata, H., Holmes, W. and Meyering, S. 1980: "Divorcees and Widows, Similarities and Differences." *Journal of Orthopsychiatry*, 50: 291–301.

Kohen, J. A. 1983: "Old But Not Alone: Informal Social Supports among the Elderly by Marital Status and Sex." *Gerontologist*, 23: 57–63.

Komter, A. 1989: "Hidden Power in Marriage." *Gender and Society*, 3: 187–216.

Lasch, C. 1977: *Haven in a Heartless World*. New York: Basic Books.

Lee, G. R. 1988: "Marital Satisfaction in Later Life: The Effects of Nonmarital Roles." *Journal of Marriage and the Family*, 50: 775–83.

Lopata, H. and Thorne, B. 1978: "On the Term 'Sex Roles'." *Signs*, 3: 718–21.

Luxton, M. 1980: *More than a Labour of Love: Three Generations of Women's Work in the Home*. Toronto: Women's Press.

Martin, T. C. and Bumpass, L. L. 1989: "Recent Trends in Marital Disruption." *Demography*, 26: 37–51.

May, M. 1987: "The Historical Problem of the Family Wage: The Ford Motor Company and the Five-Dollar Day," in N. Gerstel and H. E. Gross (eds), *Families and Work*, Philadelphia: Temple University Press.

McDonald, P. (ed.) 1993: *The Berwick Report, Australian Living Standards Study*. Melbourne: Australian Institute of Family Studies.

Milardo, R. M., Johnson, M. P. and Huston, T. L. 1983: "Developing Close Relationships: Changing Patterns of Pair Relationships." *Journal of Personality and Social Psychology*, 44: 964–76.

Moen, P. 1989: *Working Parents*. Madison, Wis.: University of Wisconsin Press.

Morgan, L. 1988: "Outcomes of Marital Separation." *Journal of Marriage and The Family*, 50: 493–8.

Mount, F. 1982: *The Subversive Family: An Alternative History of Love and Marriage*. London: Unwin.

Moxnes, K. 1985: "Parental Cooperation," in L. Cseh-Szombathy, I. Koch-Nielsen, J. Trost and I. Weda (eds), *The Aftermath of Divorce–Coping with Family Change*, Budapest: Akademiai Kiado, 199–220.

Moxnes, K. 1991: "Changes in Family Patterns–Changes in Parenting. A Change toward a More or Less Equal Sharing between Parents?," in U. Bjornborg (ed.), *European Parents in the 1990s. Contradictions and Comparisons*, New Brunswick, N.J.: Transaction Publishers, 211–28.

Murstein, B. I. 1987: "A Clarification and Extension of the SVR Theory of Diadic Pairing." *Journal of Marriage and the Family*, 49: 929–33.

Noller, P. 1984: *Nonverbal Communication and Marital Interaction*. Oxford: Pergamon.

Ostrander, S. 1984: *Women of the Upper Class*. Philadelphia: Temple University Press.

Papanek, H. 1973: "Men, Women, and Work: Reflections on the Two-Person Career," in J. Huber (ed.), *Changing Women in a Changing Society*, Chicago: University of Chicago Press, 90–110.

Parsons, T. and Bales, R. F., in collaboration with Olds, J., Zelditch, M. and Slater, P. E. 1955: *Family, Socialization and Interaction Process*. Glencoe, Ill.: Free Press.

Pleck, J. 1985: *Working Wives/Working Husbands*. Beverly Hills, Calif.: Sage Publications.

Radway, J. A. 1984: *Reading the Romance*. Chapel Hill, N.C.: University of North Carolina Press.

Rank, M. 1987: "The Formation and Dissolution of Marriages in the Welfare Population." *Journal of Marriage and the Family*, 49: 15–20.

Rapp, R. 1982: "Family and Class in Contemporary America," in Thorne and Yalom (eds), *Rethinking the Family*, 168–87.

Reibstein, J. and Richards, M. 1992: *Sexual Arrangements: Marriage and Affairs*. London: William Heinemann.

Reiger, K. 1985: *The Disenchantment of the Home: Modernizing the Australian Family*. Melbourne: Oxford University Press.

Reskin, B. 1988: "Bringing the Men Back In: Sex Differentiation and the Devaluation of Women's Work." *Gender and Society*, 2: 58–81.

Ryan, M. 1981: *The Cradle of the Middle Class*. Cambridge: Cambridge University Press.

Schapp, S., Buunk, B. and Kerskstna, A. 1988: "Marital Conflict Resolution," in P. Noller and M. A. Fitzpatrick (eds), *Perspectives on Marital Interaction*, Philadelphia: Multilingual Matters, 203–44.

Schlesinger, B. and Schlesinger, R. A. 1992: *Canadian Families in Transition*. Toronto: Canadian Scholars' Press.

Schoen, R. W., Urton, W., Woodrow, K. and Baj, J. 1985: "Marriage and Divorce in 20th-Century American Cohorts." *Demography*, 22: 101–14.

Scott, J. 1986: "Gender: A Useful Category of Historical Analysis." *American Historical Review*, 91: 1053–75.

Sen, A. 1983: "Economics and the Family." *Asian Development Review*, 1: 14–26.

Shorter, E. 1975: *The Making of the Modern Family*. New York: Basic Books.

Sillars, A. L. and Scott, M. D. 1983: "Interpersonal Perception between Inmates: An Integrative Review." *Human Communication Research*, 10: 153–76.

Spitze, G. and South, S. 1985: "Women's Employment, Time Expenditure and Divorce." *Journal of Family Issues*, 6: 307–29.

Stone, L. 1977: *The Family, Sex and Marriage in England 1500–1800*. New York: Harper and Row.

Surra, C. A. 1985: "Courtship Types: Variations in Interdependence between Partners and Social Networks." *Journal of Personality and Social Psychology*, 49: 357–75.

Surra, C. A. 1990: "Research and Theory on Mate Selection and Premarital Relationships in the 1980s." *Journal of Marriage and the Family*, 52: 844–65.

Surra, C. A. and Huston, T. L. 1987: "Mate Selection as a Social Transition," in D. Perlman and S. Duck (eds), *Intimate Relationships: Development, Dynamics and Deterioration*. Beverly Hills, Calif.: Sage Publications, 88–120.

Sweet, J. A., Bumpass, L. L. and Call, V. R. A. 1988: *The Design and Content of the National Survey of Families and Households*, NSFH Working Party No. 1. Madison, Wis: University of Wisconsin Press.

Thornton, A. 1988: "Cohabitation and Marriage in the 1980s." *Demography*, 25: 497–508.

Tiano, S. 1987: "Gender, Work and World Capitalism: Third World Women's Role in Development," in B. Hess and M. M. Ferree (eds), *Analysing Gender*, Beverly Hills, Calif.: Sage Publications, 216–43.

US Bureau of the Census 1988: *Statistical Abstract of the United States*. Washington, D.C.: US Government Printing Office.

Ve, H. 1989: "The Male Gender Role and Responsibility for Children," in K. Boh, M. Bak, C. Clason, M. Pankratoua, J. Qvortrup, G. B. Sgritta and K. Waerness (eds), *Changing Patterns of European Family Life: A Comparative Analysis of 14 European Countries*. London: Routledge, 249–61.

Weiss, R. 1987: "Men and their Wives' Work," in F. Crosby (ed.), *Spouse, Parent, Worker*, New Haven, Conn.: Yale University Press, 109–21.

Weitzman, L. 1985: *The Divorce Revolution*: New York: Free Press.

A Selected Annotated
International Bibliography

The following bibliography has been constructed from a selected number of the references found at the end of each chapter, from further suggestions submitted by the contributors, and from works considered important by the author. It is intended as a nonexhaustive guide to professional sociologists and to students. In listing the books, priority is given to classics and very recent studies.

Selected Books

Abu-Lughod, J. L. 1991: *Changing Cities: Urban Sociology*. New York: Harper Collins.
A high-level textbook containing empirical and theoretical analyses and reviews of recent debates about conditions in cities and laying out a research agenda for the study of the massive transformations of cities under the impact of economic globalization, immigration, and race relations.

Alexander, J. C. (ed.) 1985: *Neofunctionalism*. Beverly Hills, Calif.: Sage Publications.
A theoretical statement of the theoretical ingredients of neo-functionalism, with applications to a number of substantive sociological areas.

Alexander, J. C., Giesen, B., Münch, R. and Smelser, N. J. (eds). 1987: *The Micro–Macro Link*. Berkeley, Calif.: University of California Press.
A selection of synthetic treatments of the theoretical and empirical linkages between the cultural and institutional level and the social-psychological and social-process level in sociology.

Almond, G. and Verba, S. 1965: *The Civic Culture: Political Attitudes and Democracy in Five Nations*. Boston: Little, Brown.
A comparative study of five nations – the United States, West Germany, England, Italy, and Mexico – using survey information to evaluate the notion of political culture and its relevance for the institutionalization of democracy.

Alwin, F. A. (ed.) 1978: *Survey Design and Analysis*. Beverly Hills, Calif.: Sage Publications.
A standard work on the survey method, written by the Director of the Survey Research Center at the University of Michigan, who is responsible for its summer school program in data analysis.

Anderson, B. 1991: *Imagined Communities: Reflections on the Origin and Spread of Nationalism*. London: Verso.

A brief but important work which argues that the phenomenon of nationalism can be understood as a cultural and social-psychological phenomenon that integrates a nation; one of the most influential contemporary studies of nationalism.

Aries, P. 1962: *Centuries of Childhood: A Social History of Family Life*. London: Cape.
A classic treatment of the social construction of romantic love, motherhood, and the emergence of the modern conception of the child.

ASEAN 1991: *ASEAN Economic Co-operation for the 1990s. A Report Prepared for the ASEAN Standing Committee*. Jakarta: ASEAN Secretariat.
A review of current trends and future prospects with respect to internationalization in investment and trade, intra-block cooperation, and the urban and rural impact of these trends.

Badie, B. and Birnbaum, P. 1983: *The Sociology of the State*. Chicago: University of Chicago Press.
A treatise on the social and historical development of the state, regarded not as a universal phenomenon, but as a product of specific historical processes.

Banton, M. 1983: *Racial and Ethnic Competition*. Cambridge: Cambridge University Press.
A theoretical analysis from the perspective of rational-choice theory which rejects the centrality of race and emphasizes the importance of class in the advancement of racial and ethnic collectivities.

Barbash, J., Lampman, R., Levitan, S. and Tyler, G. (eds) 1983: *The Work Ethic: A Critical Analysis*. Madison, Wis.: IRRA.
A many-faceted account of the impact of the changes in post-industrial society on the Protestant work ethic.

Bell, D. 1960: *The End of Ideology*. New York: Free Press.
One of the early formulations and commentaries on the character of post-capitalist society; a critique of the Marxian theory of class conflict and the exposition of a new perspective on social integration.

Berger, B. and Berger, P. L. 1983: *The War over the Family*. London: Hutchinson.
A critique of the public–private dichotomy and discussion of problems associated with the cultural values of individualism and the conception of the family as a mediating structure.

Berger, P. and Luckmann, T. 1967: *The Social Construction of Reality*. Garden City, NY: Doubleday.
A theory of social interaction, social structure, and social control which takes a phenomenological approach to language and social experience as its theoretical starting point.

Bertaux, D. (ed.) 1981: *Biography and Society: The Life History Approach in the Social Sciences*. London: Sage Publications.
An exposition and application of the life-history method as a technique for social science investigation.

Biemer, P., Groves, R. M., Lyberg, L. E., Mathiowetz, N. A. and Sudman, S. (eds) 1991: *Measurement Errors in Surveys*. New York: Wiley.
A standard reference work concerning the kinds of errors that occur in survey research and methods for avoiding and correcting them.

Blalock, H. M. and Blalock, A. B. (eds) 1968: *Methodology in Social Research*. New York: McGraw-Hill.
A classical discussion of the principal methodological issues in social science research, brought together by two leading figures in the field of methodology.

Blankenhorn, D. (ed.) 1990: *Rebuilding the Nest: A New Commitment to American Family Life*. New York: Family Service America.

A documented analysis of family trends in American society and an articulation of ways to support private family life.

Blauner, R. 1972: *Racial Oppression in America*. New York: Harper and Row.
An analysis focusing on the oppression specifically rooted in racism which argues that such oppression is qualitatively different from class exploitation and that race and racism are central to the economy, politics, and culture of the United States.

Bloom, L. and Ottong, J. G. 1987: *Changing Africa: An Introduction to Sociology*. London: Macmillan.
One of the few introductory texts in sociology for those interested in African societies.

Blumberg, R. L. (ed.) 1991: *Gender, Family, and Economy: The Triple Overlap*. Newbury Park, Calif.: Sage Publications.
A state-of-the-art collection on the sociology of gender, which considers the interrelationships among economic, gender, and family variables and analyzes their overlap at both the micro and macro levels.

Blumer, H. 1969: *Symbolic Interactionism: Perspective and Method*. Englewood Cliffs, N.J.: Prentice-Hall.
A comprehensive statement, by the principal spokesman, of the theoretical and methodological perspectives of symbolic interactionism, a major social-psychological paradigm in sociology.

Bohrnstedt, G. W. 1983: *Handbook of Survey Research*. New York: Academic Press.
A handy and well-known reference covering the multiple aspects of research using questionnaires.

Borgatta, E. F. 1972: *Sociological Methods and Research*. Beverly Hills, Calif.: Sage Publications.
One of the major contributions to the understanding of sociological methodology by one of the leading figures in the field.

Bourdieu, P. 1984: *Distinction: A Social Critique of the Judgment of Taste*. Cambridge, Mass.: Harvard University Press.
An exposition of the author's concepts of cultural capital, stratification, and *habitus* as a theory of the orientation of individual and group action.

Bourdieu, P. *et al.* 1993: *La Misère du monde*. Paris: Seuil.
A qualitative analysis of the phenomena of marginality and poverty which makes use of the classic methods of Thomas and Znaniecki and employs intensive team collaboration (23 researchers gathering life stories from the peripheries of the world).

Braudel, F. 1979: *Civilisation, économie et capitalisme, XVe–XVIIIe sicle*. 3 vols. Paris: Arman Colin.
A monumental social and economic history from a global perspective written by one of the founders of the French historian group *Annales*.

Brubaker, W. (ed.) 1989: *Immigration and the Politics of Citizenship in Europe and North America*. Lanham, Md.: University Press of America.
A collection of essays analyzing the problems of access to citizenship and nationality on the part of immigrants in countries with contrasting histories.

Bulatao, R. and Lee, R. (eds) 1983: *Determinants of Fertility in Developing Countries*. 2 vols. New York: Academic Press.
Systematic coverage of the factors affecting fertility rates in the developing world.

Campbell, C. 1987: *The Romantic Ethic and the Spirit of Consumerism*. New York: Blackwell.
A study of the cultural and religious background, as well as the emergence and evolution of modern consumerism.

Cancian, F. M. 1987: *Love in America*. Cambridge: Cambridge University Press.

A review of gender relations and of changes affecting intimacy in contemporary times.

Cardoso, F. H. and Faletto, E. 1979: *Dependency and Development in Latin America*. Berkeley, Calif.: University of California Press.

A major statement on the "dependency" approach to development, which arose as a challenge to modernization theory and stressed the special roles of international enterprise and finance in inhibiting and/or warping the economic development of Latin American societies.

Castels, M. 1989: *The Informational City*. Oxford: Blackwell.

A theoretical and empirical examination of the urban impact of information technologies, including discussion of studies of microelectronics and telecommunications and their effects on the spatial organization of the economy. The concept of a "space of flows" is introduced.

Chafetz, J. S. 1990: *Gender Equality: An Integrated Theory of Stability and Change*. Newbury Park, Calif.: Sage Publications.

A volume that addresses the issue of change in gender systems and provides an integrated, systematic explanation of the conditions that tend to produce change in gender stratification.

Coleman, J. S. 1981: *Longitudinal Data Analysis*. New York: Basic Books.

An in-depth exposition and exploration of panel methods; that is, the systematic collection and analysis from samples followed over sustained periods of time.

Coser, L. A. 1971: *Masters of Sociological Thought: Ideas in Historical and Social Context*. New York: Harcourt, Brace, Jovanovich.

One of the best secondary accounts of the rise of sociological theory in the West.

Dahl, R. 1971: *Polyarchy: Participation and Opposition*. New Haven, Conn.: Yale University Press.

An attempt to specify the dimensions and measurements of democratic development and thus to explain the transformation of nondemocratic into democratic systems.

Dahrendorf, R. 1959: *Class and Class Conflict in Industrial Society*. Stanford, Calif.: Stanford University Press.

A challenge to the functionalist and Marxist perspectives on society and a synthetic, neo-Weberian theory of social inequality, social conflict, and social change.

Dayan, D. and Katz, E. 1992: *Media Events: The Live Broadcasting of History*. Cambridge, Mass.: Harvard University Press.

A neo-Durkheimian investigation of television live coverage of historic events, including Anwar Sadat's visit to Jerusalem, the royal marriage of Charles and Diana, and the funeral of John F. Kennedy.

Deglar, C. N. 1971: *Neither Black nor White: Slavery and Race Relations in Brazil and the United States*. New York: Macmillan.

A well-documented comparative study of slavery and race relations in Brazil and the United States, the key difference between the two countries residing in the Brazilian mulatto, who is neither white nor black.

Dierkes, M. and Biervert, B. (eds) 1992: *European Social Science in Transition: Assessment and Outlook*. Frankfurt: Campus Verlag.

A comprehensive statement prepared mainly by European scholars on the status and future directions of social science in Western Europe, with a dual emphasis on social science problems and social science disciplines.

Durkheim, E. 1958 [1895]: *The Rules of Sociological Method*. Glencoe, Ill.: Free Press.

A manifesto laying out a claim for the legitimacy of sociology as a positive science and distinguishing the social level of reality ("social facts") from other levels, especially the psychological.

Durkheim, E. 1965 [1915]: *The Elementary Forms of the Religious Life*. New York: Free Press.
   The classic sociological text for the argument that people in society are bound together by sentiment, with religion itself representing unconsciously the worship of the whole and sacralizing the collectivity.
Durkheim, E. 1984 [1893]: *The Division of Labor in Society*. New York: Free Press.
   Durkheim's first work, which lays out classic statements in the areas of social change, economic sociology, social integration, and social disorganization (anomie).
Edwards, R. 1979: *Contested Terrain*. New York: Basic Books.
   Analysis of the evolution of the labor process and the transformation of the system of control of production under capitalism.
Ehrenreich, B. 1983: *The Hearts of Men*. London: Pluto.
   A conceptualization of the male "flight from commitment" as a response to changes in the contemporary family structure.
Eisenstadt, S. N. and Rokkan, S. 1973: *Building States and Nations*. 2 vols. Beverly Hills, Calif.: Sage Publications.
   A vast theoretical work on the process of building states and nations, supplemented by a very rich collection of sources for each nation considered.
Eliade, M. 1983: *Histoire des croyances et des idées religieuses*. Paris: Payot.
   A fundamental book on the history and anthropology of religion; unusual comparisons between Western and Eastern religious philosophies.
Elias, N. 1987 [1983]: *Involvement and Detachment*. Oxford: Blackwell.
   A work in the sociology of knowledge, written in the context of the author's work on the process of civilization. The author argues that sociologists should become more detached from the world of their subject matter and more interested in, and aware of, sociological understanding and available cognitive instruments.
Essed, P. 1991: *Understanding Everyday Racism*. Newbury Park, Calif.: Sage Publications.
   A critique of contemporary theories of race and ethnicity which invokes the concept of everyday racism, emphasizes the need to distinguish between this and institutional racism, and highlights the specificity of oppression to which women are subjected.
Evans, P. M., Rueschemeyer, D. and Skocpol, T. 1985: *Bringing the State Back In*. Cambridge: Cambridge University Press.
   Instead of considering the state as an "arena" for the settlement of public conflicts, the authors assign to it a more active role in organizing collective actions, industrial relations, economic growth, and war.
Fayol, H. 1949: *General and Industrial Management*. London: Pitman.
   A classic study of the principles of organization and coordination of work.
Foucault, M. 1980: *Power–Knowledge*. New York: Pantheon.
   A representative work on the author's theoretical perspective of culture as intermeshed and sometimes indistinguishable from the institutional and informal power relations in society.
Frobel, F., Heinrichs, J. and Kreye, O. 1991: *The New International Division of Labor*. New York: Cambridge University Press.
   Originally published in German in 1977, an influential work describing the movement of manufacturing capital from Europe to Asia.
Garfinkel, H. 1967: *Studies in Ethnomethodology*. Englewood Cliffs, N.J.: Prentice-Hall.
   The original exposition of the phenomenological framework of ethnomethodology, along with some empirical illustrations and applications.
Gayer, F. and Schveitzer, D. (eds) 1981: *Alienation: Problems of Meaning. Theory and Method*. London: Routledge and Kegan Paul.

A debate on contemporary theoretical, empirical, and ideological aspects of alienation.

Gellner, E. 1983: *Nations and Nationalism*. Ithaca, N.Y.: Cornell University Press.

A brief, but very broadly informed, exposition of the concept of nationalism.

Gerstein, D. R., Luce, R. D., Smelser, N. J. and Sperlich, S. (eds) 1988: *The Behavioral and Social Sciences: Achievements and Opportunities*. Washington, D.C.: National Academy Press.

A comprehensive report of a special committee of the National Academy of Sciences/National Research Council (USA) on the most active and promising areas of social science research.

Getubig, I. P., jr. and Shams, M. K. (eds) 1991: *Reaching Out Effectively: Improving the Design, Management, and Implementation of Poverty Alleviation Programs*. Kuala Lumpur: Asian and Pacific Development Centre.

An examination of poverty and poverty policies in Asia through ten case studies showing that the poorest of the poor in both urban and rural areas are not being reached by poverty-alleviation policies and criticizing the inadequacy of criteria defining the poor, as well as the emphasis on handouts rather than empowerment.

Giddens, A. 1979: *Critical Problems in Social Theory: Action, Structure and Contradiction in Social Analysis*. London: Macmillan.

A critical study of the main currents in structuralist and Marxian thought and an exposition of the author's theory of structuration.

Giddens, A. 1992: *The Transformation of Intimacy: Sexuality, Love and Eroticism in Modern Societies*. Cambridge: Polity Press.

A critique of existing theories and a development of new views on the changing nature of relations of intimacy in modern society.

Glazer, N. and Moynihan, D. P. (eds) 1975: *Ethnicity: Theory and Experience*. Cambridge, Mass.: Harvard University Press.

A collection of papers presenting several theoretical orientations on ethnicity and analyzing a wide range of empirical settings.

Goffman, E. 1959: *The Presentation of Self in Everyday Life*. New York: Doubleday/ Anchor.

The original exposition of the dramaturgical perspective on the study of everyday life and the major statement of what is an influential perspective in social psychology.

Goldthorpe, J. H., Lockwood, E., Bechhofer, F. and Platt, J. 1968: *The Affluent Worker: Industrial Attitudes and Behaviour*. London: Cambridge University Press.

A study of high-wage workers' attitudes toward work; a challenge to the view that technology shapes the attitudes of workers.

Gordon, M. M. 1978: *Human Nature, Class and Ethnicity*. New York: Oxford University Press.

A work emphasizing psychological variables in social structure which argues that ethnicity is primordial and cannot be erased through social mobility and proposes a concept of "eth-class" which denotes the class awareness of an ethnic segment vis-à-vis other segments within or outside an ethnic community.

Gorz, A. 1982: *Farewell to the Working Class*. London: Pluto.

A reconceptualization of the relationship between work and nonwork in modern societies which argues that the utilization of human abilities is associated more with leisure.

Gramsci, A. 1971: *Selections from the Prison Notebooks*. London: Lawrence and Wishart.

An analysis in the Marxian tradition that gives special autonomy to the cultural level and develops the influential concept of hegemony.

Grawitz, M. 1976: *Méthodes des sciences sociales*. Paris: Dalloz.

A very sophisticated presentation of the main methods used in the social sciences.

Gregor, A. J. 1969: *The Ideology of Fascism*. New York: Free Press.

A study of the role of intellectuals and sub-intellectuals in the early stages of Fascist doctrine ("protofascism"); helpful in understanding embryonic authoritarianism on both the Right and the Left in a number of countries, including Third World countries.

Groves, R. M. 1989: *Survey Errors and Survey Costs*. New York: Wiley.

The best single volume on the kinds of errors that crop up in social surveys and an estimate of what it costs to reduce them and obtain more adequate data.

Habermas, J. 1975: *Legitimation Crisis*. Boston: Beacon Press.

An exposition by the most influential modern representative of the critical school, containing a comprehensive statement of the major crises facing the post-capitalist welfare state.

Habermas, J. 1987 [1981]: *Theory of Communicative Action*. 2 vols. Boston: Beacon Press.

A critical and comprehensive attempt at a theory of rational discourse in a post-Weberian and post-Kantian context; an ambitious study of social and political philosophies in the twentieth century.

Hall, P. 1986: *Governing the Economy: The Politics of State Intervention in Britain and France*. New York: Oxford University Press.

A comparative analysis of the mechanisms whereby the state controls economic activity, in terms of the logic of political systems, the role of elites, the role of political parties, etc.

Hardoy, J. E. and Satterthwaite, D. 1989: *Squatter Citizen: Life in the Urban Third World*. London: Earthscan Publications.

A critical examination of Third World cities, with discussions of the legal and illegal city, obstacles to change in housing and urban growth policies, grassroots approaches to housing, and urban environmental problems.

Harvey, D. 1989: *The Condition of Postmodernity: An Enquiry into the Origins of Cultural Change*. Oxford: Blackwell.

A broad-ranging account of recent economic changes and their cultural consequences which assigns a prominent role to flexible accumulation and time-space compression.

Hawley, A. 1950: *Human Ecology: A Theory of Community Structure*. New York: Ronald Press.

The classic statement of the relevance of spatial and temporal factors to organized social structure and functioning.

Hellman, E. and Lever, J. (eds) 1980: *Race Relations in South Africa, 1919–79*. London: Macmillan.

A collection of ten essays by analysts mainly from South Africa, covering the accelerating economic and population growth and the conflicting social and political changes in South Africa over the past 50 years, including the polarization of the races.

Hobsbawm, E. J. and Ranger, T. (eds) 1983: *The Invention of Tradition*. Cambridge: Cambridge University Press.

A collection of historical essays that demonstrate, particularly with respect to imperial Britain, the ways in which the past is socially constructed to achieve political aims in the present and a "tradition" invented to legitimize contemporary regimes.

Homans, G. C. 1974: *Social Behavior: Its Elementary Forms*. New York: Harcourt, Brace, Jovanovich.

The most complete and consistent modern statement of the behaviorist approach to sociology, which rests on principles taken from learning theory and economic theory.

Huber, J. (ed.) 1988: *Macro–Micro Linkages in Sociology*. Newbury Park, Calif.: Sage Publications.
A collection of essays that relate the macro and micro levels of analysis and establish links between processes at both levels and the direction of causation between the two levels. Several papers deal with gender stratification.

Huntington, S. P. 1991: *The Third Wave: Democratization in the Late Twentieth Century*. Norman, Okla.: University of Oklahoma Press.
The most comprehensive account of the "wave" of democracy that began in 1974 with the Portuguese Revolution and later spread to over 30 authoritarian and totalitarian countries, including those of the former Soviet Union and Eastern Europe.

Husband, C. (ed.) 1981: *"Race" in Britain: Continuity and Change*. London: Hutchinson and Co.
Seventeen articles dissecting the emergence of the concept of race in Britain, the politics of race between 1962 and 1979, the role of government in Britain's racial crisis, the personal experience of select witnesses from multiethnic backgrounds residing in Britain, and the role of cultural prejudices in structuring experiences.

Hyman, H. H. 1972: *Secondary Analysis of Sample Surveys: Principles, Procedures, and Potentialities*. New York: Wiley.
A classic source on the method of reusing previously obtained survey data, a method that has the potential of high research payoff at low research cost.

Imaga, E. U. L. 1990: *Industrial Democracy in the Third World: A Study of Nigeria and India*. New Delhi: South Asian Publishers.
A comparative study of industrial democracy in two of the largest Third World societies which traces the difficulties of achieving industrial peace in each.

Irwin-Zarecke, I. 1994: *Frames of Remembrance*. New Brunswick, N.J.: Transaction Publishers.
The best introduction to the study of social or collective memory in the social sciences, this book incorporates a large range of European and North American – especially Canadian – materials.

Israel, J. 1971: *Alienation: From Marx to Modern Sociology*. Boston: Allyn and Bacon.
A study of the meanings of the concept of alienation in the history of sociology.

Jackson, R. 1990: *Quasi-States: Sovereignty, International Relations and the Third World*. Cambridge: Cambridge University Press.
An analysis of the state in Third World societies, carried out within an international relations perspective; the work measures limitations on the sovereignty of these countries under the heading "negative sovereignty."

Kerr, C. and Rosow, J. (eds) 1979: *Work in America: The Decade Ahead*. New York: Van Nostrand.
Essays on cultural changes in the labor force associated with the process of industrialization.

King, A. (ed.) 1991: *Culture, Globalization and the World-System: Contemporary Conditions for the Representation of Identity*. London: Macmillan.
A volume of papers and discussions from a conference on global development, which lays out most of the key issues arising from the concept and the phenomenon.

Kholi, A. 1990: *Democracy and Discontent: India's Growing Crisis of Governability*. Cambridge: Cambridge University Press.
A comprehensive account of the multidimensional difficulties involved in sustaining democracy in one of the world's largest countries.

Kolakowski, L. 1978: *Main Currents of Marxism*. Oxford: Clarendon Press.
One of the major secondary sources on Marxist thought, which raises critical issues about its political and social implications.

Kuhn, T. 1962: *The Structure of Scientific Revolutions*. Chicago: University of Chicago Press.

An influential statement on the logic and history of the development of scientific paradigms which includes a fundamental criticism of the positivistic account of the nature of scientific thought.

Lepenies, W. (ed.) 1981: *Geschichte der Soziologie* (History of Sociology). 4 vols. Frankfurt: Suhrkamp.

A collection of almost all sociological approaches compiled by a leading German sociologist.

Lijphart, A. 1984: *Democracies: Patterns of Majoritarian and Consensus Government in 21 Countries*. New Haven, Conn.: Yale University Press.

A study of the "consociational" theory of democracy and an empirical application thereof to the institutional system of the world's stable democratic systems.

Likert, R. 1961: *New Patterns of Management*. New York: McGraw-Hill.

An analysis of the connections between the type of control of organization and organizational productivity.

Linz, J. and Stepan, A. (eds) 1978: *The Breakdown of Democratic Regimes*. Baltimore: Johns Hopkins University Press.

The work that placed the study of the breakdown of democracy on the agenda of the social sciences.

Lipset, S. M. 1960: *Political Man: The Social Basis of Politics*. Garden City, N.Y.: Doubleday.

A series of essays in political sociology, including statements regarding working-class authoritarianism and the economic and social correlates of democracy.

Luhmann, N. 1984: *Soziale Systeme. Grundriss einer allgemeinen Theorie* (Social Systems: Outline of a General Theory). Frankfurt: Suhrkamp.

A comprehensive exposition of the author's functional-structural systems theory.

Maffesoli, M. 1985: *La Connaissance ordinaire: précis de sociologie compréhensive*. Paris: Librairie des méridiens.

An original approach to the examination of modernity which avoids received traditions but alludes to the alternative romantic and aesthetic traditions to be employed in the analysis of everyday life.

Mannheim, K. 1955: *Ideology and Utopia*. New York: Harvest Books.

A classic work in the sociological analysis of the cultural productions and belief systems of major social movements and political ideologies.

Marsden, P. V. (ed.) 1981: *Linear Models in Social Research*. Beverly Hills, Calif.: Sage Publications.

An introduction to linear methods, among the major sets of quantitative methods in sociological data analysis.

Martinelli, A. and Smelser, N. J. (eds) 1990: *Economy and Society: Overviews in Economic Sociology*. London: Sage Publications.

A review of contributions to economic sociology, including the study of cultural and institutional contexts of the economy, economic coordination and development, and international economic linkages.

Marx, K. and Engels, F. 1968: *Selected Works in One Volume*. London: Lawrence and Wishart.

One of the largest and most comprehensive of many collections of the works of Marx and Engels.

Matras, J. 1990: *Dependency, Obligations and Entitlements*. Englewood Cliffs, N.J.: Prentice-Hall.

A review of the literature on aging and its effects on reciprocal relationships within the family.

Mayo, E. 1946: *The Social Problems of an Industrial Civilization*. Cambridge, Mass.: Harvard University Press.

A classic statement of the human relations perspective and the need for social integration of the productive organization.

Mead, G. H. 1934: *Mind, Self and Society*. Chicago: University of Chicago Press.

A systematic presentation of the outlines of Mead's social-psychological and sociological thinking, compiled from his lectures; a forerunner of symbolic interactionism, pluralistic behavioralism, and phenomenological sociology.

Merton, R. K. 1968: *Social Theory and Social Structure*, rev. enlarged edn. New York: Free Press.

An influential book on the interplay of social theory and social research, containing contributions to social theory, social psychology, deviance, and the sociology of knowledge.

Meyrowitz, J. 1985: *No Sense of Place: The Impact of Electronic Media on Social Behavior*. New York: Oxford University Press.

An argument, based in part on Erving Goffman's dramaturgical perspective, that television strongly influences and alters the texture of social life.

Miles, R. 1989: *Racism*. London: Routledge and Kegan Paul.

A work based on the argument that ''racism'' has temporally specific connotations and is not definable as a phenomenon attached especially to capitalism but rather is contradictory and historically specific.

Mills, C. W. 1959: *The Sociological Imagination*. New York: Oxford University Press.

A manifesto by a leading representative of the American radical tradition in sociology, which develops a problem-centered approach to sociological inquiry and a critique of grand-theoretical and empiricist approaches to social research.

Mingione, E. 1991: *Fragmented Societies: A Sociology of Economic Life beyond the Market Paradigm*. Oxford: Blackwell.

An account of contemporary social change in European societies which pays attention to localized and noncommodified networks of social relations and provides a counterbalance to accounts of the hegemony of internationalized market forces.

Miyamoto, K., Shigeru, Y. and Kojiro, N. 1990: *The Regional Economy* (in Japanese). Tokyo: Yichikaku.

An examination of the Japanese urban and regional economic system, which reveals growing urban and regional inequalities, the incipient deindustrialization of some cities, and the growth of corporate headquarters in the Tokyo metropolitan region.

Moore, B., jr. 1966: *Social Origins of Dictatorship and Democracy*. Boston: Beacon Press.

An original inquiry into a key question of political development: the degree of capitalist transformation in agriculture and the chances of Western-style democracy vis-à-vis right- or left-wing authoritarianism; comparisons among England, France, the United States, China, India, and Japan.

Moscovici, S. 1988: *La Machine à faire des dieux*. Paris: Fayard.

An argument that there is no reason for a division between sociology and psychology, with a stress on the psychic dimension of social phenomena and a reevaluation of the work of Comte, Durkheim, Weber, and Simmel.

Nisbet, R. A. 1966: *The Sociological Tradition*. New York: Basic Books.

A historical account of sociological thought, organized around basic concepts such as community, authority, status, the sacred, and alienation.

Odekunle, F. (ed.) 1986: *Nigeria: Corruption in Development*. Ibadan: University Press.

A discussion of corruption as an obstacle to political, economic, and social development in the Third World, focusing on Nigeria, with an emphasis on conceptual and thematic issues.

Odetola, T. O. 1982: *Military Regimes and Development: A Comparative Analysis in African Societies*. London: Allen and Unwin.
The political aspects of military regimes in Africa, following the traditions of Morris Janowitz's sociology of the military.

Ogunseye, F. A., DiDominca, C., Awosika, K. and Akinkoye, O. (eds) 1988: *Nigerian Women and Development*. Ibadan, Nigeria: Ibadan University Press.
A comprehensive survey of Nigerian women's past and present participation in various aspects of development.

Ossowski, S. 1983: *O osoblijwosciach nauk społecznych* (On Peculiarities of Social Sciences). Warsaw: Polish Scientific Publishers.
A major sociological book on sociology and society written by an outstanding Polish sociologist of the post-Second World War period.

Ouchi, W. G. 1981: *Theory Z: How American Business Can Meet the Japanese Challenge*. Reading, Mass.: Addison-Wesley.
An investigation of the role of organization culture; the role of values in the performance of an organization's employees.

Parker, S. 1983: *Leisure and Work*. London: Allen and Unwin.
An exploration of the relationships between work and leisure in the post-industrial era; an exposition of the "leisure ethic."

Parkinson, M., Bianchini, F., Dawson, J., Evans, R. and Harding, A. 1992: *Urbanisation and the Functions of Cities in the European Community: A Report to the Commission of the European Communities*. Liverpool: John Moores University, European Institute of Urban Affairs.
A multi-site, multi-year report on 24 European cities, based on primary fieldwork and emphasizing the role of networks and linkages between cities in the European Community, the impact of reunification on the German urban system, and the roles and prospects of selected cities.

Parsons, T. 1937: *The Structure of Social Action*. New York: Macmillan.
A classic theoretical statement synthesizing the works of Marshall, Pareto, Durkheim, and Weber and containing the first statement of Parsons's theory of action.

Parsons, T. 1954: *Essays in Sociological Theory*, rev. edn. Glencoe, Ill.: Free Press.
A volume of essays containing an exposition of Parsons's approach to society, as well as many of his empirical investigations of modern societies.

Piore, M. J. and Sabel, C. F. 1984: *The Second Industrial Divide: Possibilities for Prosperity*. New York: Basic Books.
A key text identifying the process of flexible specialization that creates "new industrial districts" with implications for a renewed round of regionally concentrated industrial production.

Portes, A. and Lungo, M. (eds) 1992: *Urbanizacion en Centroamerica* and *Urbanizacion en el Caribe*. San José: Flacso.
A comparative project involving research teams in Haiti, Jamaica, the Dominican Republic, Costa Rica, and Guatemala, whose goal is to understand the urban impact of periods of crisis, beginning with the oil shock of 1973.

Ragin, C. 1987: *The Comparative Method*. Berkeley, Calif.: University of California Press.
A methodological alternative to the use of multivariate statistical techniques in comparative research. Case-oriented approaches are formalized as a general method of qualitative comparison using Boolean algebra.

Reibstein, J. and Richards, M. 1992: *Sexual Arrangements: Marriage and Affairs*. London: Heinemann.
A theoretical statement arising from qualitative case studies of gender differences in responding to situations of sexuality and intimacy.

Rex, J. 1979: *Race Relations in Sociological Theory*. London: Weidenfeld and Nicolson.
An argument insisting that race relations be distinguished from other fields at three levels: that of social structure; that of benefits, ideas, and theories; and an intermediate level where principles, which may not be explicitly stated, operate in practice.

Ricoeur, P. 1983–5: *Temps et récit*. 3 vols. Paris: Seuil.
A deployment of hermeneutics in the field of sociology, especially in relation to a qualitative analysis of narratives; especially useful as a methodology applicable to life stories.

Rosenau, J. 1990: *Turbulence in World Politics*. Princeton, N.J.: Princeton University Press.
An analysis of current international relations, in which the author distinguishes between a "world of states" and a "multi-centered world" of infra-states, which are also major actors in the contemporary world.

Roussel, L. 1989: *La Famille incertaine*. Paris: Éditions Odile Jacob.
A review of the condition of European family life and the uncertainties facing the family.

Sassen, S. 1991: *The Global City: New York, London, Tokyo*. Princeton, N.J.: Princeton University Press.
An examination of the concentration of strategic functions in major cities over the past decades, including especially the new complex of specialized services for firms. The book traces the consequences – sometimes negative – of these developments on the larger social and economic structure of these cities.

Schmitter, P. and Lehmbruch, G. (eds) 1979: *Trends toward Corporatist Intermediation*. London: Sage Publications.
A work offering a general interpretation of corporate theories whereby the expression of particular interests in state structures can be analyzed. The model is compared with syndicalism and pluralism and is applied to several countries.

Schuman, H. and Presser, S. 1981: *Questions and Answers in Attitude Surveys: Experiments on Question Form, Wording, and Context*. New York: Academic Press.
The best work available on the effect of question wording, question order, and other question-related problems in constructing survey questionnaires.

Schumpeter, J. 1947: *Capitalism, Socialism, and Democracy*. New York: Harper Books.
The most influential work on the modern conceptualization of democracy. It makes a case for a minimalist definition of democracy in terms of the mechanisms of competition rather than those of values and goals.

Schwartz, H. and Jacobs, J. 1979: *Qualitative Sociology: A Method to the Madness*. New York: Free Press.
A classic presentation of the scientific but nonnumerical logic that lies behind the use of qualitative data in the social sciences.

Skocpol, T. 1979: *States and Social Revolutions*. Cambridge, Mass.: Harvard University Press.
A macroscopic, structural approach to revolutions, which develops a theory of causes and outcomes of social revolutions in which the state plays a central role, using several major revolutions (French, Russian, Chinese) as illustrations.

Shils, E. A. 1975: *Center and Periphery: Essays in Macrosociology*. Chicago: University of Chicago Press.
Several essays, including the famous title essay, on the problem of social integration.

Shryock, H. and Siegel, J. 1976: *The Methods and Materials of Demography*. New York: Academic Press.
Essential handbook for those interested in the systematic study of demography.

Sklair, L. 1991: *Sociology of the Global System*. Hemel Hempstead: Harvester Wheatsheaf.

A bold attempt to apply a systems-theoretic approach to economy, society, and polity on a global scale.

Smelser, N. J. (ed.) 1973: *Karl Marx on Society and Social Change*. Chicago: University of Chicago Press.
A collection of Marx's works designed to explicate his specifically sociological contributions to the study of the structure of society, the sweep of historical change, and the mechanisms of change.

Smelser, N. J. (ed.) 1988: *Handbook of Sociology*. Newbury Park, Calif.: Sage Publications.
A comprehensive survey of contemporary developments in sociology which refers mainly, but not exclusively, to the United States.

Smith, M. P. and Feagin, J. R. (eds) 1987: *The Capitalist City: Global Restructuring and Community Politics*. Oxford: Blackwell.
A volume of essays dealing with international economic forces, their effects on cities, and some local political strategies of accommodation and resistance to those forces.

Spencer, H. 1897: *The Principles of Sociology*. New York: D. Appleton.
The major sociological work of the dominant nineteenth-century theorist in which his distinctions between industrial and militant societies and evolutionary theories of social structure and social differentiation are developed.

Strange, S. 1988: *States and Markets*. London: Pinter.
In a book deriving from both political science and economics, the author shows that the territorial and sovereign state is no longer the principal instrument of power on the international scene.

Strauss, A. and Corbin, J. 1990: *Basics of Qualitative Research: Grounded Theories, Procedures and Techniques*. London: Sage Publications.
An elaborate statement of the methodologies to be employed in the analysis of qualitative data.

Stren, R. E. and White, R. R. 1989: *African Cities in Crisis: Managing Rapid Urban Growth*. Boulder, Colo.: Westview Press.
An examination of urban patterns in a period of sharp upheaval, and a critical discussion of policies related to meeting basic human needs and the delivery of social services.

Szacki, J. 1979: *A History of Sociological Thought*. Westport, Conn.: Greenwood Press.
One of the most comprehensive and informative stories of the development of sociological thought in the West.

Tilly, C. (ed). 1974: *The Formation of Nation States in Western Europe*. Princeton, N.J.: Princeton University Press.
A collection of essays dealing with different aspects of the building of the state and with various explanations of the rise of the state in the first place..

Touraine, A. 1977: *The Self-Production of Society*. Chicago: University of Chicago Press.
An exposition of the idea that society is a system of social interactions and that its functioning is the result of its action; a statement that society goes beyond adaptation to creative self-reproduction and transformation of its relations with its environment.

Van Den Berghe, P. L. 1967: *Race and Racism*. New York: Wiley.
A theoretical discussion and comparative analysis of race and racism in Brazil, Mexico, the United States and South Africa.

Wallerstein, I. 1974–88: *The Modern World System*. 3 vols. New York: Academic Press.
The most elaborate statement of the world-systems perspective in sociology, a perspective that constructs the history and contemporary situations of societies in terms of their involvement in the economic organization of the world. The three volumes cover the sixteenth through the nineteenth centuries.

Weber, E. 1976: *Peasants into Frenchmen*. Stanford, Calif.: Stanford University Press.
A wide-ranging history of the nineteenth-century transformation of diverse local, provincial communities into a psychologically, socially, and culturally unified France.

Weber, M. 1968: *Economy and Society: An Outline of Interpretive Sociology*. ed. G. Roth and C. Wittich. 3 vols. New York: Bedminster Press.
The most comprehensive account of Max Weber's theoretical thought, methodology, political sociology, economic sociology, sociology of religion, and sociology of law.

Wellman B. and Berkowitz, S. D. (eds) 1988: *Social Structures: A Network Approach*. N.Y.: Cambridge University Press.
The best single work presenting the social-network approach to social science research. Wellman is the founder of the International Society of Social Network Analysis.

Wilson, W. A. 1976: *Folklore and Nationalism in Modern Finland*. Bloomington, Ind.: Indiana University Press.
A case study of the role that intellectuals play in constructing nationalism, which traces the history of folkloric research in Finland and its central role in forging Finnish nationalist sentiment.

Wilson, W. J. 1978: *The Declining Significance of Race*. Chicago: University of Chicago Press.
An argument that race has receded and that class has assumed greater salience in determining the status and roles of blacks in the United States, also that racial discrimination has diminished as an impediment to the progress of blacks.

Wood, S. (ed.) 1989: *The Transformation of Work?* London: Unwin Hyman.
A debate on the changing nature of work in the post-industrial era; a contribution to the discussion about "flexibility."

World Bank 1991: *Urban Policy and Economic Development: An Agenda for the 1990s*. Washington, D.C.: World Bank.
An analysis of the linkages between the urban economy and macroeconomic performance. The report raises issues beyond housing and residential infrastructures and discusses ways to alleviate constraints on the productivity of the urban economy.

Wright, E. O. 1985: *Classes*. London: Verso.
A neo-Marxist rendition of the centrality of economic classes in the structure of contemporary societies. Game theory is used to build a model of class structure based on forms of exploitation, and class position is correlated with class consciousness as measured by survey questions.

Selected Journals in Sociology

Throughout the world there are hundreds, if not thousands, of journals and other serial publications in which articles of sociological interest appear. The following, highly selective list contains mainly journals that publish primarily in the field of sociology. Extremely specialized journals in sociology (e.g., *Sociology of Leisure*) have not been included; nor have journals that are identified primarily with another discipline (e.g., *Comparative Politics*). Many of these more specialized and outlying journals are mentioned in the references at the ends of the various chapters.

Administrative Science Quarterly (USA)
African Social Research (Zambia)

American Behavioral Scientist
American Journal of Sociology
American Sociological Review
Archives de sciences sociales des religions (France)
British Journal of Sociology
Cahiers de recherche sociologique (Canada)
Cahiers internationaux de sociologie (France)
Canadian Journal of Sociology
Canadian Review of Studies in Nationalism
Comparative Studies in Society and History (USA)
Contemporary Asia (Philippines)
Contemporary Sociology (USA)
Current Sociology (France)
Dados (Brazil)
Demography (USA)
Ethnic and Racial Studies (UK)
European Journal of Sociology (France)
Ghana Journal of Sociology
International Journal of Urban and Regional Research (UK)
International Social Science Journal (UNESCO – France)
International Sociology (International Sociological Association – Germany)
Japanese Sociology (Japan)
Journal for the Scientific Study of Religion (USA)
Journal für Sozialforschung
Journal of Democracy (USA)
Kölner Zeitschrift für Soziologie und Sozialpsychologie
Nigerian Journal of Social and Economic Research
Population and Development Review (USA)
Population Bimonthly (France)
Population Studies (UK)
Rassegna Italiania di Sociologia
Religioni e Societa. Revista di scienze sociali della religione
Revista International de Sociologia (Spain)
Revue Française de Sociologie
Sisyphus – Sociological Studies (Poland)
Social Forces (USA)
Sociological Abstracts (USA)
Sociologie et sociétés (Canada)
Sociologische Revue (Germany)
Sociology (UK)
Sociology of Religion (formerly *Sociological Analysis*) (USA)
The Sociological Review (UK)
Theory, Culture, and Society (UK)
Theory and Society (USA)
World Development (UK)

The Author

Neil J. Smelser is University Professor of Sociology at the University of California at Berkeley. His publications include *Theory of Collective Behavior* (1962), *Comparative Methods in the Social Sciences* (1976), and *Social Paralysis and Social Change* (1991), and he is the editor of *Handbook of Sociology* (1988). He is Vice-President of the International Sociological Association, and served as co-chair of its Research Committee on Economy and Society between 1978 and 1986. He has been elected to the American Academy of Arts and Sciences, the American Philosophical Society, and the National Academy of Sciences (USA).

The Contributors

Bertrand Badie is Professor at the Institut d'études politiques in Paris. He is author of *Sociologie d'état* (with Pierre Birnbaum, 1979); *Le Développement politique* (1988); *Les Deux États* (1987); *L'État importé* (1992); and *Culture et Politique* (1993).

Pierre Birnbaum holds a professorship at the University of Paris I. He is author of the following works: *The Heights of Power* (1981); *Sociology of the State* (with Bertrand Badie, 1983); *States and Collective Action: European Experiences* (1988); *Individualism* (edited with Jean Leca (1990)); *Antisemitism in Modern France* (1992).

Roberto Cipriani is Professor of Sociology of Knowledge and Sociology of Religion at the University of Rome "La Sapienze" and is President of the Research Committee for the Sociology of Religion of the International Sociological Association. His publications include *Sociology of Legitimation* (1987), *Lévi-Strauss* (1988), *La religione diffusa* (Diffused Religion) (1988), and *La religione dei valor* (Religion of Values) (1992). He has contributed articles to both Italian and international journals. His current research sites are Mexico and Greece.

Dimitrina Dimitrova is a Research Fellow in the Institute of Sociology of the Bulgarian Academy of Sciences. She also teaches the sociology of work at Sofia University. Her research interests center on labor relations and work in the global economy. She is a member of the Bulgarian Sociological Association and the International Sociological Association.

Don Edgar is Director of the Australian Institute of Family Studies, a federal government authority established to conduct research on factors that affect family stability. He is a sociologist, having taught at the University of Chicago as well as at Monash and La Trobe universities. His publications are in the areas of poverty, educational disadvantage, and early childhood; he has also concentrated on research relating to family policy.

Olayiwola A. Erinosho is Head, Department of Sociology, Ogun State University, Ago-Iwoye, Nigeria. He read sociology at the universities of Ibadan and Toronto, specializing in the areas of psychiatric and health sociology. He taught at Ibadan from 1975 to 1985 before his appointment as the Foundation Professor of Sociology and the Dean of the Faculty of Social and Management Sciences, Ogun State University, in 1985. He served as the President of the Social Science Council of Nigeria, 1990–1, and is currently President of the Nigerian Anthropological and Sociological Association.

Helen Glezer is a Fellow at the Australian Institute of Family Studies. She is a sociologist, and her research has focused on family formation, family values and behavior, work, and family responsibilities.

John Keane is Professor of Sociology and Director of the Study of Democracy at the University of Westminster. His publications include *Public Life and Late Capitalism* (1984), *Democracy and Civil Society* (1988), and *The Media and Democracy* (1991). He has edited and translated two of Claus Offe's works on the welfare state and capitalism. He was a Senior Visiting Fellow at the European University Institute in Florence in 1990 and Visiting Professor at the Central European University in Prague in 1992. He was elected a Fellow of the Royal Society of Arts in 1992.

Bolivar Lamounier received his Ph.D. from the University of California at Los Angeles in 1974. He was founder and first director (from 1980 to 1988) of IDESP (São Paulo Institute of Social, Economic, and Political Research) and remains there as a senior researcher. He serves as coordinator of a commission in charge of prospective constitutional revision established by the Institute of Advanced Study of the University of São Paulo. Among his many writings on Brazilian and comparative politics are *Depois de Transicao: Democracia e Elicoes no Governo Collor* (1991) and *Presidencialismo ou Parliamentarismo: Perspectivas sobre a Reorganizaçao Institucional Brasileira* (co-editor with Dieter Nohlen, 1993).

Valentine M. Mohadam is Senior Research Fellow and Coordinator of the Research Programme on Women and Development at the World Institute for Development of Economics Research of the United Nations University, Helsinki. A native of Iran, she has also lived in the United States, Canada, Mexico, and Finland. She earned her Ph.D. in the sociology of development at American University, Washington, D.C. Her publications include *Modernizing Women: Gender and Social Change in the Middle East* (1993). She is currently studying the issues of populism, class, and gender in the Iranian revolution.

T. K. Oommen has been Professor of Sociology at the Centre for the Study of Social Systems, School of Social Sciences, Jawaharlal Nehru University, New Delhi, India, since 1976. His first book *Charisma, Stability and Change* was published in 1972. Two of his books have won awards: *Doctors and Nurses: A Study in Occupational Role Structures* (1978) won the V.K.R.V. Prize in Sociology awarded once in three years to an Indian sociologist below the age of 45, and *From Mobilization to Institutionalization* (1985) won the G. S. Ghurye Award given for the best book published in Indian sociology and social anthropology in the award year. His latest books are *Protest and Change* (1990) and *State and Society* (1990). Currently he is President of the International Sociological Association (1990–4).

Saskia Sassen is Professor of Urban Planning at Columbia University, New York. Among her published works are *The Mobility of Labor and Capital* (1988) and *The Global City: New York, London, Tokyo* (1993). She is now working on the topic of governance and accountability in a world economy. She has served with a number of international research groups, among them the New York–London Comparative Study sponsored by the Economic and Social Research Council of the UK and the Project on Economic Restructuring in the US and Japan sponsored by the United Nations Centre on Regional Development. Professor Sassen wishes to thank the Russell Sage Foundation for general support and Ms. Vivian Kaufman for assistance in preparing her contribution.

Michael Schudson is Professor of Communication and Sociology at the University of California at San Diego. His writings include *Discovering the News: A Social History of American Newspapers* (1978), *Advertising, the Uneasy Persuasion* (1984), and *Watergate in American Memory: How We Remember, Forget, and Reconstruct the Past* (1992). He is now working on a history of the "public sphere" in American life from colonial days to the present. He is a MacArthur Prize Fellow. He held a Guggenheim Fellowship in 1990–1 and was a fellow at the Center for Advanced Study in the Behavioral Sciences in 1992–3.

Sudha Shreeniwas received her M.A. from the University of Delhi in 1986 and her Ph.D. from the University of Michigan in 1992. She is currently serving as a Mellon Post-Doctoral Fellow in the Department of Demography of the University of California at Berkeley. Her research interests include the demographic problems of Third World countries and gender issues in the study of demography.

Heinz R. Sonntag is Professor of Sociology at the Universidad Central de Venezuela and Head Researcher of the University Centre of Studies for Development (CENDES), of which he was Director between 1983 and 1987. He is currently vice-chairman of the Latin America Sociology Association (ALAS) and has published numerous books and articles on problems of development and underdevelopment.

György Széll is Professor of Sociology at the University of Osnabrück, Germany. He is a native of Hungary. Among his publications are *International Handbook of Participation in Organizations* (1989), *Labour Relations in Transition in Eastern Europe* (1992), and *Concise Encyclopaedia of Participation and Co-Management* (1992). He is a member of the Executive Committee of the International Sociological Association and President of its Research Committee on Environment and Society. He has been Visiting Professor at the Hungarian and Bulgarian academies of science, at the École des hautes études en sciences sociales in Paris, and at numerous European and Asian universities.

Karl M. Van Meter, who holds both French and American citizenship, has a research appointment at the French National Scientific Research Center. He has degrees in social sciences and mathematics from universities in the United States, the United Kingdom and France. His publications are mainly in sociology but also in political science, anthropology, psychology, and mathematics. He has worked with a number of French governmental ministries. In 1983 he founded and has continued to direct the *Bulletin de Méthodologie Sociologique*. He is currently a member of the Executive Committee of the International Sociological Association and President of its Research Committee on Logic and Methodology. He is Vice-President of the International Institute of Sociology.

Alan Warde is a Senior Lecturer in Sociology at Lancaster University and works in urban and regional sociology, political sociology, economic sociology, and the sociology of consumption. His recent writings include a special edition of the journal *Sociology* on consumption (1990); *Restructuring: Place, Class and Gender* (with P. Bagguley and others in the Lancaster Regionalism Group, 1990); *Social Change in Contemporary Britain* (with M. Savage, 1993). He is a member of the Urban Sociology and Social Class and Social Movements research committees of the International Sociological Association.

Edmund Wnuk-Lipiński is Professor of Sociology in the Institute of Political Studies at the Polish Academy of Sciences. Among his publications are *Praca i wypoczynek w budzecie czasu* (Work and Leisure in Time Budgets) (1972), *Rozumienie kultury* (Understanding of Culture) (1975), and *Grupy i wiezi społeczne w monocentrycznym społeczenstwie masowym* (Groups and Social Bonds in a Monocentric Mass Society) (1990). He has served in several capacities with Solidarity and in a number of Polish governmental offices and ministries. He is Editor-in-Chief of *Sisyphus – Sociological Studies*, published by the Polish Academy of Sciences.

Index